AHMADIYYAT

The Renaissance of Islam

OTHER BOOKS BY

MUHAMMAD ZAFRULLA KHAN

English translation of the Holy Quran
with Arabic text

English translation of the *Riyadh-as-Salihin*
or *Gardens of the Righteous*

English translation of *Tadhkirah*
being dreams,visions and verbal revelations
vouchsafed to the Promised Messiah

The Prophet at Home

Pilgrimage to the House of Allah

Islamic Worship

Wisdom of the Holy Prophet

Islam and Human Rights

Deliverance from the Cross

Islam–its Meaning for Modern Man

The Agony of Pakistan

The Excellent Exemplar

Tahdith Nimat (Urdu, autobiography)

AHMADIYYAT

The Renaissance of Islam

Muhammad Zafrulla Khan

1978
TABSHIR PUBLICATIONS

Published in Great Britain by Tabshir Publications
care of the London Mosque
16 Gressenhall Road, Southfields, London SW 18

ISBN 0 85525 015 1

Printed in Great Britain at the Alden Press, Oxford

FOREWORD

The Ahmadiyya Movement is the most dynamic organization within the vast body of Islam today. This is a brief account of its origin, doctrines, teachings and activities. It is designed to assist one engaged in the comparative study of religion to assess the standing and position of the Movement in the field of religion.

The Movement was founded in March 1889 by Hazrat Mirza Ghulam Ahmad (1835–1908) of Qadian, India. It has thus completed 89 years of its first century and already occupies an assured position in the religious pattern of the world. Its branches are spread around the globe and it is acknowledged as the most powerful living force within contemporary Islam. The number of its adherents and its significance in the world of religion are daily, almost hourly, on the increase. No student of religion can afford to neglect or ignore it.

The Movement is established at the very centre of Islam and represents the essence of Islam, shorn of all encrustations that have through the centuries gradually been patched upon the body of Islam and have thus defaced and disfigured it. The Movement does not depart from Islam in the very least, nor does it add one iota to the doctrines and teachings of Islam. Yet it is a fresh presentation of Islam, and more particularly of the wisdom and the philosophy that underlies its doctrines and teachings based upon and deriving entirely from the Holy Quran and the pronouncements and practice of the Holy Prophet of Islam. It is not a new religion nor is it an innovation. It sets forth only that which has been inherent in Islam from the very beginning, but which had been overlaid in the last few centuries or the need of which had not yet arisen.

All references, unless otherwise specified, are to the Holy Quran.

MIRZA MUBARAK AHMAD VAKILUTTABSHIR

Rabwah, Pakistan

INTRODUCTION

The world of religion is familiar with the concept of the second advent of great religious teachers who have passed away, but curiously enough all those who are looking forward to the fulfilment of the prophecies relating to the second advent of a great teacher expect that he would return to the earth in his physical body. This concept has been responsible for great confusion, bewilderment and conflict.

In 62:4, 'And among others, from among them who have not yet joined them', the Quran indicates a second spiritual advent of the Holy Prophet. In this case, however, there has never been any expectation that the Holy Prophet would return to earth in his physical body. His second advent was expected to be fulfilled through the appearance of one so completely devoted to hims as to be a spiritual reflection of him. He was to be so completely identified with him spiritually, that the Holy Prophet said: 'He will be buried with me in my grave.' This was no indication of the burial of a dead body along with the body of the Holy Prophet in his grave; that would be an unthinkable outrage. What it meant was that he would be spiritually identified completely with the Holy Prophet, as if in spirit he was the Holy Prophet himself.

There are prophecies attributed to the Holy Prophet of the advent of a Mahdi and a Messiah, in the latter days. The Holy Prophet specified that these prophecies would be fulfilled in the appearance of the same person who would be both Mahdi and Messiah and thus there was no doubt left that the spiritual second advent of the Holy Prophet indicated in 62:4 would be fulfilled in that person. The Holy Prophet indicated that he would be of Persian descent.

The bulk of the Muslims, however, being influenced by the traditions of the large body of Christians who entered the fold of Islam, gradually developed the entirely erroneous concept that Jesus had been raised to heaven in his physical body and would descend to earth in that physical body in the latter days in fulfilment of the prophecies of the Holy Prophet in that behalf.

The Christians believe that Jesus died on the cross, a misconception which has now been completely exposed, that he was resurrected and ascended to heaven in his physical body and would descend to the earth in that body in the latter days. Yet Jesus himself had explained clearly the meaning of a second coming of one who had passed away. One factor that reinforced the opposition and hostility of the Jewish divines to his claim of being the Messiah, whose advent had been foretold in their scriptures, was that it had been prophesied in Mal. 4:5 that Elijah, the Prophet, would be sent before the advent of the Messiah.

> His disciples asked him, saying, why then say the scribes that Elias must first come? And Jesus answered and said unto them Elias truly shall first come and restore all things. But I say unto you that Elias has come already, and they knew him not, but have done unto him whatsoever they listed . . . then the disciples understood that he spoke unto them of John the Baptist [Matt. 17:10–13]. If ye will receive it, this is Elias which was for to come [Matt. 11:14]. And he shall go before him in the spirit and power of Elias . . . [Luke 1:17].

Thus, Jesus made it clear that a second coming of one who has passed away means the coming of someone in his power and spirit.

One question that needs to be considered in respect of the almost universal expectation of the second advent in the latter days of a great teacher is, what would be the message and function of that teacher? Such an advent has been prophesied in almost all the principal faiths that flourish today upon the earth. Would the message and function of everyone of them be identical or would each of them have his own message different from and in conflict with the messages of the other great teachers in their second advent? If the messages of all of them are to be identical then not more than one would be.

needed to convey that message and to set an example in conformity with it. If the messages are to be different and conflicting, the advent of so many teachers, instead of promoting unity, peace, accord and spiritual fulfilment, would only foster hostility, discord, enmity and chaos.

If every one of these great teachers is to appear within the dispensation of each respective faith, would he uphold the values of that faith as originally set forth, or would he depart from them; and if the latter, what would be the scope of his doctrines and teachings? Either contingency would raise problems that would be difficult to resolve.

Mankind has, during the last two centuries or so, been pressing forward towards a unity of aim and purpose, and all the developments that have taken place towards bringing different sections into closer relations with each other afford the strongest indication that the great teacher of the latter days would be a single person and that there would not be a plurality of personages.

It is agreed among the Muslims that the prophecy, 'He it is Who sent His Messenger with guidance and the Religion of Truth, that he may make it prevail over every other religion, even though those who associate partners with God may dislike it' (9:33), will be fulfilled through the advent of the prophet of the latter days, that is to say, one who will be the Mahdi and the Promised Messiah.

There is a very strong presumption that the great teacher of the latter days would appear within the dispensation of Islam. This presumption is upheld by many factors, into a detailed exposition of which it is not necessary to enter here. It would be enough to mention some of the oustanding ones.

(1) The scripture of Islam, the Holy Quran, clearly and definitely proclaims the universality of the mission of the Holy Prophet. For instance:

Proclaim, O Prophet: O mankind verily I am God's Messenger to you all [7:159]. We have sent thee as a bearer of glad tidings and a Warner for the whole of mankind, but most people know not [34:29]. We have sent thee as a mercy for the universe [21:108].

(2) The scripture of Islam contains comprehensive guidance for the whole of mankind for all time, as is said:

A Messenger from God reciting pure scriptures wherein are lasting commandments [98:4]. The Quran is a Reminder for all peoples [38:88]. The Quran is a source of honour for the whole of mankind [68:53]. Blessed is He Who has sent down the Discriminating Book to His servant that he may be a Warner to all the peoples [25:2].

(3) The Quran is the only scripture that has been safeguarded against perversion under divine decree, as is said, 'Surely, We Ourself have sent down this Exhortation, and We will, most surely, safeguard it' (15:10). The Quran has the unique distinction that of all the scriptures it alone is, from beginning to end, entirely verbal revelation. That in itself is a guarantee that it would not be perverted or twisted. All non-Muslim scholars who have made a research into the integrity of the text of the Holy Quran are unanimous that it is an exact and accurate version of the verbal revelation that Muhammad, the Prophet of Islam, claimed God had vouchsafed to him. But the divine guarantee of safeguarding the Quran that has just been set out, is not confined to preserving the integrity of its text alone. It extends to all the factors that bear upon the preservation of the Quran as the perfect source of divine guidance for the whole of mankind for all time. For instance, it is a guarantee that the language in which the Quran was revealed, namely classical Arabic, would always continue a living language in current use so that no difficulty might be encountered in determining and comprehending the meaning of the Quran. Classical Arabic is today spoken and written over a much vaster area of the earth and by many hundred times the number of people than was the case when the Quran was revealed. Besides, the Holy Prophet predicted that at the beginning of every century God would raise someone from among his followers who would set forth from the Quran the guidance that might be needed by mankind from time to time. In the case of no other scripture has the integrity of its text, its language and its guidance been maintained.

(4) There is the promise contained in the Quran already referred to that in the latter days a Prophet would be raised in Islam who would not only defend Islam against the concerted attacks of the followers and exponents of other faiths but would establish the superiority of Islam in every respect over all other religions (9:33). The commentators of the Quran are agreed that the promise contained in this verse would be fulfilled through the Mahdi-Messiah whose advent in the latter days had been foretold by the Holy Prophet. He would be a spiritual reflection of the Holy Prophet himself as is indicated in 62:4.

(5) Islam is the only faith that requires belief in all the Prophets wherever and whenever they might have appeared. The Quran affirms: 'Verily, We have sent thee with enduring truth, as a bearer of glad tidings and as a Warner; and there is no people to whom a Warner has not been sent' (35:25). Even more explicitly are the Muslims commanded:

> Affirm: We believe in God and in that which has been sent down to us and in that which was sent down to Abraham and Ishmael and Isaac and Jacob and his children and in that which was given to Moses and Jesus, and in that which was given to all other Prophets from their Lord. We make no discrimination between any of them and to Him do we wholly submit ourselves [2:137].

This again is a sure indication that the great teacher who is to appear in the latter days must appear in the dispensation of Islam, as he would then be a believer in the righteousness of all the Prophets and would not deny or reject any of them. If he were to appear in any other dispensation he would not be acceptable to those whose Prophets he denied or rejected. He must be the champion of God in the mantles of all the Prophets.

(6) It is obvious that the great teacher, whose advent in the latter days has been foretold in every one of the principal revealed religions of the world, would be divinely guided, that is to say, he would be the recipient of divine revelation. This is also an important factor that would persuade a seeker after truth to determine that the promised great teacher must

appear within the dispensation of Islam, inasmuch as the door of divine revelation has long been closed in all faiths other than Islam, and the followers of all those faiths hold firmly to the notion that divine revelation is no longer possible. Thus, the advent of a divinely inspired teacher is possible only in Islam.

There has been general agreement among the Muslims that the Mahdi-Messiah would appear at the beginning of the 14th century of the Hegira correspondingly roughly to the last decade of the 19th century of the Christian era.

Jesus had indicated that the signs of the time of his second coming would be earthquakes, plagues, epidemics, wars and rumours of wars and general tribulations. These signs have been manifested from the end of the 19th century onwards. Among several Christian denominations the end of the 19th and the beginning of the 20th century have been considered as the time of the second coming of Jesus.

These were expectations based upon a variety of general indications contained in prophecies mentioned in the scriptures and sacred writings of Christianity and Islam. The Holy Prophet, however, had announced a very clear and definite sign of the appearance of the Mahdi which it was not in the power of anyone to manufacture or improvise. Darqutni, an eminent and recognized authority on *hadees,* had recorded that the Holy Prophet said:

> For our Mahdi there are appointed two signs which have never been manifested for any other claimant since the creation of the heavens and the earth. They are that at his advent there shall occur an eclipse of the moon on the first of its appointed nights, and an eclipse of the sun on the middle one of its appointed days and both will occur in the same month of Ramazan.

The eclipse of the moon normally occurs on the 13th, 14th or 15th night of a lunar month, and the eclipse of the sun takes place on the 27th, 28th or 29th of the lunar month. The sign mentioned by the Holy Prophet, therefore, was that the moon would be eclipsed on the 13th night of the lunar month, and the eclipse of the sun would take place on the 28th of the same lunar month, which will be the month of Ramazan. This sign was to appear after and not before the advent of the Mahdi. It so happened that an eclipse of the moon occurred on Thursday night, the 13th of Ramazan, 1311 Hegira (21 March 1894), and the eclipse of the sun occurred on the 28th of the same month of Ramazan (6 April 1894), in exact accord with the prophecy of the Holy Prophet. The same phenomenon was repeated in the United States of America in 1895.

Hazrat Mirza Ghulman Ahmad began to receive revelation in 1876, and as time passed his experience of revelation multiplied progressively. Every one of his revelations was clearly fulfilled according to its tenor at its due time; some of them that related to future events have been fulfilled from time to time since his death and some await fulfilment.

In 1889, under divine direction, he claimed to be the Mahdi whose advent had been foretold by the Holy Prophet. Thereafter it was revealed to him that he was also the Promised Messiah and was indeed the Prophet whose advent had been foretold in the principal religions of the world. One of the revelations vouchsafed to him was: 'Champion of God in the mantles of all the Prophets' He was, however, at pains to emphasize all the time and on every occasion that whatever God Almighty had bestowed upon him, out of His grace, was in consequence of his utter devotion and obedience to the Holy Prophet, peace and blessings of Allah be upon him, and that in himself he was nothing and claimed no merit. He was thus a perfect spiritual reflection of the Holy Prophet and in him was fulfilled the second advent of the Holy Prophet, promised in 62:4.

We shall now enter upon a brief study of his life, character, claims, status, doctrines, teachings, the purpose of the Movement instituted by him and the progress made by it in the achievement of its purpose so far.

CHAPTER ONE

In 1530 Mirza Hadi Beg, a Central Asian chieftain of Persian descent, moved out of Samarkand, accompanied by the members of his family and about two hundred of his retainers, and entered the Punjab and settled down in an open area in the district of Gurdaspur. Mirza Hadi Beg was a descendant of Haji Barlas, uncle of the famous Amir Taimur whose tomb in Samarkand continues to be an attraction for tourists. The place he selected for settling down was about seventy miles due east of Lahore. He founded a walled village there which he named Islampur.

As he was a scion of the royal family of Emperor Babar, he was granted a *jagir* of several hundred villages by the Emperor and was appointed Qazi of the surrounding district. Thus the village founded by him became known as Islampur Qazi. In course of time Islampur was dropped and the village began to be called Qazian which could also be pronounced Qadian.

Though the seat of the family was situated far from the Imperial capital at Delhi, members of the family from time to time held important offices under the Imperial Government. In the days of the decline of Mughal rule Mirza Faiz Muhammad, the then head of the family, adopted strong measures to suppress the anarchy that prevailed in the Punjab, in appreciation of which the Emperor Farrukhsiyar bestowed upon him the rank of Haft Hazari in 1716. The holder of this rank was entitled to maintain a regular force of seven thousand soldiers. This rank was generally bestowed only upon the members of the Imperial family. The emperor also conferred upon Mirza Faiz Muhammad the title of Azadud Daulah, meaning the Strong Arm of the Government.

After the death of Mirza Faiz Muhammad his son, Mirza Gul Muhammad, had to put up a desperate struggle against the forces of anarchy in the Punjab. This phase continued during the reigns of Muhammad Shah, Shah Alam and Alamgir II. From the Imperial despatches that were addressed to him it appears that Mirza Faiz Muhammad had repeatedly warned the authorities at Delhi of the dangers that loomed ahead and appealed for assistance in containing the forces of disorder and rebellion. He was given promises of support but received no concrete aid. He continued his struggle for the maintenance of the Imperial authority in his surrounding area but with declining success. The Punjab was being torn up between rival petty chieftains who defied the Imperial authority with impunity. Mirza Gul Muhammad, who possessed considerable ability, consolidated his authority over a tract of land which comprised eighty-five villages and became in effect a ruler of his small estate. He was a person of great piety and benevolence and was a patron of learning. He held his own against rival chieftains with the help of a small force. He was very open-handed and students and scholars flocked to him in large numbers and were maintained by him. He was, however, fighting a losing battle against the forces of disorder around him and the Imperial authority was being rapidly displaced by the Sikhs, particularly in the central districts of the Punjab.

Mirza Gul Muhammad was succeeded by his son, Mirza Ata Muhammad, who was pressed hard by the Sikhs and lost control of the surrounding villages. His authority was confined in the end to Qadian itself which in effect became a besieged fortress. About 1802 the Sikhs of Ramgarh managed to make their way into Qadian through treachery, and Mirza Ata Muhammad and the members of his family were all made prisoners. Everything was looted, mosques and other buildings were pulled down, and one of the mosques was turned into a Sikh temple, and such it remains to this day. The library of the family containing a large number of valuable books and manuscripts was burned down. A number of people were killed but the members of the family were spared and were expelled from Qadian. They moved, in great distress, across the River Beas to Begowal where Sardar Fateh Singh Ahluvalia, ancestor of the Maharaja of Kapurthala, treated them with kindness and extended to them a practical sympathy that they had neither solicited nor expected. He made them an allowance which was by no means adequate for their needs, but which was greatly appreciated. The family remained there for about fifteen years. Mirza Ata Muhammad's death was brought about by poison administered to him at the instance of his enemies. His son, Mirza Ghulam Murtaza, brought his father's body to Qadian for burial in the family graveyard. The Sikhs were opposed to this, but the local population became so excited that the Sikhs, apprehending a repudiation of their authority, gave in.

At that time Maharaja Ranjit Singh had consolidated his authority and had brought all the petty chiefs under his sway. About 1818 he permitted Mirza Ghulam Murtaza and the members of his family to return to Qadian. Mirza Ghulam Murtaza and his brothers joined the army of the Maharaja and rendered excellent service to the Maharaja in several places, including the frontier of Kashmir which was annexed by the Maharaja in 1819.

During the period of his military service under the Maharaja, the burden of affliction upon Mirza Ghulam Murtaza was to some degree reduced but the family continued in a state of adversity. It was not till 1834 that the Maharaja, being impressed with the goodness and loyalty of Mirza Ghulam Murtaza, restored to him five villages out of his ancestral estate. This was about the time when, on 13 February 1835, Mirza Ghulam Murtaza was blessed with a second son whom he named Ghulam Ahmad. Thus the child's very birth became a signal of the good fortune of his family. Their period of extreme adversity came to an end and an era of peace and prosperity appeared to open out before them.

Maharaja Ranjit Singh died in 1839, the Sikh power broke up and within a few years the British established their authority in the Punjab.

The Punjab Chiefs, compiled by Sir Lepel Griffin and

Colonel Massey, revised by Mr (later Sir) Henry Craik (1910), contains the following account of the family.

In 1530, the last year of the Emperor Babar's reign, Hadi Beg, a Mughal of Samarkand, emigrated to the Punjab and settled in the Gurdaspur District. He was a man of some learning and was appointed Qazi or Magistrate over 70 villages in the neighbourhood of Qadian, which town he is said to have founded, naming it Islampur Qazi, from which Qadian has by a natural change arisen. For several generations the family held offices of respectability under the Imperial government, and it was only when the Sikhs became powerful that it fell into poverty. Gul Muhammad and his son Ata Muhammad were engaged in perpetual quarrels with Ramgarhia and Kanhaya Misals, who had held the country in the neighbourhood of Qadian; and at last having lost all his estates Ata Muhammad retired to Begowal, where under the protection of Sardar Fateh Singh Ahluvalia (ancestor of the present ruling chief of the Kapurthala State) he lived quietly for twelve years. On his death Ranjit Singh, who had taken possession of all the lands of the Ramgarhia Misal, invited Ghulam Murtaza to Qadian and restored to him a large portion of his ancestral estate.

He then, with his brothers, entered the army of the Maharaja, and performed efficient service on the Kashmir frontier.

During the time of Nao Nihal Singh, Sher Singh and the Darbar, Ghulam Murtaza was continually employed on active service. In 1841 he was sent with General Ventura to Mandi and Kulu, and in 1843 to Peshawar in command of an infantry regiment. He distinguished himself in Hazara at the time of the insurrection there; and when the rebellion of 1848 broke out, he remained faithful to his Government and fought on its side. His brother Ghulam Muhi-ud-Din also did good service at this time. When Bhai Maharaja Singh was marching with his force to Multan to the assistance of Diwan Mul Raj, Ghulam Muhi-ud-Din, with other *Jagirdars*, Langar Khan Sahiwal and Sahib Khan Tiwana, raised the Mohammedan population and with the force of Sahib Dayal attacked the rebels and completely defeated them, driving them into the Chenab, where upwards of 600 perished.

At annexation the *jagirs* of the family were resumed, but a pension of Rs. 700 was granted to Ghulam Murtaza and his brother and they retained their property rights in Qadian and the neighbouring villages. The family did excellent service during the mutiny of 1857. Ghulam Murtaza enlisted many men and his son Ghulman Kadir was serving in the force of Gen. Nicholson when that officer destroyed the mutineers of the 46th Native Infantry who had fled from Sialkot at Trimughat.

General Nicholson gave Ghulam Kadir a certificate stating that in 1857 the Qadian family showed greater loyalty than any other in the district.

Mirza Ghulam Murtaza was an expert physician. He treated people freely but would not accept a fee. He was very generous and openhanded. He had an imposing appearance and most people stood in awe of him.

He was of a literary bent of mind and was also by way of being a poet.

Towards the end of his life he built the central mosque in Qadian which is known as the Masjad-i-Aqsa. Though by that time his resources had been much reduced he spent a large amount of money in constructing the mosque.

He made continuous efforts to regain possession of his ancestral estate. He approached the government authorities in that behalf and also had recourse to judicial proceedings on several occasions but nothing availed. He disposed of a considerable portion of his properties to defray the expenses of the series of litigation upon which he embarked in the effort to recover portions of his ancestral estate.

His wife, who belonged to a respectable Mughal family of Aima, a village in the Hoshiarpur district, and was named Charagh Bibi (Lady of the Lamp), was a generous, hospitable, cheerful and good-hearted woman of exemplary piety. She looked after the poor and administered relief to them while they lived and arranged for their decent burial when they died. She proved herself a devoted wife and an excellent companion to Mirza Ghulam Murtaza both in adversity and in prosperity. He esteemed her highly and constantly sought her advice in his affairs.

She was a most loving mother and lavished her most tender care on her children. As her son Ghulam Ahmad grew up and gave evidence of his being completely withdrawn from the world and its affairs, she esteemed his other-worldliness, while the other members of the family looked down upon it. She died in 1868 and was buried in the family graveyard to the west of Qadian. Mirza Ghulam Ahmad had loved her deeply and cherished her memory tenderly. Whenever he spoke of her his eyes would be filled with tears. He often visited her grave and supplicated the Divine in her behalf.

Mirza Ghulam Ahmad was born a twin. His birth was preceded by the birth of a baby sister who died within a few days. There is a reported prediction of the famous saint and scholar Hazrat Muhyuddin Ibn Arabi that the Promised Messiah would be born a twin.

During his childhood he accompanied his mother several times when she visited her parents at Aima, in the Hoshiarpur district, where he played about in the dry beds of the hill streams that ran through the valley in the rainy season. His childhood was distinguished from that of other children of his age by the fact that he was never rowdy and possessed a serene temperament which was seldom ruffled. His gravity and earnestness were remarked upon by all observers. While he participated in pursuits, common among children of his age, he displayed a serious bent of mind and a certain degree of aloofness that were noticeable.

CHAPTER TWO

We have available Mirza Ghulam Ahmad's own account of the arrangements made by his father for his education. He says:

My elementary education was arranged at home. When I was six or seven years old a tutor was engaged for me who taught me the Holy Quran and a few Persian books. His name was Fazal Ilahi. When I was about ten years old another tutor was appointed for my instruction whose name was Fazal Ahmad. I conceive that as, by the grace of God Almighty, the purpose of my elementary education was to sow the seed of His grace (Fazal) in my mind, the names of both my tutors began with Fazal (Grace). Maulvi Fazal Ahmad Sahib, who was a pious and respectable gentleman, taught me with great attention and diligence. He instructed me in grammar and cognate subjects. When I was seventeen or eighteen I read with another Maulvi Sahib for some time whose name was Gul Ali Shah. He had also been appointed by my father for my tuition at Qadian. From him I acquired further knowledge of grammar and studied logic and philosophy with him according to the then current syllabus, as far as God Almighty so willed. My father was an expert physician and I read some books on medicine with him.

By that time I had become very fond of reading books, so much so that I paid little attention to anything else. My father repeatedly admonished me to reduce my study of books as he was afraid that too much concentration on books might have an adverse effect on my health and also because he was desirous that, laying aside books, I should begin to take interest in his affairs and should become involved in the problems with which he was preoccupied. He was at that time engaged in litigation in the British courts for the recovery of some of our ancestral villages and he finally succeeded in employing me also in that pursuit. I was so occupied for a long period. I have always regretted that so much of my precious time was wasted in this useless pursuit. My father also committed the superintendence and management of our landed property to me. I had little interest in these matters and in consequence my father was often upset with me. He was most kind and affectionate towards me, but he desired that I should pursue worldly affairs like my contemporaries and I was much adverse to it [Kitabul Bariyyah, pp. 175–7, footnote].

While his first teachers, Maulvi Fazal Ilahi Sahib and Maulvi Fazal Ahmad Sahib, carried on their tuition of him in Qadian, Maulvi Gul Ali Shah Sahib, after a short while, moved back to Batala where he belonged, and Mirza Ghulam Ahmad had to take up his residence in Batala for a time so as to continue his education with his tutor.

At that stage Mirza Ghulam Ahmad had already started taking an interest in religious studies, among which his deep study of the Holy Quran always held pride of place. But he did not confine himself to the study of Islamic subjects alone, and began to take an interest in the study of Christian religious literature also. He was much struck by the aggressive and often highly offensive Christian polemics directed against Islam and the Holy Prophet. This left a deep impress upon his mind.

In the meantime, as was customary in those days, Mirza Ghulam Ahmad's marriage to a first cousin was arranged. The bride's name was Hurmat Bibi. From her he had two sons, Mirza Sultan Ahmad and Mirza Fazal Ahmad, born in 1853 and 1855 respectively.

At the time of his marriage Mirza Ghulam Ahmad was still engaged in his studies and he did not permit his marriage to affect in any manner his programme of studies or his manner of life, which became progressively more studious and contemplative. The only change was that he began to devote more and more time to divine worship, prayer and the study of the Holy Quran. He spent a good deal of his time in the family mosque, walking up and down most of the time engaged in deep thought and contemplation.

He had learned swimming and riding at an early age but his principal form of exercise was brisk walking. He kept to it all through his life, even during its busiest periods.

When he had finished his formal schooling his father

became anxious to engage his interest in and attention to the secular affairs of the family, but nothing of that kind appealed to him at all. He observed:

My father was desirous that I should be completely occupied with worldly affairs, which was contrary to my disposition. Nevertheless, out of goodwill and in order to earn spiritual merit, but not for the sake of any worldly gain, I devoted myself to serving my father and for his sake I occupied myself with worldly affairs and also continued to supplicate the Divine in his behalf. He was assured that I was dutiful towards my parents and he often said that he desired me to participate in worldly affairs out of a feeling of sympathy for me, though he realized that the subject in which I was deeply interested, that is to say, religion, was alone worth pursuing and that he himself was only wasting his time [*Kitabul Bariyyah*, pp. 175–8, footnote].

At one time, casting about for some means that might prove effective in engaging his interest in secular affairs, his father procured his appointment to a minor post in the civil administration of Sialkot district, and in compliance with his father's wishes Mirza Ghulam Ahmad took up his residence at Sialkot some time in 1864. While he performed the duties of his office diligently and conscientiously he led a somewhat secluded life and continued to devote his spare time to religious study and exercises. He had few intimate acquaintances and absolutely refused to receive anyone at his simple lodging in connection with the discharge of his official duties. His only intimate friends were Lala Bhim Sen, a Hindu lawyer, who had been one of his fellow pupils when he had studied with Maulvi Gul Ali Shah at Batala and whom he esteemed highly, Maulvi Syed Mir Hasan Sahib, a revered scholar and teacher and Mir Hussamuddin Sahib, a physician who received some instruction from Mirza Ghulam Ahmad and became his devoted friend.

During his stay at Sialkot, Mirza Ghulam Ahmad also came to know two or three Christian missionaries with whom he exchanged views on religious subjects. One of them, the Revd Mr Butler M.A. who was a learned cleric and often had occasion to carry on religious discussions with Mirza Ghulam Ahmad, held him in high esteem. When the time came for Mr Butler to return to Britain he made it a point to call on Mirza Ghulam Ahmad in his office to say goodbye to him.

One curious incident that happened during his stay in Sialkot was that one night, when he was asleep in a room in the second storey of a house, he heard a sound which appeared to proceed from the beam of the roof as if a bird was pecking at it. It occurred to Mirza Ghulam Ahmad that the beam might break and the roof might fall down. There were several other people asleep in the room. He awakened them and urged them to go out of the room with him. They put him off with the explanation that the sound probably indicated the movement of a rat, and they all went back to sleep. A short while later the sound was repeated and Mirza Ghulam Ahmad urged his companions again to go out of the room, but they paid no attention to him. He heard the sound again and this time he insisted that they should all go out of the room. He saw all of them go out and was himself the last to leave the room. He had hardly gone out when the roof fell down and carried down with it the floor of the room which was the roof of the lower storey. Thus all of them escaped the risk of serious injury.

In 1868 Mirza Ghulam Ahmad's mother died and his father sent a messenger to him apprising him of the tragedy and directing him to resign his post and return to Qadian. Mirza Ghulam Ahmad complied immediately with his father's direction and proceeded to Qadian. He has summed up his impressions of his stay at Sialkot as follows:

> While I was under my father's care I had most unwillingly spent a few years in the employ of the British government, but my father finding that separation from me sat heavy on him directed me to resign my appointment which I did gladly and returned to my father. This brief experience of official life made me realize that most people in that position lead very undesirable lives. Very few

of them carry out their religious duties properly and few of them restrain themselves from indulgence in illicit pursuits. I was surprised at their manner of life. I found that most of them were eager to collect money lawfully or unlawfully and all their efforts in this brief life were directed towards the world. I found few of them who, out of regard for the Divine Majesty, cultivated the higher moral values like meekness, nobility, chastity, lowliness, sympathy, purity.

I found most of them afflicted with arrogance, misconduct, neglect of religious values and all types of evil morals. As the wisdom of God Almighty had decreed that I should have experience of all types of people, I had to keep company with those of every kind. All that time I passed in great constraint and unease [*Kitabul Barriyyah*, pp. 179–80, footnote].

Mirza Ghulam Ahmad has given an account of his life at Qadian after his return from Sialkot in which he has observed:

When I returned to my father I became occupied with the management of our lands but the greater part of my time was devoted to the study of the Holy Quran and of the commentaries on it and of the traditions of the Holy Prophet. Often I would read out portions from those books to my father who was mostly melancholy on account of the failure of his efforts to recover a part of his patrimony. He had spent 70,000 rupees in the prosecution of those cases, but the result was failure. We had lost those villages since a long time and their recovery was a chimera. On account of this failure my father was always plunged in grief and observing his condition, I was enabled to carry out a pure change in my own life. The bitter life led by my father taught me to value a clean life free from all worldly impurities. My father owned a few villages and was in receipt of a stipend from the British Government and also enjoyed a pension for his service but all this was as nothing compared with what he had been accustomed to in his younger days. That is why he was always melancholy and often said that had he striven for the faith as much as he had striven for the world he would have been a saint.

His last days were saddened by the thought that he would face his Maker empty handed. He often regretted that he had wasted his life in the pursuit of a useless worldly objective. On one occasion he related that he had seen the Holy Prophet, peace be upon him, in his dream proceeding with great dignity towards my father's house like a mighty monarch. My father advanced towards him to welcome him. When he arrived near him he thought he should make a present to him and put his hand in his pocket where he found only one rupee and looking closely discovered that it was a false coin. Perceiving this, my father's eyes became wet and he woke up. He interpreted the dream as meaning that love of God and of the Holy Prophet mixed with wordly ambitions was like a false coin.

In his old age my father's grief and sorrow had multiplied manifold. Towards the end of his life he had a mosque constructed in the middle of the town which is the principal mosque in the place and he directed that he should be buried in a corner of the mosque so that he should constantly hear the Word of God Almighty being glorified, which might perchance become the means of his procuring forgiveness. It so happened that when the construction of the mosque was almost completed my father died of dysentery after a few days' illness and was buried in a corner of the mosque which he had himself specified. May Allah have mercy on him and admit him to paradise. Amen. He was 80 or 85 years of age.

His sorrow over wasting his life in the pursuit of the world still affects me painfully and I realize that everyone who seeks the world must carry this sorrow with him. Let him who seeks understanding understand this [*Kitabul Bariyyah*, pp. 184–9, footnote].

Soon after Mirza Ghulam Ahmad's return to Qadian an incident took place which illustrates his perfect intellectual integrity. It so happened that about that time Maulvi Muhammad Husain of Batala returned to his native town, having qualified as a Maulvi after his theological studies in Delhi. He belonged to the Ahle Hadees sect and his views were not approved by a majority of his fellow citizens who were of the Hanafi persuasion. They sent one of their number to Qadian to convey to Mirza Ghulam Ahmad their earnest request that he might go to Batala and hold a public discussion with Maulvi Muhammad Husain on the principal points of difference between the Ahle Hadees and the Hanafis. Mirza Ghulam Ahmad agreed and proceeded to Batala and presented himself in the mosque where the discussion was to take place. At the time appointed Maulvi Muhammad Husain opened the proceedings with a statement of the doctrines in which he believed. Having heard the statement Mirza Ghulam Ahmad declared that there was nothing in it which called for a refutation. This created an uproar. The Ahle Hadees interpreted this as a triumph for their side and the Hanafis were deeply chagrined and felt that they had been let down and humiliated. Thus Mirza Ghulam Ahmad incurred the displeasure of both parties, but he was completely indifferent to the reactions of both sides. His love of truth and honesty was unaffected by the approval or disapproval of his friends or foes. He was prepared to suffer every humility and indignity with a cheerful countenanace for the sake of truth. That night he was greatly cheered and comforted by the divine assurance conveyed to him by way of revelation that God was pleased by the attitude that he had adopted in the matter of the discussion and that He would bless him greatly, so much so that kings would seek blessings from his garments. He was also shown in a vision some of those kings, six or seven in number, mounted on their steeds.

In his representation of his father from time to time in judicial proceedings he was not much concerned with the result of the particular case. He adhered to truth in all circumstances, behaved with extreme courtesy towards everyone and held aloft his principal objective which was to establish and strengthen his relationship with God. In connection with these proceedings he had often to proceed to Batala, Gurdaspur, Dalhousie, Amritsar and Lahore. These journeys had sometimes to be performed on foot or by very indifferent types of vehicles. Dalhousie was a hill station about seven thousand feet above sea level and on occasion no means of transportation was available. The distance between

Qadian and Dalhousie was more than a hundred miles, which he traversed on foot, when that became inevitable. Whenever he had occasion to go to Dalhousie he was much impressed by the mountainous scenery through which he had to pass, and these views impelled him towards contemplation and appreciation of God's creation and His bounties.

It sometimes happened that the opposite party to the proceedings would intimate to the presiding officer of the court that it was willing to abide by the statement of Mirza Ghulam Ahmad regarding the facts in dispute. He would then be called upon to make a statement and would set forth the facts according to his knowledge of them, which often resulted in the case being decided against his father's interests. On one such occasion his father was much upset and reproved him severely, bidding him to leave the house. He withdrew to Batala where he stayed for a couple of months till his father recalled him to Qadian.

He has set out some of these instances in his writings. Attention might be drawn to one or two of them by way of illustration.

At one place he has stated:

> My son Sultan Ahmad filed a suit against a Hindu alleging that the defendant had built a structure on a site belonging to us and praying for its demolition. One of the facts involved in the case, if established in favour of the defendant, would have led to the dismissal of the suit causing loss both to Sultan Ahmad and to me. The defendant cited me as a witness in the case and I went to Batala to give evidence. When I arrived there Sultan Ahmad's lawyer came to me and told me that the case was likely to be called soon and asked me what statement would I make as a witness in the case. I told him that I would set forth the true facts. On this he observed that in that case it was not necessary for me to go into the court room. When the case was called he went in and made a statement withdrawing the suit [*Ayena Kamalati Islam*, pp. 299–300].

His elder brother Mirza Ghulam Qadir instituted a suit against a Hindu resident of Qadian for the removal of a platform which had been constructed upon a site adjacent to the defendant's house but which was the property of the plaintiff. The defendant pleaded that the platform had been in existence long enough to vest the title to the site in the defendant. As proof he called Mirza Ghulam Ahmad as a witness who made a statement supporting the defendant's allegation, in consequence of which his brother's suit was dismissed. His brother was much chagrined and expressed his grave displeasure with Mirza Ghulam Ahmad, whose only response was that he could not be expected to deny a fact.

On one occasion he had gone to Batala in prosecution of a civil suit on behalf of his father. While he was waiting for the case to be called it became time for the performance of the noon service. He withdrew to a vacant spot at a short distance from the courtroom and engaged himself in divine worship. While he was so occupied the case was called and the defendant urged the Judge that the suit should be dismissed in default, but the Judge rejected his plea and after a study of the papers, and after some inquiry from the defendant, decreed the suit. When Mirza Ghulam Ahmad returned to the courtroom he was informed by the peon of the court that the case had been called in his absence and had been disposed of. He entered the courtroom and imagining that the suit had been dismissed in default submitted to the Judge that when the case was called he had been engaged in worship. The Judge smiled and told him that he had decreed the suit. (*Hayat-en-Nabi*, Vol. I, p. 56).

During that period of his life Mirza Ghulam Ahmad had frequent experience of true dreams which he related to those residents of Qadian, both Hindu and Muslim, who were in the habit of calling on him and keeping company with him for a while. These dreams always came true and those people to whom he related them became witnesses of their truth. Among them were two prominent Hindus, Lala Sharmpat, Secretary of the Arya Samaj of Qadian and Lala Mulawa Mal.

At one time Lala Mulawa Mal began to suffer from

tuberculosis and requested Mirza Ghulam Ahmad to pray for his recovery, which he did and told Lala Mulawa Mal that he had an indication that his prayer was accepted. Lala Mulawa Mal recovered from his illness and died in 1951 at the age of 95.

From about 1872 onwards Mirza Ghulam Ahmad began to emerge as a champion of Islam, defending it against the attacks of Christians, Arya Samajists and Bramho Samajists and setting forth the excellence of its teachings in every sphere. He did this by writing articles for publication in newspapers and journals. His earliest article was published in *Manshur Muhammadi*, which used to be published every ten days from Bangalore, Mysore, South India. In addition to *Manshur Muhammadi*, he subscribed regularly to *Vakil, Safeer Hind, Vidya Prakash* and *Riaz Hind* all of which were published from Amritsar, and *Brother Hind* (Lahore), *Aftab Punjab* (Lahore), *Wazir Hind* (Sialkot), *Noor Afshan* (Ludhiana) and *Ishaatas Sunnah* edited by his friend Maulvi Muhammad Husain of Batala. Occasionally he contributed his own articles to some of them. At a later period he also subscribed to *Akhbar-i-Aam* of Lahore.

In his first article published in *Manshur Muhammadi* of 25 August 1872, he announced that his experience and observation extending over more than a score of years had convinced him that the basis of all goodness in human affairs and relationships was truth and that an easy way of determining the truth of a religion was to discover to what degree it had put forth an effective and emphatic teaching designed to establish its followers firmly on truth. He challenged the followers of all religions to set forth from their recognized religious books their respective teachings in this behalf. He promised to award a prize of Rs 500 to any non-Muslim who would set forth from his own religious books one-half or even one-third of the teachings in support of truth that he himself would set forth from the recognized and authoritative books on Islam. No one came forward to take up the challenge.

Thereafter Mirza Ghulam Ahmad challenged every statement that was published in an article or book which was in conflict with the fundamental teachings of Islam and refuted every such statement so effectively that every intelligent person was convinced of the correctness and rightness of his views. One out of many instances might be mentioned by way of illustration. In the issue of *Vakil*, Amritsar, of 7 December 1877, a statement was published on behalf of the Arya Samaj, on the authority of Swami Dayanand, founder of the Arya Samaj, to the effect that the number of human souls was infinite and was not known even to God, so that however many of them might attain salvation their number would not be exhausted. Mirza Ghulam Ahmad wrote a series of articles refuting this position which were published in the *Safeer Hind* of Amritsar from 9 February to 9 March 1878. Swami Dayanand was touring in the Punjab at the time. In his article Mirza Ghulam Ahmad challenged the Arya Samaj to vindicate its position and offered a prize of Rs 500 to anyone who would establish the correctness of the statement mentioned above. The arguments put forward by him were so conclusive and convincing that Lala Jiwan Das, Secretary of the Central Samaj of the Punjab, issued a statement that the doctrine refuted by Mirza Ghulam Ahmad did not form part of the basic principles of the Arya Samaj. He added that the members of the Ayra Samaj were not blind followers of Swami Dayanand. They did not accept all that the Swami said unless it was found reasonable. Swami Dayanand himself put forward no refutation of the articles of Mirza Ghulam Ahmad and declared that the number of souls was not in fact infinite, but through perpetual transmigration their number was not exhausted. He invited Mirza Ghulam Ahmad to a debate on the point in a letter addressed to him. The invitation was accepted by him in an open letter dated 10 June 1878 published in *Brother Hind* of Lahore, edited by Pandit Shiv Narain Agni Hotri, who commented on the letter as follows:

So far the Arya Samaj had staunchly held, according to the teachings of Dayanand, based on the authority of the Vedas, that the number of souls is infinite, but it now appears that when Mirza Ghulam Ahmad refuted this doctrine, Dayanand was compelled to declare that the number of souls is not infinite but that the transmigration of souls is established. What we wish to observe is that Dayanand had instructed his followers, on the authority of the Vedas, that the number of souls was infinite and that they were self-existing. Now that his belief has been refuted, his confession that the number of souls is not infinite clearly shows that Dayanand is going against the Vedas. If the Vedas really teach that which Dayanand has now declared, this is a serious reflection upon his position as a Leader, as he has set forth two contradictory teachings from the Vedas. If the Vedas are silent on the point, it is a reflection on the Vedas.

There is no evidence of any response from Swami Dayanand, but Pandit Kharak Singh, a member of the Arya Samaj of Amritsar, came to Qadian and offered to hold a debate with Mirza Ghulam Ahmad. It was agreed that the subject of the debate should be transmigration of souls, and a comparison of the teachings of the Vedas and the Quran on the subject. Accordingly Mirza Ghulam Ahmad wrote a paper which was read out in a public meeting held for the purpose. The Pandit tried to make an answer but felt unequal to the task, lost his temper and returned to his home, whence he wrote to Mirza Ghulam Ahmad that he would like to continue the debate through the columns of a newspaper. Mirza Ghulam Ahmad promptly notified his willingness and suggested that the columns of the *Safeer Hind* (Amritsar) or *Brother Hind* (Lahore) or *Arya Darpan* (Shahjahanpur) might be used for the purpose. He also promised to award Pandit Kharak Singh Rs 500 if, in the opinion of judges to be appointed for the purpose, he should be declared to have established his thesis, and proposed that the Rev. Mr Rajab Ali, a Christian missionary, and Pandit Shiv Narain, a Brahmo Samajist, be appointed as judges. Mirza Ghulam Ahmad wrote a paper in support of the thesis that God is the

Creator of the universe, that human souls are not co-existent with God, and that they are all created by God. Pandit Kharak Singh made no response to the proposal of Mirza Ghulam Ahmad. Sometime later he became a Christian and wrote several pamphlets condemning the teachings of the Arya Samaj.

In 1879 Mirza Ghulam Ahmad had an exchange of views with Pandit Shiv Narain Agni Hotri on the subject of revelation, through correspondence which was later published. Pandit Shiv Narain Agni Hotri was a teacher in the Lahore Government High School. He was also editor and proprietor of the *Hindu Bandu* and was looked upon as a leader of the Bramho Samaj which denied the possibility of verbal revelation. The exchange of views continued from 21 May to 17 June 1879.

Kharak Singh's experience was repeated in the case of Agni Hotri. In later life he ceased to be a member of the Bramho Samaj and claimed that he himself was a recipient of divine revelation and founded a new sect called Dev Samaj.

In 1878 Mirza Ghulam Ahmad sent the manuscript of an article for publication to the Vakil Press, Amritsar, in a packet stamped at the rate prescribed for postal packets. He also placed in the packet a letter addressed to the Manager of the Press giving him instructions about the article. This was a contravention of the Post Office regulations which was punishable with fine or imprisonment. The Press belonged to Ralya Ram, a lawyer, who was a bigoted Christian. He made a complaint against Mirza Ghulam Ahmad to the postal authorities and a prosecution was instituted against him. He was summoned to Gurdaspur to answer the charge and engaged a lawyer, who was a friend of his, to defend him. The lawyer advised him very strongly to deny that he had put the letter in the packet. Mirza Ghulam Ahmad emphatically rejected the advice of the lawyer and told him that he could not depart from the truth in the least degree. The lawyer told him that in that case he was bound to be convicted and that it was no use for the lawyer to make an attempt to defend him. Mirza Ghulam Ahmad said that he regretted the lawyer's decision to leave him to his own devices but that there was no help for it. When the case was called he appeared before the magistrate without a lawyer, the prosecution being represented by a European Superintendent of Post Offices. The magistrate was also a European. In answer to his question Mirza Ghulam Ahmad stated that the packet and the letter had been despatched by him, but by placing the letter in the packet he had not intended to defraud or occasion loss to the Post Office. As the subject matter of the letter only contained directions with regard to the manuscript enclosed in the packet he had in good faith thought that the letter formed a part of the manuscript. The prosecutor argued that this was a clear case of contravention of the relevant Post Office regulation and that the statement of the accused amounted to a confession of guilt and he should be convicted and sentenced. The magistrate rejected the plea of the prosecutor and discharged Mirza Ghulam Ahmad.

It is worthy of note that the burden of proof, as had been pointed out to Mirza Ghulam Ahmad by his lawyer, was on the prosecution to establish that Mirza Ghulam Ahmad had placed the letter inside the packet. In case of his denial that he had done so, it would have been difficult for the prosecution to establish in fact that he had himself placed the letter in the packet. But he would not adopt a subterfuge and felt that he had no choice but to state the truth.

In 1874 Mirza Ghulam Ahmad saw in a dream a very handsome boy, about seven years of age, who he thought in his dream was an angel. The boy was sitting on a raised platform and gave him a large, delicious and luminous loaf of bread and said: 'This is for you and the dervishes who are with you.' This was a most significant dream; bread being a symbol of life and an indication of the establishment of the kingdom of God on earth. Mirza Ghulam Ahmad had already established the practice of sharing his food with others and some years later he instituted at Qadian a hostel and a kitchen for the entertainment of all those who came to visit him.

As a rule Mirza Ghulam Ahmad did not seek the company of other men, but he was always eager to visit righteous persons. Maulvi Abdullah Sahib of Ghazni, Afghanistan, was an eminent Muslim divine. He was persecuted in his native country by fanatics, and having been declared a disbeliever was expelled from Ghazni. He arrived in the Punjab and settled down in the neighbourhood of Amritsar. Mirza Ghulam Ahmad visited him on two occasions and requested him to pray for the welfare of Islam. Maulvi Abdullah Sahib complied with his request and told him later that he had received the revelation: 'Thou art our Master, so grant us succour against those who reject Thee' (2:287).

On a later occasion Maulvi Abdullah Sahib declared that he had seen in a vision that a heavenly light had descended on Qadian but that his descendants had failed to derive any benefit from it.

Towards the end of 1875 Mirza Ghulam Ahmad was advised in a vision by an angelic presence that it would be appropriate if, following the example set by many prophets, he would undertake the observation of a fast for a certain period. In pursuance of this suggestion he arranged to embark upon this discipline secretly, without disclosing his purpose to anyone. He arranged to distribute his food among some poor children whom he had told to come to him at certain appointed times. He took only one meal after sunset; but after two or three weeks of this discipline he began to reduce the quantity of that meal also, so that in the end he partook only of a few ounces of bread in 24 hours. He has described his experience in the following terms:

I continued this discipline over a period of eight or nine months and despite the extreme meagreness of the nourishment that I took, God Almighty safeguarded me against every kind of disorder. During this period of fasting I experienced many spiritual mysteries. I met several previous prophets and some outstanding Muslim saints who had passed away. On one occasion, in a state of complete wakefulness, I beheld the Holy Prophet, peace and blessings of Allah be upon him, who was accompanied by his two grandsons, his daughter Fatima and his cousin and son-in-law Ali, may Allah be pleased with all of them. This was not any kind of dream but was a species of complete wakefulness.

Besides this kind of experience, I beheld columns of spiritual light of different colours white, green and red, that were beautiful and impressive beyond description. These columns were so related to my heart that observing them my heart experienced an ecstacy the delight of which has no comparison. I imagined that these columns were an illustration of the mutual love between God and man. One light proceeded from the heart and ascended upwards and another light descended from above. When the two met they assumed the shape of a column. These are spiritual experiences which are not within the ken of worldly people, but there are also those in the world who are bestowed knowledge of such matters.

Another benefit that I derived from this exercise was that I discovered that, on need arising, I could endure starvation for a long period. I feel that if a stout wrestler were to compete with me in enduring starvation, he would die long before I would need any nourishment. I also feel that till a person's body is enured to such hardship he is not capable of experiencing the higher spiritual mysteries. But I would not advise everyone to embark upon such an exercise, nor did I undertake it on my own volition. I adopted it under divine direction that was conveyed to me in a clear vision. At the end of eight or nine months I terminated it and have since reverted to it only on rare occasions [*Kitabul Bariyyah*, pp. 164–7, footnote].

In 1876 Mirza Ghulam Ahmad happened to be in Lahore when he saw a dream which indicated that the death of his father was approaching. As he has said:

I hastened back to Qadian. My father was suffering from dysentery but I had no apprehension that he would die the following day. In fact there had been some improvement in his condition and he appeared quite steadfast. The following day we were all with him at noon when he kindly suggested that I should go and have some rest, for it was the month of June and the heat was intense. I retired into an upper room and a servant began to massage my feet. Presently I fell into a light slumber and received the revelation [Arabic]: 'We call to witness the heavens where all decrees originate, and We call to witness that which will happen after sunset.' I understood that what was to happen after sunset was my father's death, and that this revelation was by way of condolence on behalf of God Almighty. Holy is Allah! How Glorious is He that He conveyed His condolence on the approaching death of a person who was dying sorrowful over the waste of his life. Most people would be surprised at this interpretation that God Almighty should have condoled with me. It should, however, be remembered that when God, Glorified be His name, treats someone mercifully He deals with him like a friend.

When I received this revelation, which presaged the death of my father, the thought passed through my mind, due to my humanity, that some of the means of income which were available to my father would now be closed and we might be confronted with difficulties. Thereupon I received another revelation [Arabic]: Is not Allah sufficient for His servant?' This revelation conveyed great comfort to me and it found a firm place in my heart. I call God Almighty, in Whose hand is my life, Himself to witness that He has fulfilled this comforting revelation in a manner which I could not have imagined. He has provided for me as no father could have provided for anyone. I have been the recipient of His continuous bounties which I find impossible to count.

My father died the same day after sunset. This was the first day on which I experienced a sign of divine mercy through revelation, concerning which I cannot imagine that it would ever cease to have effect during my lifetime. I had the words of the revelation engraved on a semi-precious stone and set in a ring which I have with me securely. Nearly forty years of my life passed under the care of my father, and with his departure from this life I began to receive divine revelation continuously [*Kitabul Bariyyah*, pp. 190–5, footnote].

CHAPTER THREE

With the death of his father, his elder brother Mirza Ghulam Qadir became the head of the family and took over the administration of its affairs. Mirza Ghulam Qadir at that time held a civil office at Gurdaspur and visited Qadian at frequent intervals. Mirza Ghulam Ahmad was entitled to half of the property left by his father, but he paid no attention to these matters and let his brother appropriate the entire income from the property, being content with the provision of his own modest needs. He made no demand upon his brother, wore such clothes as he was furnished with and partook very sparingly of the food that was sent to him by his brother's wife. More often that not he would distribute the food among some poor people and would himself subsist on a little roast gram purchased with no more than a farthing. On some occasions he went without food altogether. By his own choice he led not only a simple but austere life. He occupied himself mainly with the worship and remembrance of God, study of and reflection upon the Holy Quran and other relevant religious literature. He subscribed to one or two papers, and on one occasion he sent a request to his brother for a trifling amount of money to pay for one of these papers. His request was turned down on the ground that reading a paper was a waste of time and to spend money on it was extravagance.

His brother respected him and was glad to provide the necessaries of life for him, but felt that his devotion to religion was a useless hobby and that he should address himself to some gainful occupation. Thus during the remaining years of his brother's life (1876–83) Mirza Ghulam Ahmad's life was much restricted and circumscribed in several respects.

The other members of the family were not much interested in his way of life and some of them did not conceal their hostility towards him and their contempt for the tenor of his life. He did not let any of this disturb his serenity and accepted whatever came in a spirit of cheerful resignation, deeming it a trial which he had been called upon by God to endure.

About that time the activities of the Arya Samaj, which had been founded by Swami Dayanand and had spread very rapidly in the Punjab began to be directed towards a harsh and even abusive criticism of Islam, its doctrines and teachings. In its polemics even the person of the Holy Prophet of Islam was not spared and his character was scandalously misrepresented in the vilest terms. Another quarter from which Islam was under constant attack were the Christian missionary organizations, whose fierce assault against Islam was couched in most offensive terms. In this situation the Muslims found themselves utterly helpless and exhibited extreme listlessness. Those of them who were alive to the perils to which Islam and the Muslims were exposed could not think of any effective means of meeting and overcoming them. Mirza Ghulam Ahmad proved to be the one great exception. His study of the Holy Quran, his deep reflection over the eternal verities, his complete reliance upon the grace and bounty of God, and his experience of communion with Him had already equipped him with the qualities of an effective champion of Islam. Under a divinely inspired urge he was moved to embark on a project which would not only help to safeguard Islam against hostile attacks, but would clearly and demonstrably establish its superiority over all other faiths. He resolved to set forth the excellences of Islam in a monumental work which he designated *Braheen Ahmadiyya*.

By May 1879 he had made enough progress with the composition of his great work to make a public announcement concerning its scope and purpose. The principal difficulty in his way was lack of funds for its publication. He made an appeal that those who could easily afford it should come forward to help him with its publication by subscribing to it in advance. But on account of the prevailing poverty of the Muslims, and their lack of enthusiasm for the faith, the response was not encouraging. A few of the well-to-do Muslims, however, made donations in excess of the price of the planned volumes that enabled the author to start publication of his work. The first two parts were published in 1880. The first part put forth a challenge that if a follower of any religion other than Islam would set forth on behalf of his religion one-half, or one-fourth or even one-fifth of the excellences that he himself proposed to formulate as the basis of Islam, he would make a present to him of all his property, which he valued at ten thousand rupees.

The composition and publication of this great, comprehensive work was a tremendous undertaking beset with difficulties of different types. The author himself was a profound scholar of Islam and of comparative religion and already enjoyed the experience of communion with the Divine. He was a constant recipient of revelation. He also had the advantage of access to the family library which, despite its destruction by the Sikhs in the time of his grandfather, had been restored to a respectable size. But that was the end of the facilities available to him. As already mentioned, Qadian, the place of residence of Mirza Ghulam Ahmad, was situated at a distance of eleven miles from the nearest railway station and telegraph office. It was a small town boasting few amenities. The nearest printing press available for the printing of this book was situated at Amritsar, a matter of thirty-five miles from Qadian. There was no one at that time available in Qadian who could have in any way assisted the author in the writing and production of his great work. He wrote out the entire manuscript with his own hand and when the time came for committing it to the printing press, he had to take it himself to Amritsar and make suitable arrangements for its printing. This involved a journey of eleven miles on a dirt track studded with potholes, which it was easier to traverse on foot than by means of one of the uncomfortable and perilous springless horse-drawn contraptions that were occasionally available for this purpose, followed by a railway journey of 24 miles. He had to undertake this journey to Amritsar and back on several occasions in connection with the printing of *Braheen Ahmadiyya*. The book was thus conceived, written and published entirely through the efforts of a single individual assisted only by the grace and bounty of the Divine.

The first two parts of the book were published in 1880, the third followed in 1882 and the fourth in 1884. Further work on the book was then laid aside as Mirza Ghulam Ahmad's attention was diverted from 1882 onwards to a much wider field. In that year he was commissioned by God Almighty, through revelation, as the Reformer of the century.

On the publication of the first two parts of the *Braheen Ahmadiyya*, tributes in superlative terms were paid to the book and its author by leading Muslim divines and outstanding Muslim personalities. Attention may here be drawn to some of the published reviews of the book.

Maulvi Muhammad Husain Sahib of Batala, leader of the Ahle Hadees sect, published in his journal *Ishaatas Sunnah* (Vol. VII, Nos. 6–11) a detailed review of the book extending over two hundred pages. In the opening part of the review he observed:

In our opinion, keeping in mind this age and its circumstances, this is a book the equal of which has not been published in Islam to this day, whatever might happen hereafter. The author has proved himself so steadfast in the service of Islam through his pen, his money, his tongue, etc., that few such instances are to be found among the Muslims.

If anyone should be disposed to consider our language an instance of Asiatic exaggeration he should point out at least one book which refutes the opponents of Islam, particularly the Arya Samaj and Brahmo Samaj, so emphatically and forcefully and should name three or four such helpers of Islam who are determined to serve Islam not only with money, pen and tongue but also with their persons and who have challenged the opponents of

Islam and those who deny the possibility of revelation to come and satisfy themselves that the challenger is himself a recipient of revelation.

He added: The author of *Braheen Ahmadiyya,* according to the testimony of friends and foes, regulates his life according to the law of Islam and is a pious and truthful person. It is well known that Satanic suggestions are mostly false but not one of the revelations received by the author of *Braheen Ahmadiyya* has been proved false up to this day. not, therefore, be considered Satanic suggestions. Can any Muslim follower of the Quran believe that Satan can be given knowledge, like the Prophets and the angels, of that which is hidden so that not one of his disclosures of the hidden should lack truth?

This detailed review concluded with the following appeal: The excellence of this book and its benefit for Islam will be recognized by those who read it with an open mind and by those who go through our review of it. Therefore, acting upon the principle that the only return for beneficence is beneficence, we wish to point out that helping the publication of this book through contributions towards the cost of its printing is a duty laid upon the entire Muslim community. The author of *Braheen Ahmadiyya* has, by writing this book, safeguarded the honour of the Muslims and has challenged the opponents of Islam emphatically and forcefully. He has announced to the whole world that anyone who doubts the truth of Islam should come to him and should witness the intellectual and spiritual proofs based on the Quran, and the miraculous manifestations of the prophethood of Muhammad (peace be on him) in support of the truth of Islam.

Another great admirer of *Braheen Ahmadiyya,* Hazrat Sufi Ahmad Jan Sahib of Ludhiana, who was himself a great saintly Sufi, wrote about the book as follows:

That great personage, benefactor of mankind, source of benevolence and beneficence, personal proof of Islam, honoured above the commonalty and the nobility, Hazrat Mirza Ghulam Ahmad Sahib, may his blessings endure, Chief of Qadian, in the district of Gurdaspur, Punjab, has written a book designated *Braheen Ahmadiyya* in Urdu, of which two parts have been published and the rest will continue to be published from time to time and will reach the subscribers in due course.

This book establishes the truth of Islam and of the Prophethood of Muhammad, peace and blessings of Allah be upon him, and of the Holy Quran, through three hundred strong proofs of various types and refutes the Christian, Arya, Hindu, Brahmo Samaj and all other religions opposed to Islam, by means of convincing reasoning. The author has announced in the first part of *Braheen Ahmadiyya* that if an opponent of Islam would set forth a refutation of all his arguments or half of them or even of one-fifth of them he would transfer the whole of his property, valued at ten thousand rupees, to him. This book completely frustrates all the opponents of Islam and demonstrates the truth of Islamic teachings in such excellent manner that everyone realizes what a grand bounty are faith and Islam, and what a treasure is the Holy Quran, and what a grand verity is the faith of Muhammad. The verses of the Holy Quran that are quoted on their appropriate occasions in this book amount to two-thirds of the whole Quran. The book convinces the disbelievers, activates the indifferent, warns the neglectful, perfects the understanding of the believers, strengthens the roots of Islamic doctrines and wipes out the doubts that are expressed by the opponents of Islam. In this 14th century of Islam great confusion prevails among the followers of every religion. As someone has said, new disbelievers and new Muslims emerge every day. At this time a book was needed like the *Braheen Ahmadiyya* and a Reformer was needed like our revered master Mirza Ghulam Ahmad Sahib who is ready to prove the claims of Islam to the satisfaction of its opponents.

The author of *Braheen Ahmadiyya* is not one of the common run of divines and spiritual preceptors, but has been specially commissioned by God and is a recipient of revelation. Hundreds of revelations and messages and prophecies and true dreams and Divine directions and glad tidings relating to this book and comprising intimations of triumph and Divine help and Divine guidance couched in various languages, such as Arabic, Persian, Urdu, and even English, though the author is not at all well versed in English, have been set out in this book, supported by the testimony of hundreds of opponents of Islam, which establishes their truth and proves that the author is doubtlessly writing this book under Divine instruction. It is also clear that, according to the *hadees* of the Holy Prophet, peace and blessings of Allah be upon him, that Allah, Lord of Glory and Honour, would raise among the Muslims at the beginning of every century one who would revive the faith, the author of this book is the Reformer of the 14th century and is a profound scholar and is one of the most perfect individuals of the Muslim community. This is also supported by another *hadees* of the Holy Prophet, peace and blessings of Allah be upon him, wherein he is reported to have said: The true divines among my followers will be like the prophets of Israel.

He concluded his review of *Braheen Ahmadiyya* by describing the character and qualities of its author in superlative terms.

Another appreciative review of the book was published by Maulvi Muhammad Sharif Sahib of Bangalore, Mysore, South India, who was the editor of *Manshoor Muhammedi*. He headed his review with the verse of the Holy Quran: 'Truth has arrived and falsehood has vanished; falsehood was bound to disappear (17.82).' In the course of his review he observed:

Islam is being attacked from all directions. Atheism is flourishing and irreligion is on the increase. Those of the Brahmo Samaj are making every effort to establish the superiority of their creed over Islam through their philosophic writings. Our Christian brothers are devoting the whole of their effort towards wiping out Islam. They are convinced that so long as the sun of Islam continues to shed its light upon the world all the efforts on behalf of Christianity would prove vain and trinity would gain no support. In short, the followers of all religions are eager to put out the light of Islam.

We had been most anxious over a long period that of the body of Muslim divines someone, who may be inspired by God to stand up in support and defence of the faith, should write a book which should be in accord with the need of the times, and which should set out on the basis of reason and scriptural arguments to prove that the Holy Quran is the Word of God and that the Holy Prophet, peace and blessings of Allah be upon him, was a righteous Prophet of God. We are deeply grateful to God that this desire of ours has at last been fulfilled. Here is the book the writing of which we had been awaiting for a long time. It's title is *Braheen Ahmadiyya*, and the author has set out in it three hundred conclusive arguments in proof of the truth of the Holy Quran and the prophethood of Muhammad, peace and blessings of Allah be upon him. The author of this book is the best of the divines, an accomplished scholar, pride of the Muslims of India, the accepted one of God Almighty, Maulvi Mirza Ghulam Ahmad Sahib, chief of Qadian, district Gurdaspur, Punjab. Allah be praised! What a wonderful compilation this is whose every word proves the truth of Islam and displays the righteousness of the Quran and of the prophethood of Muhammad. The opponents of Islam have been presented with bright conclusive arguments. Every claim is reasonable and is supported by brilliant arguments of a character so positive that no one can question them and everyone must yield to them provided everyone approaches them with a open and just mind.

This is the book which in truth is matchless. The author claims that it cannot be controverted. If anyone writes a reply to it, according to the conditions laid down in the announcement, he would be awarded ten thousand rupees. The truth is that if the opponents of Islam have any fear of God in their hearts they should, after perusing the book, affirm that there is no one worthy of worship save Allah and Muhammad is His righteous Messenger. We affirm with confidence and pride that no reply is possible to this book, indeed not till the day of Judgment. We too urge the opponents of Islam that if they truly believe in their respective religions they should come into the field and write a reply to this book. The author has offered an award of ten thousand rupees to anyone who writes a reply to the book. We, on our part, add one thousand rupees in the same way to this amount. We shall now see whether those of our brethren who are opposed to us will be roused to take up this challenge or will continue to repeat their old slogans.

He continued: Now we address ourselves to our Muslim brethren. This book, *Braheen Ahmadiyya,* is a peerless publication in its proof of the truth of the Quran and of the Prophethood of the Holy Prophet. The author has proved the truth of Isalm by such positive arguments that every just person would acknowledge that the Quran is the Book of Allah, that the Prophethood of the Holy Prophet is righteous, that Islam is a faith established by God and that a Muslim is instructed in the truth. There is here such a multiplicity of proofs that no way of escape and no possibility of denial has been left open to an opponent. Every argument is clear, every proof is bright. The book is a mirror of faith and is full of the Quran to the brim. It leads to the straight path, it is a torch that lights up the true way. It is a treasury of truth, it is a mine of guidance, it acts as lightning on the stores of the enemy and burns up all his arguments. For the Muslims it is a strong support for the Holy Book and is a bright proof of the Mother of the Book. It has unsettled and disturbed every enemy of religion.

A few minor Muslim divines were critical of parts of the book and merely betrayed their own lack of knowledge by giving expression to their critical views. No one paid any serious attention to them.

But the book aroused great indignation in certain non-Muslim sections. They expressed themselves in defamatory and contemptuous language against the author and announced in indignant terms their intention of writing a refutation of the book. But their indignation subsided fairly quickly. They were prodded by the author of the book in an announcement which was couched in these terms:

> I put all these gentlemen on oath that they should not delay for one moment in entering the lists against me. Let them put on the guise of Plato, Aristotle and Bacon. Let them supplicate their false deities, and then see whether our God is proved Supreme or their false deities.

Despite the original challenge in the first part of *Braheen Ahmadiyya*, and this reminder in the second part, no one of any standing undertook a refutation of the book. Here and there a self-styled leader among the Hindus or the Christians announced his intention of taking up the challenge of the author but took no step in pursuit of that objective.

Only one notoriously foul-mouthed Arya Samajist, of the name of Pandit Lekh Ram, published a collection of absurdities under the name of *Refutation of Braheen Ahmadiyya*, the senselessness of which was speedily exposed by Maulvi Hakim Nooruddin Sahib (may Allah be pleased with him) in his book designated *Confirmation of Braheen Ahmadiyya*. This was, however, only the beginning of the mischief of Pandit Lekh Ram to whose tragic end we shall revert later.

Hazrat Mirza Ghulam Ahmad had two sons, Mirza Sultan Ahmad and Mirza Fazal Ahmad, from his first wife. His near relatives had not the slightest inclination towards religion and led lives divorced altogether from the higher moral qualities, and had no concept at all of spirituality. His wife had also adopted their ways and was not in the least interested in matters that were considered vital by her husband and to which he attached the greatest importance. The result was that in course of time their lives drifted apart and in the end their marriage was terminated. Thereafter, Hazrat Mirza Ghulam Ahmad's whole attention was devoted to Divine worship and service of the faith and he became indifferent altogether to the values of a marital life.

His health had for some time been indifferent. He had begun to suffer from diabetes and migraine and he had lost all interest in the other sex. In this situation he received a revelation in 1881, when he was 46 years old, in Arabic: 'We give thee glad tidings of a handsome son.' He mentioned this revelation to some people who were in touch with him, including his two non-Muslim friends, Lala Sharmpat and Lala Mulawamal, who were all greatly surprised, considering that he had divorced his first wife, was not interested in a second marriage, and was in a state of indifferent health.

Some months later he received another revelation (Arabic): 'Be grateful for My bounty that thou hast found My KHADEEJAH.' As Khadeejah was the name of the first wife of the Holy Prophet, the meaning of the revelation clearly was that God had planned a second marriage for him.

This was followed after a short interval by another revelation (Arabic): 'All praise belongs to Allah who has bestowed upon you a noble relationship through marriage and a noble descent.' A short while after he received a revelation, part of which was in Urdu and part was in Persian: 'I have designed another marriage for you, and shall Myself arrange and provide everything connected with it. You will not be put to any inconvenience concerning it.'

It thus became clear, through these successive revelations,

that God Almighty desired him to arrange a second marriage which would carry Divine blessings with itself. Despite his own disinclination towards marriage and the state of his health and his somewhat advanced age, he bowed to the Divine will and it so happened that by the sheer grace of God his second marriage was celebrated on 17 November 1884 with a young lady of a noble Syed family of Delhi whose name was Nusrat Jahan Begum (meaning the lady who helps the whole world). Her father's name was Mir Nasir Nawab Sahib, the meaning of Nasir Nawab being the Prince helper. Both names were of very good augury, as they indicated that the marriage would prove a source of Divine help and blessings.

Concerning this marriage, Hazrat Mirza Ghulam Ahmad wrote several years later as follows:

> Approximately sixteen years ago I informed some of those people who were in touch with me that God had revealed to me that He would arrange for my marriage in a noble Syed family and that He would bless this marriage and would make it fruitful. This had been conveyed to me at a time when I suffered from certain disorders and had become physically very weak and infirm. I had only a short while before recovered from tuberculosis. On account of the retired life that I led my mind shrank from undertaking the responsibilities of married life. In this pitiful condition I received a revelation [Persian:] 'I shall provide all that may be needed in respect of your marriage.' I call to witness Him in Whose hand is my life, that in accord with His promises He relieved me after this marriage from every burden relating to it and provided me with great comfort. No father provides for his son as He provided for me. No mother takes such good care of her child as He took of me. A long time before this marriage He had promised me in a revelation [Arabic] which was mentioned in *Braheen Ahmadiyya:* 'O Ahmad, dwell thou and thy wife in paradise'; and He fulfilled this promise to the utmost. He did not let me worry in the least concerning the means of my subsistence, nor did He let me suffer any anxiety about my household affairs.
>
> As my heart and brain had become weak in consequence of the two disorders, namely diabetes and migraine, from which I suf-

fered permanently, some of my friends expressed their concern over my marriage. Out of sympathy for me Maulvi Muhammad Husain Sahib of Batala wrote to me: 'You have married a second time and I understand from Hakim Maulvi Muhammad Sharif that on account of extreme weakness you are not fit for marriage. If this matter relates to your spiritual state I have no right to raise any objection, for I am not unaware of the extraordinary spiritual powers of the saintly ones. Otherwise, I fear lest you might encounter some trial.'

In this situation I supplicated the Divine and He intimated to me through revelation the medicines that would prove effective for me and I saw in a vision that an angel was administering those medicines to me. God so blessed me that I was convinced that He had bestowed on me the full health and strength that are enjoyed by a person in normal health. He bestowed four sons on me. Were I not afraid that I might be suspected of exaggeration, I would have set out in detail the miraculous change that was brought about in me so that it might be known that the signs of our Powerful God are exhibited in every shape and form particularly for those of His servants whom He esteems [*Taryaqul Qulub*, pp. 35–6].

Even before this marriage Hazrat Mirza Ghulam Ahmad had had in mind that he should go into retreat at some solitary place for 40 days and devote himself entirely in solitude to Divine Worship and supplication. In 1884 he decided to go to Sujanpur, in the district of Gurdaspur, for the purpose of this retreat; but he received a revelation (Urdu): 'Your purpose would be achieved in Hoshiarpur.'

Eventually in January 1886 he went to Hoshiarpur, accompanied by three attendants, and took up his residence on the first floor of a secluded building belonging to Sheikh Mehr Ali Sahib, a leading citizen of Hoshiarpur. He instructed his attendants that one of them should bring up his two daily meals to him and should leave them with him without any comment. He also told them that no one should be permitted to come up and intrude upon him.

Having completed this period of 40 days he published an announcement on 20 February 1886, from Hoshiarpur, that during his retreat he had been honoured by God Almighty with the disclosure of many matters with regard to the unknown which he would set out in detail subsequently. Out of them he mentioned in the announcement one particular prophecy which related to his own person. He stated:

God Almighty, the Lord of Honour and Glory, Merciful, Benevolent, Exalted, Who has power to do all that He wills (glory be to Him and exalted be His name) has vouchsafed to me the following revelation.

I confer upon thee a sign of My mercy according to thy entreaties and have honoured thy prayers with acceptance through My mercy and have blessed this thy journey. A Sign of power, mercy and nearness to Me is bestowed on thee, a Sign of grace and beneficence is awarded to thee, and thou art granted the key of success and victory. Peace on thee, O victorious one. Thus does God speak so that those who desire life may be rescued from the grip of death, and those who are buried in the graves may emerge therefrom, so that the superiority of Islam and the dignity of God's Word may become manifest unto the people, and so that truth may arrive with all its blessings and falsehood may depart with all its ills; so that people may understand that I am the Lord of Power and do what I will and so that they may believe that I am with thee, and so that those who do not believe in God and deny and reject His religion and His Book and His Holy Messenger, Muhammad the chosen one, on whom be peace, may be confronted with a clear Sign and the way of the guilty ones may become manifest.

Rejoice, therefore, that a handsome and pure boy will be bestowed on thee. Thou wilt receive an intelligent youth who will be of thy seed and will be of thy progeny. A handsome and pure boy will come as your guest. His name is Emmanuel and Bashir. He has been invested with a holy spirit, and he will be free from all impurity. He is the light of Allah. Blessed is he who comes from heaven. He will be accompanied by grace which shall arrive with him. He will be characterized by grandeur, greatness and wealth. He will come into the world and will heal many of their ills through his Messianic qualities and through the blessings of the Holy Spirit. He is the Word of Allah, for Allah's mercy and honour have equipped him with the Word of Majesty. He will be extremely intelligent and understanding and will be meek of heart and will be filled with secular and spiritual knowledge. He will convert three into four (of this the meaning is not clear). It is Monday, a blessed Monday. Son, delight of the heart, high ranking, noble; a manifestation of the First and the Last, a manifestation of the True and the High; as if Allah has descended from heaven. His advent will be greatly blessed and will be a source of the manifestation of Divine Majesty. Behold a light cometh, a light anointed by God with the perfume of His pleasure. He will pour His spirit upon him and he will be sheltered under the shadow of God. He will grow rapidly in stature and will be the means of procuring the release of those held in bondage. His fame will spread to the ends of the earth and people will be blessed through him. He will then be raised to his spiritual station in heaven. This is a matter decreed.

Thy house will be filled with blessings and I shall perfect My favours unto thee and thou wilt have a large progeny from blessed women some of whom thou wilt find hereafter, and I will cause a great increase in thy progeny and will bless it; but some of them will die in early age and thy progeny will spread greatly in different lands. Every branch of thy collaterals will be cut off and will come to an end soon through childlessness, if they do not repent. Their houses will be filled with widows and God's wrath will descend upon their walls. But if they turn to God, He will turn to them in mercy. God will spread thy blessings about and will revive through thee a house that is ruined and will fill a fearful house with blessings. Thy progeny will not be cut off and will flourish to the end of days. God will maintain thy name with honour till the day when the world comes to an end, and will convey thy message to the ends of the earth. I shall exalt thee and shall call thee to Myself, but thy name will never be erased from the face of the earth. It will so happen that all those who seek to humiliate thee and to cause thee to fail and wish to ruin thee will be frustrated and will die, being brought to naught. God will bestow every success upon thee and will grant thee all that thou dost desire. I will cause an increase of thy true sincere friends and will bless their lives and their properties and they will grow in number, and they will always prevail over the other Muslims who are jealous of thee and are hostile to thee. God will not forget thy supporters and will not overlook them and they will have their reward according to the degree of their devotion. Thou art to Me as the prophets of

Bani Israel. Thou art to Me as My Unity. Thou art of me and I am of thee. The time is approaching, indeed it is near, when God will put thy love in the hearts of Kings and nobles, so much so that they will seek blessings from thy garments. O you who deny and oppose the truth, if you are in doubt concerning My servant, if you deny the grace and bounty that I have bestowed upon him, then produce some true sign concerning yourselves like this Sign of mercy, if you are truthful. But if you are unable to produce it, and be sure you will never be able to produce it, then he mindful of the Fire which has been prepared for the disobedient, the liars and the transgressors.

In his announcement of 22 March 1886, he stated:

This is not only a prophecy, it is a grand heavenly Sign, which Almighty God has shown for demonstrating the truth and greatness of the gentle and compassionate Prophet, Muhammad, the chosen one, peace and blessings of Allah be on him and his people. This Sign is a hundred times greater, better, more perfect, more exalted and more complete than bringing a dead one back to life. Such an event, the possibility of which is open to question, merely means to bring a spirit back to life by supplication to God. In this instance God, the Almighty, has through His great grace and benevolence and through the blessings of the Seal of the Prophets, peace and blessings of Allah be upon him and his people, by accepting the supplications of this humble one, promised to send a blessed spirit whose manifest and hidden blessings will spread throughout the earth. It might, on the surface, appear like bringing to life a dead person, but reflection would show that it is a far better Sign than reviving a dead person. Reviving a dead person means to win back a soul through supplication, but what a tremendous difference is there between those souls and this soul.

In the same announcement he specified that the promised son would surely be born within nine years. In another announcement, of 8 April 1886, he pointed out:

The grandeur of the prophecy relating to the birth of a son whose various high qualities have been set out, is not reduced by any long period that might be specified for its fulfillment, even though it might be the double of nine years. The heart of every just person will bear clear witness that the fulfilment of such a high prediction which comprises the birth of such an outstanding and special personality is beyond human power. The revelation of such good news in consequence of the acceptance of prayer is not only a prophecy but is a grand heavenly Sign.

In an announcement of 1 December 1886, he explained that in the announcement of 20 February, the words beginning with 'A handsome and pure boy' and ending with 'he who comes from heaven' indicate a short life, for a guest is one who stays for a few days and then departs before one's eyes. The succeeding sentence refers to the Promised Reformer who is named FAZAL in the revelation.

In a footnote to that announcement he stated: 'According to the Divine Promise, he will certainly be born within the term announced. Heaven and earth can move away but it is not possible that His promise may not be fulfilled.'

According to the earlier part of the prophecy a son was born to Hazrat Mirza Ghulam Ahmad on 7 August 1887 but proved only a guest and died on 4 November 1888. He was named Bashir Ahmad and has become known as Bashir I.

In an announcement of 12 January 1889, Hazrat Mirza Ghulam Ahmad affirmed:

I know with complete certainty that God Almighty will deal with me according to His promise. If the time of the birth of the promised son is not yet, he will appear later. If there is left only one day of the term announced, God, the Lord of Honour and Glory, will not let that day end till He has fulfilled His promise.

On Saturday 12 January 1889, Hazrat Mirza Ghulam Ahmad was blessed with a son whom he named Mahmud. On the same day he issued a leaflet announcing the birth of the child, in which he stated that he had not yet been informed whether this boy was the one who would be the Promised Reformer. Later, at different times, he declared in his books definitely that Mahmud was the promised son whose birth had been predicted in the announcement of 20 February 1886.

Approximately a year earlier Hazrat Ahmad had been directed through revelation to lay the foundation of a Community of his followers by inviting them to enter into a convenant of spiritual allegiance to him. He waited for some time before making an announcement that he had been authorized to invite people to enter into a convenant of spiritual allegiance to him. Eventually he made such an announcement on 1 December 1888, and on 12 January 1889 he announced conditions of initiation into the Movement. These conditions were:

A person who desires to make the covenant should make up his mind firmly:

First, that up to the date of his death he shall abstain altogether from associating anything with Allah in his worship;

Secondly, that he shall keep away altogether from falsehood, adultery, gazing at women outside the prohibited degrees, cruelty, dishonesty, disorder, rebellion and every kind of evil; and shall not allow himself to be carried away by his passions, however strong they may be;

Thirdly, that he shall perform the five daily acts of worship, according to the divine command and the directions of the Holy Prophet, and shall try to the best of his ability to offer the late night voluntary prayers to invoke the blessings of Allah upon the Holy Prophet, to ask forgiveness for his own sins and for supplicating Allah for His help; and that reminding himself of Allah's bounties, shall praise Him continuously;

Fourthly, that he shall in no way do harm to any of Allah's creatures in general and to Muslims in particular by giving way to his passions, neither with his hands, nor with his tongue, nor by any other means;

Fifthly, that in every state whether of joy or of sorrow, of prosperity or adversity, he shall prove himself faithful to Allah and shall be ready to endure every kind of insult and pain, and that in the hour of misfortune he shall not turn away from God but shall rather draw closer to Him;

Sixthly, that he shall not follow vulgar customs and shall guard against all evil inclinations, and shall submit himself completely to the authority of the Holy Quran and shall make the Word of Allah and the practice of the Holy Prophet the guiding principles of his life;

Seventhly, that he shall discard pride and haughtiness and shall pass his days in humility, lowliness, courtesy and meekness;

Eighthly, that he shall hold his religion and the dignity and welfare of Islam dearer than his life, wealth and children and everything else;

Ninethly, that he shall, for the sake of Allah, have sympathy for Allah's creatures and shall, to the best of his ability, devote his natural talents towards the promotion of their welfare; and

Tenthly, that he shall establish a relationship of brotherhood with me on condition of obeying me in all good things and adhere to it till the day of his death and that this relationship shall be of such high order that the like of it shall not be found in any worldly relationship either of family or between master and servant.

In March 1889 Hazrat Ahmad went to Ludhiana, and on the 4th of that month he issued a leaflet in which he stated:

God desires to found a community of the faithful to manifest His Glory and Power. He will make the Community grow and prosper, to establish the love of God, righteousness, purity, piety, peace and goodwill among men. This shall be a group of persons devoted to God. He shall strengthen them with His own spirit, and bless them and purify them. He shall multiply them exceedingly as He has promised. Thousands of truthful people shall join His ranks. He shall Himself look after them and shall make the Community grow, so much so that its numbers and progress shall amaze the world. The Community shall be a lighthouse so high as to illumine the four corners of the world. The members thereof shall serve as models of Islamic blessings. My true followers shall excel every other people. There shall always rise among them, till the Judgment Day, personages who will be the chosen ones of God in every respect. So has the Almighty decreed. He does as He wills.

The formal initiation started on 23 March 1889. Hazrat Maulvi Nurud-din Sahib had the honour of being the first to be invited to make the covenant, which was as follows:

I repent today, at the hand of Ahmad, of all the sins and evil habits to which I was addicted; and most truly and solemnly promise that to the last day of my life, I shall eschew, to the best of my ability, all manner of sin. I will uphold my faith above all worldly considerations. I shall try, as far as may be within my power, to observe the ten conditions of initiation set out in the leaflet dated 12 January 1889. I seek the forgiveness of God for my past sins. [These words were repeated in Urdu, and, thereafter, the following supplication was made in Arabic:] I ask forgiveness of Allah, my Lord, for all sins and turn to Him in repentance. I bear witness that there is no one worthy of worship save God, the One without associate; and I bear witness that Muhammad is His Servant and Messenger. Lord, I have wronged my soul and confess my sins. Do Thou forgive my sins for no one can forgive sins save Thyself.

Thus was laid the foundation of the Ahmadiyya Movement in Islam, the branches of which are to be found in every part of the world.

CHAPTER FOUR

In 1890 Ahmad wrote two books, *Fateh Islam* and *Tauzih Maram*. To these was later added his book *Izalah Auham*. All three were published early in 1891. In these three books he set forth his claim of being the Mahdi, and the Promised Messiah, whose advent in the latter days had been foretold by the Holy Prophet of Islam, peace and blessings of Allah be upon him.

There is a whole mass of traditions attributed to the Holy Prophet, on whom be peace, which present a confusing variety of the signs and particulars relating to the Mahdi and the Messiah. Most of these traditions have been declared by eminent Muslim theologians as of doubtful authenticity. That which emerges positively from this body of traditions may be summarized very briefly as follows.

(1) The Mahdi and the Messiah would appear in the latter days.

(2) They will not be distinct and separate personalities but would be one person whose main function would be the renaissance of Islam.

(3) Within this overall framework, the Promised Messiah would effectively refute the doctrine of the cross, and expose the falsity of the doctrines of the Church like the Trinity, Atonement and Salvation through the blood of Jesus.

(4) He would be the champion of Islam against all comers, and would establish the superiority of Islam over all other faiths as is indicated in 9:33.

At the time of the advent of Ahmad, there was a widespread misconception among the members of the so-called orthodox sects of Islam that Jesus had been taken up bodily unto heaven and would descend upon earth in the latter days. Ahmad demonstrated the falsity and absurdity of this notion so effectively, both from the Holy Quran and from the traditions of the Holy Prophet, peace be on him, that today there is scarcely an enlightened divine among the orthodox sects who adheres to this concept. Those Muslims who had believed that Jesus had been taken bodily up into heaven held that he was not put upon the cross and was taken up to heaven before someone resembling him having been mistakenly taken for Jesus was put upon the cross. Therefore, the question whether Jesus died on the cross has relevance only *vis-à-vis* the Christian Church and does not concern the orthodox body of Muslims. However, the notion that Jesus had been taken bodily up to heaven and would descend to earth in his physical body in the latter days was considered an effective refutation of the claim of Ahmad that he was the Promised Messiah. During Ahmad's lifetime fierce controversy raged around this phenomenon.

His claim of being the Mahdi-Messiah aroused bitter opposition and the then Muslim divines, led by Maulvi Muhammad Husain of Batala, who, up to that time had been a great admirer and enthusiastic supporter of Ahmad, almost unanimously declared him an infidel, outside the pale of Islam. They hurled vile abuse at him, denounced him as an apostate from Islam, and some of them went so far as to declare that his assassination would be a highly meritorious act and that whoever brought it about would be straightaway admitted to paradise. He and his followers were held up to ridicule, were vituperated, were boycotted and were persecuted in diverse ways. He himself was prosecuted on false or untenable charges but was in each case honourably discharged or acquitted, according to his own previously announced revelations which conveyed to him Divine assurance of support and protection.

The principal points of doctrinal controversy between him and his opponents were:

(1) Whether Jesus had died a natural death on earth, as Ahmad affirmed, or whether he was taken bodily up to heaven as his opponents alleged.

(2) Whether the Holy Prophet's being the Seal of the

Prophets as mentioned in the Holy Quran (33:41) precluded altogether the appearance of a prophet among the Muslims, even by way of reflection of the prophethood of the Holy Prophet, peace be on him, as claimed by Ahmad.

(3) Whether Ahmad's claim of being a recipient of revelation and being a subordinate prophet by way of reflection of the Holy Prophet, peace be on him, was justified on the merits.

I

The Holy Quran is perfectly clear that Jesus died a natural death, and is most emphatic that no human being can ascend to heaven in his physical body. For instance, it is said:

> The enemies of Jesus devised their plan and Allah devised His plan; Allah is the best of planners. Allah reassured Jesus: 'I shall cause thee to die a natural death, and shall exalt thee to Myself, and shall clear thee from the calumnies of those who disbelieve, and shall place those who follow thee above those who disbelieve, until the Day of Judgment; then to Me shall be your return and I will judge between you concerning that wherein you differ' (3:55–6).

This makes it absolutely clear that Jesus died a natural death and not the accursed death of the cross and was spiritually exalted like all the righteous. The calumny of Jesus, that having died on the cross he had become accursed in accordance with the pronouncement contained in Deut. 21:23, is refuted in this verse, which established that Jesus did not die upon the cross and died a natural death in due course.

Those of the Muslims who believe in the bodily ascent of Jesus to heaven seek to pervert the sequence of this verse and claim that the exaltation of Jesus to heaven was to precede his eventual death after his descent upon earth in the latter days. In adopting this attitude they perpetrate several enormities. The sequence of the whole of the Quran was determined by God Almighty and cannot be interferred with or differently construed by anyone. But even their daring attempt does not advance their atrocious and absurd purpose. The exaltation mentioned in the verse is clearly spiritual exaltation which follows upon the death of a righteous person. The whole purpose of the mention of such exaltation in this verse is to clear Jesus of the calumny of the Jews that he had died an accursed death and had thus been rejected by God. Therefore, this verse affirms that Jesus died a natural death and was spiritually exalted to God and was not rejected by Him. This is reaffirmed in another verse, where it is stated: 'They certainly did not slay him; indeed, Allah exalted him to Himself; Allah is Mighty, Wise' (4:158–9).

The term employed in these two verses for exaltation is used at other places in the Quran in the same sense of spiritual exaltation. For instance, it is said with regard to Prophet Idris (Enoch): 'Recite the account of Idris according to this Book; he was indeed a righteous person and a prophet, and We exalted him to a lofty station' (19:57–8). In another verse it is stated: 'Recall to them the case of him to whom We gave Our Signs but he passed them by. Then Satan went after him and he became one of those who had gone astray. Had We so willed We would have exalted him by means of Our Signs, but he leaned towards the earth and followed his vain desires' (7:176–7).

Besides, it is worthy of note that the exaltation promised to Jesus and indeed to all the righteous is to God Himself, which can only be spiritual exaltation. There is no mention or indication here of any physical ascent to heaven.

The matter is conclusively settled by the clear affirmation of the Quran that it is not possible for a human being to ascend bodily to heaven. The opponents of the Holy Prophet, peace be on him, assured him that they would believe in him if he would ascend up into heaven and bring down therefrom a book which they might read. The Holy Prophet was directed to tell them in answer to their demand: 'Holy is my Lord. I am but a human being sent as a Messenger' (17:94). Therefore, there can be no doubt whatever that it is out of the question for any human being to ascend bodily unto heaven.

The physical survival of Jesus in heaven is also refuted by the Quran in the verse: 'Muhammad is but a Messenger; of a surety all Messengers before him have passed away. If then he should die or be slain, will you turn back on your heels?' (3:145). This establishes definitely that all prophets who had preceded the Holy Prophet, peace be on him, had died and that none of them was physically alive. When the Holy Prophet himself died, some of his companions were so overwhelmed with grief that they asserted that he had not died and would soon be revived. Hazrat Abu Bakr drew their attention to this verse that all prophets who had appeared before the Holy Prophet had died, and that his death was in accord with the divine law that everyone who is born must die in due course. On that occasion he made his famous pronouncement: 'Hearken! Let him out of you who worshipped Muhammad know that he has died, and let him who worshipped Allah draw comfort from the realization that He is Ever-Living and is not subject to death.'

The earth has been appointed man's natural habitat, as it is said: 'There is an abode for you and a provision for a time on this earth. Therein shall you live, and therein shall you die, and therefrom shall you be brought forth' (7:25–6).

At another place it is said: 'Have We not made the earth vast enough to gather the living and the dead?' (77:26–7).

A good deal of confusion has resulted from the double connotation of the word heaven. It means both the sky and all that it comprises as a geographical entity, and also the spiritual state and condition that the righteous would enjoy after they pass on from this life. The human body is so designed and is invested with such faculties as enable it to function properly in the conditions that prevail upon the earth. It cannot survive under any other conditions. If by ascent to heaven of any person it is meant to convey that such a person has departed physically from the earth and has taken up his abode somewhere in or beyond the atmosphere of the earth with his physical body, or has been admitted with that body into the conditions of the spiritual state which is promised to the righteous after their demise, in either case the statement amounts to an absurdity.

Another difficulty in the way of the bodily ascent of Jesus to heaven is, what became of his habitat after such an ascent and how are his physical needs being met?

There is a well-known saying of the Holy Prophet: 'Had Moses and Jesus been alive they would have had no choice but to follow me.' This clearly means that in the estimation of the Holy Prophet, peace be on him, Jesus was as dead as Moses. That should be conclusive even in the eyes of the orthodox divines.

II

The finality of the prophethood of the Holy Prophet, peace be on him, is still a matter of fierce controversy between the bulk of the orthodox Muslims and the members of the Ahmadiyya Movement. The central issue in this context is the verse of the Holy Quran: 'Muhammad is not the father of any of your males, but he is the Messenger of Allah and Seal of the Prophets; Allah has full knowledge of all things' (33:41). Thus the issue resolves itself into the exact connotation of the expression Seal of the Prophets, keeping in mind the context of the verse.

There is not the least doubt that the Founder of the Ahmadiyya Movement believed sincerely and whole-heartedly that the Holy Prophet, peace be on him, was the Seal of the Prophets in its truest and most exalted connotation. For instance, he has said:

> I call to witness the Glory of God and His Majesty that I am one of the faithful, a Muslim, and I believe in Allah, the Exalted, in His Books, in His Messengers, in His angels and in the life after death. I believe that our Prophet Muhammad, the Elect of God, peace and blessings of Allah be upon him, is the most eminent of the prophets and the Seal of the Prophets [*Hamamatul Bushra*, p. 8].

Again, he has said: The charge made against me and my Community that we do not believe the Messenger of Allah, peace be on him, to be the Seal of the Prophets is utterly false. The faith, the conviction, the certitude and the absoluteness that characterize our belief in the Holy Prophet, peace be on him, as the Seal of the Prophets, are entirely absent from the belief of our opponents [*Al-Hakam*, 19 March 1905].

He elaborated this in his statement as follows: We believe that the Quran is the last Book and Final Law and that after it there can be no prophet till the end of days, in the sense of a law-giver or a recipient of the word of God independently of the Holy Prophet, peace be on him. As God Almighty has pronounced the Holy Prophet, peace be on him, to be the Seal of the Prophets, He implies that because of his spiritual eminence the Holy Prophet is like a father unto the righteous whose inner perfection is achieved through subordination to him and who are honoured with the bounties of Divine revelation. Thus it is said: 'Muhammad is not the father of any of your males, but he is the Messenger of Allah and the Seal of the Prophets.'

The use of the conjunction 'but' after the opening affirmation of the verse, introduces a qualification of the affirmation to the effect that though the Holy Prophet does not enjoy the physical fatherhood of any male, his spiritual fatherhood is so comprehensive that after him an independent grant of the blessings of prophethood has been terminated and that thereafter prophethood would be granted only to a person bearing the Seal of, and acknowledging subservience to, the Holy Prophet. Such a one would thus become a son and heir of the Holy Prophet.

Thus while the fatherhood of the Holy Prophet in respect of males has been negatived, yet his spiritual fatherhood has been affirmed so that the criticism of his enemies, based on the verse 'Surely, it is thy enemy whose line will be cut off', might be confounded. In short, what is meant is that prophethood, even unaccompanied by a new law, is barred as a direct bounty, yet it is attainable as a bounty through the light of Muhammad, peace be on him. (Review on the Debate between Chakralvi and Batalvi, pp. 6–7.)

Yet again he has said: The Seal of the Prophets indicates that no prophethood can be valid without the attestation of the Seal. When a seal is stamped on a paper the paper is attested as authentic. Thus a prophethood not bearing the seal and attestation of the Holy Prophet, peace be on him, is not valid [*Al-Hakam*, 17 October 1902].

He has said further: Allah made the Holy Prophet, peace be on him, the Lord of the Seal and granted him as proof of his eminence the Seal that He granted to no other prophet. Therefore was he styled Seal of the Prophets, meaning that subservience to him imports the excellences of prophethood and that his spiritual grace has a prophet-raising quality and that such holy eminence was not granted to any other prophet [*Haqeeqatul Wahi*, pp. 96–7].

In explanation of his own claim he has said: I received this honour through obedience to the Holy Prophet, peace be on him. Had I not been one of his followers, I would never have been honoured with the Divine word, even if my striving and my deeds had matched the grandeur and height of all the mountains, for, all prophethoods, except the prophethood of Muhammad, have come to an end. No law-bearing prophet can now arise, but a prophet without law may arrive, provided he is primarily a follower of the Holy Prophet, peace be on him. Thus I am both a follower and a prophet [*Tajalliyate Ilahiyya*, pp. 24–5].

Prophethood in Islam is of three types. One, the principal and only real type of prophethood which is law-bearing; two, non-law-bearing prophethood which is independent of any other prophethood and is a direct Divine gift, such as the prophethood of the line of prophets who followed after Moses, whose prophethood was not derived from allegiance to Moses; and three, non-law-bearing prophethood which is bestowed through allegiance to a law-bearing prophet as a reflection of his light and his excellences. Such was the prophethood claimed by the Promised Messiah who was simultaneously a follower of the Holy Prophet, peace be on him, and a prophet as a reflection of the prophethood of Muhammad, peace be on him. Such a prophethood does not in any way contravene or violate the Seal of Prophethood, nor is it at all derogatory to the dignity of the Holy Prophet, peace be on him. Indeed it upholds and uplifts the dignity of the Holy Prophet.

This position is supported fully by the Holy Quran. For instance, we are taught the supplication in the Surah Fatiha: 'Guide us along the right path, the path of those on whom Thou hast bestowed Thy favours.' This supplication is made by every pious Muslim in full earnestness more than thirty times in a day. It is thus surely to be hoped that the Divine bounties referred to in this supplication would from time to time be bestowed upon righteous Muslims. What are those bounties? They are set out in the following verse of the Holy Quran: 'Whoso obeys Allah and the Messenger shall be among those upon whom Allah has bestowed His favours—the Prophets, the Faithful ones, the Martyrs and the Righteous; and excellent companions these are. This is Allah's grace and Allah is All-Comprehending' (4:70–1).

God Almighty having Himself urged the believers to supplicate Him repeatedly and continuously that they might become the recipients of His favours and having specified the categories of those favours, would not close the doors of any of those favours upon His righteous servants. Reading these verses together it follows inevitably that the permissible category of prophethood is, throughout, open to the righteous among the Muslims.

Sometimes it is suggested that the use of the expression 'among', in the verse last cited, means only that those who obey Allah and His Messenger would be in the company of those upon whom Allah has bestowed His favours, and not that they would themselves belong to those categories. This is an utterly untenable interpretation and is inconsistent with the use of the expression 'among' in other verses of the Holy Quran. For instance, it is said: 'Lord, forgive us our sins, cover up our faults and cause us to die with the virtuous.' Here the same expression has been used but obviously means that in our death we should be accounted virtuous.

The Holy Quran clearly contemplates the advent of prophets among the Muslims. For instance, it is said:

Children of Adam, if Messengers come to you from among yourselves, rehearsing My commandments unto you, then whoso is mindful of his duty to Allah and acts righteously, on such shall come no fear nor shall they grieve. But those who reject Our Signs and turn away from them in disdain, these shall be the inmates of the Fire; therein shall they abide [7:36–7].

The context in which the Holy Prophet was designated the Seal of the Prophets was that all his male children, born of his first marrige, had died while he was still in Mecca. His opponents took up the position that as he was without male issue there would be no one to carry on his mission after him and that with his death the religion founded by him would automatically come to an end. He thereupon received the revelation: 'Surely We have bestowed upon thee abundance of every kind of good. So supplicate thy Lord in gratitude and offer Him sacrifice. Surely, it is thine enemy whose line will be cut off' (108:2–4). The Holy Prophet had adopted Zaid as his son in Mecca. After his migration to Medina the institution of adoption was abrogated under divine commandment, and this furnished another opportunity to his opponents to charge him with lack of male heirs. To repel this charge the verse in question was revealed to him, namely: 'Muhammad is not the father of any of your males, but he is the Messenger of Allah and the Seal of the Prophets. Allah has full knowledge of all things' (33:41). This was designed to draw the attention of friend and foe to the verity that the dispensation instituted by the Holy Prophet, peace be on him, was not in the nature of a secular hereditary kingdom which would terminate on his death without male heirs, but was a spiritual dispensation which would be carried on by his spiritual successors who would include among them prophets, whose prophethood would be authenticated with his Seal. It was also indicated that with his advent all other prophethoods had been terminated and that henceforth the only prophethood that would survive would be his prophethood.

It is worthy of note that up to the advent of the Holy

Prophet, peace be on him, the prophethoods of all other prophets were in operation. For instance, a follower of Moses, who believed in Moses and the prophets who were raised in Bani Israel after Moses, was not under any obligation to believe, for instance, in Zoroaster or Krishna, or any other prophet. In the same way a follower of Zoroaster was not called upon to believe in Moses or Jesus. A Christian was not under obligation to believe in Zoroaster or Krishna or Buddha. The prophethoods of these prophets remained current and alive among their respective peoples; but with the advent of the Holy Prophet, peace be on him, all those prophethoods were terminated and it became obligatory upon everyone to believe in the Holy Prophet and in all the other prophets who had appeared before him. Thus he authenticated with his Seal the prophethood of all previous prophets, and would authenticate the prophethood of any prophet that God might raise among his followers. There would, henceforth, be no prophet who was not his subordinate and follower and did not bear his Seal.

The expression the Seal of the Prophets is susceptible of only two interpretations. First, that though Muhammad, peace be on him, is not the father of any male issue, yet being the Messenger of Allah he is the spiritual father of all the faithful, and that he is so exalted that he is invested with the Seal of Prophethood and as such is the spiritual father of any prophet that might be raised after him, who will be his spiritual descendant and his devoted follower whose prophethood would bear the authenticating Seal of the Holy Prophet. Secondly, Muhammad is not the father of any males but as the Messenger of Allah he is the spiritual father of all the faithful and is pre-eminent among the prophets as he occupies the highest position in the pinnacle of the excellences of prophethood.

This leaves no room for the interpretation adopted by the opponents of Ahmad. The expression Seal of the Prophets has obviously been employed in this verse as stressing the pre-eminence of the Holy Prophet among the other Prophets. According to their interpretation, the verse would mean that though Muhammad was not the father of any males but with his advent prophethood of every type had been terminated. Surely this would not import any preeminence for the Holy Prophet but would amount to denigration of him. At the very best it would be meaningless and disjointed.

We shall proceed to consider some of the sayings of the Holy Prophet, peace be on him, which have a bearing on this question. On the death of his son Ibrahim, he said:

> Had Ibrahim lived he would have certainly been a righteous Prophet (Ibne Maja, Kitabal Janaiz). This is all the more remarkable as Ibrahim died five years after the revelation of the verse in which the Holy Prophet was designated the Seal of the Prophets.

Hazrat Mullah Ali bin Muhammad Sultanal Qari, a highly respected and most eminent divine of the Hanafi sect has said:

> If Ibrahim had lived and had become a prophet, he would have been one of the followers of the Holy Prophet and his Prophethood would not have been in contradiction of the divine word that the Holy Prophet was the Seal of the Prophets, as the meaning of this expression is there would not arise after the Holy Prophet any Prophet who would abrogate his law and may not be one of his followers [*Mauzuat Kabir*, pp. 66–7].

Again the Holy Prophet, peace be on him, is reported to have said: 'Abu Bakr is the best of my followers except anyone who might be a prophet' (Dalmy quoted by *Kanazul Haqaiq* of Imam Monadi, p. 7); or: 'Abu Bakr is the best of the people except one who may be a prophet' (Tabrani Kabir Kamil Ibne Adi quoted in *Jame Saghir* by Imam Suyuti, p. 5). This is a clear indication of the possibility of prophets arising among Muslims after the Holy Prophet, peace be on him.

Another tradition reported on the authority of Abu Hurairah states that the Holy Prophet, peace be on him, said: 'There will be no Prophet between me and Jesus [meaning in his second advent]; he will surely appear, so as you see him accept him. He will be a man of medium height, of fair complexion. He will fight on behalf of Islam, will break the Cross, will kill swine and will abolish the poll-tax' (Abu Daud, Book *Al-Malaham*, Ch. 'Khurujuddajjal'). This tradition is clear that there would be no prophet in Islam after the Holy Prophet, peace be on him, till the appearance of the Promised Messiah.

This finds support from another tradition mentioned in Muslim where the Holy Prophet, peace be on him, has described the Promised Messiah repeatedly as a prophet of Allah. In the course of this long tradition the Holy Prophet said: 'The Prophet of Allah, Isa, and his companions will be besieged . . . then Isa, Prophet of Allah, and his companions will turn to Allah . . . then Isa, Prophet of Allah, and his companions will invade the camps of the enemy . . ., and again, Isa, the Prophet of Allah, and his companions will turn to Allah . . .' (Muslim, Ch. 'Zikruddajjal'). This tradition makes it absolutely clear that the status of the Promised Messiah will be that of a Prophet.

We shall now advert to some of the traditions of the Holy Prophet, peace be on him, which are relied upon by the opponents of the Promised Messiah in support of their contention that no type of prophet can appear in Islam after the Holy Prophet, peace be on him. The first of these is: 'There is no Prophet after me.' The Holy Prophet, peace be on him, is reported to have expressed himself in this manner on an occasion when he was about to depart on an expedition and appointed Hazrat Ali, his cousin, to be in charge at Medina during his absence therefrom. Hazrat Ali was distressed that he would thus be deprived of the opportunity of serving at the front under the command of the Holy Prophet. To reassure him the Holy Prophet said to him: 'You are to me in the position in which Aaron was to Moses, except that there is no Prophet after me.' It is perfectly clear that in this context the expression 'after me' means during my absence and does not mean, and cannot mean, after my death, for the simple reason that Aaron had died in the lifetime of Moses and, though he was a prophet along with Moses during his lifetime, he did not survive Moses and was not a Prophet after his death.

Be that as it may, a well-known tradition attributed to Hazrat Ayesha makes it quite clear that the meaning of the saying of the Holy Prophet cannot be what the opponents of the Promised Messiah seek to establish. Hazrat Ayesha admonished some of the companions of the Holy Prophet in the terms: 'Say by all means that he is the Seal of the Prophets, but do not say that there will be no Prophet after him' (*Tukmila Majma' ul-Bihar*, p. 85).

It is further contended that the Holy Prophet, peace be on him, has himself said that he is the last of the prophets; and on the basis of this it is urged that there can be no prophet of any kind after him. It is true that the Holy Prophet, peace be on him, has used the expression 'last of the prophets' with references to himself, but the complete *hadees* in which he employed this expression is: 'I am the last of the prophets and this mosque of mine is the last of the mosques.' Now it is clear that by designating his mosque the last of mosques he obviously did not mean that no other mosque would be built anywhere in the future. The only meaning of the expression can be that there shall be no mosque to replace his mosque and that all mosques to be built henceforth would be copies of his mosque and its reflections. Similarly, the expression 'last of the prophets' means that there would be no prophet after him who would abrogate his law or who would receive the bounty of prophethood independently of him.

Another *hadees* relied upon by our opponents is: 'Had there been a prophet after me it would have been Umar.' The short answer is that the Holy Prophet himself has furnished the key to the meaning of this *hadees* by saying: 'Had I not been raised among you, Umar would have been raised instead' (Ibne-Adee quoted in *Kanazul Haqaiq*, Vol. II, p. 151). It is well known that in Arabic idiom the expression *ba'ad* (after) also connotes 'instead of', as is said in the Holy Quran: 'There are the Signs of Allah that We rehearse unto thee with truth. What is it then that they will believe instead of [*ba'ad*] Allah and His Signs?' (45:7).

Hazrat Imam Sha'rani has very clearly affirmed that the statement of the Holy Prophet, peace be on him, that there would be no prophet after him simply means that there will be no prophet after him bearing a new law (*Al-Yawaqitwal Jawāhar,* Vol. II, p. 27). Hazrat Sheikh Akbar Muhyuddin Ibne Arabi has stated: 'The prophethood that terminated with the person of the Holy Prophet, peace be on him, was the law-bearing prophethood and not just prophethood itself. . . .' This is the meaning of his statement that Messengership and prophethood had been terminated and that there would be no messenger or prophet after him, that is to say, there would be no prophet with a law other than his law and that anyone who comes would be subject to his law (*Futuhate-Makkiyya,* Vol. II, p. 73).

In another place the same eminent, saintly divine has said: 'Prophethood would continue to be open to people till the Day of Judgment, though law-making has terminated, yet law-making is but one element of prophethood' (*Futuhate-Makkiyya,* p. 100).

He has also said: 'So far as law-bearing prophethood is concerned, it came to an end with Muhammad, peace be on him, and therefore, there can be no law-bearing prophet after him . . . but Allah in His graciousness towards His servants has continued general prophethood shorn of law-bearing' (*Feisusal Hikam,* pp. 140–1).

Hazrat Shah Waliullah Muhaddis of Delhi, who was acclaimed as the Reformer of the 12th century of the Hegira, and was highly revered for his wide learning and great erudition, has stated: 'Prophets ended with the Holy Prophet, that is to say, there shall not be after him one whom Allah the Holy invests with a new law binding over people' (*Tafhimate-Ilahiyya,* No. 35).

Hazrat Maulvi Abul Qasem Nanotvi, the renowned founder of the Deoband Academy, who died in 1889, stated: 'In the conception of the masses the Holy Prophet, peace be on him, was Khatam in the sense that he came after all the other prophets and that he was the last prophet of all. But it is evident that in the estimation of the wise no superiority whatever attaches to precedence in time or its reverse' (*Tahzirunnas*, Saharanpur, p. 3).

In the same publication, at page 28, he stated: 'If a prophet appeared after the Holy Prophet, peace be on him, it would in no way affect his finality.'

The members of the Ahmadiyya Movement believe that the Holy Prophet, peace be on him, is the Seal of the Prophets as proclaimed in the Holy Quran (33:41). In him all the excellences of prophethood reached their climax. There can be no prophet after him who might be bestowed the bounty of prophethood independently of him, for henceforth every type of grace is attainable only through obedience to him. A prophet can now appear only through allegiance to him, receiving light from his light as a reflection, and not otherwise.

III

The third question that needs consideration is whether, assuming the possibility of a prophet or prophets appearing after the Holy Prophet, peace be on him, Hazrat Mirza Ghulam Ahmad was in fact the recipient of Divine revelation and was a prophet, subordinate to the Holy Prophet, peace be on him, and a spiritual reflection of him.

Hazrat Ahmad began to receive Divine revelation in the early seventies of the 19th century of the Christian era. This experience began to be multiplied and became continuous after the death of his father in 1876, and terminated only with his own death on 26 May 1908. Thus the period during which he continuously received Divine revelation extends to well over thirty years.

It is the unanimous and firm belief of all Muslims that according to the Holy Quran a person who fabricates something himself and attributes it to the Divine is bound to be frustrated and ruined by God and cannot at all flourish. This doctrine is based upon the following verses of the Holy Quran:

> We cite in evidence all that which you see and all that which you see not, that the Quran is surely the Word brought by a noble Messenger; and is not the word of a poet; little it is that you believe. Nor is it the word of a soothsayer; little it is that you heed. It is a revelation from the Lord of the worlds. If he had fabricated any saying and attributed it to Us, We would surely have seized him by the right hand and then surely We would have severed his large artery; and not one of you could have kept Us from it [69:39–48].

This is an awesome warning to every daring impostor. A person, wholly misguided or out of his mind, might claim that he is God and may not come to any visible harm. The Divine mercy might be pleased to overlook his aberration, inasmuch as such a claim is not likely to mislead or to confuse any sensible person. The case is entirely different where a person claims to be the recipient of Divine revelation. If his claim is false and he persists in it deliberately, he might become the cause of the error and misguidance of a large number of people. God Almighty has, therefore, set forth in these verses His firm and clear warning that an impostor would not escape God's chastisement and His wrath.

Muslim divines and scholars have specified that if a claimant of the receipt of Divine revelation persists in his claim over a period equal to the period of the prophethood of the Holy Prophet, peace be on him (23 years), his claim must be accepted as true. This does not mean that an impostor would in all cases be granted immunity over such a long period. He is bound to be overtaken by Divine wrath much earlier. The period of 23 years is, in the opinion of the Muslim divines, the maximum limit which is treated as decisive.

Since the time of the Holy Prophet, peace be on him, there have been many false claimants of Divine revelation and in no single instance has any of them been spared the doom that is pronounced in these verses. In every such case divine judgment has overtaken the offender and he has been visibly ruined.

In the case of Ahmad, as has been mentioned, the receipt of Divine revelation continued over a period well beyond thirty years. The revelation vouchsafed to him carried within itself numberless proofs of its genuineness and truth. It was replete with grand prophecies, spiritual insights, knowledge of things divine, glad tidings and warnings for friend and foe and spiritual guidance at the highest level. It comprised shining and convincing proofs of its own truth, to some of which we shall draw attention later by way of illustration.

Not only did Ahmad enjoy complete immunity from Divine chastisement, which is appointed as the portion of an impostor, he marched from triumph to triumph throughout his life and was obviously one who was greatly favoured by God within the meaning of the final verse of Sura Fatiha. Far from being exposed to Divine wrath for his daring imposture, as was imagined and alleged by his opponents, he had been bestowed a Divine guarantee of security in the same words in which the Holy Prophet, peace be on him, had been guaranteed security. These words were: 'O Messenger, proclaim widely that which has been sent down to thee from thy Lord; for if thou do it not, thou will not have conveyed His Message at all. Allah will safeguard thee against harm by people. Allah guides not the disbelieving people' (5:68). Ahmad had also received the same assurance in exactly the same words: 'Allah will safeguard thee against harm by people'; and this guarantee was as completely fulfilled in his case as it had been fulfilled in the case of his master the Holy Prophet, peace be on him.

He had been condemned as an infidel, an apostate from Islam. Leading Muslim divines had declared that his assassination would be a highly meritorious act and that whoever brought about his death would prove himself deserving of paradise.

His life was exposed to every hazard. Qadian, where he resided permanently, was a small town which boasted no police station, where not a single police constable was posted, nor was there any military guard. Ahmad did not seek any kind of protection at the hands of the authorities. He did not appoint anyone from among his followers to watch over him or to make any arrangements for his security. He went into the mosque to join the five daily services, and at the end of the service often stayed in the mosque to meet visitors of all descriptions and carried on a discourse aimed at the training of his people in the exercise of high moral qualities and to encourage them to develop the higher grades of spirituality.

During the forenoon he went for a walk extending over several miles when he was accompanied by some of his followers who did not deny anyone free access to him.

From time to time he visited other places both far and near and during these journeys also he was exposed to danger all the time. In these circumstances, and in view of the bitter hostility of his enemies, the complete security that he enjoyed under Divine protection was so remarkable that it was considered miraculous or supernatural.

Not only was his physical security fully safeguarded, he was also completely safeguarded in respect of his freedom, dignity and honour. False charges were brought against him and he was hauled into court to answer them. In every case he was honourably discharged or acquitted and all the unholy designs of his enemies were completely frustrated. In one of these cases he was charged with so grave an offence as conspiracy to murder. Yet the proceedings took a course in which his honour, his dignity and his innocence were so completely upheld and vindicated that not only were his opponents utterly frustrated in their evil designs, but were subjected to great humiliation and were exposed to ridicule and contempt. At the end of the proceedings the District Magistrate who had tried the case against him intimated to him that if he would be inclined to institute criminal proceedings against his prosecutor, the Magistrate would grant him leave to do so. Ahmad declined to take advantage of the offer of the Magistrate, declaring that his case was pending before God Almighty and that he would not initiate proceedings against his enemies in a court of law.

The complete security of life, limb, honour, property and good name that he continued to enjoy all through his life, despite the bitter hostility of some of his opponents, was a matter of wonder for friend and foe alike.

Whenever God Almighty designs to exalt one of His servants to the level of prophethood, He lays the foundations of His design long before the birth of such a person. From the moment of his birth He places him under His own guardianship. He safeguards him against all evil and develops all his faculties beneficently so as to prepare his mind for the reception of His message and to prepare his physical form and capacities to endure all that he might have to encounter in the cause of God. For instance, with regard to Moses it is said in the Holy Quran: 'I have been gracious towards thee before also, when I revealed to thy mother all that was needed to be revealed. . . . I surrounded thee with My love, so that thou might'st be reared under My care. Then . . . We proved thee in diverse ways and thou didst tarry several years among the people of Midian. Then thou camest up to the standard, Moses, and I chose thee for Myself' (20:37–42). As with Moses, so with all prophets, particularly with the Holy Prophet, peace be on him, who was safeguarded against all evil since the moment of his birth and was brought up under the care and guardianship of God Who developed his mind and his faculties in a manner that prepared him for the discharge of the responsibilities that God intended to place upon his shoulders.

This is recalled in the Holy Quran, where it is said: 'Tell them: Had Allah so willed, I would not have recited it to you, nor would He have made it known to you. I have spent a whole lifetime among you before this. Will you not then understand?' (10:17). The attention of the disbelievers is here drawn to the entire purity of the Holy Prophet's life even before the Divine call came to him, so as to impress upon them that he who had throughout led a righteous life would not suddenly, on arriving at full maturity, start fabricating lies against God. Indeed the Holy Prophet's truthfulness had become a proverb among his contemporaries, so that he had become known as AL-AMEEN, meaning the trustworthy. Even after the call came to him his opponents did not charge him with falsehood, but only rejected that which he had brought, as is said: 'We know well that what they say grieves thee sorely; for they charge not thee with falsehood but it is the Signs of Allah that the evil-doers reject' (6:34).

In the case of Hazrat Ahmad also, in the revelation vouchsafed to him, God Almighty invited attention to the purity of his life from the very beginning as a proof of the truth of his claim, in the same words as had been employed in the Holy Quran with reference to the Holy Prophet, peace be on him. In his case also there is the testimony of both friends and opponents that he had led an absolutely pure and blameless life. For instance, Maulvi Muhammad Husain Sahib of Batala said: 'The author of *Braheen Ahmadiyya,* according to the experience and observation of his friends and opponents, adheres to the commandments of the Islamic law and leads a pious and truthful life, subject to his accountability to God' (*Ishaatas-Sunnah,* Vol. VII, No. 9).

Ahmad himself has invited attention to the purity of his life in the following words:

> You cannot point to any fault, imposture, falsehood or deceit in my previous life so that you could say that a person who was already given to falsehood and imposture has only added to his previous falsehoods another imposture. Which of you can criticize anything in my previous life? It is the grace of God that from the very beginning He established my life along the lines of righteousness. This is a proof for those who reflect [*Tazkaratush Shahadatain,* p. 62].

There is a whole mass of evidence in support of this statement of his, some of which has been mentioned earlier. It should be enough to mention here that throughout his life no one had ever charged him with having uttered a falsehood. It is not to be imagined, therefore, that a person who was so wholly committed to the truth in all aspects of his life would be guilty of the mose despicable falsehood that God spoke to him, if in fact He did not.

All commentators of the Holy Quran and eminent Muslim divines have been agreed that the prophecy set forth in the Holy Quran in the following words, 'He it is Who sent His Messenger with guidance and the Religion of Truth, that He may make it prevail over every other religion, even though those who associate partners with Allah may dislike it' (9:33), would be fulfilled through the Promised Messiah and Mahdi.

At the time of the advent of Ahmad, Islam was in the situation of one who is encircled by bitter enemies and is assaulted continuously from every direction. The Hindus, and more particularly the Ayra Samaj and Brahmo Samaj, were looking forward to the acceptance of their creeds throughout India and were making rapid progress in certain parts of the country towards the achievement of that objective. Christian missionaries had put forward a similar claim on behalf of their faith, and prominent British statesmen had announced that God had bestowed the sovereignty of India upon the British for the purpose that, through the efforts of Christian missionaries, the whole of India might be redeemed by and find its salvation in Jesus Christ. It was against this background that Ahmad proclaimed his challenge in *Braheen Ahmadiyya* that he would hand over the whole of his property, then valued at ten thousand rupees, to any non-Muslim, Arya, Brahmo, Sanatan Dharmist or Christian, who would set forth from the sacred books of his religion even as little as one-fifth of the proofs in support of the teachings of his religion as Ahmad proposed to expound in *Braheen Ahmadiyya* in support of the teachings of Islam. No one took up the challenge seriously during his lifetime or has done so since. Pandit Lekh Ram, of tragic memory, purported to do so in a most offensive manner which clearly betrayed that his only purpose was to seek an opportunity of unburdening his mind of part of the filth with which it was saturated. Through his terrible end he set a seal on his falsehood, as we shall demonstrate later.

Beginning with the publication of *Braheen Ahmadiyya*, the whole of the rest of Ahmad's life was devoted towards establishing the supremacy of Islam over all other religions in every aspect of teaching, doctrines, beliefs and the upholding of moral and spiritual values and standards. The practical results of his persistent and intensive campaign soon began to make themselves manifest. Within a very short period all those who carried on an aggressive campaign against Islam were put upon the defensive in respect of their own religions.

Ahmad's campaign in support of Islam was not confined to reasoning and argument alone. He claimed that Islam was the only religion that was living, in the sense that it brought forth life-giving spiritual fruit which should be the purpose of every religion, and that no other religion even claimed to do so. He put forward himself as proof of the truth of the claim that he made on behalf of Islam. He drew attention to the fact that he was a constant recipient of Divine revelation, which was the pure and delicious fruit of Islam and a proof of Divine grace, while all other religions denied even the possibility of Divine revelation in this age.

He proclaimed that the truth of his claim could be judged by any of the recognized, relevant, criteria that were applicable to such a claim and which are clearly set forth in the Holy Quran. The only response made to his challenge was derisive and contemptuous rejection of it, which demonstrated the utter poverty and emptiness of all rival religions. This challenge did not expire with his life. Its effectiveness continues to be demonstrated even today both through the fulfilment of some of his prophecies from time to time and the manifestation of the blessings of Islam in the lives and conduct of a large number of the members of the Movement founded by him.

In his own case, ample proof of the righteousness of his claim continued to be furnished throughout his life. For instance, as has been mentioned earlier, he had received very little formal schooling so that when he put forth his claim as Reformer, Mahdi and Promised Messiah, some of the opposing Muslim divines pointed to his lack of scholarship and his inadequate mastery of Arabic as proof that he had not the capacity to penetrate to the true meaning of the Holy Quran and that, therefore, he could not have been chosen by the Divine as an instrument for establishing the superiority of Islam over all other religions.

He has referred to this objection of the divines at page 6 of his Arabic book, *Sirrul Khilafah*, in the following words:

> These divines state that one of the qualifications of a Reformer who calls people to Islam is that he should be an eminent scholar and they allege that I have no knowledge of Arabic and possess no literary qualification and that they consider me an ignoramus. What they say is true; and so I supplicated the Divine that if He so pleased, He might bestow upon me adequate knowledge of Arabic. He granted my prayer and by His grace I acquired mastery in this language and was bestowed the capacity to express myself in it at a high level. Under Divine direction I wrote two books in Arabic and challenged my opponents to produce their match, but they ran away and went into hiding.

The two books referred to here were *Karamatus Sadiqeen* and *Nurul Haq*. Thereafter he wrote several books in Arabic and composed a number of Odes in that language, all of which are held in high esteem by recognized masters of the Arabic language. He also compiled a book which he designated *Minanur Rahman*, in which he set forth his thesis that Arabic was the mother of all languages, that it originated in revelation, and that is why the most perfect Divine guidance, the Holy Quran, was revealed in this language. Among other things that he set forth in support of his thesis was that Arabic comprises more than two and a half million roots as compared, for instance, with Sanskrit, which has no more than four hundred roots.

On 13 April 1900, which was the day of the Festival of Sacrifice, Ahmad was divinely directed to deliver the sermon himself in Arabic. He carried out the direction in a performance of the most extraordinary character. He appointed his two foremost disciples, Hazrat Maulvi Nurud Din Sahib and Hazrat Maulvi Abdul Karim Sahib, to take down the text of the sermon as it issued from his lips. He stood with his eyes half closed as if he was in a trance, and the sermon rolled out from his lips in a sustained succession of grand periods as if he was reading out a text that was spread out before his half-closed eyes. The delivery of the sermon occupied more than an hour. After he had finished speaking, Maulvi Abdul Karim Sahib conveyed the substance of the address to the congregation in Urdu. While this was being done Ahmad, overtaken suddenly by a rush of gratitude towards God for the great bounty He had bestowed on him, went into prostration and the whole congregation followed his example. After the prostration Ahmad mentioned that he had just seen the word MOBARAK (Felicitations) spelt out in scarlet letters in front of him. The sermon was an extraordinary sign of Divine bounty which deeply impressed all those who were present. Later, Ahmad added four chapters to it in Arabic and the full text, together with its translation into Persian and Urdu, was published in book form in October 1902 under the title *Khutbah Ilhamiyyah*. The main topic of the sermon, as delivered, was the philosophy of sacrifice. It stands as a unique example of his mastery of the Arabic language and the deep insight of spiritual values that had been bestowed upon him by Divine grace.

He was also bestowed a deep and comprehensive understanding of the Holy Quran from which he set forth all that was needed in the way of moral and spiritual guidance in the era that was opening out before him. He had pointed out that his age was related to the future of mankind as the age of Adam was related to the centuries that had passed before his own advent. He repeatedly challenged all Muslim divines, scholars and spiritual preceptors to compete with him in writing a commentary in Arabic on any group of Quranic verses that might be selected for the purpose. But no one took up the challenge seriously. Pir Mehr Ali Shah of Golara, near

Rawalpindi, professed to take up the challenge but failed miserably and earned only ridicule and humiliation in consequence.

His championship of Islam was blessed by God to such a degree that after their first encounter with him, the advocates of other religions always avoided being placed in juxtaposition to him in any religious discussion or debate. In the case of Christian missionaries a directive was issued by the authorities of the Anglican Church that no one of their clergy should get involved in a discussion with any member of the Ahmadiyya Movement.

One of the functions of the Promised Messiah as indicated by the Holy Prophet, peace be on him, was to refute the Christian claim that Jesus had died upon the cross in order to take over the burden of the sins of mankind and thus to redeem humanity through his atonement. Ahmad took up the refutation of this claim with great vigour and established from the Gospel accounts of the crucifixion that Jesus was taken down from the cross before life had become extinct and was ministered unto and resuscitated, and having met his disciples and convinced them that he was still alive in his physical body, he departed from Judaea in search of the lost tribes of Israel.

In 1899 Ahmad wrote a book under the title *Jesus in India* in which he recited briefly the course of the journey of Jesus in search of the lost tribes through Mesopotamia, Iran, Afghanistan and Kashmir. He established that Jesus had finally settled down in Kashmir and had died in Srinagar where he lies buried. Historical evidence that has since become available fully confirms the account given by Ahmad of the journey of Jesus to Kashmir, his sojourn there and his death and burial in Srinagar. He thus effectively gave the quietus to the series of myths concerning the death of Jesus upon the cross, his resurrection and his ascension to heaven in his physical body.

CHAPTER FIVE

In his pamphlet designated *Asmani Faislah* (Heavenly Decision), Ahmad invited his opponents to agree upon some method whereby the truth or falsehood of his claim might be decisively determined. One of the four criteria that he suggested for the purpose was the acceptance of prayer. He proposed that an association might be established in Lahore, the members of which should be selected by agreement between the parties, and the association might be charged with announcing their decision in accordance with the procedure proposed by him. The decision could be unanimous or by a majority.

He proposed that the association should call for the names and particulars of people who might be sorely afflicted with any kind of calamity or misfortune. A person professing any religion could send in his name and particulars if he found himself in the grip of a severe calamity or affliction. A list of such afflicted persons would be prepared by the association, entries into which would continue to be inscribed for a period of one month or any longer period that the association might consider appropriate. At the end of this period copies of this list, together with all the particulars, should be drawn up and on a date to be appointed these lists should be placed before each of the participants in this trial, and the afflicted persons would be asked to appear in person so that the participants in the trial may be able to check up on them, and thereafter lots would be drawn whereby the sufferers would be distributed among the participants in the trial. Each participant would be provided with a list of the persons allotted to him by drawing lots, and copies of these lists would be preserved in the office of the association. Ahmad offered to bear the cost of all the announcements that might have to be made for the purpose of inviting sufferers to send in names and particulars and informing them of the day on which they would be required to present themselves to meet the participants in the trial. Beginning with that day each participant in the trial would continue to supplicate during the period of one year for deliverance from their sufferings of the persons allotted to him by the drawing of lots. The association would maintain a record of the progress of the trial. If any of the participants should die before the expiry of the period of one year and before a clear estimation could be made of the success or failure of the respective participants in the trial, the deceased would be deemed to have failed in the trial; as it would be assumed that God Almighty had by His special design removed him in the middle of the trial so as to make it manifest that his claim was false. The result of the trial would be determined on the basis of the condition of a large majority of sufferers in each list. Ahmad pointed out that it was necessary for such a trial that there should be a large number of sufferers for otherwise the trial might prove inconclusive. For instance, if there were only two or three persons in a list it was possible that their sufferings might be under an irrevocable Divine decree so that they could not be helped by any prayer or supplication. A saintly person was recognized through the acceptance of a large majority of his supplications and not through the acceptance of every one of them. This was a well-recognized principle.

He said: I have suggested the inclusion in the list of sufferers of people who are afflicted with diverse types of calamities so that Divine mercy may be manifested in diverse forms and people of different temperaments might be able to arrive at a true estimation of the result reached from different points of view.

I promise and state it on oath that if I am defeated in this trial I shall myself announce my confession of failure and my falsehood. There will remain no further need for any of my opponents to adjudge me an infidel or impostor. In such case I shall deserve every humiliation and disgrace and contempt. I shall also confess in the public sitting of the association in which the result of the trial is announced that I have not been sent by God Almighty and that all my claims are false. But I believe firmly that God will surely not so determine and will not let me be ruined. If the divines to whom this challenge of mine is addressed fail to respond to it no seeker after truth and no just person would approve of their attitude. Indeed they would look upon it with deep regret [*Asmani Faisalah*, pp. 16–21].

It is indeed a matter of deep regret that none of his opponents to whom his challenge was addressed dared to enter the field against him. By their failure to do so they set a seal upon his truth.

There have been countless instances in the life of Ahmad of the acceptance of prayer in a remarkable and extraordinary manner. Many of them have been mentioned in his writings.

We would here draw attention to the period of his retreat, which he spent in Hoshiarpur, at the end of which he announced that as a result of his supplications God Almighty, out of His pure grace and mercy, had conveyed to him the grand news of the birth of a son who would be equipped with moral, intellectual and spiritual qualities of the highest order. That son was born on 12 January 1889, and in his illustrious career he manifested all the great qualities that Divine revelation had indicated as his characteristics. We shall return to that aspect of the prophecy of 1886 in due course.

One of the earliest revelations (Urdu) vouchsafed to Ahmad was: 'I shall carry thy message to the ends of the earth.' We have described earlier the circumstances and conditions of his life at the time. When he received this revelation he did not possess, nor had access to, even elementary means that he could have utilized for the purpose of conveying his message within the Province in which Qadian was situated. Yet today his message has been conveyed to the ends of the earth and branches of the Movement founded by him are strung around the globe in many different countries. Had he been an impostor his name would have been forgotten altogether by this time as one of the unregretted and unmourned. The revelation found fulfilment through his earnest supplications.

In the early years of his ministry a young man of the name of Abdul Karim was sent by his widowed mother from Hyderabad, South India, to Qadian for the prosecution of Islamic studies. By ill chance he was bitten by a mad dog and was immediately despatched to Kasauli for treatment in the Pasteur Institute so as to make him immune against the onset of rabies. Having gone through a full course of treatment at Kasauli he returned to Qadian. A few days later he exhibited unmistaken signs of hydrophobia. A telegram was sent to the Director of the Pasteur Institute at Kasauli describing his symptoms and asking for directions. His reply came back by telegram: 'Sorry nothing can be done for Abdul Karim.' Ahmad had been advised of the condition of Abdul Karim and was kept informed of the progress of his symptoms. When he was told of the reply received from Kasauli, he was much distressed and was deeply moved out of pity for Abdul Karim and his widowed mother, a thousand miles away from Qadian. He occupied himself with earnest supplications on behalf of Abdul Karim. From that moment the progress of Abdul Karim's symptoms was arrested, and his condition began to mend. Within less than twenty-four hours he made a complete recovery, his health was fully restored and he resumed the course of his studies. Till a few years ago there had not been a single case of the restoration to health of a person in whom the symptoms of hydrophobia had manifested themselves. A few years back, however, a case was reported in the United States of America where a boy who had been bitten by a mad dog and who had begun to manifest symptoms of hydrophobia was restored to health through intensive medical care and the use of recently discovered drugs. This case, however, does not in the least detract from the striking character of the healing bestowed upon Abdul Karim by Divine grace through the prayers and supplications of Ahmad.

We shall now draw attention to some equally striking

cases which furnish illustrations both of the acceptance of prayer and of foreknowledge of future events bestowed upon Ahmad in accordance with the verse of the Holy Quran: 'He is the Knower of the unseen; and He reveals not His secrets, except to him whom He chooses from among His Messengers' (72:26–7). Mention has been made of Pandit Lekh Ram of Peshawar who was a very zealous apologist of the Arya Samaj, whose zeal outran all considerations of goodwill, courtesy and good manners. He had served for a number of years as a subordinate officer in the state police force, but had retired at an early age and devoted himself to polemics of the lowest type. His venom was particularly directed against the Holy Prophet of Islam, peace be on him. He referred to the Holy Quran in derisive and contemptuous terms and even spoke irreverently of God Almighty. Ahmad had tried to persuade him to adopt a more moderate style when writing or speaking on such grave matters, but to no purpose. Finally, on 20 February 1893, Ahmad made the following announcement concerning him:

Be it known that in my announcement of 20 February 1886 I had suggested to Inderman of Moradabad and Lekh Ram of Peshawar that if they would so desire I might announce some prophecies concerning their future. Inderman objected to this and died a short time after, but Lehk Ram sent me a postcard in which he told me that I could publish whatever I desired concerning him and that he would take no objection to it. So I supplicated the Divine concerning him and received from God, the Glorious, the revelation [Arabic]: 'He is a lifeless calf from which issues an unpleasant sound. In respect of his impertinent abuse, punishment and torment and suffering has been decreed for him.' I was given to understand that within six years from today, February 20 1893, this man will be overtaken by severe torment as a punishment for the disrespect which he has manifested towards the Holy Prophet, peace be on him. Now by announcing the prophecy I am seeking to inform all Muslims, Christians, and followers of all other religions, that if this person is not overtaken within the period of six years from today by a torment that should be distinguishable from ordinary sufferings and should bear an extraordinary character and should be in the nature of Divine chastisement, then it might be concluded that I have not been sent by God Almighty, nor do I speak under the urge of His Spirit. If I am proved false in respect of this prophecy I will be ready to undergo any punishment and would be willing that a rope might be drawn round my neck and I might be hanged from a gibbet. Besides, apart from this agreement of mine, it is obvious that a person's being proved false in his prediction is in itself the highest degradation. Now all the Aryas should join together in supplicating that their advocate might be spared this torment. It should be understood that this man has offered such insult to the Holy Prophet, peace be on him, the contemplation of which makes one's body tremble. His books are full of contempt and defamation and vile abuse. There is no Muslim whose heart and liver would not be cut into pieces by listening to their contents. Despite his insolence this man is most ignorant, has not the slightest knowledge of Arabic and cannot even write in literary Urdu. This prophecy is not a mere casual utterance. This humble one supplicated in this particular regard and received the reply that has been set out above. This prophecy is a sign for the Muslims also. Would that they could realize the truth and their hearts could be softened. I now conclude with the name of God, the Lord of honour and glory, with Whose name I began. All praise belongs to Allah and may His peace and blessings be upon His Messenger Muhammad, the chosen one, the most exalted of the Messengers, the best of creation, our master, and master of all those that are in the earth and in heaven.

In a Persian poem published at the same time, Ahmad made reference to Lekh Ram in the words: 'Beware, O foolish and misguided enemy, and tremble with fear, of the sharp sword of Muhammad.'

This prophecy was criticized in certain quarters. In reply Ahmad declared, in his book *Barakatud Dua:*

If in consequence of the prophecy nothing more happened than a fever or an ordinary ache or cholera after which normal health is restored, that would not be a fulfilment of the prophecy, and the prophecy would turn out to be a deception and a snare, for no one is free from such disorders; we all fall ill sometime or the other. In such case I would certainly deserve the punishment that I have mentioned in my announcement. But if the prophecy is fulfilled in a manner in which the operation of Divine wrath is clearly perceived then you must understand that it is from God. . . . It is quite untrue that I bear any personal enmity towards Lekh Ram or towards any other person. This man has proved himself the enemy of truth and has spoken contemptuously of the perfect and holy being who is the fountainhead of all truth. Therefore, God Almighty decided to uphold the honour of his loved one.

On 2 April 1893 Ahmad wrote: This morning in the course of a light slumber I saw that I was sitting in a large room where some of my friends were present when a well-built man of terrible appearance, as if blood would burst forth from his face, came and stood before me. When I raised my eyes towards him I perceived that he was a person of strange build and character, as if he was not a man but was one of the severe terrible angels who overawe all hearts. As I looked at him he asked me: 'Where is Lekh Ram?' and he also named another person and inquired where he was. Then I understood that this one had been appointed for the chastisement of Lehk Ram and the other person. But I do not now remember the name of the other person, though I am certain that he is one of those whom I have mentioned in my announcement. This was Saturday, at 4 a.m. All praise belongs to Allah for all this.

In his book *Karamatus Sadiqeen,* which he wrote in the latter part of 1893, Ahmad reaffirmed the period of six years mentioned in the prophecy concerning Lekh Ram, and in one of his Arabic odes included in that book he stated: 'God has given me the good news and said: "You will recognize the day of joy which will be closest to the day of the Festival." ' He pointed out that this verse referred to Lekh Ram and that the day of his chastisement would be next to the day of Eid.

Lekh Ram on his side announced that Ahmad would die of cholera within three years, for he was an impostor (*Takzeeb Braheen Ahmadiyya,* p. 311).

On 6 March 1897, on the day following the Festival of Sacrifice, Pandit Lekh Ram was attacked in his own house in Lahore by a well-built person who thrust a dagger into his abdomen and rotated it in his body, thus severing his entrails at several places and inducing heavy loss of blood. His mother and wife were in an adjoining room and rushed out immediately to aid Pandit Lekh Ram and to intercept his assailant. The house was situated in a populous street in the middle of the town and the attack on Pandit Lekh Ram was carried out between 6 and 7 p.m. before sunset. It is alleged that Lekh Ram's mother tried to take hold of the assailant but he struck her on the head with a wooden roller and in the confusion that ensued made his escape from the house. Pandit Lekh Ram's entrails had protruded from his body and he was bleeding profusely. He was immediately conveyed to the hospital where he was at once attended to by two surgeons who employed all their skill to staunch the bleeding and to stitch together the injured portions of his entrails, but to no purpose. He continued in great agony till shortly after midnight when he succumbed to his injuries. No trace of the assassin could be discovered.

Pandit Lekh Ram's tragic end came as a great shock to the Aryas who immediately raised the cry that the assassination must have been carried out under the directions of Hazrat Mirza Ghulam Ahmad who had prophecied the death of Pandit Lekh Ram with such striking accuracy as could not have been predicted by anyone who had not himself planned and organized the tragedy. At their instance Hazrat Ahmad's house at Qadian was thoroughly searched by the district police of Gurdaspur and the houses of several prominent Ahmadis were searched in different parts of the Province. None of these searches disclosed anything that could raise the slightest suspicion that Ahmad or any of his followers had been concerned even remotely with the tragic event.

As the Aryas continued to give currency to their suspicion that Ahmad had been concerned with the assassination of Pandit Lekh Ram, he made an announcement on 15 March 1897 to the following effect:

If anyone still suspects me of having conspired to bring about the death of Pandit Lekh Ram, as has been alleged in some of the

Hindu papers, I would make a suggestion which would clear up the whole matter. Such a person should take an oath in my presence and state: 'I know as a certainty that Mirza Ghulam Ahmad was concerned in the conspiracy to murder Pandit Lekh Ram, or that he was murdered under the directions of Mirza Ghulam Ahmad. If this statement of mine is not true may God Almighty impose upon me some terrible torment which should not be the work of any man nor the result of any human planning.' Then if such a person survives for a year after his statement on oath, I may be deemed guilty of the murder and might be punished as a murderer. Now if there is any courageous Arya who can rescue the whole world from the suspicions that trouble people's minds by adopting this mode of seeking a decision, let him come forward to do so.

But no one came forward to take up this challenge. Had anyone responded to the challenge, the world would have witnessed another terrible sign.

On the 16th anniversary of the assassination of Pandit Lekh Ram, a leading member of the Arya Samaj, Babu Ghansi Ram M.A., Ll.B., wrote in the *Musafir Agra* Martyr Number of 6 March 1913:

This murder took place in Lahore, the capital of the Punjab Province, but the police utterly failed to trace the assassin. It was a coincidence that the prophecy of Ghulam Ahmad was fulfilled and Pandit Lekh Ram suffered martyrdom. God alone knows whether this was a torment afflicted by Him, or was the result of human planning.

The assassination of Lekh Ram within the period specified in the prophecy, and in exact accord with the other particulars published from time to time was a great Sign, particularly for the Hindu community of India and more especially for the Aryas.

In 1895, the Promised Messiah learnt that the principal relic of Baba Nanak, the Founder of the Sikh religion, who flourished in the 16th century, was preserved in a temple situated at Dera Baba Nanak, in the district of Gurdaspur, at a distance of approximately twenty-five miles from Qadian. The relic was a cloak of cotton stuff, which had a certain number of writings worked into its fabric. The Sikh tradition was that this cloak had been sent down fron heaven by God Almighty as a mark of honour for Baba Sahib and also as a means of providing security for him against all dangers.

Baba Nanak had been born into a Hindu family, but had, early in his life, exhibited deep devotion to the doctrine of the Unity of God and a marked aversion towards everything that savoured of polytheism or association of any person, idol, or thing as partner with God. As he grew up it became apparent that he held the Holy Prophet of Islam, peace be on him, in high honour and believed in the Holy Quran as the Word of God. He is reputed to have travelled far and wide in his search after truth, and Sikh tradition confirms that he even performed the pilgrimage to Mecca.

When the Promised Messiah learned of the relic at Dera Baba Nanak and heard rumours about its divine origin, he became anxious to discover what evidence this relic would disclose of its origin and what significance could be attached to the writings which had reputedly been worked into its fabric. He despatched a delegation composed of four of his followers to Dera Baba Nanak for the purpose of investigating the existence, condition and significance of the relic. On their return they reported that they had succeeded in having a view of the cloak and had found to their joy and delight that the writings which the cloak bore were all in Arabic, and that besides the credo of Islam, 'There is no one worthy of worship save Allah and Muhammad is the Messenger of Allah', all the writings were verses of the Holy Quran. The Promised Messiah, on hearing the report, felt that this was a grand proof that Baba Nanak was a Muslim saint and that he should personally follow up the matter and make sure what exactly was inscribed on the cloak.

On 30 September 1895, the Promised Messiah proceeded to Dera Baba Nanak in the company of ten of his devoted followers. He visited the temple in which the relic was preserved and requested the keeper of the relic to let them view the sacred cloak. It was discovered that the cloak was wrapped in about three hundred coverings of silk, cotton and the finest wool. Some of them bore the name and description of the donor. These indicated that the cloak had been held in high honour ever since the death of Baba Nanak.

These coverings were removed slowly, a few at a time, as a certain degree of persuasion was needed in the shape of discreet tips to induce the keeper to proceed with the removal of the whole body of covers. The process took more than an hour and in the end the cloak came into view in its full glory. It was found to be a blessed fabric into which the Islamic credo and several verses of the Holy Quran, including the entire Sura Fatiha, had been worked. Among other verses, the verses of the brief Chapter 112 of the Holy Quran were also thus inscribed. No other writing appeared on the cloak.

The cloak was spread out before the eyes of the visitors and, under the direction of the Promised Messiah, a sketch was made of the cloak and of the writings that appeared on it.

The Promised Messiah set forth the whole story about the cloak, together with an explanation of its different aspects, in his book *Sat Bachan*. The publication of this book roused great interest on the part of the Sikh community and among students of comparative religion. Several prominent Sikh gentlemen, after a study of the whole matter, became Muslims and joined the Ahmadiyya Movement; some of them rendered devoted service to the cause of Islam. Their descendants continue zealous and dedicated members of the Movement. Some time later the Promised Messiah learnt that another relic of Baba Nanak was preserved in a gurdawara at Guru Har Sahai, in the Ferozepur District. He despatched three of his followers to discover what the relic was. It was known as the Pothi (prayer book) of Baba Nanak. It turned out to be a copy of the Holy Quran!

As the result of the efforts of a Hindu ascetic, Swami Shugan Chandra, who was keenly interested in religion, a

Conference of Great Religions was proposed to be held in Lahore on 26, 27 and 28 December 1896, in which the representatives of the principal religions were invited to read papers on five themes on the basis of the teachings of their respective faiths. The themes were:

(1) The Physical, Moral and Spiritual States of Man.

(2) Life After Death.

(3) The True Purpose of Human Life and How it May Be Achieved.

(4) The Effect of Human Actions on Life Here and Hereafter.

(5) The Sources of Divine Knowledge.

Ahmad was invited to prepare and read a paper in the Conference setting forth the teachings of Islam on the five selected themes, and he agreed to write a paper to be read by one of his devoted followers, Maulvi Abdul Karim Sahib of Sialkot.

Five days before the opening of the Conference Ahmad published an announcement, headed *Great News for Seekers after Truth*, in the following terms:

> The Conference of Great Religions, to be held in the Lahore Town Hall on 26, 27, 28 December 1896, includes in its programme a paper by this humble one, the subject of which is the excellences and miracles of the Holy Quran. This paper does not represent the result of ordinary human effort but is one of the Signs of God written with His special grace and help. It sets forth the beauties and truths of the Holy Quran and proves like the noon-day sun that the Holy Quran is in truth God's own word, a book revealed by the Lord of all creation. Anyone who listens to this paper from beginning to end, paying attention to my treatment of the five themes set down for discussion, will receive, I am sure, a new faith and a new light. He will come upon a commentary on the whole of the Holy Book. The paper is free from human weaknesses, empty boasts and vain assertions.
>
> I feel moved on this occasion by sympathy for my fellow human beings to issue this notice. I invite one and all to come and witness the beauties of the Holy Quran, to come and see how unjust are our critics who love darkness and hate light. God, the All-Knowing,

has revealed to me that my paper will be acclaimed superior to all other papers that are read out in the Conference. Its light, truth, wisdom and knowledge will put all other parties in the shade, provided those who come to listen to it will stay from beginning to end. It will not avail the other participants in the Conference to try and set forth anything similar on the basis of their holy books, be they Christians, Sanatanists or Arya Hindus, or others. This is so, because Almighty God has decreed that on that day His Holy Book should reveal its resplendent countenance. I saw in a vision an invisible hand striking at my mansion, at which a shining light shot out and spread in all directions. Some of it fell on my hands. Then someone who stood by proclaimed in a loud voice: 'Allahu Akbar, Kharibat Khaibar' [Great is God, Khaibar is in ruins]. The interpretation of it is, that my mansion which appeared to be the aim and focus of this flood of heavenly light is symbolic of my heart; the light with which the place is flooded is symbolic of the truths of the Holy Quran; and Khaibar is symbolic of religions which are corrupted by false and ungodly ideas and which seek to install man in the place of God and to detract in different ways from the full meaning of His most perfect attributes. It has been revealed to me that when the contents of this paper of mine become widely known, the falsehood of other religions will be exposed and the truth of the Quran will spread all round till it fulfils its destiny. From the state of vision I passed to the state of reception of revelation and received the revelation [Arabic:] 'Verily God is with you, verily God stands where you stand. This was an assurance of Divine help in metaphorical language.

I need not write any more. I inform everyone that they should come on the appointed day to listen to my paper even at some personal inconvenience. If they do so the increase in their understanding and faith will be beyond their expectation. Peace be on those who follow the guidance.

Ahmad's paper was to be read at the Conference on 27 December from 1.30 to 3.30 p.m. It was read out by Maulvi Abdul Karim and was listened to with rapt attention. By 3.30 the reading of the answer to the first question had not yet been completed. Maulvi Mubarak Ali of Sialkot, who was scheduled to read out his paper at that time, announced that the time allotted to him for reading his paper might be used for the further reading of Ahmad's paper. This announcement was joyfully acclaimed by the audience. But even by 4.30 the reading of the answer to the first question could not be completed and it was suggested that the session which was to be concluded at 4.30 p.m. might be prolonged till the reading of the answer to the first question was finished. The directors of the Conference agreed to the suggestion and the reading of the paper continued until 5.30 p.m. As a good part of the paper had still to be read out the audience requested that the sessions of the Conference might be continued through an extra day to enable the whole of the paper to be read out. Accordingly arrangements were made to extend the sessions of the Conference over 29 December.

The paper was unanimously acclaimed as by far the best one read out at the Conference. In the official report of the Conference glowing tributes were paid to the paper. The *Civil and Military Gazette* of Lahore, in its issue of 29 December 1896, in the course of its comments on the Conference observed:

> Particular interest centered in the lecture of Mirza Ghulam Ahmad of Qadian, a master in the apologetics of Islam. An immense gathering of all sects from far and near assembled to hear the lecture, which, as the Mirza was himself unable to attend in person, was read by one of his able scholars, Maulvi Abdul Karim of Sialkot. On the 27th the lecture lasted for about three and a half hours and was listened to with rapt attention, though so far it dealt only with the first question. The speaker promised to treat with the remaining questions if time was allowed, so the president and the executive committee resolved to extend the sitting of the Conference to the 29th.

An English translation of the paper published under the title *The Teachings of Islam,* met with a very warm reception in Europe and America. Count Leo Tolstoy wrote: 'I approved very much two articles: "How to Get Rid of Sin", and "The Life to Come". The ideas are very profound and very true.'

The *Theosophical Notes* observed: 'The best and most

attractive presentation of the faith of Muhammad which we have yet come across.'

The *Indian Spectator* commented: 'An exposition of the teachings of the Quran in a very attractive form . . . there is nothing disputatious and nothing which is not drawn directly from the Quran.'

The *Indian Review* wrote: 'Very entertaining and pleasant reading, lucid, comprehensive and philosophical . . . evokes admiration. The book deserves to be in the hands of every Muhammadan student and also in the libraries of those who wish to know something of the Muhammadan religion.'

The *Spiritual Journal*, Boston, summed it up as: 'Pure Gospel.'

The *Bristol Times and Mirror* opined: 'Clearly it is no ordinary person who thus addresses himself to the West.'

Sahibzada Syed Abdul Latif was a descendant of the well-known saint Hazrat Sheikh Abul Hasan Ali Hajveri, who is generally known as Data Ganj Bakhsh and is buried in Lahore. Sahibzada Abdul Latif's home was Sayyadgah in the Province of Khost in Afganistan. He was a very learned divine, a great religious leader and a man of saintly life. He was a recipient of revelation, and had frequent experience of true visions. He was a spiritual preceptor of note, and had a large number of disciples and followers in Afghanistan. He possessed large properties in Khost as well as in adjoining British territory. He had a high standing at court and was nominated one of the two representatives of Afghanistan on the Boundary Commission appointed in 1894 to demarcate the boundary between Afghanistan and British India, which came to be know as the Durand Commission, after Sir Mortimer Durand who was the senior British representative on the Commission.

Sahibzada Abdul Latif had become aware fairly early of the advent of the Promised Messiah. During the sittings of the Commission one of the members of the staff of the British representatives presented a copy of the Promised Messiah's book *Ayena Kamalat Islam* to Sahibzada Abdul Latif, who was deeply impressed by its perusal and conceived great respect and affection for its author.

After the Commission had concluded its work Sahibzada Abdul Latif established contact with the Promised Messiah through some of his disciples, whom he sent from time to time to Qadian and who reported back to him and brought back with them the latest books, pamphlets and announcements of the Promised Messiah.

Among these disciples of Sahibzada Abdul Latif was Maulvi Abdur Rahman who visited Qadian several times as his emissary. In December 1900 the Sahibzada despatched his covenant of *Ba'iat* to the Promised Messiah, together with some robes through Maulvi Abdur Rahman and some other disciples.

At that time in view of the agitation that had been set afoot in the Frontier areas against the British and which was described by the Mullas as Jehad, in consequence of which several British officers had been treacherously murdered, the Promised Messiah issued some pamphlets condemning such activities and set forth the correct teachings of Islam on the question of Jehad.

Maulvi Abdur Rahman studied the pamphlets and, having fully grasped their import, gave expression to the views set forth in them on his return to Kabul. This was brought to the notice of Amir Abdur Rahman, the then ruler of Afghanistan, who was greatly incensed and directed the arrest and incarceration of Maulvi Abdur Rahman. In the middle of 1901 Maulvi Abdur Rahman was strangled to death in his cell at the instance of the Amir. He thus became the first martyr from among the followers of the Promised Messiah. Through his martyrdom a portion of the revelation 'Two goats would be slaughtered', which had been vouchsafed to the Promised Messiah several years earlier, was fulfilled.

A few weeks after the assassination of Maulvi Abdur Rahman, on 10 September 1901, Amir Abdur Rahman suffered a severe paralytic stroke which made him bed-ridden and to which he succumbed on 3 October 1901.

Towards the end of 1902 Sahibzada Abdul Latif set out from his home, with the permission of Amir Habibullah Khan, with the intention of proceeding on pilgrimage by way of Lahore, accompanied by two of his disciples and another divine. He had also in mind to pay a visit to Qadian so that he could have an opportunity of meeting the Promised Messiah in person. Thus he arrived in Qadian and was received by the Promised Messiah, who recorded the impression that he conceived of him in the following words:

> I call God Almighty, in Whose hand is my life, to witness that when I met him I found him so completely committed and devoted to my obedience and the confirmation of my claim that it is not possible to conceive more of it in respect of any person. I perceived that he was as full of love for me as a crystal vial filled with perfume. It seemed to me that his heart was as illumined as was his countenance.

He had intended to stop at Qadian for only a few days, but his meeting with the Promised Messiah and the members of the Movement at that time present in Qadian affected him so powerfully that he postponed his proceeding on pilgrimage and stayed on in Qadian for several months.

As has been mentioned Sahibzada Sahib himself had experience of visions and revelation. He was, therefore, able to appreciate deeply and appraise accurately the spiritual status of the Promised Messiah, and was so much overcome that he could not tear himself away from him. When in the end he asked for permission to return to Afghanistan and was granted it, the Promised Messiah accompanied him for two or three miles on his way. The moment of separation proved deeply affecting for both, and particularly painful for Sahibzada Abdul Latif. By the time he departed from Qadian he was convinced that on his return home he would have to lay down his life in the cause of truth. He told some of his friends that during the last few days of his stay he had repeatedly received the revelation: 'Offer your head! Offer your head!' He also received the revelation: 'Go to Pharaoh.'

While the Sahibzada Sahib was still in British territory he wrote a letter to Brigadier Muhammad Husain, Commissioner of Police, Kabul, explaining why he had not been able to go on pilgrimage and requested that the Brigadier should submit his explanation to Amir Habibullah Khan and ascertain whether the Amir would permit him to proceed to Kabul to pay his respects to him. The Amir sent back word that he should proceed to Kabul by all means and personally explain everything to the Amir to enable him to decide whether the claim of Hazrat Mirza Ghulam Ahmad was true, in which case he himself would also accept him. Sahibzada Abdul Latif proceeded to his home in Khost, and shortly after was summoned to Kabul under guard. On his arrival there he found that the Amir was much incensed against him. Without any inquiry from him, the Amir directed that he should be committed to a cell in the citadel in which the Amir himself was residing and should be kept in durance vile pending the pleasure of the Amir. His person was secured with heavy chains and fetters. He passed four months in a wretched condition in this cell. On several occasions it was intimated to him that if he would repudiate the claim of Hazrat Mirza Ghulam Ahmad that he was the Promised Messiah, he would be set at liberty, and would be restored to all the privileges, dignities and honour that he had previously enjoyed. But the Sahibzada Sahib remained firm in his belief and each time sent back the reply that he was an intelligent and knowledgable person who was equipped by God with the faculty of distinguishing between truth and falsehood. He was convinced after full study and investigation that Hazrat Mirza Ghulam Ahmad was the Promised Messiah. He realized that in making this affirmation he was putting his life in jeopardy and was inviting the ruin of his family, but he held his faith above every worldly comfort and consideration.

The Sahibzada Sahib had held a very high position in the country and had up to then passed his life in great comfort.

He had a large family and a great number of followers. The conditions of his imprisonment were painful in the extreme, but all the privations and pains and discomfort that he suffered over this long period did not in the least shake his determination to adhere firmly to his faith.

It appears that the Amir himself did not consider that the Sahibzada Sahib had been guilty of any serious offence and was anxious to find, if possible, some excuse to deal gently with him, but was afraid of a head-on collision with the orthodox divines to whom the Sahibzada Sahib's newly accepted doctrine was anathema and who were determined to bring about his ruin. The Amir had directed the incarceration of the Sahibzada Sahib in the citadel in which he himself resided so that he should have no difficulty in approaching the Sahibzada Sahib himself, or through his emissaries, for the purpose of persuading him to repudiate his erroneous doctrine. His continuous efforts in that behalf did not, however, have the least effect upon the Sahibzada Sahib.

One matter that must have upset the Amir was that the Sahibzada Sahib during his imprisonment did not hesitate to affirm that there was no justification in the present time to carry on Jehad with the sword and that the teaching of the Promised Messiah in this context was that this was the time of propagating Islam through reason and argument and that the concept of Jehad by the sword that was current among the Muslims was not in accord with the teachings of Islam.

After the expiry of four months the Amir summoned the Sahibzada Sahib into his presence and adjured him publicly that if he would repudiate the claim of the Qadiani pretender and his teachings, his life would be spared and he would be set at liberty with honour. The Sahibzada Sahib replied that it was not possible for him to resile from the truth and that the torment that a government could inflict upon him would end with his death, but that he could not offend Him Whose torment would be everlasting. He urged, however, that the divines who were opposed to his belief should enter into a discussion with him on the question of the correctness of the doctrines to which they objected, and that if the arguments in support of his belief were effectively refuted he could be condemned and punished. The Amir approved of his suggestion and Khan Mulla Khan and eight Muftis were selected to enter into discussion with the Sahibzada Sahib. A doctor from the Punjab, of the name of Abdul Ghani, who was bitterly opposed to the Promised Messiah's claim and teachings was appointed as umpire.

The discussion started at 7.00 a.m. and continued till 3.00 p.m. There was a large gathering in the mosque where the discussion was being held, but the exchange of views was carried on in writing and nothing was said orally. At the end of the written discussion the Sahibzada Sahib was asked that if this Qaisani was the Promised Messiah, what did he think about the second coming of Jesus? The Sahibzada Sahib affirmed stoutly that Jesus had died and would not appear again, and that the Holy Quran proclaimed his death and stood in the way of his coming again. Upon this the Muftis burst out in abuse against him and proclaimed that no doubt was left of his infidelity; and they prepared and subscribed to the formal declaration of his apostacy. Thereafter Sahibzada Sahib was returned to his cell burdened with his heavy chains and fetters. Throughout the course of the discussion eight guards with drawn swords had stood around the Sahibzada Sahib.

The declaration of the Muftis was submitted to the Amir at night without the record of the discussion, which is a strong indication that the Muftis had not been able to refute the arguments of Sahibzada Sahib. The Amir acting solely upon the declaration of the Muftis passed the sentence of death on him.

This was a most irresponsible action for which the Amir laid himself open to serious blame. Indeed the whole procedure was most unjust and tyrannical.

There was not the slightest justification for subjecting the Sahibzada Sahib to the torment of the most painful kind of durance for a period of four months without charging him with an offence and affording him an opportunity of clearing himself. When at long last such an opportunity was granted, he was brought to the trial, if it can be so described, loaded with his heavy chains and fetters and eight guards with drawn swords kept watch over him, so that he might be overawed and handicapped in replying to the charges preferred against him.

The Amir realized that the discussion might lead to the loss of the life of an innocent person, he should, therefore, have been present himself in the course of the discussion; but not having done so he should have insisted that the written record of the discussion should be submitted to him. Indeed, not only should he have himself perused the record of the discussion to satisfy himself of the guilt of the accused person, he should have directed the publication of the entire record to show that the Sahibzada Sahib had failed to set forth any proof in support of the claim of the Qadiani Promised Messiah, or in support of the prohibition of Jehad by the sword, or in support of the death of Jesus. He should at least have inquired from the Muftis on what was their condemnation of the Sahibzada based, and whether, in view of the differences that divided the various sects of Muslims, all of them, except one, should be similarly condemned.

The next morning the Sahibzada Sahib was summoned to the Salam Khana where a large crowd was gathered. The Amir left the citadel and on his way to the Salam Khana noticed the Sahibzada Sahib at one place and asked him what had been decided in the discussion. He returned no answer to the Amir's query, but one of the guards said that he had been condemned. When the Amir arrived in the Salam Khana he called for Sahibzada Sahib and said to him: 'You have been declared an apostate. Will you now repent, or will you submit to the penalty?' He replied that he could not repent of the truth and would not subscribe to falsehood to save his life. The Amir urged him again to repent and promised to let him go free if he would recant. The Sahibzada Sahib firmly declined and said that he would never give up the truth. The

Amir then wrote out an order in his own hand, and basing himself on the declaration of the Muftis condemned Sahibzada Sahib to death by stoning. This document was suspended round Sahibzada Sahib's neck and the Amir directed that a hole should be bored through his nose and a rope should be run through it and he should in this manner be led to the place of execution. This painful operation was carried out and Sahibzada Sahib was led outside the town to the place appointed for his execution, through the reviling and cursing crowd. The Amir also proceeded to the place of execution accompanied by his courtiers, Qazis, Muftis and other high officials.

At the place of execution a pit had been dug and Sahibzada Sahib was made to stand in it and it was then filled up to his waist. The Amir, his brother Sardar Nasrullah Khan and the Chief Qazi and commandant Abdul Ahad were mounted on their horses, and everyone else was on foot. The Amir again approached Sahibzada Sahib and told him that if he repudiated the Qadiani Promised Messiah even now, he would be delivered from death. He adjured him to have mercy on himself and the members of his family and comply with the Amir's suggestion. The Sahibzada Sahib affirmed he could in no wise deny the truth and could not abjure his faith to save his own life and to safeguard the members of his family. Thereupon the Qazis and jurists raised a clamour that he was an infidel and should be destroyed forthwith. Thereupon the Amir directed the Chief Qazi to throw the first stone. The Qazi said that the Amir should do so, as he was the sovereign. The Amir rejoined that the Qazi was the repository of the law and that it was his sentence that was to be carried out. The Qazi then dismounted and aimed a stone at Sahibzada Sahib which struck him with great force and made him lower his head. The Amir then aimed another stone at him and thereupon stones began to be hurled at him from every direction till a mound of stones rose up above him. The day of execution was 14 July 1903.

The Promised Messiah expressed himself in the following

terms about this tragic event:

> The martyrdom that was appointed for Sahibzada Abdul Latif was thus accomplished. The recompense of the tyrant is now awaited: 'The portion of him who comes to his Lord a sinner is hell; he shall neither die therein nor live' [20:75]. The Amir placed himself within the operation of the verse: 'Whoso kills a believer deliberately, his reward shall be hell, wherein he shall abide and Allah will be wroth with him and cast him away and will prepare for him a great punishment.' The Amir cast aside the fear of God and became guilty of killing a believer who had no equal in the whole of Afghanistan. He was one of those who laid down their lives with full sincerity in the cause of faith and truth and have no care for wife and children.
>
> I call down a thousand blessings on you, O Abdul Latif, that you proved your sincerity in my lifetime, for I do not know how those of my Community will behave who will survive me [*Tazkaratush Shahadatain*, pp. 47–58].

The Promised Messiah further observed:

> The merciless killing of Sahibzada Abdul Latif is a most grievous event; but it is also full of blessings that will be manifested with the passage of time and the land of Afghanistan will see what consequences the shedding of his blood will entail. His blood will not go waste. Before this, poor Abdur Rahman, a member of my Community, was unjustly killed, and God took no action. But after this tragedy He will not remain silent, and grave consequences will manifest themselves. It is understood that soon after the martyrdom of the Sahibzada a severe epidemic of cholera broke out in Kabul and many notable people, including some near relatives of the Amir, passed out of this world. This was a most merciless killing which has no match in this age. What folly has this Amir committed that he has ruined himself by his merciless killing of such an innocent person. O land of Afghanistan, bear witness that a grave offence has been committed in thee. O unfortunate land, thou hast fallen in the estimation of God in that this great tragedy was enacted in thee [*Tazkaratush Shahadatain*, p. 72].

Sahibzada Abdul Latif left behind his widow and five sons. They were all subjected to severe persecution and torment at the instance and under the direction of the government of

Afghanistan for nearly a quarter of a century, yet they all remained steadfast in their faith. Two of his sons died of fever in jail in Afghanistan. Eventually his widow, three sons, a sister and some of his grandchildren moved out of Afghanistan on 2 February 1926, and came to Bannu, in British Indian territory, where there was some property belonging to the family.

The assassination of Sahibzada Abdul Latif was followed by a number of significant events. On the day of his execution a fierce storm of extraordinary violence passed over certain parts of the country, a little after sunset. On the following day a severe epidemic of cholera broke out in the city of Kabul and its environs which carried away large numbers of people everyday over a period of weeks. The wife of Sardar Nasrullah Khan and one of his sons and several members of the royal family died of cholera, and also some of the Muftis who had condemned the Sahibzada Sahib.

The Punjabis who had been instrumental in inciting the Afghan Mullas against the Sahibzada Sahib were three brothers, Dr Abdul Ghani, Maulvi Najaf Ali and Muhammad Charagh. Amir Habibullah Khan condemned them to 11 years' imprisonment for treason. Dr Abdul Ghani had been the umpire in the discussion between Sahibzada Abdul Latif and the Muftis. He was still in prison when his wife died in Landi Kotal and his grown up son was murdered in broad daylight in Kabul. After he had served out his sentence he was expelled from the country. His brother Maulvi Nataf Ali was declared an infidel and an apostate in the time of Nadir Shah and was sentenced to be stoned to death, but was permitted to return to India through the intervention of the British Ambassador in Kabul. His brother Muhammad Charagh was also expelled along with him.

The condemnation of Sahibzada Sahib had been certified by Qazi Abdur Razzaq and Qazi Abdur Rauf, of whom the former was the superintendent of schools and was the Mullah in attendance upon the Amir. He was subsequently charged with some offence and having been found guilty forfeited all his property, and his limbs were cut off bit by bit in public till in great torment only his torso was left. It was then skinned and he finally perished. Qazi Abdur Rauf left Kabul and his son, Qazi Abdul Wase, who was appointed his successor, was cruelly murdered in 1929.

Sardar Nasrullah Khan, brother of Amir Habibullah Khan, had behind the scenes taken keen interest in the incarceration and condemnation of Sahibzada Sahib. He was also present at his execution. He was later suspected of treason and was brought to Kabul in chains by the order of Amir Amanullah Khan and was committed to prison. The shock upset his mind and sometime later he was killed in his cell by suffocation. One of his sons had died of cholera which followed on the martrydom of Sahibzada Sahib and another son was assassinated after his father's death. Amir Habibullah Khan himself was shot dead by some person unknown on 20 February 1919 at night in his camp near Jalalabad and was buried there. The rebels of Shinwar raided Jalalabad and stoned his grave. His son Sardar Hayatullah Khan was subsequently secretly hanged under the order of Bacha Saqua.

The Promised Messiah set out in some detail the particulars of the two martyrdoms of Maulvi Abdur Rahman and Sahibzada Abdul Latif in his book *Tazkaratush Shahadatain* which was published in 1903. In this book he admonished the members of his Community in the following terms:

> If you will adhere to truth and faith, angels will instruct you, heavenly comfort will descend upon you, you will be helped by the Holy Spirit, God will be with you at every step and no one will be able to overcome you. Await the grace of God steadfastly. Listen to abuse and keep silent. Endure being beaten and be steadfast. As far as possible do not resist evil, so that you may be accounted acceptable in heaven.

At the end of the book he announced:

> Harken, all ye people. This is a prophecy of Him Who had created heaven and earth. He will spread this Community of His in all countries and will make it supreme over all, through reason and

arguments. The days are coming, indeed they are near, when this will be the only religion which will be held in honour. God will bestow extraordinary blessings on this religion and Movement. He will frustrate everyone who seeks to destroy it. This supremacy will last till the Judgment Day.

Remember, that no one will descend from heaven. All our opponents who are alive today will die and no one will see Jesus son of Mary descending from heaven. Then their next generation will pass away and no one of them will see this spectacle. Then the generation next after that will pass away without seeing the son of Mary descending from heaven. Then God will make them anxious that though the time of the supremacy of the cross had passed away and the world had undergone great changes, yet the son of Mary had not descended from heaven. Then the wise people will suddenly discard this belief. The third century after today will not yet have come to a close when those who hold this belief, whether Muslims or Christians, will lose all hope and will give up this belief in disgust. There will then be only one religion that will prevail in the world and only one leader. I have come only to sow the seed, which has been sown by my hand. Now it will sprout and grow and flourish and no one can arrest its growth [*Tazkaratush Shadatain*, pp. 64–5].

On 15 April 1905 Hazrat Ahmad announced that it had been revealed to him that within a short time the world would be overtaken by a widespread calamity of a terrible character which would not only affect human beings but even birds, animals and trees. He indicated that in the course of it rivers of blood would flow and terror would spread and that the Czar of Russia would be afflicted with great misery. He admonished his opponents not to rush into denial but to treat the prophecy as a proof of his righteousness. He affirmed emphatically that as the prophecy was based on divine revelation it was bound to be fulfilled without doubt and that all that was needed was that his opponents should wait for some time for its fulfilment in a spirit of righteousness and steadfastness.

The whole world is witness to the terrible tragedy that overtook the Czar and the members of his family and culminated in the dishonour and destruction of the Czar and his family on 16 July 1918. It is not necessary to describe its gruesome details. They are now part of history. This historical event alone would be sufficient in the estimation of any just and reasonable person to establish the truth and righteousness of Ahmad beyond the least doubt. In 1905, when the prophecy was published, the Czar was, without a doubt, the most powerful and most absolute monarch of his time. In the eyes of his people he was a demigod, above and set apart from normal human beings. His territories were vaster than those of any other ruler. They stretched across the whole of the old world. His wealth and resources staggered the imagination.

Ahmad was the resident of a small town in a backward province of India, a town which was not in touch with the rest of the world even by telegraph or railway. He had no special interest in the vast dominions of the Czar or in the personal affairs of that monarch. When he published his prophecy it was completely ignored as a meaningless pronouncement of a person on the verge of insanity. Anticipating such a reception he had emphasized that his truth and righteousness would be judged through the fulfilment of the prophecy. He repeated that the prophecy was based on divine revelation which would not be frustrated under any circumstances. All that was necessary was to await its fulfilment in a spirit of righteousness and steadfastness. It is worthy of note that the prophecy presented a lurid picture of the horrors of the First World War. The miserable end of the Czar was only one of the dozen or so features of the war described in the prophecy though it was the most striking one of them.

CHAPTER SIX

John Alexander Dowie was by birth a Scotsman. He was born in Edinburgh in 1847 and studied for the Church in his early years.

In 1872 he went to Australia as a cleric and acquired a certain degree of reputation for healing. In 1888 he went over to the United States of America and started the publication of a paper called *Leaves of Healing*. In 1896 he founded the Christian Catholic sect. In 1901 he started building a town in the State of Illinois which he called Zion City. He established many factories within the area of the town and became in effect the uncrowned king of Zion City. In the same year he claimed to be Elijah III.

Dowie was a bitter enemy of Islam and of the Holy Prophet, peace be on him. He gave repeated expression to his hostility towards Islam in his speeches and writings which were published in the *Leaves of Healing*. On one occasion he delivered himself of the following despicable verbal caricature of Islam:

I think of the falsehood of Muhammad with great contempt. If I were to accept those falsehoods I would have to believe that in this gathering and indeed in any part of God's earth there is no single woman who possesses an immortal soul. I would have to acknowledge that you women are but wild animals which can be used for an hour or a day as playthings and that you have no eternal existence, and that when those who are dominated by bestial passions have satisfied their lust with you, you would die the death of dogs. This would be your end. This is the religion of Muhammad [*Leaves of Healing*, Vol. VII, No. 5, 26 May 1900].

On another occasion he said: I warn the Christian people of America and Europe that Islam is not dead. Islam has great strength, though Islam and Muhammadanism must be destroyed. The ruin of Islam will not be compassed through the supine Latin church or the powerless Greek church [*Leaves of Healing*, 25 August 1900, p. 7].

Being provoked by his reviling of Islam and the Holy Prophet, peace be on him, and his eagerness to destroy Islam and the Muslims, Ahmad confronted him with the following challenge in September 1902:

I am surprised at the attitude of some Christian missionaries who have studied philosophy, physics, astronomy, etc., and yet invite people to accept a weak human being as God. Recently there has appeared in the United States of America a man, apostle of Jesus, whose name is Dowie. He claims that Jesus in his capacity of God has sent him into the world to invite people to the doctrine that there is no God besides Jesus. But what kind of a God is he who could not safeguard himself against the Jews, who was betrayed by a treacherous disciple against whose mischief he proved helpless, He ran to a fig tree to eat of its fruit and did not know that it bore no fruit; when he was asked when would the Day of Judgment arrive, he confessed his ignorance of it. He became accursed, which means that his heart had become impure and had turned away from God and that he had been cast away from God and His mercy. He climbed towards heaven because the Father was very far from him, even by millions of miles, and this distance could not be overcome unless he ascended to heaven in his physical body. What a contradiction is here! On the one hand he asserts: 'The Father and I are one'; and on the other he journeyed over millions of miles to meet Him. If the father and son were one why did he have to endure the fatigue of such a long journey? The father was where he himself was, as both were one. Then on whose right hand did he sit?

Now we address ourselves to Dowie who deifies Jesus and calls himself his apostle and says that the prophecy mentioned in Deut. 18:15 is fulfilled in his advent and that he is himself Elijah and the apostle of this age. He does not know that his artificial god was never conceived of by Moses, and that Moses repeatedly admonished the children of Israel that they must not deify any creature, whether man or animal, neither in heaven nor on earth. He reminded them that God had spoken to them, yet they had not seen Him; and that their God was above having a shape or a body.

But Dowie, repudiating the God of Moses, presents a god who has four brothers and a mother. He has repeatedly declared in his paper that his god Jesus has told him that all Muslims will be destroyed and not one of them will survive, except those who should acknowledge the son of Mary as their god and Dowie as the apostle of that artificial god.

We have a message for Dowie that he need not be anxious to destroy all the Muslims. How can they acknowledge the godhead of the humble son of poor Mary, especially as in this age the tomb of Dowie's god has been discovered in this country and there is present among them the Promised Messiah, who has appeared at the end of the sixth and the beginning of the seventh millennia, with whose advent many Signs have been manifested? Dowie's claim, that all Muslims will be destroyed and only those will be saved who will acknowledge Jesus as god and Dowie as the apostle of the god, spells danger for even those Christians who believe in the son of Mary as god but do not acknowledge Dowie the false apostle. Dowie has clearly proclaimed in the revelation alleged to have been received by him that it is not enough to acknowledge Jesus as god unless Dowie is also acknowledged as Elijah and an apostle for the age, according to the prophecy mentioned in Deut. 18:15. They would not be saved unless they acknowledge all this, in default of which they would be destroyed. In this situation the Christians of Europe and America should make haste to acknowledge Dowie, lest they should be ruined. Having accepted one absurd doctrine, namely, the godhead of Jesus, they should have no difficulty in accepting another absurd doctrine that Dowie is the apostle of that god.

As regards the Muslims, we wish to point out respectfully to Mr Dowie that there is no need for the fulfilment of his purpose to subject millions of Muslims to destruction. There is a very easy way of determining whether Dowie's god is true or our God. That way is that Mr Dowie need not repeatedly announce his prophecy of the destruction of all Muslims, but should keep me alone in his mind and should pray that of the two of us, the one who is false may die before the other. Dowie believes in Jesus as god and I consider him a humble creature and a prophet. The matter in issue is which of us two is in the right? Mr Dowie should publish this prayer which should bear the testimony of at least one thousand persons. When the issue of the paper that contains this announcement reaches me I too will pray accordingly and shall append to my prayer the testimony of a thousand persons, if God so wills. I am sure that through the adoption of this course a way shall be opened for Mr Dowie and all the Christians for the recognition of the truth.

I have not been the first to propose such a prayer. It is Mr Dowie who, through his announcements, has put himself in that position. Observing this, God, Who is jealous, has urged me towards this confrontation. It should be remembered that I am not just an average citizen of this country. I am the Promised Messiah, who is being awaited by Mr Dowie. The only difference is that Mr Dowie says that the Promised Messiah will appear within twenty-five years, and I proclaim that he has appeared already and that I am that person. Hundreds of Signs have appeared in my support in the earth and from heaven. My Community numbers approximately a hundred thousand and is rapidly increasing.

Mr Dowie boasts that he has healed thousands of sufferers through his attention. We retort: Why then was he not able to heal his own daughter and let her die, and still mourns her loss? Why was he not able to heal the wife of his follower who was in extremity in childbirth and Mr Dowie was summoned to her side and she died? It is noteworthy that hundreds of people in this country practise the art of healing and many of them become experts in it and yet no one acknowledges that they possess spiritual merit. It is surprising how the simple people of America are trapped by Mr Dowie. Were they not carrying the burden of unduly deifying Jesus that they took over this second burden also? If Mr Dowie is true in his claim and Jesus is indeed god, this matter can be determined by the death of only one person; there is no need of destroying the Muslims of all countries. But if Mr Dowie does not respond to this notice and offers a prayer according to his boasts and then is removed from this world before my death, this would be a sign for all the people of America. The only condition is that the death of either of us should not be compassed by human hands but should be brought about by illness or by lightning, or snakebite or by the attack of a wild beast, I grant Mr Dowie a period of three months to make up his mind to comply with my request and I pray that God be with those who are true.

The method I propose is that Mr Dowie should come into the field against me with the permission of his false god. I am an old man of more than sixty-six years of age. I suffer from diabetes, dysentery, migraine, and deficiency of blood. I realize, however, that my life depends not upon the condition of my health but upon the command of my God. If the false god of Mr Dowie possesses any power he will certainly permit him to come forth against me. If instead of the destruction of all the Muslims Mr Dowie's purpose can be served by my death alone, he will have established a great sign, in consequence of which millions of people will acknowledge the son of Mary as god and will also believe in Dowie as his apostle. I affirm it truly that if the disgust that the Muslims of the world feel towards the god of the Christians were to be placed on one side of the scale and the disgust that I feel towards him were to be placed on the other side of the scale my disgust would be found to be heavier than the disgust of all the Muslims of the world. The truth is that Jesus son of Mary is from me and I am from God. Blessed is he who recognizes me and most unfortunate is he from whose eyes I am hidden [*Review of Religions, Urdu*, Vol. I, No. 9, pp. 342–8].

The challenge of the Promised Messiah was given great publicity in the American Press, in some organs of which its substance was published almost verbatim, among them the *Literary Digest* of 20 June 1903, the *Burlington Free Press* of 27 June 1903, the *New York Commercial Advertiser* of 26 October 1903.

The *Argonaut* of San Francisco, in its issue of 1 December 1902, gave an account of the challenge under the caption, 'English versus Arabic Prayer Contest', and concluded as follows: 'In brief the Mirza has written to Dowie: You are the leader of a community. I too have several followers. The decision as to who is from God can be easily sought. Each of us should pray that whoever is false God should take him away in the lifetime of the other. The one whose prayer is heard shall be considered from the true God.'

The paper commented: 'This indeed is a most reasonable and just position.'

Dowie gave no reply to Ahmad's challenge but announced in the *Leaves of Healing* of 14 February 1903: 'I pray to God that Islam should soon disappear from the world. O God, accept this prayer of mine. O God destroy Islam.'

On 23 August 1903 Ahmad published another statement addressed to Mr Dowie, in the course of which he said:

I do not say merely out of my own mouth that I am the Promised Messiah. God Who has created the heavens and the earth bears witness for me. To complete His witness He has manifested and continues to manifest hundreds of signs in my support. I say truly that His grace upon me is in excess of his grace that He bestowed upon the Messiah who appeared before me. His countenance has been exhibited in my mirror more widely than it was reflected in his mirror. If I say this only out of my own mouth, I am false; but if He bears witness for me, no one can call me false. I have thousands of His testimonies in my support, which I cannot number . . . One testimony is that if Mr Dowie will accept my challenge and will put himself in opposition to me expressly or impliedly, he will depart this life with great sorrow and torment during my lifetime.

Dowie has not so far replied to my challenge nor has he referred to it in his paper. I, therefore, grant him time for seven months from today, the 23rd of August 1903. If during this period he comes forth in opposition to me and makes an announcement in his paper that he accepts fully the plan that I have put forward, the world shall soon see the end of this contest. I am about seventy years of age and Dowie, according to his own statement, is a young man of fifty years. I am not concerned about this disparity in our ages as the issue is not to be decided on the merits of age. It rests entirely with God Who is the God of heaven and earth and is the best Judge. If Mr Dowie runs away from this contest I would call upon the people of America and Europe as witnesses that this would also be deemed to be his defeat, and in such case it should be concluded that his claim of being Elijah is a mere boast and deceit. He may try to flee from death in this manner, but he should realize that his flight from the proposed contest is also a species of death. Be sure, therefore, that a calamity will most certainly befall his Zion very soon.

At last Mr Dowie announced in the *Leaves of Healing* of December 1903:

In India, there is a Mohammedan Messiah who keeps on writing to me that Jesus Christ lies buried in Kashmir. People ask me why do I not send him the necessary reply? Do you think that I should answer such gnats and flies? If I were to put my foot on them I would trample them to death. The fact is that I merely give them a chance to fly away and survive.

Thus the issue was squarely joined between Ahmad and Dowie. From that moment Dowie entered upon a progressive decline of all his affairs. His health began to deteriorate, his followers began to have doubts and questioned his claims, he began to encounter financial difficulties. In 1905 he suffered a severe stroke of paralysis and was directed by his physician to move to a warmer climate. He was taken to Mexico and later to Jamaica. The affairs of Zion were handed over to a nominee of his who soon turned against him. His wife and children deserted him and he was charged with diverse illicit and immoral practices. On 9 March 1907 he died a miserable death. The prophecy of the Promised Messiah was truly and completely fulfilled.

The *Dunville Gazette* of 7 June 1907 wrote: 'Ahmad and his adherents may be pardoned for taking some credit for the accuracy with which the prophecy was fulfilled a few months ago.'

The *Truth-Seeker* of 15 June 1907 wrote: 'The Qadian man predicted that if Dowie accepted the challenge, he would leave the world before his eyes with great sorrow and torment. If Dowie declined, the Mirza said, the end would only be deferred; death awaited him just the same and calamity would soon overtake Zion. That was the grand prophecy: Zion would fall and Dowie would die before Ahmad.'

The *Herald of Boston*, in its issue of 23 June 1907, observed: 'Dowie died a miserable death with Zion city torn and frayed by internal dissensions.'

Ahmad had often confessed that the keenest distress that oppressed his mind was the deification of Jesus by the Christian Church, and that he was most anxious to discover some means by which this matter might be conclusively settled and mankind might be rid of this enormity. He missed no opportunity of expounding the truth on the basis of the Holy Quran, the Christian scriptures and human reason. While exposing the baselessness of the doctrine of the divinity of Jesus, he always took care to point out that, according to the teaching of the Holy Quran, he himself believed in Jesus as a true Prophet of God and revered him as such.

The Christian missionaries on their part were not only aggressively occupied with propounding the doctrines of the Church and inviting people to their acceptance, but carried on an offensive, scurrilous and abusive campaign against Islam, the Holy Quran and the Holy Prophet of Islam, on whom be peace. By the begining of 1893 the Christian mission had gained a footing in Jandiala, a small village in the Amritsar district. This roused the local Muslims to rally together in the defence of Islam and they began to ask questions and raise objections in the open-air meetings that the Christians held in the village from time to time. The mission authorities began to feel uneasy at this reaction on the part of the local Muslims and conveyed their apprehensions to the Rev Dr Henry Martyn Clark, medical missionary in charge of the Amritsar district, who wrote a letter to one of the Muslims of Jandiala, in which he suggested that a public debate might be arranged between accredited representatives of the two faiths, so that a final decision could be taken on their relative merits and it might be determined which of them was true. When this letter was received by the addressee he approached Ahmad in a letter, dated 11 April 1893, with the request that Ahmad might be pleased to represent the Muslims in the proposed debate. Upon this a certain amount of correspondence was exchanged between Ahmad and Dr Henry Martyn Clark through which an agreement was reached upon the holding of the debate at Amritsar from 22 May to 3 June 1893. In this debate Ahmad was to represent the Muslims and Mr Abdullah Athim, a retired civil servant, was to represent the Christian Mission. The venue of the debate was the bungalow of Dr Henry Martyn Clark at Amritsar. The subjects of the debate were to be the truth of

Islam, of the Holy Quran and of the Holy Prophet, peace be on him, and the divinity of Jesus.

A fortnight before the debate was scheduled to begin Ahmad wrote to Dr Clark that as a debate was only an academic discussion which might help some people but which might not prove conclusive, the parties should agree to supplicate the Divine for the exhibition of a definite sign in support of the party that was in the right; but Dr Clark did not think that this was a feasible proposal. Ahmad repeated his suggestion during the course of the debate. While Dr Clark was still reluctant, Mr Abdullah Athim adopted a more reasonable attitude and intimated that though he himself would not participate in the supplication, he would have no objection to Ahmad making the supplication.

The debate contined during a fortnight in which papers dictated in the meeting by the representative of each side on the subject of discussion set for the day were read out and exchanged. At the close of the debate Ahmad concluded his last paper with the following announcement:

> When I prayed to God, in all humility and earnestness, that He might give His judgment in the debate as we were weak mortals and without His judgment we could not accomplish anything, I was given the sign, by way of glad tidings, that of the two parties to the debate the one who was deliberately following a falsehood and forsaking the true God and deifying a weak mortal would be thrown into hell within fifteen months, each month corresponding to each day of the debate, and that he would suffer open disgrace if he did not turn to the truth; and that the one who was following the truth and believed in the true God would be openly honoured. . . . Now, I ask Deputy Sahib [Athim]: If this sign is fulfilled, would you accept it as a perfect and a divine prophecy according to your liking? Would it not be a strong proof that the Holy Prophet, on whom be peace, whom you have called a *Dajjal* [Anti-Christ] in your book *Androonai Bible*, is a true Prophet?

When Athim heard these words he trembled visibly and turned pale. He raised his hands to his ears, put out his tongue and shook his head to indicate in the Eastern manner that he had not intended to abuse the Holy Prophet. He repeatedly uttered the words: 'I repent, I repent. I did not mean to be disrespectful and I have never called the Prophet Anti-Christ.'

After the debate, Athim withdrew altogether from public life, made no public speech, nor said a word against Islam or the Holy Prophet, peace be on him. He moved about from place to place, became the subject of illusions and hallucinations, and was haunted by the fear of death. He was being tortured by his own diseased imagination. The period of fifteen months expired and he survived it. There was a clamour on the part of Ahmad's opponents that his prophecy had not been fulfilled.

Ahmad issued a leaflet on 5 September 1894, and another one four days later, in which he explained the background and the implications of the prophecy. He claimed that Athim's declaration on hearing the prophecy and his passive attitude thereafter were proof that he had turned to the truth and had changed his attitude towards Islam. Ahmad invited him to deny this openly on oath and stated that if he did so he would die within one year from the date of taking the oath. Ahmad further declared that if, after making the oath, Athim survived for a year Ahmad would pay him the sum of 1,000 Rs by way of acknowledgment of defeat. Athim made no response. Ahmad then sent registered letters to Athim, Dr Clark and the Rev Mr Imadud Din, inviting Athim to take the oath and calling upon the other two gentlemen to persuade him to do so. Dr Clark wrote back to say that Athim was not prepared to take the oath. Thereupon Ahmad issued another leaflet on 20 September 1894 calling upon Athim to take the oath and offered to pay him Rs 2,000 if he would do so. To this Athim replied in a letter that he was still a Christian and that he did not believe in Islam. Ahmad issued still another leaflet on 5 October 1894 which contained an answer to about a score of different points that had been raised by various people and challenged Athim again to declare on oath in a public meeting that during the fifteen months he had not changed his attitude towards Islam. The only response that Athim made was that he wrote in the *Noor Afshan* (a Christian paper) of 10 October that it was not permissible for him to take an oath except in the course of a judicial proceeding, as his religion did not allow him to take an oath on any other occasion. He confessed that he had been afraid of death during the period of fifteen months as he apprehended that Ahmad, or any of his followers, might make an attempt to kill him. Ahmad issued still another leaflet on 27 October in which he emphatically denied that he or any of his followers were in any way concerned to bring about Athim's death and raised the amount of the award that he had offered to Athim to Rs 4,000. He also explained that it was not against the teachings of Christianity to take an oath in the name of God. He further wrote that God would not leave Athim long unpunished even if he did not take the oath because he had tried to deceive the world by his silence and refusal to take the oath.

The *Noor Afshan* of 13 September 1895 published an article in which it pointed out that twelve months had passed and Athim was still alive. In answer to this article Ahmad issued a leaflet in which he explained that no time limit had yet been declared for Athims's death as he had not yet taken the required oath.

In December 1895, a Christian missionary, Fateh Masih, said to a friend of Ahmad that Athim did not come forward to take the oath because Ahmad had only a handful of followers. Ahmad at once issued a leaflet in which he asked Fateh Masih how many people should urge Athim to take the oath. If he wanted a petition signed by one, two, three, or four thousand Muslims, Ahmad would arrange it immediately, provided Athim could be persuaded to take the oath. But nothing came of it.

Within less than seven months of the issue of this last leaflet Athim died at Ferozepur, where he was buried. The repeated efforts of Ahmad, and even of some of the colleagues of Athim, to persuade him to take the required oath failed to move him from his determined stand that he would not take the oath. This was proof enough that he was afraid to do so lest divine wrath should overtake him for taking a false oath.

The proceedings of the debate had effectively exposed the hollowness of the claim that Jesus was God, as taught by the Church, and had afforded an excellent opportunity to Ahmad to set forth the excellence of the teachings of Islam in their proper perspective. This had proved a great setback for Christianity in the Punjab in general and for the Amritsar mission and its head Dr Henry Martyn Clark in particular.

An amusing incident in the course of the debate, engineered by Dr Clark and his colleagues, served to bring them into ridicule and to show that their attitude towards religion lacked all seriousness and that they considered the whole subject as a joke. One day they procured the presence of three persons, one of them lame, another blind and a third dumb, at Dr Clark's bungalow, and when the sitting commenced they pretended that they desired to test the truth of the claim of the Promised Messiah through a sign. They alleged that Jesus used to cure the maimed and the blind by virtue of his spiritual power, and that as Ahmad claimed to be the Promised Messiah, he should be able to heal such afflicted persons in the same way. They added that in order to facilitate matters they had three such persons ready at hand for Ahmad to heal. Ahmad was not at all perturbed by the demand and pointed out that it was the Gospels that mentioned these so-called miracles of Jesus, and they also reported Jesus as saying that if his disciples had faith as much as a grain of mustard seed, they would also be able to heal the sick with their touch and even perform greater wonders. He thanked them for having provided the opportunity for their own faith to be tested. If what Jesus said was true they should now proceed to establish its truth by healing the three persons whose attendance they had themselves arranged. He himself had not made any claim that he could heal the afflicted with his touch and was not called upon to demonstrate any such sign. The Christian divines were completely frustrated by

Ahmad's reply and speedily arranged to get rid of the three specimens whom they had assembled together.

The debate was followed by the controversy whether Athim's attitude towards Islam had been affected by the prophecy that Ahmad had made concerning Athim, which terminated in the death of Athim on 27 July 1896. This was followed on 6 March 1897 by the terrible death of Pandit Lekh Ram, in exact accord with the prophecies of Ahmad. Thus, by the middle of 1897, both the Christians and the Hindus were highly incensed against Ahmad. The orthodox Muslims had already pronounced him an apostate from Islam and had declared that his assassination would be a highly meritorious act. In this atmosphere of almost universal hostility towards Ahmad, Dr Henry Martyn Clark devised a plan to bring about the humiliation and disgrace of Ahmad which further illustrated his utter lack of moral principles. Human degradation could scarcely have sunk lower. It is true that the device to which he had recourse was applauded by the Aryas as well as some of the Muslim divines who were ready to lend it their approval and support, but this proved of little comfort to Dr Clark when it boomeranged upon him and made him an object of ridicule and contempt. This is what happened.

On 1 August 1897 Dr Clark filed a complaint in the Court of the District Magistrate of Amritsar charging Ahmad with conspiracy to murder him. In support of his charge he produced a youth by the name of Abdul Hamid, who made a statement on oath before the District Magistrate that Ahmad had instructed him to proceed to Amritsar and assassinate Dr Clark. On the basis of Abdul Hamid's statement the District Magistrate issued a warrant for the arrest of Ahmad and sent the warrant for execution to the District Magistrate of Gurdaspur. Soon after, the District Magistrate of Amritsar realized that he had no jurisdiction in the matter and he forwarded Dr Clark's complaint to the District Magistrate of Gurdaspur and requested that the warrant that he had previously sent to the latter officer for execution might be returned to him. This could not be done, as the warrant had not reached the District Magistrate of Gurdaspur and it could not be discovered where and how it had miscarried.

The District Magistrate of Gurdaspur, Captain M. W. Douglas, issued a notice to Ahmad to appear and show cause why he sould not be bound over to keep the peace. He appeared in court on 10 August and the statements of Abdul Hamid and some other witnesses began to be taken down. This kept the Magistrate occupied till 13 August. He found that there were serious discrepancies between the statement of Abdul Hamid made before the District Magistrate of Amritsar and his statement before him. He was also not satisfied with Abdul Hamid's demeanour in the witness box. He found that Abdul Hamid was living under the care of the Mission authorities at Batala, and as his statement was being constantly enlarged and added to, Captain Douglas asked the District Superintendent of Police, Gurdaspur, to take charge of him and question him independently.

Mr le Marchand, the District Superintendent, sent for Abdul Hamid and began to examine him. He had taken down a part of his statement when Abdul Hamid burst into tears, fell at Mr le Marchand's feet and confessed that he had made a false statement at the instance of some of the missionaries. He had been guarded by them for several days, was in a state of great misery and had even comtemplated suicide. He subsequently made a similar statement in court and Captain Douglas, on putting him through a thorough examination, was satisfied that the charge against Ahmad was utterly false and baseless. Thus, the only course open to him was to discharge Ahmad honourably, which he did, and he told Ahmad that if he desired to prosecute Dr Clark for malicious prosecution, he, the District Magistrate, would grant him leave to do so. Ahmad replied that he had no desire to prosecute Dr Clark before an earthly court. His complaint was pending before the Highest Judge. Dr Clark died on 16 May 1900.

The Rt Rev George Alfred Lefroy was Bishop of Lahore in

the early years of this century. His attitude towards Islam might be gathered from the following incident recorded in the *Life and Letters of George Alfred Lefroy* by H. H. Montgomery (London: Longmans, Green & Co. 1920), where it is said:

> Archbishop Bensen made a speech at the annual meeting of the Society for the Propagation of the Gospel in St James's Hall on 16 June 1892 in the course of which he said: 'We know what the sins of Mohammadenism are, but do we not know what the sins of Europe and London are? . . . Mohammadenism does form high character. No one can go into a Mohammaden place of worship without being struck with the evidence of sincerity, gravity, absorbedness and solemnity in the worshippers.' Commenting on this Lefroy said: 'It must be with the extremest deference that I venture to dissent from the views of his Grace.'

Bishop Lefroy knew Hebrew, Arabic and Persian and could speak with great facility in Urdu. He was fond of public speaking and often addressed meetings in the spirit of an evangelist. He was appointed Bishop of Lahore in 1899. During the spring and early summer of 1900 the Bishop delivered public addresses at different places in Lahore on the thesis that Jesus alone, out of all the prophets, was sinless and compared him with the other prophets, especially with the Holy Prophet of Islam, to the disadvantage of all the other prophets.

When Ahmad heard of these lectures, he wrote and published two leaflets on 25 May 1900 for distribution at the Bishop's lecture which was due to be delivered the same afternoon. This was done and at the end of his address the Bishop was asked to comment on the subject matter of the leaflets. The Bishop excused himself on the plea that the points raised in the leaflets were new to him and that he had come to know of them for the first time. The leaflets dealt with the subjects on which the Bishop had spoken on earlier occasions. At the end of the second leaflet, Ahmad wrote that if the Bishop of Lahore was in earnest and was really interested in the truth, he should come forward and announce that he was prepared to hold a public discussion with Muslims on the topic whether Jesus or Muhammad was the greater Prophet in respect of knowledge, personal example and spiritual influence.

A large number of Muslims also addressed a letter to Bishop Lefroy inviting him to agree to a public discussion on five questions affecting the truth of Christianity and Islam with Hazrat Mirza Ghulam Ahmad of Qadian, over a period of five days. They set out the regulations for the conduct of the meeting and appealed to the Rt Rev gentleman, in the name of Jesus, not to fail to provide an opportunity for the seekers after truth to come to a decision on the proposed questions after listening to the discussion.

The well-known English daily, *The Pioneer,* published from Allahabad, said in the course of its observations on the letter: 'The letter has a great many signatures, of which the first few names will be sufficient to indicate the widespread interest and expectation with which the Mohammedan community are looking forward to the encounter.'

On 12 June 1900, the Bishop sent a reply to the letter from Simla in which he put forward a number of reasons or excuses why he could not comply with the request submitted to him in the letter. One of these was:

> The Mirza Sahib, in venturing to call himself the Messiah, assumes, with no shadow of authority, that name by which we Christians are called and which we regard with profoundest reverence, and offers in my opinion a most grievous insult and dishonour to Him Whom I worship as my Lord and Master. How then can I possibly consent to meet him in a friendly way?

A reasoned and courteous rejoinder was sent, on behalf of the signatories to the original letter, to the Bishop on 10 July 1900. In the course of it the writer pointed out:

> Your lordship has declined to meet Mirza Ghulam Ahmad in any friendly relationship for his having assumed a name which the Christians honour and worship as their Lord and Master. Had it

been even as your Lordship thinks, it could not have been a good ground for hatred and the cessation of friendly relations, for the Holy Bible inculcates love towards enemies. Treatment of this nature towards an adversary cannot be expected from the followers of any religion, not to say anything of a Christian and especially of a Church dignitary, whose duty it is not only himself to act upon Matt. 5:44, but also to teach that doctrine to the laity and to preach it to the non-Christians. But I may assure you that Mirza Sahib does not assert that he is Jesus Christ in person, but one coming in that Prophet's spirit and character and preaching after his manner, as John came in the spirit and power of Elias. Moreover, the Muslims honour Jesus as a true and eminent prophet and the Mirza Sahib, being the foremost Muslim of his day, does so pre-eminently, whereas millions of people who do not profess the Christian or Muslim faith do not look upon him even as a prophet and thus offer the greatest affront to his dignity, and your lordship must often, I suppose, have come into contact with such persons. Yet, I do not think that your Lordship has ever expressed the same feeling of hatred towards them as you have expressed towards Mirza Sahib in your letter.

In conclusion it was stated: When this matter was referred to the Mirza Sahib and he was asked whether, as your Lordship had declined to meet him in a friendly way, he too was disposed to entertain similar feelings towards your Lordship, he gave the following reply:

'I do not look upon anyone in the world as my enemy. I hate not individuals but the false beliefs they entertain. As regards individuals, my feelings towards them are of the utmost sympathy and goodwill. How can I then regard anyone as my enemy who enjoys respectability among his co-religionists and is honoured for his position and learning? I love him though I do not like his doctrines, but my hatred towards these doctrines extends only so far as the attributes of God are ascribed to human beings, and human faults and weaknesses are ascribed to the Lord of the universe. I am not averse to meeting his Lordship in a friendly way, for it is possible that either party may reap some advantage from the other, as the seed of sincerity must bear fruit. It is the first requisite in the performance of a person's duties as a reformer or a preacher that he should receive those who hold views differing from his own in the most cordial and cheerful manner. In truth, I would not only be departing from my functions as a reformer, but dealing at the same time a death-blow to all moral laws, if I were to regard as my enemies persons who deserve compassion for having unfortunately fallen into error. Such a step on my part would only deprive a large majority of those noble and holy truths which it is my duty to preach to all.

'The Holy Quran says: "We have sent unto you a Prophet whose heart is full of sympathy for you, so much so that all your cares and anxieties grieve him in the same manner as if they were his own, and he is always anxious for your comfort and happiness" (9:128). Again it says: "Shalt thou, O Prophet, put an end to thy life out of grief that these people do not accept the truth?" (26:4). The last verse makes a reference to the true sacrifice of life which the prophets of God make for the reformation of the people. These are the verses upon which I act, and one can easily understand from this the nature of my feelings towards those who regard themselves as my enemies.'

But nothing could induce his Lordship to change his mind. He wrote in reply on 12 July 1900: 'I have received your letter of the 10th instant, but I have nothing to alter in, or add to, the reasons assigned in my former letter for declining to enter into a controversy with Mirza Ghulam Ahmad to which you invited me.'

The comments of two impartial papers would give a fair idea of the validity of the reasons put forward by Bishop Lefroy for declining the invitation addressed to him. The Indian *Daily Telegraph* of 19 June 1900 wrote as follows:

We reproduce on another page a most interesting religious challenge, from the school of Islam in this country which follows Mirza Ghulam Ahmad of Qadian, to the Bishop of Lahore. It is interesting because it seems to be put forward in an earnest and sincere spirit. Mirza Ghulam Ahmad is the Chief of Qadian, and, according to the wording of the challenge, not only lays claim to the Promised Messiahship, but has made good that claim by strong and conclusive arguments, and has proved himself to be the Promised One whose appearance has been foretold in the Holy

Quran and the Bible. It seems that the following of this somewhat remarkable personage numbers about thirty thousand in different parts of the world, and his friends and disciples are anxious that he should hold an elaborate and learned argument on the respective truth of Christianity and Islam with the Bishop of Lahore, whose lectures at that place have convinced the Mohammedans that he is unrivalled in religious learning in this country. His vast and practical knowledge, his acquaintance with Arabic, Persian and Urdu and his amicable and polished manners are also enumerated as further reasons why he should be asked to enter into a controversy with this Champion of Islam. The challenge throughout is worded in conciliatory terms and exhibits an evidently keen desire for a formal and set controversy on fair terms to both parties on the comparative merits and excellences of Christianity and Islam. The challengers, who are large in numbers and hail from all parts of India, hope by adjuring the Bishop in the name of Jesus Christ to gain his consent to a controversy.

We are of the opinion that the Bishop would do well to accept the challenge. To assume a superiority that cannot stoop to controversy would be a mistake, as the challengers would be entitled from their point of view to conclude that the case being undefended went by default and to claim the victory. Also, the fact that Mirza Ghulam Ahmad of Qadiani is not the promised one whose appearance has been foretold in the Holy Quran and the Bible ought not to influence the learned Bishop towards a refusal to enter into an argument with him. This question is not to be discussed in the proposed controversy, but the Bishop may possibly convince his opponent of error if the challenge is accepted. The fact that the Muslims desire to pit their Messiah against the Bishop is the highest compliment they could desire to pay to his learning. They wish to intimate that they recognize him as the first authority in India. Again, we do not see how the Bishop can plead that such an elaborate controversy would take up too much of his time. He should on no account lose an opportunity of refuting, silencing and convincing such opponents, especially where he is desired to prove which of the two religions, Christianity or Islam, can be called the living faith; and of the teaching inculcated in the Holy Quran and the Bible, which is the more excellent and natural? We should like to see the challenge accepted because we think it would prove highly interesting.

On the Bishop's refusal the Indian *Spectator* commented as follows:

The Bishop of Lahore seems to have retired with more haste than dignity from a challenge which he had himself provoked. His Lordship, some time back, set before himself the task of proving to Mohammedan audiences that Christ was a true Messiah and the challenge was taken up by Mirza Ghulam Ahmad of Qadian to whose claim of Messiahship we referred some time ago in these columns. Now Mirza Ahmad may, for aught we know, be a rank impostor, or he may really believe himself to be what he claims to be. In either case, we do not see why the Bishop should decline to argue with him. His Lordship speaks of Mirza Sahib as offering a grievous insult and dishonour to Christ by venturing to call himself the Messiah. The Jews of two thousand years ago crucified Christ for the self-same reason. They felt insulted by his venturing to call himself the Messiah. What is even more strange is the Bishop pointing to the fact of Mirza Ahmad's claims being treated with ridicule and contempt by an overwhelming majority of Punjab Mohammedans as conclusive proof of the falsity of those claims. When Pilate asked the assembled Jews whom would they like to be liberated on the day of the Passover, Christ or Barabbas, they unanimously voted for the impenitent thief. Did that prove that Christ's claim to Messiahship was unfounded? We are not among the followers of Mirza Ahmad and have no intention of upholding his claims in preference to those of Christ, but we object to the logic of the hustings being introduced in a discussion on religion. If the whole Muslim world would have acclaimed the Mirza, would the Rt Rev Prelate of Lahore have altered his opinion of his mission? Religious beliefs in his country are in a state of dissolution just now. It behoves those who are anxious to see them crystallized round the truth not to employ arguments which are not of the purest temper.

No comment is called for.

CHAPTER SEVEN

The Holy Prophet had mentioned among the functions of the Promised Messiah that he would revive the faith, which was an indication that at the time of the advent of the Promised Messiah Islam and the Muslims would have arrived at a state which could be described as devoid of life. Indeed the Holy Prophet, peace be on him, specified several aspects of the decline of the values of Islam in the daily life of the Muslims at that time. For instance, he had said that the Muslims of the time of the Mahdi-Messiah would subordinate the values of their faith to their worldly interests. At the time of the advent of the Promised Messiah this grievous spectacle presented itself all over the Muslim world and more particularly in the land in which the Mahdi-Messiah appeared. In his book *Fateh Islam*, published in 1890, he described the condition of Islam and Muslims in Persian verse as follows:

It behoves the eyes of every faithful one to shed tears of blood over the distress of Islam and the disappearance of true Muslims. He whose soul is bereft of all good, dares to attribute all sorts of defects to the best of Divine Messengers. He who is held prisoner in the bondage of vice finds fault in the character of the Leader of the righteous. An ill-starred wicked one shoots his arrows at the immaculate one, so that it behoves heaven to hurl rocks on the earth. Before your very eyes Islam has fallen into the dust, what excuse will you offer to God, O Muslims, who pass your lives in the lap of luxury? Disbelief is surging up in all directions like the forces of Yazeed, while the true faith lies ill and helpless like Zainul Abideen. The well-to-do are eager in pursuit of their joys and pleasures, passing their time in laughter and badinage in the company of beautiful women. The divines are at loggerheads with each other day and night over trifles, and the pious are entirely unaware of the needs of the faith. O Muslims, are these the signs of your religiosity that while the faith is in such distress you are occupied wholly with the pursuit of the carrion of the world?

The Holy Prophet, peace be on him, also indicated that at that time Muslims would neglect the observance of the five daily prayers. The situation at the time of the advent of the Madhi-Messiah was that though there were plenty of mosques there were few worshippers. Many of the mosques had fallen into ruin and had become the resort of animals.

The Holy Prophet also indicated that the worship of the Muslims would be reduced to the formal postures of the *Salat* and would become empty of spirit. This could be observed everywhere that those who gathered in the mosques participated in the services only formally, without concentration, and went through them as speedily as possible.

The Holy Prophet, peace be on him, also foretold that at the time of the advent of the Mahdi-Messiah, nothing would have been left of Islam but its name, and nothing would have been left of the Quran but its bare words. He also said that the Muslims would neglect the guidance contained in the Quran but would pay great attention to beautifying and decoarting it, preserving it in silken covers.

All this came to pass and to a large degree still persists among the Muslims of today. There are few who concentrate on the study of the Quran and seek to make its guidance the rule of their lives.

Another prediction of the Holy Prophet was that in the latter days the Muslims would build mosques in rich styles and would spend large amounts of money on their internal decoration, contrary to the simplicity that should be the characteristic of Islamic places of worship. It is common knowledge that many of the famous mosques resemble museums more than places of worship.

The Holy Prophet, peace be on him, also predicted that in the latter days the Arabs would stray far away from their faith and would derive no benefit from the Quran. The condition of the Arab countries proclaims eloquently the truth of this prediction.

This was the situation of the Muslims, but the condition of the rest of the world was not much better. The Holy Prophet had predicted the spread of pornography and of immodesty and shamelessness. so much so that the people would take pride in vice. It was also predicted that promiscuity would become common. Today the West presents a pattern of culture in which all that is condemned as vice in the law of Islam has become the insignia of social behaviour and a civilized way of life. It is not necessary to set out the details of the degraded aspects of the cultural and social life of the West in illustration of this grievous situation. Promiscuity has become so much the rule of life that marriage has come to be regarded as an undesirable restriction on the freedom of social life.

It is reported that the Holy Prophet, peace be on him, said that the signs of the approach of the Last Day would be that true knowledge would disappear, ignorance would spread, adultery would be multiplied and addiction to liquor would become widespread, so much so that it would be consumed openly in the streets. All this needs no comment or illustration.

It is also reported that the Holy Prophet, peace be on him, said that the signs of the approach of the Last Day would be that the forms of gambling would be greatly multiplied.

Among other indications of the approach of the Last Day, mentioned by the Holy Prophet, peace be on him, are that righteousness would disappear, integrity and trust would fall away and respect for, doing honour to and good behaviour towards parents would decline.

It would thus be realized that the function of the Mahdi-Messiah in respect of the revival of Islam, and giving practical effect to its guidance and values in one's daily life, was an objective that could only be achieved by one who was honoured with constant communion with the Divine and was wholly and completely committed to winning the pleasure of God, through service of his fellow beings. This was fully illustrated in the life of the Promised Messiah.

Of the problems confronting him were not only the hostility of the followers of all other faiths towards Islam, and their complete indifference towards moral and spiritual values, but also the condition of the House of Islam itself, which was riddled with mutual strife and pitiful ignorance of the values inculcated by Islam for the regulation of all aspects of human life, let alone putting them into practice in all matters big and small.

The condition of the Muslims of his time, and indeed of our own present time, was summed up by the Holy Prophet, peace be on him, as follows:

> A time would arrive when the Muslims will praise a person for his courage, his agreeableness, his grand manners and his wisdom, while there would not be a particle of faith in his heart. This is well illustrated today in that if a person, who is not in the least conversant with the values of the faith, stands up and begins to clamour vociferously for the rights of the Muslims, they at once proclaim him their leader. No one dares to say a word against him or to inquire how such a person, who has never taken a single step in the cause of Islam, has become a leader of the Muslims. They consider it enough that he makes excellent speeches, refutes his rivals very cleverly or is so anxious to achieve his political objectives that he puts his own life in danger in their pursuit.

The Holy Prophet, peace be on him, also indicated that in the latter days the true believers would not be honoured and would remain hidden on account of the enmity of people. He also indicated that the knowledge of Arabic and its use as a medium of communication between Muslims would decline and the Muslims would thereby be deprived of many social, religious and political benefits that they could have derived from greater knowledge and use of the Arabic language.

He also indicated that women would take to dressing in a manner that would make their beauty manifest rather than cover it up; and that women would take part in trade and commerce along with men and would become dominant over men. He also prophecied that the proportion of women in the population of the world would become much larger than that of men.

He indicated that means of transportation by land and sea would be multiplied and camels would no longer serve as a normal means of transportation.

He also indicated that currency would be multiplied manifold and credit and the lending of money on interest would be developed enormously.

He pointed out that Muslims would fall into decline and would become divided among themselves. He predicted the rise of labour and its coming into political power.

All this and a great deal more that the Holy Prophet, peace be on him, had indicated with regard to the latter days manifested itself at the time of the advent of the Promised Messiah and became progressively more noticeable and predominant.

Confronted and distressed with this pitiable situation of Islam and Muslims, Hazrat Mirza Ghulam Ahmad addressed himself at an early age, long before the Divine call came to him, to the exposition of the verities and the guidance contained in the Holy Quran, so as to foster a sense of trust, confidence and pride in the Muslims through the appreciation of the tremendous Divine bounty which is the Holy Quran.

He discovered that the Muslims laboured under numerous misconceptions concerning the Quran. One of his great services to the cause of Islam was the removal of these misconceptions and the generation in the hearts of the Muslims sentiments of deep love and honour for the Quran, and the Holy Prophet, peace be on him, and firm faith and reliance upon God, the Lord of Honour and Glory.

One or two illustrations of his efforts in that direction may usefully be set out here. With regard to the Quran itself he found the Muslims divided into two groups. There were those who were prepared to assign a position of pre-eminence to the Holy Quran but were altogether averse to seeking any benefit from the *hadees* (sayings of the Holy

Prophet) as they considered the *ahadees* as neither authentic nor reliable and, therefore, not a source of guidance. The other group attached so much importance to the *ahadees* that they tended to subordinate the Quran to them. The Promised Messiah rejected both those positions as extremes and harmful. He pointed out that the Holy Quran was fundamental and supreme, and the *ahadees* were a very valuable source of light and guidance for the understanding of the Quran. He admitted the possibility that some *ahadees* lacked authenticity and validity. He drew attention to a saying of the Holy Prophet himself that if anything was attributed to him which was in conflict with the Quran it should be rejected, as he could not possibly have said it. Therefore, according to the Promised Messiah, the criterion was that unless a reported *hadees* was irreconcilable with the Holy Quran, it should be accepted as a source of the interpretation of the Quran. He also pointed out that a distinction must be drawn between the practice of the Holy Prophet (Sunnah) which had been transmitted to us through the centuries having been illustrated by the conduct of the Muslims throughout the world, and the sayings of the Holy Prophet, peace be on him, which had been transmitted in the early stages orally from mouth to mouth, before they were collated through the efforts of the great Imams of *hadees*. The Sunnah was, therefore, a much surer source of guidance than the *ahadees*. Through this exposition, the Promised Messiah, on the one hand preserved a great treasury of understanding and insight contained in the *ahadees*, and on the other hand provided a sure criterion for excluding such *ahadees* from consideration whose authenticity was open to question. He also pointed out that though crtieria laid down by the Imams of *hadees* for judging the reliability of a *hadees* were of great value, nevertheless, if events confirmed the authenticity of a *hadees* any technical factors that might tend to weaken the authority of the particular *hadees* could be overlooked.

At the time of the advent of the Promised Messiah one of the great misconceptions current among the Muslim divines of all persuasions was that a large number of the verses of the Holy Quran, according to some as many as six hundred, had been abrogated by subsequently revealed verses, and that the abrogated verses and the abrogating verses were all part of the Quran. This was a great error. Its logical effect was that it destroyed the reliability of the Holy Quran and laid it open to serious criticism. The Promised Messiah emphatically rejected any notion of the abrogation of even a single verse or part of a verse or even a single word of the Holy Quran and offered to satisfy anyone who had any doubt on the matter that any idea of abrogation was wholly unjustified and had no basis whatsoever in fact.

Those who had given currency to the notion of abrogation relied upon verse 107 of the second chapter of the Holy Quran in which the expression abrogation occurs. They failed to pay attention to the content of that verse. The previous verse runs as follows: 'Those ones from among the People of the Book and from among those who associated partners with Allah, who have disbelieved, desire not that any good may be sent down to you from your Lord. They forget that Allah chooses as the recipient of His mercy whomsoever He pleases. Allah is Lord of exceeding bounty.' This verse has reference to the contention of the People of the Book that as their scriptures were also Divine revelation and contained all the guidance that was needed, the Quran was superfluous; and also that they could not accept as binding commandments contained in the Quran which were in conflict with their scriptures and amounted to abrogation of them. God Almighty reminded them that all guidance proceeds from Him and that He sends down whatever may be needed through whomsoever He pleases as a bounty for mankind.

The succeeding verse runs: 'Whatever previous commandment We abrogate or cause to be forgotten, We reveal in this Quran one better or the like thereof. Knowest thou not that Allah has full power to do all that He wills?' Thus this verse establishes that whatever commandment laid down in any previous scriptures is abrogated by the Quran it is replaced by a better commandment and, whatever commandment previously revealed is forgotten but is still needed, is revived in the Quran. This is all part of the wisdom of the Divine Who has full power to do all that He wills. This brings out the progressive character of the teaching of the Holy Quran as compared with the previous scriptures, which undoubtedly contained fundamental teachings, that have been repeated in the Quran; but they also contained directions that were of a temporary or a local character and were no longer needed. These latter were abrogated by the Quran. Also in the previous scriptures certain directives were given which were suited to the circumstances of those times, but were of an intermediary character. These were replaced in the Quran by more perfect, more comprehensive and more definite directions than the intermediary directives. For instance, liquor was not totally and absolutely forbidden in previous scriptures; only its excessive use was restrained. This was a wise directive because at those stages of human development the harm done by the moderate use of liquor was not greater than the benefit that could be derived from it in the then conditions of human existence. By the time of the advent of the Holy Prophet, the stage had been reached in which on the one side human intellect and human spiritual capacity had been developed to a degree where the harm to be apprehended from the use of the smallest quantity of liquor had increased manyfold, and on the other side the benefit that could be derived from its moderate use could be obtained in alternative ways that had been developed and had become available. Therefore, Divine wisdom forbade the use of liquor altogether. The Holy Quran has pointed this out: 'They ask thee concerning liquor and gambling: Tell them there is great harm in both and also some benefit for people, but their harm is greater than their benefit' (2:220). In view of this total abstention was prescribed: 'O Ye who believe, liquor, gambling, idols and divining arrows are but abominations and Satanic devices. So turn wholly away from each one of them that you may prosper. Satan desires only to create enmity and hatred between you by means of liquor and gambling and to keep you back from the remembrance of Allah and from Prayer. Will you, then, desist?' (5:91–2).

Another error into which the Muslims had fallen since sometime before the advent of the Promised Messiah, and were deeply involved in, was their assumption that the Holy Quran made it obligatory upon them to have recourse to the use of force for the propagation of Islam. This was an emormity that constituted a grave affront to the Holy Quran and its teachings, and amounted to a confession that Islam could not successfuly appeal to human reason and could not persuade intelligent people to accept it by virtue of its inherent qualities of truth and wisdom. The Quran has laid great stress on freedom of conscience. For instance, it proclaims: 'There shall be no compulsion in religion, for guidance and error have been already distinguished' (2:57). Again it says: 'Proclaim: This is the truth from your Lord, then let him who will, believe, and let him who will, disbelieve' (18:30).

Faith is a matter of conscience, and conscience cannot be forced. A person may be compelled by pressure, coercion or force to say that he believes, but he cannot be forced to believe. Faith is bestowed by God alone, and even He does not force anyone to believe. How then can anyone else bring about faith by force or compulsion? This is pointed out by the Holy Quran: 'If thy Lord had enforced His Will, surely all those on the earth would have believed, without exception. Wilt thou, then take it upon thyself to force people to become believers? No one can believe, except by Allah's leave' (10:100–1). Again it is said: 'Tell them: O ye people! the truth has indeed come to you from your Lord. Then whoso follows the guidance, follows it only for the good of his own self, and whoso errs does so only to his own detriment. I am not appointed a keeper over you' (10:109).

This leaves no doubt whatever that the Quran does not permit recourse to any type of force or compulsion for the purpose of making a person affirm faith in Islam, yet it does positively and repeatedly lay stress upon the obligation of every Muslim to strive constantly in the cause of Allah with all his faculties and resources. For instance, it is said: 'O ye who believe, bow down and prostrate yourselves in Prayer, and worship your Lord, and work righteousnes that you may prosper. Strive in the cause of Allah a perfect striving, for He has exalted you and has laid no hardship upon you in the matter of religion' (22:78–9).

Again the Prophet was commanded: 'So do not give way to the disbelievers and put forth against them by means of the Quran a great effort' (25:53). It needs to be noted that this verse was revealed at Mecca, when there was no question of taking up arms in defence. Another verse, also revealed in Mecca, says: 'We will surely guide in Our ways those who strive after Us' (29:70). There are many other verses in the Holy Quran that urge the Muslims to strive in the cause of Allah with their belongings and their lives.

The Arabic expression for striving is *jehad,* and no doubt when after the migration to Medina the Muslims were permitted to take up arms for the purpose of repelling the aggression of the Quraish and of other tribes, fighting in the cause of Allah became one of the forms of striving in His path. The object of such fighting was not to compel anyone to believe in Islam, but to frustrate the designs of the Quraish and other hostile tribes to stamp out Islam and to force the Muslims to repudiate their allegiance to it.

Unfortunately, however, in the course of the centuries when spiritual and moral values began to suffer a decline, an impression gradually gained ground that to force a person at the point of the sword to declare himself a Muslim was a highly meritorious act and was an obligation imposed upon every Muslim as part of his faith. This was a fundamental and most harmful error. The verses cited above, and there are many others to the same effect, establish quite clearly that no kind of compulsion in matters of religion is permissible in Islam.

The Holy Prophet, peace be on him, has also made it clear

that fighting in the cause of Allah is only one of the forms of striving *(jehad)*, the pursuit of which is obligatory only in the contingencies specified in the Holy Quran. For instance:

Permission to fight is granted to those against whom war is made, because they have been wronged, and Allah indeed has the power to help them. They are those who have been driven out of their homes unjustly, only because they affirmed: Our Lord is Allah. If Allah did not repel aggression of some people by means of others, cloisters and churches and synagogues and mosques, wherein the name of Allah is oft commemorated would surely be destroyed. Allah will surely help him who helps His cause; Allah is indeed Powerful, Mighty [22:40–1].

Again, there is the clear direction:

Fight in the cause of Allah against those who fight against you, but transgress not. Surely, Allah loves not the transgressors. Once they start the fighting, kill them wherever you meet them, and drive them out from where they have driven you out; for aggression is more heinous than killing. But fight them not in the proximity of the Sacred Mosque, unless they fight you therein; should they fight you even there, then fight with them, such is the requital of disbelievers. Then if they desist, surely Allah is Most Forgiving, Ever Merciful. Fight them until all aggression ceases and religion is professed for the pleasure of Allah alone. If they desist, then be mindful that no retaliation is permissible, except against the aggressors [2:191–4].

Should the enemy be inclined towards making a truce the Muslims are urged to respond positively, as is said: 'Then if they should be inclined to make peace, do thou incline towards it also and put thy trust in Allah. Surely, it is He Who is All-Hearing, All-Knowing. Should they design to deceive thee, then surely Allah is sufficient for thee as Protector' (8:62–3).

There are a host of directions in the Quran designed to regulate fighting once it should break out and to bring it to a speedy end. War in the view of Allah is a non-beneficent activity which should be resorted to only when it becomes inescapable and should be brought to an end as speedily as possible, as is said: 'Whenever they kindle a fire to start a war, Allah puts it out. They strive to create disorder in the land and Allah loves not those who create disorder' (5:65).

On returning from an expedition when the Holy Prophet, peace be on him, and his companions approached Medina, he reminded them of the priority of values in the matter of striving in the cause of Allah by admonishing them: 'We are returning from the lesser striving to the greater striving'; meaning that striving after self-improvement and righteousness was higher in value than fighting in the cause of Allah.

By the time of the advent of the Promised Messiah the concept of *jehad* had been thoroughly vitiated by the Muslim divines and had become a reproach to Islam. A prominent religio-political figure has laid down the preposterous doctrine that it is obligatory on a Muslim state to call on non-Muslim states of neighbouring countries to accept Islam, and in case of their failure to do so to go to war with them to compel compliance with its demand. If this utterly false notion were to find favour with Muslim governments, or with any of them, it would constitute the gravest single threat to the maintenance of international peace, and would eventually destroy the independence of all Muslim states.

This erroneous and destructive concept was not confined in its application to states alone, but was put into effect by and against individuals also. Incidents occurred frequently in the territories designated as tribal areas along the North West Frontier of India in which a tribesman coming upon a peaceful non-Muslim, in a situation in which he was at a disadvantage, would insist upon his formal acceptance of Islam in default of which his life would be forfeit. Often in such a case the threat was carried into effect and the innocent non-Muslim, was despatched on the spot.

Raids were carried out against Indian territory from time to time under the cloak of *jehad*, so that life in the neighbouring areas had become most insecure not only for the non-Muslims but for the Muslims also. The government of India had to maintain a large force along the frontier to check and restrain the mischievous activities of the forces of disorder.

In these circumstances the Promised Messiah considered it essential, as part of his service to the cause of Islam and humanity, to make a detailed and reasoned exposition of the true concept of *jehad* as propounded in the Holy Quran and as illustrated by the Holy Prophet, peace be on him, in his practice. This roused a fierce storm of hostility against him on the part of a certain type of Muslim divine, the principal object of which was to bring him into hatred and contempt in the estimation of the common run of the Muslims who were not conversant with the teaching of the Holy Quran on this, or on any other, philosophic question.

In his exposition of this problem he called attention to the general policies of the government of India, one of the cardinal principles of which was complete non-interference in religious matters and a guarantee of freedom of the profession and practice of religion. This invited a charge from his opponents that he was a stooge and an instrument of the alien government of India and that his claim of being the Mahdi-Messiah had been inspired by the British so that they might make use of him for the purpose of promoting their own interests.

This was a somewhat ironic situation, because those very divines who sought to make him out to be an instrument of the British were diligent in carrying tales to government officials that he was contemplating a rebellion against the government and that he would prove even more dangerous than the Sudanese Mahdi. In actual fact, loyalty towards the established government of every country by its people was inculcated by the Promised Messiah as one of the cardinal principles of Islam to which the members of his Movement were constantly admonished to adhere.

The instances of the exposition of Islamic doctrines and teachings that we have mentioned above were only a fraction of his great service to the cause of Islam. In his voluminous writings, in his speeches and addresses and in the course of conversation he based everything that he set forth on the

Holy Quran and the practice and pronouncements of the Holy Prophet, peace be on him. The great body of his writings and the reports of his speeches and addresses thus constitute a detailed commentary on the Holy Quran in which is set forth the guidance that mankind needs in the era that opened with his advent. At one place he observed that his age bears the same relationship to the era that was now opening out before mankind as the age of Adam bore to his age. One of the revelations vouchsafed to him was: 'We are about to create a new heaven and a new earth.' He was the Adam of this new heaven and new earth.

The Promised Messiah on the one side weeded out the innovations and superstitions which had been encrusted over the body of Islam, and had to a large degree choked out its true spirit like poison ivy that was strangling the tree of Islam, so that it had ceased to flourish and to yield the beneficence that it was intended to provide; and on the other side set forth clearly the true and pure teachings of the Holy Quran by acting upon which Islam and the Muslims could be revivified and restored to their full moral and spiritual vigour. He forbade recourse to all practices that were inconsistent with faith in the Unity of God and the teachings of the Holy Quran and the practice of the Holy Prophet, peace be on him. The bulk of Muslims had taken to a glorification of saints, making offerings to them, addressing supplications to them and making vows for the purpose of propitiating them and winning their pleasure. All this was utterly inconsistent with faith in the Unity of God and was opposed to the true spirit of Islamic teachings. The Muslims had, like the rest of mankind, come to place their reliance entirely upon means, ignoring that all good proceeds from God and that means should not be exalted to the position of the true source of all good and beneficence.

Prayer and supplication had been reduced into mere cermonial and formality and no longer served as the principal means of approach to God and of establishing communion with Him. The Promised Messiah expounded the great significance of prayer and supplication for the purpose of cultivating moral and spiritual qualities and repeatedly urged recourse to prayer, supplication and remembrance of God as a lively experience that yielded pure and delicious fruit.

He stressed the great importance of the cultivation of moral and spiritual qualities and conforming to them strictly in every sphere of life.

The result was that he succeeded in building up a Community whose members, under his instructions and following his example, illustrated in their daily lives the beneficence of Islamic teachings, according to their faculties and capacities. The patterns and traditions established by him have become the warp and woof of the texture of their lives, so that it might be truly said that the Community founded by him is today the only one that illustrates in the lives of the greater part of its members the true purpose of human life and the manner of its achievement.

CHAPTER EIGHT

We shall now proceed to set out, in the words of Ahmad himself, his own concept of his status, his claims and the purpose of his Movement. He has said:

God Almighty has, through the blessings of my obedience to and love for the Holy Prophet, peace be on him, and through my following His Holy Word, honoured this humble one with His revelation and with inner knowledge. He has enlightened me with the disclosure of many mysteries, and has filled my bosom with many verities and realities. He has informed me many times that all these gifts, bounties, exaltations, favours, kindnesses, attention, awards, supports and revelations have been bestowed upon me by virtue of the blessings of obedience to and love for the Seal of the Prophets, peace be on him. [*Braheen Ahmadiyya*, p. 623, footnote 1].

I believe in the Divine revelation that is vouchsafed to me in the same way as I believe in the Torah and the Gospel and the Holy Quran, and I know and recognize the God Who revealed them. Thus I have been accorded as perfect a portion of this revelation as may be bestowed upon anyone who enjoys perfect nearness to God Almighty. When a person is thrown into the fire of eager love, as was the case with all the prophets, the revelation that is vouchsafed to him is free of all confusion. In such a case all fancies and imaginings are consumed as dry grass is consumed in the oven, and Divine revelation emerges in all its purity. Such revelation is vouchsafed only to those who, by virtue of utter purity, love and devotion take on the colour of Prophets. As is set out in line eighteen of page five hundred and four of the *Braheen Ahmadiyya*, I have been described in my revelation as one sent by Allah in the mantles of the prophets. Thus, I receive certain and absolute revelation. I call God in Whose hand is my life as witness, that I have been informed by convincing and conclusive reasons, which are continuously repeated, that whatever is conveyed to me and is vouchsafed to me as revelation is from God and not from Satan. I believe in it as I believe in the existence of the sun and the moon, or as I believe that two and two make four [*Tableegh Risalat*, Vol. VIII, pp. 64–5].

I am the water that has descended from heaven at its due time. I am the Divine light that has illumined the day [*Braheen Ahmadiyya*, Pt V, p. 115].

I have, by the sheer grace of God, and not on account of any merit of my own, been accorded a full measure of the bounty that was bestowed before me on the Prophets and Messengers and the chosen ones of God. It would not have been possible for me to be granted this bounty had I not followed the ways of my lord and master, the pride of the Prophets, the best of mankind, Muhammad, the chosen one, peace be on him. Whatever I have been given I have been given by following him and I know through true and perfect knowledge that no man can reach God except by following the Holy Prophet, peace be on him, nor can anyone arrive at a full understanding of God except through him [*Haqeeqatul Wahi*, p. 68].

When the 13th century of the *Hegira* drew to a close and the beginning of the 14th century approached, I was informed by God Almighty, through revelation, that I was the Reformer for the 14th century. I received the revelation [Arabic]: 'The Gracious One has taught thee the Quran and has expounded its true meaning to thee, so that thou mayest warn people of their evil end, those who through generations of neglect and through not having been warned have fallen into error, so that the way of those offenders may be made manifest who do not desire to follow the guidance after it has been openly declared. Tell them: I have been commissioned by God and am the foremost of believers' [*Kitabul Bariyya*, p. 201, footnote].

When God Almighty, observing the condition of the world and finding the earth filled with every type of disobedience, sin and misguidance, appointed me for the propagation of the truth and the reform of the people, then I, in obedience to this Divine command, sent forth the call through written and oral announcements that I was the person who was to arrive at the beginning of the century for revival of the faith. My purpose was to re-establish the faith which had disappeared from the earth and to pull mankind towards reform and righteousness and truthfulness through the power and strength that God had bestowed upon me, and through the magnetic power of His hand. It was also my purpose to correct their doctrinal errors and to reform their conduct. A few years thereafter, it was made quite clear to me through Divine revelation that the Messiah, whose advent among the Muslims had been promised from the beginning, and the Mahdi whose advent had been Divinely decreed at the time of the decline of Islam and the spread of error, and who was to be guided directly by God, and who was to invite people to partake of the heavenly banquet, and whose coming had been foretold by the Holy Prophet, peace be on him, thirteen hundred years in advance, was myself. Divine revelation to this effect was vouchsafed to me so clearly and so continuously that it left no room for doubt. It was replete with grand prophecies that were fulfilled clearly as bright day. Its frequency and number and miraculous power compelled me to affirm that it comprehended the words of the One God, without an associate, Whose Word is the Holy Quran [*Tazkaratush Shahadatain*, pp. 1–2].

In order to win the pleasure of Allah, I hereby inform you all of the important fact that Almighty God has, at the beginning of this 14th century, appointed me from Himself for the revival and support of the true faith of Islam. It is my function in this disturbed age to proclaim the excellences of the Holy Quran and the greatness of the Holy Prophet, peace be on him. It is also my function to repel all enemies of Islam who are attacking it, by means of the light and blessings and the miracles and inner knowledge that have been bestowed upon me [*Barakatud Dua*, p. 24].

The author has been informed that he is the Reformer of the age and that his spiritual excellences bear a resemblance to the spiritual excellences of Jesus, son of Mary, and that the two are closely related to each other and resemble each other [*Ayena Kamalat Islam*, p. 657].

In this age the Holy Prophet, peace be on him, has been reviled in abusive writings to a degree to which no other prophet has been reviled in any age. In truth in this age Satan, with the help of all his progeny, is trying his utmost to destroy Islam. As doubtless this is the last battle between truth and falsehood, the age demanded the advent of a Divinely commissioned one for its reform. That one is the Promised Messiah, who is present among you. [*Chashmah Maarifat*, p. 86].

As I am the Promised Messiah and God has manifested heavenly signs in my support, everyone who in the estimation of God has been sufficiently warned of my advent as the Promised Messiah and has become aware of my claim, will be accountable to God, for no one can turn away with impunity from those who have been sent by God. In this situation, I am not the complainant, the complainant is one for whose support I have been sent, that is to say, Muhammad, the chosen one, peace be on him. He who does not accept me, does not disobey me but disobeys him who had prophesied my coming [*Haqeeqatul Wahi,* p. 187].

In the beginning I believed that I stood no comparison with the Messiah, son of Mary. He was a Prophet and was a distinguished one from among those who were near to God. Whenever in my revelation something appeared to exalt me above him I interpreted it as partial exaltation. But later Divine revelation which descended upon me like plentiful rain, did not permit me to continue to adhere to this belief, and the title of Prophet was clearly bestowed upon me, but with the proviso that I was a Prophet from one point of view and the follower of the Holy Prophet from another point of view. . . . It is to be observed that Jesus, son of Mary, was the last Khalifah of Moses and I am the last Khalifah of the Holy Prophet, who is the best of the Messengers. Therefore God willed that I should not be deficient in any aspect compared with him [*Haqeeqatul Wahi,* p. 149].

Blessed is he who has recognized me. Of all the paths that lead to God I am the last, and of all his lights, I am the last light. Unfortunate is the one who departs from me, for without me all is darkness [*Kashti Nuh,* p. 77].

The Christians were proclaiming loudly that Jesus, on account of his nearness to God and on account of his high status was unique, without an equal. Now God has proclaimed that He has created a second Jesus who is better than the first one and who is a servant of Ahmad, peace be on him [*Dafeul Balaa,* p. 20].

It is set out in true *hadees* that he who fails to recognize the Imam of his age will die the death of the time of ignorance [*Zurooratul Imam,* p. 2].

The question remains who is the Imam of the age today who must, under Divine Command, be obeyed by all Muslims, the pious, the recipients of revelation and dreams. I have no hesitation in affirming that I am the Imam of the age. God Almighty has combined all the signs and the conditions of the Imam in my person and has caused me to appear at the beginning of the century.

It must be borne in mind that the expression 'the Imam of the age' comprises prophets, messengers, muhaddaseen and reformers, all of them. Those who are not Divinely appointed for the reform and guidance of mankind and are not invested with the requisite excellences, cannot be described as Imam of the age even if they are saints and abdal [*Zurooratul Imam*, p. 24].

As I am the follower of a Prophet who was invested with all human excellences and whose law is perfect and is designed for the reform of the whole world, I have been invested with all the capacities that are needed for the reform of the whole world. There can be no doubt that Jesus was not invested with the capacities with which I have been invested, for he was sent to one particlar people only [*Haqeeqatul Wahi*, p. 153].

I can call God to witness that as He spoke to Abraham and Isaac and Ishmael and to Jacob and to Joseph and to Moses and to Jesus, son of Mary, and last of all spoke to our Holy Prophet, peace be on him, in such manner that He vouchsafed to him the most brilliant and excellent revelation, so has He honoured me with His converse. This honour has been bestowed upon me only on account of my obedience to the Holy Prophet, peace be on him. Had I not been one of his followers and had I not obeyed him, I would never have been honoured with God's word even if my good deeds had been piled up as high as the mountains. All Prophethood has now come to an end except the Prophethood of Muhammad. No law-bearing Prophet can now arise, but a non-law-bearing prophet can arise provided he is a follower of the Holy Prophet. In this way I am both a follower and a Prophet, and my Prophethood is a reflection of the Prophethood of the Holy Prophet. Apart from that it is nothing. It is the same Prophethood as that of Muhammad which has manifested itself in me [*Tajalliat Ilahiyyah*, p. 24].

I have repeatedly affirmed that the revelation that I put forth is certainly and absolutely the word of God, as the Holy Quran and the Torah are the word of God, and I am a Prophet of God by way of reflection. Every Muslim is bound to obey me in religious matters, and is bound to accept me as the Promised Messiah. Everyone whom my call has reached, though he is a Muslim, and he does not accept me as arbiter and does not believe in me as the Promised Messiah, and does not esteem the revelation that is vouchsafed to me as coming from God, is accountable before heaven, for he rejects that which he was under obligation to accept at its due time. I do not say only that had I been an impostor I would surely have been destroyed, but I affirm that I am truly like Moses and Jesus and David and the Holy Prophet, peace be on him. God has exhibited more than ten thousand signs in my support. The Quran bears witness for me and so does the Holy Prophet, peace be on him [*Tohfatun Nadawah*, p. 4].

As the period of the Prophethood of the Holy Prophet, peace be on him, extends to the Day of Judgment and he is the last law-bearing Prophet, God did not design that the unity of all minkind should be perfected during his lifetime, for this would have indicated that the period of his Prophethood was coming to an end, inasmuch as his last task would have been completed and perfected. Therefore, God timed the unification of mankind and their acceptance of one faith for the latter part of the period of the Prophethood of Muhammad, which will be the time of the approach of the Judgment. For the achievement of this purpose God appointed a deputy from among the people of Muhammad, who was named the Promised Messiah, as the Khatamal Khulafa. Thus the Holy Prophet, peace be on him, stands at the beginning of the period of his Prophethood, and the Promised Messiah stands towards the end of it.

It was necessary that this dispensation of the world should not be cut off till after his appearance, as the function of the unification of mankind was destined for his time. This is set out in the verse: 'He it is who has sent His Messenger with guidance and the religion of truth so that He may bring about its triumph over all religions' (9:33). This means that the Promised Messiah would enjoy a world-wide triumph. All those who have preceded me are agreed that this supreme triumph of Islam would be achieved in the time of the Promised Messiah [*Chashmah Maarifat*, pp. 82–3].

I have been bestowed two titles by God Almighty. One of my titles is a follower, as is indicated by my name Ghulam Ahmad. My second title, by way of reflection, is that of Prophet. God Almighty named me Ahmad in *Braheen Ahmadiyya* and called me repeatedly by this name. This was an indication that I am a Prophet by way of reflection. This is also indicated in the revelation set out in *Braheen Ahmadiyya:* 'Every blessing is from Muhammad, peace be on him, and so blessed is he who taught, that is to say, the Holy Prophet, peace be on him, and blessed is he who was taught, that is to say, this humble one' [*Zameema Braheen Ahmadiyya*, Pt V, pp. 188–9].

Whenever I have denied being a Prophet or a Messenger, it means that I am not a law-bearer, nor am I a Prophet in my own right. But I am a Messenger and a Prophet without a new law in the sense that God reveals to me that which is hidden, and because of the inner grace that has been bestowed upon me on account of my obedience to the Holy Prophet, and because of having received his name. I have never denied being a Prophet in this sense. It is in this sense that God has called me a Prophet and a Messenger. My having said, I am not a Messenger and have not brought a book; means that I am not the bearer of a new law. It must, however, be remembered and should never be forgotten, that despite my having been called Prophet and Messenger, I have been informed by God that all this grace is not bestowed directly upon me but that there is one in heaven, that is to say, Muhammad, the chosen one, peace be on him, whose spiritual grace accompanies me. In this way the Seal of Prophethood has been fully safeguarded, for I have been given these names by way of reflection through the mirror of love. If a person is chagrined over the revelation that has been vouchsafed to me in which God Almighty has called me a Prophet and a Messenger, it is foolish on his part, for my being Prophet and Messenger, as I have explained, does not contravene the Divine Seal [*Ek Ghalati Ka Izalah*, pp. 8–9].

It is God's design that whoever out of the Muslims remains away from me will be cut off, whether he is a ruler or a subject [*Tazkirah*, p. 307].

God Almighty has disclosed to me that whoever has been apprised of my advent and does not accept me is not a Muslim and is accountable to God [*Tazkirah*, p. 600].

I am the Garden of God, the Holy; whoever designs to cut me down would himself be cut down [*Nishan Asmani*, p. 37].

I announce it plainly that it is not easy to denounce me. He who calls me a kafir would have himself to become a kafir first. He who describes me as faithless and astray would have to confess his own error and humiliation. He who charges me with departing from the Quran and the Hadith would have himself first departed from them. I am an affirmant of the Quran and the Hadith and am in turn affirmed by them. I am not astray but am the Mahdi. I am not a kafir but am the foremost of the believers. God has assured me that whatever I say is the truth. He who believes in God and accepts the Quran and the Holy Prophet, peace be on him, as true, should find it enough proof to silence him that I say so, but I have no remedy for him who is daring and heedless in his denial. God himself will admonish him. I, therefore, desire that you should reflect upon this for the sake of God alone and you should also advise your friends so that they should reflect upon these matters honestly and impartially [*Malfoozat*, Vol. IV, p. 16].

On one occasion I saw in a vision that I created a new heaven and a new earth and I said: 'Let us now create man.' Thereupon the stupid maulvis raised a clamour that I had claimed to be God; whereas the meaning of the vision is that through me God would bring about such a change as if heaven and earth had been renewed and true men will be created [*Chashmah Masihi*, p. 58, footnote].

People pay lip-service to God but their hearts are alienated from Him. That is why God has said He will create a new heaven and a new earth. This means that the earth has died, that is to say, the hearts of the people of the earth have become so hardened that they are practically dead, for the face of God has become hidden from them and heavenly signs that had been shown in the past have become like myths. So God has designed a new heaven and a new earth. The new earth are the pure hearts whom God is preparing with His own hand, who will be manifested by God and through whom God will be made manifest. The new heaven are the Signs that are being manifested by His command through His servant [*Kashti Nuh*, pp. 10–11].

(1) God has bestowed upon me the understanding of the Quran.

(2) God has taught me the language of the Quran in a miraculous manner.

(3) God accepts my prayers more than of any other person.

(4) God has supported me with heavenly Signs.

(5) God has bestowed upon me Signs from the earth.

(6) God has promised me that I shall triumph over everyone who comes forward to oppose me.

(7) God has given me the good tidings that my followers will always triumph over others through their reasoning in support of the truth, and that they and their progeny will be greatly honoured in the world. so that they should see that he who comes to God never suffers loss.

(8) God has promised me that till the Day of Judgment He will continue to manifest my blessings so much so that kings will seek blessings from my garments.

(9) Twenty years ago, I was informed by God that I would be denied and that people would not accept me but that God would accept me and would manifest my truth through powerful assaults.

(10) God has promised me that for the purpose of repeating the light of my blessings, a person will be raised from among my progeny into whom God will breathe the blessings of the Holy Spirit. He will be characterized by inner purity and will have a close holy relationship with God. He will be a manifestation of the True and the High as if God had descended from Heaven.

The time is coming and is near when God will spread far and wide the acceptance of this Movement. It will spread in the East and the West and the North and the South and Islam will become synonymous with this Movement. This is not said by any man. This is revelation from God for Whom nothing is impossible [*Tohfah Golarviah*, p. 90].

Had my claim been put forward on my own, you would have been free to reject me, but if God's Holy Prophet bears witness for me in his prophecies and God manifests His Signs in my support, then do not wrong yourselves by rejecting me. Say not that you are Muslims and have no need of accepting any Messiah.

I tell you truly that he who accepts me accepts him who had prophesied about me thirteen hundred years in advance, and had indicated the time of my appearance, and had specified my function; and he who rejects me rejects him who had commanded that I should be accepted [*Ayyamus Solh*, p. 93].

He who accepts me accepts afresh all the prophets and their miracles, and he who does not accept me will lose his previous faith also, for he has only tales to fall back on and his own observation. I am the mirror of God Almighty. He who comes to me and accepts me will see afresh the God concerning Whom other people have only old tales to tell. I believe in the God Whom those who deny me do not recognize. I state truly that what they believe in are the idols of their imagination and not God. That is why those idols cannot help them, cannot give them any strength, cannot bring about a holy change in them, and cannot show them any signs [*Nazoolul Masih*, pp. 84–5].

The great purpose of the advent of the Prophets, peace be on them, and the grand objective of their teaching and propaganda is that mankind should recognize God Almighty and should be delivered from the sinful life which leads to hell and ruin. Now that God Almighty has established a dispensation and has raised me, the same common purpose of all the Prophets is my purpose also. I wish to expound and to exhibit what God is and I guide towards the way of escaping sin [*Malfoozat*, Vol. III, p. 11].

When the Imam of the age appears in the world, a thousand lights accompany him, and there is joy in heaven and the good qualities of people are stimulated through the spread of spirituality and illumination. He who possesses the capacity of receiving revelation begins to receive revelation, and he who has the capacity to reflect upon matters of the faith experiences an increase of the power of reflection and understadning, and he whose heart is drawn towards worship begins to find pleasure in worship and religious exercises, and he who carries on discussions with the followers of other faiths is bestowed the power of reasoning and carrying conviction through relevant proofs. All this results from the spread of spirituality which descends from heaven with the Imam of the age and activates every eager heart. This is a Divine law which is expounded in the Holy Quran and the true *ahadees* and the working of which is observable through personal experience. The age of the Promised Messiah has this special characteristic that in the ancient scriptures and the *ahadees* it is recorded that at the time of his advent this spread of spirituality will reach a degree in which women will also receive revelation, and minor children will be able to prophecy, and the common people will speak with the power of the Holy Spirit. All this will be a manifestation of the spirituality of the Promised Messiah [*Zurooratul Imam*, pp. 4–5].

The purpose for which God has appointed me is that I should remove the malaise that afflicts the relationship between God and His creatures and should restore the relationship of love and sincerity between them. Through the proclamation of truth I should bring about peace by putting an end to religious wars and should manifest the verities which have become hidden from the eyes of the world. I am called upon to demonstrate that spirituality which has been overlaid by selfish darknesses. It is for me to demonstrate in practice and not only in words, the Divine attributes which penetrate into the hearts of people and are manifested through prayer and concentration. Most of all it is my purpose to plant once more in the hearts of people the pure and shining unity of God which is free from every suspicion of paganism and which has completely disappeared. All this will be accomplished not through my power, but through the Power of Him Who is the God of heaven and earth [*Lecture Lahore*, p. 47].

God has sent me into the world so that through gentleness, kindness and meekness, I should draw towards God and His Holy Guidance such people as are involved in error and should make them tread along the path of righteousness to the light which has been bestowed upon me. Man stands in need of such reasoning as would convince him that God exists, inasmuch as a great part of the world is being driven to ruin for lack of faith in the existence of God Almighty and His revealed Guidance. There is no clearer and easier way of believing in the existence of God than that He reveals to His special servants that which is hidden and will come to pass in the future. He discloses to those who are close to Him the hidden secrets which it is beyond the power of human intellect and faculties to discover. There is no way for man to be enlightened through his own efforts about the secrets of the future, which are beyond the reach of human faculties, especially those matters which are related to the exercise of Divine power and command.

God, of His beneficence, has chosen me out of the whole world so that through manifestations of His Signs He should bring back to the right path those who have gone astray [*Tiryaqul Quloob*, p. 13].

In addition to the natural resemblance which this humble one possesses to other great ones which is set out in detail in *Braheen Ahmadiyya*, I have a special resemblance to Jesus, on account of which I have been sent with his name so that I should demolish the doctrine of the cross. I have been sent to break the cross and to slaughter the swine. I have descended from heaven with angels on my right and left whom God, Who is ever with me, will cause to enter, and indeed is already causing to enter, into every eager heart for the achievement of my purpose. Even if I were to remain silent and my pen were to refrain from writing, the angels that have descended with me would not stop their function. They have been furnished with powerful maces with which to break the cross and to demolish the temple of the worship of creatures [*Fateh Islam*, p. 11, footnote].

God Almighty desires to draw all those souls to His Unity who are scattered throughout the earth, whether in Europe or Asia, who possess a righteous nature, and to gather them together under the banner of one faith. This is the Divine purpose for which I have been sent into the world. So you should follow this purpose, through gentleness and high moral qualities and supplications; and till someone rises under the direction of the Holy Spirit proceeding from God, you should all work together after me [*Al-Wasiyyat*, pp. 10–11].

What is needed today is not the sword but the pen. On account of the doubts which our opponents have raised concerning Islam, and on account of the assault that they have planned to mount against the true religion revealed by God Almighty, basing themselves on different sciences and pretences, my mind has moved in the direction that equipping myself with the armament of the pen, I should enter this field of science and intellectual progress, and should demonstrate the spiritual gallantry and inner power of Islam. I was not myself fitted for this field. It is the grace of God Almighty and His limitless bounty that He desires that the honour of the faith should be demonstrated at the hands of a humble one like myself [*Malfoozat*, Vol I, p. 57].

It is clear that those who have accpeted this humble one as the Promised Messiah are secure against every danger and will be accounted as deserving several kinds of merits and regards together with the strengthening of their faith.

(1) They thought well of a brother and did not declare him an impostor or a liar and did not admit into their hearts any doubts concerning him. They are, therefore, deserving of the merit which is earned by those who think well of a brother.

(2) They have not been afraid of anyone's reproaches in the matter of accepting the truth, nor did they yield to passion or prejudice. They have, therefore, become deserving of merit in that having heard the call of a divinely inspired caller they accepted His message and did not hold back for any reason.

(3) Having believed in one who has appeared in fulfilment of prophecy, they have been freed of all troublesome thoughts which are generated by a long period of waiting, and in the case of disappointment occasion a loss of faith. These fortunate people have not only been delivered from such risk but having observed the fulfilment of a divine Sign and of a prophecy of the Holy Prophet, their faith has been much strengthened and has taken on

the colour of reality. They have now been relieved of all anxiety that invades the hearts in the matter of the prophecies that do not arrive at fulfilment.

(4) Having believed in one sent by God Almighty they have been rescued from Divine wrath which pursues the disobedient ones who persist in denial and in calling the claimant a liar.

(5) They have become deserving of the graces and blessings which descend upon those sincere people who, out of thinking well of a claimant, accept the one who comes from God Almighty.

These are the benefits which will, God willing, be bestowed by Him on those fortunate ones who have accepted this humble one. Those who do not accept me are deprived of all this good fortune [*Izala Auham*, pp. 86–7].

The system of *Ba'it* has been instituted solely with the purpose of gathering a group of the righteous together so that a large group of such people should create a good effect in the world and their being united together should be a source of blessing and greatness and good results for Islam. Being agreed upon one formula they should, through its blessings, be readily available for the pure and holy service of Islam. They should not be lazy, miserly and purposeless Muslims, nor should they be like the worthless ones who have done great harm to Islam through their differences and injustices and who have stained its beautiful face by leading vicious lives, nor should they be like heedless dervishes who have withdrawn from the world and who are not aware of the needs of Islam and have no concern with the welfare of their brethren, and who feel no eagerness for promoting the good of mankind. They should have such sympathy with the people that they should become the refuge of the poor, they should be like fathers of the orphans and should be ready to sacrifice themselves like eager lovers for performing Islamic tasks. They should put forth every effort that their blessings should spread in the world and that the pure fountain of love for the Divine and of sympathy for His servants should issue forth from every heart and should be seen as flowing in the form of a river. God Almighty has determined that by His special grace He would make the prayers and the attention of this humble one the means of the manifestation of their pure capacities. That Holy and Glorious One has inspired me with eagerness that I should occupy myself with the inner training of these seekers, and that I should beg for them that light whereby a person is delivered from the bondage of his ego and of Satan, and develops a natural love for the ways of God Almighty. I would also demand for them the holy spirit which is generated by the combination of perfect providence and sincere service of the Divine. I would also endeavour to obtain their deliverance from the vicious spirit which is generated by the combination of the evil ego and Satan. Thus with the help of Allah, I will not be backward and inattentive and will not be heedless in seeking the reform of my friends who have joined this Movement in full sincerity. Indeed, I shall be ready to face death so that they might live. I shall seek for them from God Almighty the spiritual power which should activate their entire beings like an electric current. I am sure that for those who, having joined the Movement, shall wait steadfastly, all this will come about, for God Almighty has determined to create this group and to promote it for the manifestation of His Glory and His Power. God desires to spread in the world love for Himself and sincere repentance and purity and real goodness and peace and sympathy for mankind. Therefore, this group will be a special one and He will strengthen it with His Own Spirit. He will purify them from all impurity and will bring about a pure change in their lives as He has promised in His Holy prophecies. He will cause this group to grow greatly and will cause thousands of the righteous to enter it. He Himself will water them and cause them to flourish, so much so, that their numbers and the blessings that they enjoy will be looked upon as a wonder. Like a lamp that is placed at a height they will spread their light in all directions and will be examples of Islamic blessings [*Izala Auham*, p. 460].

O my friends who have entered into a covenant with me, may God enable you to do that which should please Him. Today your number is small and you are treated with contempt. You will be persecuted in every way and you will have to bear all sorts of disagreeable things. Everyone who causes you hurt by word or deed will imagine that he is helping Islam, and you will have to pass through some heavenly trials also that you may be tried in every way. Therefore, listen with attention that your way to victory and supremacy will not be through your dry logic or through your returning mockery or abuse with abuse, for if you adopt these ways, you will be left with nothing but words, which God Almighty hates and looks upon with aversion. So do not behave in a manner whereby you should become subject to two curses, the curse of men and the curse of God.

Remember well that if the curse of men is not accompanied by the curse of God Almighty, it amounts to nothing. If God does not wish to destroy us, we cannot be destroyed by anyone; but if He should become our enemy, no one can afford us shelter. Then how shall we please God Almighty and how shall we win His support? He has repeatedly given me the answer to this question. Through righteousness. So my dear brethren, put forth every effort that you should become righteous. Without sincerity no action is acceptable. Righteousness means that eschewing all harmful ways you should march forward to God Almighty, being mindful of th smallest factor of piety.

First of all cultivate humility, straightforwardness and sincerity, and become truly meek and submissive and humble, for every seed of good and ill first sprouts in the heart. If your heart is empty of evil, your tongue will also be empty of evil and so will your eyes and all your limbs. Every light and darkness takes birth initially in the heart, and then gradually envelops the whole body. So check up on your hearts every moment, As an eater of betel leaves constantly rotates the leaves and snips off their rotten parts and throws them away, in the same way you should keep rotating before your mind's eye, the secret thoughts and habits and passions and capacities of your hearts, and whenever you encounter a rotten thought or habit or capacity, snip it off and throw it out lest it should pollute the whole heart and you may be cut off.

God is great wealth. To find Him you should be ready to encounter misfortunes. He is a great purpose. To achieve it be ready to lay down your lives. Do not slight the commandments of God Almighty. Let not the poison of current philosophy affect you. Submit to His commandments like a child. Be constant in Prayer, be constant in prayer, for Prayer is the key to all good fortune. Do not stand up in Prayer as if you are performing a ceremony. As you make a physical ablution in preparation for Prayer, so perform an inner ablution whereby you should wash out from your mind and body all thoughts besides that of Allah. Then stand up in prayer after both the purifying ablutions and supplicate intensively in the course of your Prayer and make crying and weeping your habit so that you may have mercy.

Be truthful, be truthful, for He is observing your hearts. Can man deceive Him? Can cunning devices succeed with Him?

Greatly unfortunate is the person who carries his disobedience to a degree as if there were no God. Such a one is destroyed quickly and God Almighty cares not at all for him.

The teachings of the Holy Quran are designed to carry you to the highest stage of righteousness. Lend ear to them and comfort yourselves with them. The Quran does not teach like the Bible that you should not look at women with the eye of lust. The object of its perfect teachings is that you should not look heedlessly at a woman who is not related to you within the prohibited degrees, neither with lust nor without lust. You should shut your eyes so that you may not be affected. Remember well this commandment of your Lord and safeguard yourselves against the adultery of the eyes and be fearful of the wrath of One Whose wrath can destroy in an instant. The Holy Quran also prescribes that you should safeguard your ears against listening to any discourse concerning women outside the prohibited degrees and also against every discourse that is otherwise improper. It is not necessary for me to admonish you not to commit murder, for no one except a wholly wicked person advances towards murder. But I do admonish you that you should not insist upon injustice and thus slay the truth. Accept the truth even if it should proceed from a child. If you find your opponent uttering the truth then immediately give up your dry logic. Adhere to the truth and bear true witness. As God the Glorious has said: 'Shun the abomination of idols and shun all words of falsehood' (22:31). Falsehood is not less than an idol. That which turns you away from the Qibla of truth is an idol in your path. Bear true witness even if it should be against your fathers or brothers or friends. Let no enmity incite you to injustice.

Be united and give up all miserliness, rancour, jealousy and lack of compassion. There are two great commandments of the Holy Quran. One is Unity, love and obedience of the Lord, hallowed be His name; and, secondly, sympathy with your brethren and with the whole of mankind [*Izala Auham*, pp. 446–52].

The members of my Community, wherever they might be, should listen with attention to this admonition. The purpose of their joining the Movement and establishing the relationship of spiritual preceptor and disciple with me is that they should achieve a high degree of good conduct, good behaviour and righteousness. No wrongdoing, or mischief, or misconduct should even approach them. They should perform the five daily Prayer services regularly, and should not utter a falsehood, and should cause no one any hurt by their tongues. They should be guilty of no vice and should not let even a thought of any mischief or wrong or disorderliness or turmoil pass through their minds. They should shun every type of sin and offence and undesirable action and passion and unmannerly behaviour. They should become pure-hearted and meek servants of God Almighty, and no poisonous germ should flourish in their beings. They should be sincerely loyal and obedient to the British Government under whom their properties and lives and honour are secure. Sympathy with mankind should be their principle and they should fear God Almighty. They should safeguard their tongues and their hands and their thoughts against every kind of impurity and disorderliness and dishonesty. They should join the five daily Prayer services without fail. They should refrain from every kind of wrong, transgression, dishonesty, bribery, trespass and partiality. They should not participate in any evil company. If it should be proved that one who frequents their company does not obey God's commandments, or is not loyal to the benevolent government, or is not mindful of the rights of people, or is cruel or mischievous, or is ill-behaved, or is seeking to deceive the servants of God Almighty by speaking ill or abusively of, or is guilty of imposture towards, the person with whom they have entered into a covenant of *Ba'it,* it should be their duty to repel him and to keep away from such a dangerous one. They should not design harm against the followers of any religion or the members of any tribe or group. Be the true well-wishers of everyone and take care that no mischief-maker, or vicious person, or disorderly one, or ill-behaved one should be ever of your company, or should dwell among you; for such a one could at any time become the cause of yout stumbling.

These are matters and conditions that I have been urging from the beginning, and it is the duty of every member of my Community to act upon them. You should indulge in no impurity, or mockery, or derision. Walk upon the earth with good hearts, and pure tempers, and pure thoughts. Not every evil is worth fighting, so cultivate the habit of forgiveness and forbearance and behave with steadfastness and meekness. Do not attack anyone improperly and keep your passions under complete control. If you take part in a discussion, or in an exchange of views on a religious subject, express yourself gently and be courteous. If anyone misbehaves towards you, withdraw from such company exchanging greetings of peace. If you are persecuted or reviled be mindful that you should not meet stupidity with stupidity, for otherwise you will be accounted in the same category as your opponents. God Almighty desires that you should become a Community that should set an example of goodness and truthfulness for the whole world. Hasten to exclude everyone from your company who sets an example of evil, and mischief, and provocation, and ill-behaviour. He who cannot dwell among us in meekness, goodness and piety, using gentle words and comporting himself in ways of good conduct should depart from us quickly, for God does not desire that such a one should dwell among us. He will die miserably, for he did not adopt a good way. Be alert, therefore, and be truly good-hearted, and gentle, and righteous. You will be known by your regular attendance at Prayer services and your high moral qualities. He who has the seed of evil embedded in him will not be able to conform to this admonition.

Your hearts should be purified of deceit, your hands should be innocent of wrong, your eyes should be free from impurity and there should be nothing inside you except truth and sympathy for mankind. I trust that my friends who dwell with me in Qadian will set a high example in respect of all their faculties. I do not desire that among our pious Community there should be anyone of suspicious conduct or to whose behaviour any exception might be taken, or who should be inclined towards disorderliness or should suffer from any other kind of impurity. If we hear any complaint against anyone that he deliberately disregards the obligations due to God Almighty, or keeps company which indulges in mockery or nonsense, or is guilty of any kind of misconduct, he will be immediately excluded from the Community and will no longer be able to remain with us. . . . A harvest that is prepared with labour and ripens, also contains some weeds that have to be cut down and burnt; such is the law of nature from which our Community cannot be exempt. I know that those who are truly the members of my Community have been bestowed hearts by God Almighty which naturally hate evil and love goodness, and I hope that they will set a good example for people [*Tableegh Risalat,* Vol. VII, pp. 42–5].

The world is a passing panorama. If a person does not exert himself fully to carry out a good work at its proper time he cannot thereafter recover the time that he has lost. I have lived the greater part of my life, and I know through divine revelation, and also estimate myself, that what remains is a small portion. He who helps me during my lifetime and in my presence, in achieving my purpose according to my desire, will, I hope, be with me on the Judgment Day also. He who spends money in carrying out these important projects will, I apprehend, suffer no decline in his wealth. Indeed, his wealth would be blessed. Therefore, trusting in God Almighty, they should act with full sincerity and eagerness and courage, for this is the time of fruitful service. Thereafter a time will come when the spending of a mountain of gold in this cause will not equal in merit the spending of one penny now. This is the blessed time when he who has been sent by God, and whose advent had been awaited through centuries, is present among you, and every day fresh revelation, full of new signs, is vouchsafed by God Almighty. It has been made clear throughout by God Almighty, that he alone will be considered as having truly and conclusively joined this Community who spends his property, which he holds dear, in the cause. . . . Do not imagine that you gain your wealth with your own efforts. It is bestowed upon you by God Almighty; nor should you imagine that by spending a portion of your wealth, or by serving in some other way, you put God Almighty, or the one He has sent, under obligation to you. Indeed, He lays you under obligation that He calls you for such service. I tell you truly that if all of you should leave me or should hold back from service and help, He will create another people who will carry out the needed service. Be sure that all this affair is from heaven and your service is for your own good, so let no pride enter your heart, nor have any consciouness that you are helping financially or otherwise. I admonish you repeatedly that God is not in need of your service, it is His bounty that He provides you with the opportunity to serve. . . . I have no greater anxiety than this that I may die leaving my Community in a state of imperfection. I know for certain that miserliness and faith cannot co-exist in a heart. . . . I will not remain long among you and the time is coming when you will not see me any more. Many will wish that they had performed some valuable service while I was alive. Now is the time to carry out this wish. As previous prophets and messengers did not dwell forever among their followers, I too will not remain among you; so appreciate the present opportunity.

Even if you perform such service that you have to sell your immovable properties to carry it out, it would be disrespectful of you to imagine that you have performed any service at all. You are not aware that Divine mercy is eager in support of this faith and that His angels are descending upon the hearts. Every matter of reason and understanding that arises in your hearts is not from yourselves but is from God. A wonderful system of lights is descending from heaven. I admonish you repeatedly to serve to the utmost limit of your capacities, but let not a thought pass through your minds that you have done something. If you think so, you will be ruined. All such thoughts are disrespectful. A disrespectful one is ruined more quickly than anyone else [*Tableegh Risalat,* Vol. X, pp. 54–5].

To affirm the convenant of *Ba'iat* with the tongue alone amounts to nothing, unless it is carried into effect fully with determination. He who acts fully on my teachings enters my house, concerning which there is a promise in divine revelation: I shall safeguard all that are in the house. Do not imagine that only those people are dwellers in my house who live in this house of bricks that belongs to me. Those also are dwellers in my spiritual house who follow me completely. To follow me it is necessary for them to believe that they have a Mighty, Self-Existing and All-Creating God, Whose attributes are eternal and unchangeable. He has no father and no son. He is exempt from suffering and being put upon the cross and being killed. He is far, and yet near. He is near, and yet far. He is One, but has diverse manifestations. Thus a person experiences a change in God according to the change in himself. Yet, no change takes place in God, for He is eternally unchangeable and perfect; but when a person moves towards goodness, God manifests Himself to him in a new way. At the time of every improved condition that manifests itself in a person God Almighty also manifests Himself in an improved manner. He manifests His might in an extraordinary way, where an extraordinary change takes place in a person. This is at the root of all extraordinary happenings and miracles. This is the God Who is presented by our Movement. Believe in Him and prefer Him to your own souls and your comforts and all your relationships; and exhibit sincerity and loyalty in His cause with courage in a practical way. People of the world do not prefer Him to their resources and to their relatives, but you must prefer Him to everything, so that you might be recorded in heaven as belonging to His Community. To display signs of His mercy has been the way of God from of old, but you can participate in it only when nothing separates you from Him and your will is subordinated to His will and your desire is identified with His desire. Your head should lie prostrate at His threshold in all conditions, whether of success or failure, so that He may do whatever He wills. If you do this, that God will manifest Himself in you Who has hidden His countenance since a long time. Is there any one of you who is prepared to act in this way, so as to seek His pleasure and not to be disquieted by His decrees? When you encounter misfortune, you should step forth even more eagerly, for this is the only means of your progress. Try with all your might to spread His Unity in the earth, have mercy on His creatures, do not wrong them by your tongue or your hand or by any other means, and strive to promote their welfare. Entertain no pride against anyone, even if he is your subordinate, and revile not anyone, even if he should revile you. Become meek and good-intentioned and sympathizers with God's creatures, so that you may be accepted.

There are many who appear meek but they are wolves inside. There are many who appear clean but are serpents inside. You cannot be accepted by Him unless you are the same inside and out. Being great, have mercy on the small and do not look down upon them. Possessing knowledge, admonish the ignorant ones, but do not humiliate them by showing off your knowledge. Being wealthy serve the poor and behave not arrogantly towards them out of self-love. Be fearful of the ways of ruin and fear God and adopt the ways of righteousness, and worship no creature and cut asunder from everything to turn to your Lord. Turn your hearts away from the world and becone wholly His, and live for Him and hate every impurity and sin, for He is Holy. Let every morning bear witness that you have spent the night in righteousness, and let every evening bear witness that you have spent the day in His fear. Be not afraid of the curses of the world, for they are apt to disappear like smoke, and they cannot convert day into night. You should be fearful of God's curse which descends from heaven and upon whomsoever it falls it consumes him in both worlds. You cannot save yourselves with hypocrisy, for your God's eye penetrates you through and through; then can you deceive Him? Be straightforward, and clean, and pure, and true. If you have any darkness left in you it will dispel all your light, and if you have any portion of arrogance, of hypocrisy, or self-love, or sloth, you are not something that would find acceptance. Do not deceive yourselves, with your few accomplishments, that whatever you had to do has been done, for God desires a complete revolution in your beings and He demands from you a death whereafter He would revive you. Hasten to make peace and forgive your brethren their defaults, for he who is not inclined to make peace with his brother is wicked and will be cut off because he is the cause of dissension. Give up your selfishness from every point of view and do not cultivate ill-will. Being in the right, humiliate yourselves as if you are in the wrong, so that you may be forgiven. Discard the fatness of your ego, for a fat person cannot enter through the door from which you have been called.

How unfortunate is the person who does not accept that which has issued from the mouth of God and which I have set forth. If you desire that God should be pleased with you in heaven become to each other like real brothers. He is the greater among you who forgives his brother more, and unfortunate is the one who is obstinate and does not forgive. Such a one has no part in me. Be fearful of God's curse, for He is Holy and jealous. A vicious one cannot attain to nearness to God, nor an arrogant one, nor a wrongdoer, nor a dishonest one, nor one who is not jealous for the sake of His name, nor those who fall upon the world like dogs, and ants, and vultures, and find their whole comfort in the world. Every impure eye is far from Him, every impure heart is unaware of Him. He who is afire for His sake will be delivered from the Fire. He who weeps for His sake will laugh, and he who cuts asunder from the world for His sake will find Him. Become the friends of God with a true heart and full sincerity and complete eagerness, so that He should become your friend. Have mercy on your subordinates, and on your wives, and on your brethren. Become truly His, so that He should become yours. The world is full of calamities, one of which is the plague. Hold fast to God with sincerity so that He should safeguard you against all calamities. No calamity overtakes the earth till there is a command from heaven, and no calamity is repelled till mercy descends from heaven. Wisdom demands that you should take hold of the root and not the branch. You are not prohibited from having recourse to proper devices and remedies, but you are forbidden to put your reliance upon them. In the end that will come about which will be decreed by God. If one has the strength, complete trust in God has a higher status than any other virtue.

An essential teaching for you is that you should not discard the Holy Quran, for therein is your life. Those who honour the Quran will be honoured in heaven. Those who prefer the Quran to every *hadees* and every other saying, will receive preference in heaven. For mankind there is no book in the world except the Quran, and for all children of Adam, there is no Messenger and intercessor but Muhammad, the chosen one, peace be on him. Then endeavour to cultivate true love for that dignified and majestic Prophet and do not give any kind of preference over him to anyone else, so that in heaven you may be counted as those who have attained salvation. Remember that salvation will not be manifested only after death, but true salvation is that which exhibits its light in this very world. Who attains salvation? He who believes that God is true, that Muhammad, on whom be peace, is the intercessor between God and all His creatures, and that there is no Messenger equal to him in rank under heaven, nor is there any book equal in rank to the Holy Quran. God did not desire immortality for anyone but this exalted Prophet is alive forever [*Kashti Nuh,* pp. 15–20].

I repeat that you should not be content with having made the covenant of *Ba'ait* overtly, for that amounts to nothing. God looks at your hearts and will deal with you accordingly. I hereby discharge my obligation of conveying my message by warning you that sin is a poison, so do not swallow that poison. Disobedience of God is dirty death, so safeguard yourselves against it. Supplicate so that you might be granted strength. He who at the time of supplication does not believe that God has power to do everything except that which might be contrary to His promise is not one of my Community. He who does not give up lying and deceit, he who is caught up all the time in the world and does not lift his eye to look at the hereafter, he who does not in truth prefer the faith to the world, he who does not shun every vice and every ill, that is to say liquor, gambling, impure looks, deceit, bribery, and every improper acquisition, is not of my Community. He who is not regular in performing the five daily Prayer services, he who is not constant in Prayer and does not remember God with humility, he who does not discard the company of an evil one who influences him towards vice, he who does not honour his parents and does not obey them in all matters that are not contrary to the Quran and is careless in serving Him diligently, is not of my Community. He who does not treat his wife and her relatives with gentleness and benevolence and he who refrains from doing even the least good to his neighbour is not of my Community. He who does not forgive an offender and entertains rancour, and every husband who deceives his wife, and every wife who deceives her husband, is not of my Community. He who breaks the covenant of *Ba'iat* in any respect and does not believe in me as the Promised Messiah and Mahdi, and he who is not willing to obey me in all good matters, and he who consorts with my opponents and endorses what they say,is not of my Community. Every adulterer, disobedient one, wine-bibber, murderer, thief, gambler, deceiver, bribe-taker, usurper, tyrant, liar, forger and their companions, and everyone who calumniates his brothers or sisters, and does not repent of his vices, and does not refrain from joining evil company, is not of my Community.

All this is poison. You cannot swallow poison and survive; light and darkness cannot exist together. Everyone who has a crooked disposition and is not straightforward with God can never achieve the blessing that is bestowed on the pure hearted. How fortunate are those who cleanse their hearts and purify them of every impurity and are faithful to God, for they will not be destroyed. It is not possible that God should humiliate them, for they are God's and God is theirs. They will be safeguarded against every calamity. Foolish is the enemy who moves against them, for they are in the lap of God and enjoy God's support. Who believes truly in God? Only those who are such as we have just described. He too is foolish who follows a fearless sinner, vicious and evil-minded, for such a one will destroy himself in due course. Ever since God has created the heaven and the earth, it has never chanced that He should have ruined or destroyed or obliterated the good. On the contrary, He has always shown wonders in their behalf and will also show them now. He is a very faithful God and for the faithful He manifests wondrous works. The world desires to devour them, and every enemy grinds his teeth at them, but He, Who is their Friend, delivers them from every place of danger and bestows victory upon them in every field. How fortunate is the person who never lets go of the robe of God. We have believed in Him and we have recognized Him. The God of the whole world is He Who has sent down His revelation to me, Who has shown mighty signs in my support, and Who has sent me as the Promised Messiah for this age. There is no god beside Him, neither in heaven, nor in earth. He who does not believe in Him is bereft of all good fortune and is caught in humiliation. I have received God's revelation which is as bright as the sun. I have seen that He is the God of the world and that there is none other. How Mighty and Self-Supporting is the God Whom we have found! How great are the powers that belong to Him! The truth is that nothing is beyond Him except that which is contrary to His books and His promise. Therefore, when you pray do not be like those ignorant ones who pretend to follow nature and have devised a natural law which does not bear the seal of God's Book. They are the rejected ones whose prayers will not be heard. They are blind and not seeing, they are dead and not alive. They present to God their self-devised law and presume to limit His limitless powers and deem Him weak. So he will treat them accordingly. But when you stand up in Prayer, you should have full faith that your God has power to do all that He wills. Your Prayer will then be accepted and you will experience the wonders of the powers of God which I have experienced. My testimony is by seeing and not as a tale [*Kashti Nuh*, pp. 26–9].

If you become God's then be sure that God is yours. You will be asleep and God Almighty will keep awake for you. You will be heedless of the enemy and God will watch him and will frustrate his designs. You still do not know the extent of God's powers. Had you known you would not have sorrowed after the world on any day. Does he who owns a treasure weep and cry and become sorrowful unto death by losing a penny? Had you been aware of the treasure that at every time of need God would do the needful, you would not have been so restless after the world. God is a dear treasure, then value Him accordingly, For He is your Helper at every step; without Him you are nothing, nor do your resources and your devices amount to anything. Do not follow other people for they have become wholly dependent upon means. I do not forbid you to employ means within reason, but I do forbid you to become slaves of means like other people and to forget God, Who provides the means also. Had you possessed true insight, you would have seen that God is everything and all else is nothing. You can neither stretch forth your hand, nor hold it back, but only under His command. A dead one might laugh at this, but had he truly died it would have been better for him than this laughter. . . . I do not forbid you the pursuit of the commerce and industry of the world, but follow not those whose world is their all. Continue to supplicate God for strength and ability in all your works, whether they are worldly or relate to the faith. Your supplications should not be confined to your lips, but you must believe truly that every blessing descends from heaven. You will become righteous only when, before embarking upon a project, you shut your door and fall down at the threshold of the Divine, urging your difficulty and supplicating Him to resolve it by His grace. You will then be helped by the Holy Spirit and a hidden path will be disclosed to you. Have mercy on your souls and do not follow those who have cut asunder altogether from God and depend wholly upon means, so much so that they do not even say: If God so wills. May God open your eyes so that you should realize that He is the cross-beam of all your plans. If the cross-beam should fall, can the rafters continue to support the roof? In the same way, your plans cannot succeed without the help of God. If you will not supplicate Him for help and will not make it your rule to seek strength from Him, you will achieve no success and will die in sorrow. Do not wonder why other people seem to succeed while they are not even aware of the existence of God Who is your Perfect and Mighty Lord. The answer is that they have been subjected to the trial of the world on account of their abandoning God. He sometimes tries a person who abandons Him and seeks the joys of the world and runs after the riches of the world, by opening the doors of the world to him. Such a one is wholly deprived of faith and is naked on that side. In the end he dies with his mind devoted wholly to the world and is cast into eternal hell. Sometimes such a one is tried by being deprived of the world also, but this latter kind of trial is not so fearful as the former, for the one who is tried with plenty becomes more arrogant. In any case both these ways earn the wrath of God. The fountainhead of true prosperity is God. While these people are unaware of the Ever-Living and Self-Supporting God and are heedless of Him and turn away from Him, how can they attain true prosperity? Blessed is he who understands this mystery and ruined is the one who does not realize it.

You should not follow the philosophers of this world, nor look upon them with honour, for they only pursue follies. The true philosphy is that which God has taught you in His Word. It is acquired through the Holy Spirit which you have been promised. Through the spirit you will be carried to the pure knowledge to which others have no access. You will obtain such knowledge if you will ask sincerely, and you will then find that that is the knowledge which bestows freshness and light upon the heart and guides you to the tower of certainty. He who feeds upon carrion cannot bring you pure food. He who is sightless cannot show you the right path. Every pure wisdom descends from heaven; then what are you seeking from earthly ones? Those whose souls ascend to heaven are the true heirs of wisdom. He who is not satisfied himself cannot bestow satisfaction upon you; but the first condition is the purity of the heart. If you have sincerity and purity everything will be bestowed upon you [*Kashti Nuh*, pp. 32–4].

Now you can reflect and decide in your own minds that having made the covenant of *Ba'iat* with me, and having accpted me as the Promised Messiah, arbiter and judge, if your hearts feel constrained over any decision or action of mine you should be concerned about the sincerity of your faith. No good can be expected from faith that is full of doubts and superstitions. If you have accepted truly that the Promised Messiah is in fact the arbiter, then submit to his order and his action and look upon his decisions with respect so that you may be counted among those who honour the word of the Holy Prophet, peace be on him, and esteem it highly. Sufficient is the evidence of the Holy Prophet, peace be on him. He assures you that the Promised Messiah will be imam, and arbiter, and judge. If this is not enough to satisfy you then how will you be satisfied? [*Malfoozat*, Vol III, p. 73].

Be it known to all sincere ones who have entered into the covenant of *Ba'iat* that the purpose of the covenant is that the love of the world should grow cold and love of God and of the Holy Prophet, peace be on him, should fill the heart, and the soul should be weaned away from the world, so that the journey to the hereafter should not appear disagreeable. But for the achievement of this purpose it is necessary to spend some time in my company, so that, if God should so will, by the witnessing of some sure signs all weakness and indifference may be removed. This should be kept in mind and there should be constant supplication that God Almighty should make this possible.

The human heart is like the Black Stone and a man's bosom resembles the House of Allah. The thoughts of that which is beside

Allah are the idols installed in this House. The idols of Mecca were obliterated when the Holy Prophet, peace be on him, accompanied by ten thousand saints, arrived at Mecca and Mecca surrendered. To defeat and obliterate the idols that are besides Allah, it is necessary that they should be invaded in the same manner. A *jehad* is needed for clearing this house of its idols and I shall point out the way of this *jehad* to you; and I assure you that if you follow that way, you will succeed in breaking those idols. This way is not devised by me. God has appointed me to disclose it to you. What is that way? It is that you should follow me and obey me. This is not a new voice. To clear Mecca of idols, the Holy Prophet, peace be on him, also announced: 'Tell them: If you love Allah, then follow me, Allah will then love you' (3:32). In the same way, if you will follow me you will be able to break the idols that are inside you and you will be able to purify your bosoms which are filled with idols of many kinds. No hard disciplines are needed for the purification of self. The Companions of the Holy Prophet, peace be on him, were not subjected to any hard discipline or purposeless repetition of formulas. They were wholly committed to obedience of the Holy Prophet, peace be on him. The light that was in him passed through the pipe of obedience and fell upon the hearts of his companions and wiped out all thoughts of whatever was beside Allah. Their bosoms were filled with light in place of darkness. The same is the situation today. Your eyes cannot be purified till the light which comes through the divine pipe falls upon your heart. The human bosom is the place of descent of divine light, that is why it is called the house of Allah. The grand design is that the idols that fill it should be broken and Allah alone should dwell in it [*Malfoozat*, Vol I, pp. 174–180].

Consider well whether anyone else has experienced such a prophetic age during the last thirteen hundred years. Our Community resembles in many respects the Companions of the Holy Prophet, may Allah be pleased with them. Our people witness miracles and signs such as the Companions witnessed and gain light and certainty from them as the Companions gained. They are enduring, in the cause of Allah, the mockery, and derision, and reproaches of people, and bear persecution and the cutting-off of ties of kinship, as the Companions endured. They lead pure lives, being helped by clear signs and heavenly supports and wise teachings, as did the Companions. There are many among them who weep during their Prayers as the Comapnions wept. Many of them see true dreams and are honoured with divine revelation, as was the case with the Comapnions. Many of them spend their hard-earned wages in promoting the activities of the Movement, purely for the sake of winning the pleasure of God Almighty, as did the Companions. Among them will be found many who keep death in mind and are gentle of heart and are treading the way of true righteousness, as was the case of the Companions. They are the party of God who are supported by Him and whose hearts He is purifying daily and whose bosoms He is filling with the wisdom of faith, and whom He is drawing towards Himself through heavenly signs, as He did with the Companions. In short this Community exhibits all those signs which are implied in the verse: 'Among others from among them' (62:4). The Word of God Almighty was bound to be fulfilled [*Ayyamus Solh,* pp. 72–3].

God, Who is hidden from human eyes but is shining brighter than everything else, and of Whose majesty even the angels stand in awe, does not like insolence and cunning. He has mercy upon those who fear Him, so be afraid of Him and utter everything with deliberation. You are His Community whom He has chosen to set an example of goodness. He who does not discard vice, whose lips do not shun falsehood, and whose heart does not exclude inpure thoughts, will be cut off from this Community. Servants of God, cleanse your hearts and wash out your insides. You can please everyone with hypocrisy and double-dealing, but thereby you will only earn the wrath of God. Have mercy upon yourselves and safefguard your progeny against ruin. It is not possible that God should be pleased with you while in your heart there is someone who is dearer to you than Him. Spend yourselves in His way and be devoted to Him and become wholly His if you desire that you should see Him in this very life [*Raze Haqeeqat,* pp. 4–5].

The purpose of God Almighty in setting up this Community is that true understanding of God, which has disappeared from the world, and true righteousness and purity, which are not to be found in this age, might be re-established. Arrogance is rife. The divines are caught in the pride and vanity of their learning. Those who pretend to have withdrawn from the world have no concern with self-improvement. All the disciplines which they practise are error and innovation; they are only words and outer form and have no spiritual reality. They cannot be traced back to the Holy

Prophet. They pay no attention to inner purification, nor can their artificial disciplines purify their hearts, nor can they acquire the light of true understanding through them. This age has become empty of true righteousness and purity. The way of the Holy Prophet, which is the means of purification, has been discarded. Now God Almighty desires that the time of prophethood should be revived in this age and the same righteousness and purity may be re-established. Thus the purpose of God Almighty in setting up this Community is that the lost understanding might be re-established in the world through this Community [*Speeches*, pp. 21–2].

O ye dear ones, O ye the flourishing branches of the tree of my being, who are, by the mercy of God Almighty, which you enjoy because of having entered into the covenant of *Ba'iat* with me, devoting your lives, your comfort and your properties to this cause, I am aware that you will deem it your good fortune to carry out whatever I might impose upon you to the full extent of your capacity, but I do not desire to lay down myself anything as an obligation upon you, so that your service should not be the result of my directive, but should proceed out of your own free will. Who is my friend and who is dear to me? Only he who recognizes me, only he who believes that I have been sent and who accepts me as those are accepted who are sent. The world cannot accept me because I am not of the world, but those whose nature has been invested with a portion of the other world accept me and will accept me. He who turns aside from me turns aside from Him Who has sent me, and he who establishes a relationship with me, establishes a relationship with Him from Whom I have come. I hold a lamp in my hand. He who comes to me will surely partake of its light, but he who, out of ill-thinking, runs away will be cast into the darkness. I am the citadel of security for this age. He who enters therein will be secure against thieves, robbers and wild beasts. He who seeks to remain away from my walls will be confronted with death from every direction and even his dead body will not be saved. Who is it who enters my citadel? Only he who discards vice, and adopts goodness, and gives up crookedness, and treads along the path of truth, and frees himself from the bondage of Satan and becomes an obedient servant of God Almighty. Everyone who does that is in me and I am in him. But only he has the power to attain to this upon whom God Almighty bestows a pure ego. Then He puts His foot in the hell of such a one's ego and it becomes cool as if there had never been any fire in it. Then he marches forward till the spirit of God Almighty dwells in him and with a special manifestion the Lord of the worlds establishes Himself in his heart. Then his old humanity is consumed and a new and pure humanity is bestowed on him. For him God Almighty becomes a new God and establishes a special relationship with him and he is equipped in this very life with the pure fittings of a heavenly life [*Fateh Islam*, pp. 34–5, footnote].

O my Community, may God Almighty be with you. May that Mighty Benefactor prepare you for the journey to the hereafter as the Companions of the Holy Prophet, peace be on him, were prepared. Bear well in mind that this world is nothing. Cursed is the life which is only for this world and unfortunate is the person all whose grief and sorrow are for the sake of the world. If there is such a one in my Community, vain is his membership of the Community, for he is like a dry branch that will not bear fruit.

O fortunate ones, follow eagerly the teaching which has been given to me for your salvation. Believe in God as One, without associate, and do not associate anything with Him in heaven or in earth. God does not forbid you to employ means, but he who turns aside from God and depends entirely upon means is a pagan. God has ever affirmed that there is no salvation without a pure heart, so become pure-hearted and cast aside rancour and anger. Man's ego has many impurities, but the greatest of all is arrogance. Had there been no arrogance, no one would have disbelieved. So become meek of heart and have sympathy with mankind. You preach to them about Paradise, but how can your preaching be effective if you should wish them ill in this ephemeral world? Discharge your obligations to God Almighty with fear in your heart, for you will be called to account in respect of them. Supplicate earnestly in your Prayers so that God might draw you to Himself and purify your heart. Man is weak; vice can be overcome only by the power of God Almighty and unless one is bestowed power by God one cannot succeed in overcoming vice. Islam does not mean that you should merely repeat the credo verbally. The reality of Islam is that your souls should fall prostrate at the threshold of God Almighty and God and His commandments should, from every point of view, have preference over the world [*Tazkaratush Shahadatain*, pp. 61–2].

It is our principle to have sympathy for the whole of mankind. If a person sees that fire has broken out in the house of a Hindu neighbour and he does not get up to help in putting it out, I tell you truly he is not of me. If one of my followers sees a Christian being killed and he does not go to his assistance to rescue him, then I tell you quite truly that he is not of us. I say it on oath that I have no enmity with any people. I do, however, desire, as far as it may be possible, to reform their beliefs. If anyone abuses me my plaint is preferred to God and not to any court. Despite all this we claim it as our right that we should have sympathy with the whole of mankind.

It is my principle that till one prays for one's enemy, one's mind is not wholly cleared. God has said: 'Call on Me, I shall respond to you' (40:61). He has not said that He will not accept a prayer in respect of an enemy. I believe that to pray for an enemy was the practice of the Holy Prophet, peace be on him; that is how Hazrat Umar, may Allah be pleased with him, became a Muslim. There should be no personal enmity with anyone and one should not be miserly and tyrannical. I am grateful that I can recall not one among my enemies for whom I have not prayed more than once. That is what I tell you and teach you. God Almighty is as much averse to anyone being persecuted and being treated as an enemy as He is averse to anyone being associated with Him. In one relationship He does not desire cutting asunder, and in another relationship He does not desire association. He does not desire that mankind should cut asunder from each other, and He does not desire that anyone should be associated with Him. This is the way that entails praying for those who deny us. Thereby one's mind is cleansed and expands and one's resolve becomes firm. . . . It is an attribute of God that He forgives the evil ones for the sake of the good ones. You, who have established a relationship with me, should become a people concerning whom it has been said that whosoever keeps company with them will not encounter misfortune. This is the purport of the teaching: Adorn yourselves with the qualities of God [*Malfoozat,* Vol III, pp. 26–7].

As you are the heirs of truth you are bound to be treated with enmity. Then be warned and let not your egos prevail over you. Endure every hardship and reply gently to all abuse so that you may be rewarded in heaven.

You should not use any harsh language concerning the rishis and elders of the Aryas lest they should revile God, the Holy, and His

Holy Messenger. As they are not endowed with true understanding they do not realize whom are they reviling. Bear in mind that a person who is liable to be carried away by his passions is not the one whose lips could set forth wisdom and understanding. . . . Do not deride and do not indulge in mockery. Your speech should betray no meanness or ribaldry, so that the fountain of wisdom may be opened for you. Wise words conquer hearts. Coarse and vulgar language promises disorder [*Naseem Dawat*, pp. 3–4].

I consider it right to declare that not all those who have entered into the covenant of *Ba'iat* with me are such that I could express a good opinion about them. I view some of them as dry branches whom my God, Who is my Guardian, will cut off from me and cast among fuel. There are some who were sincere in the beginning and possessed burning hearts, but now they are greatly constricted and no longer exhibit the eagerness of sincerity and the light of loving discipleship; like Balaam they are only left with cunning and like a rotten tooth deserve only to be pulled out of the mouth and cast underfoot. They have become tired and are fatigued and this worthless world has enveloped them in its cunning and deceit. I tell you truly that they will soon be cut asunder from me, except such of them whom the hand of God Almighty should take hold of afresh. However, there are many whom God has given me forever and they are the flourishing branches of the tree of my being [*Fateh Islam*, p. 40].

Though I am grateful to God Almighty for such perfect friends, yet, it is part of my faith that even if not a single one remains with me and all of them go their way leaving me alone, I would still have no fear. I know that God Almighty is with me. Even if I am ground down and am crushed and become less than a particle and experience persecution and abuse and curses from every direction, yet shall I be victorious in the end. No one knows me, but He is with me. I cannot be destroyed. Vain are the efforts of my enemies and useless are the designs of the envious ones.

O ye foolish blind ones, which one out of the righteous before me was ruined, so that I might be ruined? Which truly faithful one was destroyed in humiliation by God, that He will destroy me? Listen with attention and remember, that my soul is not liable to destruction and that my nature is not prone to failure. I have been bestowed such courage and fortitude as mountains cannot match. I care for no one. I was alone and was not displeased at being alone;

will God then desert me? Never. Will He destroy me? Never. My enemies will be humiliated and those who are envious of me will be put to shame, but God will bestow victory in every field upon His servant. I am with Him and He is with me. Nothing can break our relationship. I swear by His honour and His glory that I hold nothing dearer in this world and in the hereafter than that the greatness of His religion may be manifested, His glory may shine forth, and His Word may be exalted. By His grace I am not afraid of any trial, even if I am confronted not with one but with ten million trials. I have been bestowed strength for the field of trials and the jungle of persecutions.

He who does not wish to follow me can depart from me. I do not know how many terrible and thorny forests I may have to traverse. Why do those who are tender-footed put themselves to trouble with me? Those who are mine will not depart from me, neither on account of misfortune, nor in consequence of the vilification of people, nor through heavenly trials and tribulations. Those who are not mine, vain are their affirmations of friendship, for they will soon be separated from me and their last state would be worse than their first [*Anwarul Islam*, p. 23].

I pray earnestly that all members of my Community should be such as fear God Almighty and are constant in Prayer and get up at night and fall upon the earth and weep and discharge their obligations to God and are not avaricious or miserly, or heedless and insects of the earth. I hope that God Almighty will accept my prayers and will show me that I am leaving such people behind. But those whose eyes commit adultery and whose hearts are more foul than privies are, who do not remember death and with whom God is disgusted are welcome to cut asunder; and it will please me greatly if they would do so, for God desires to make this Community a people observing whom others should remember God, and who should be established at the highest level of righteousness and purity and who in practice and in truth prefer their faith to the world. But those wicked ones who, having placed their hands in my hand and having professed that they will uphold their faith above the world, return to their homes and occupy themselves with purely worldly matters, whose glances are not pure, nor their hearts, no good issues from their hands, nor do they move their feet for the achieving of any good, are like rats who are nurtured in darkness and dwell in darkness and die in darkness. In heaven they have been cut off from our Movement. Vain is their assertion that they are members of this Community, for in heaven they are not accounted as such. He who does not comply with my admonitions and does not in truth uphold the faith above the world, and does not carry out a pure change in his life, and does not become pure-hearted and pure-intentioned, and does not cast aside the garment of impurity and foul living, and does not sympathize with mankind, and does not become truly obedient to God, and does not follow me, abandoning his own designs, is like a dog who cannot keep away from the place where carrion is thrown. Am I in need of people who should profess with their tongues that they are with me, so that I should have a large Community for show? I tell you truly that if all people were to abandon me and not one of them would remain with me, my God will create another people who will be better than these in their sincerity and loyalty. It is through a heavenly attraction that good-hearted people are being drawn towards me and no one can obstruct this heavenly attraction. Some people rely more upon their own cunning and deceit than upon God. Perhaps in their secret hearts they entertain the notion that all prophethood and messengership is a pretence and that such people acquire fame and are accepted by chance. No concept is more corrupt than this one. He who thinks like this has no faith in God, without Whose command not a leaf falls from a tree. Accursed are such hearts and such dispositions. God will destroy them in humiliation, for they are the enemies of God's designs. Such people are atheists and have only impurity in their hearts. They carry on a hellish life and after death they can look forward to nothing but the fire of hell [*Tableegh Risalat,* Vol. X, pp. 61–2].

The name which is appropriate for this Movement and which we prefer for ourselves is Muslims of the Ahmadiyya sect. We have chosen this name because the Holy Prophet, peace be on him, had two names Muhammad and Ahmad; Muhammad was his name of glory and Ahmad was his name of beauty. In the name of Muhammad was implicit a prophecy that the Holy Prophet, peace be on him, would punish with the sword such enemies as would attack Islam with the sword and slaughter hundreds of Muslims. His name Ahmad indicated that he would spread peace and security in the world. God so arranged the life of the Holy Prophet, peace be on him, that his Meccan life was a manifestation of his name

Ahmad and the Muslims were taught patience and endurance. In his life in Medina, his name Muhammad was manifested, and God in His wisdom decided to chastise his enemies. But there was a prophecy that the name Ahmad would be manifested again in the latter days and that a person would appear through whom the qualities of beauty, which characterize Ahmad, would be manifested, and all fighting would come to an end. For this reason it has been considered appropriate that the name of this sect should be Ahmadiyya sect, so that everyone hearing this name should realize that this sect has come into being for the spread of peace and security and that it would have nothing to do with war and fighting [*Tableegh Risalat,* Vol IX, pp. 90–1].

I consider those maulvis in error who oppose the study of modern subjects. They do so to cover up their own weakness. They are of the view that research into modern subjects leads to error and alienates a person from Islam. They seem to hold that reason and science are inconsistent with Islam. As they have not the capacity to expose the weaknesses of philosophy, they seek to cover up their own shortcomings by propounding that it is not permissible to study modern subjects. Their souls tremble before philosophy and prostrate themselves before new research. They have not been bestowed the true philosophy which is born of divine revelation and of which the Holy Quran is full to the brim. This philosophy is bestowed only upon those who prostrate themselves at the threshold of God Almighty with extreme humility and nothingness, whose minds and hearts exclude all arrogance and who, confessing their weaknesses, affirm humbly that they are the true servants of God.

In the service of the faith and for upholding the Word of Allah, by all means study modern subjects and study them diligently. I must, however, utter the warning that it is within my experience that those who have pursued this study one-sidedly and were so taken up by it that they had no opportunity of keeping company with the righteous, and who did not themselves possess inner divine light, stumbled and turned away from Islam. Instead of subordinating their learning to Islam, they embarked upon the vain effort to subordinate Islam to modern subjects and in their own estimation they acquired the monopoly of religious and national service. Remember, however, that he alone is capable of performing religious service who is guided by heavenly light

[*Malfoozat*, Vol. I, pp. 65–6].

I used to admonish the members of my Community that they should learn Arabic, for without the study of Arabic they can derive no benefit from the Holy Quran. In order to understand the Holy Quran it is necessary and proper that they should make some effort to learn Arabic. In these days many facilities have become available for learning Arabic. It is the duty of every Muslim to study the Holy Quran. It is not right, therefore, that no attention should be paid to the learning of Arabic, and that one's whole life should be devoted to the learning of English and other language [*Malfoozat*, Vol. I, p. 285].

CHAPTER NINE

The Russo-Japanese war started on 6 February 1904. About the same time the Promised Messiah received a revelation (Urdu): 'An Eastern power and the delicate situation of Korea.' Quite unexpectedly Russia suffered a series of defeats at the hands of Japan and eventually, in the Treaty of Portsmouth of 5 September 1905 which terminated the war, Japan's full authority over Korea was acknowledged, and the prophecy was fulfilled.

This prophecy was fulfilled once again in 1950, by which time Japan had been reduced from its position of an Eastern power and the U.S.S.R. had emerged as a strong Eastern power. Korea had, in the meantime, been divided into North and South, and North Korea had established an accord with communist China, which in turn had become another great Eastern power. In 1950 Communist North Korea invaded Democratic South Korea, and for a time the situation gravely threatened the maintenance of International peace. Ever since then the relationship between North and South Korea has been a delicate one.

On 15 January 1906 the Promised Messiah received a revelation (Persian): 'The palace of the Emperor of Iran has been shaken.' At the time Muzaffarud Din Shah sat securely on his Imperial throne. He had announced the setting up of a parliament in 1905 and everyone seemed happy. Parliament was opened in October 1906 and the Shah died on 8 January 1907. He was succeeded by his son Muhammad Ali Shah who immediately confirmed his predecessor's constitutional reforms; but signs of political unrest soon appeared and there were incidents between the royal guards and patriotic crowds. The Shah dissolved parliament, whereupon the republicans took over the administration of the country, while civil war broke out on a large scale. Eventually the

Shah abdicated on 15 July 1909 and took refuge in the Russian Embassy. Muhammad Ali Shah made half-hearted attempts to regain the throne but all his efforts were frustrated and the prophecy of the Promised Messiah was clearly fulfilled.

Lord Curzon, the famous Viceroy of India in the early years of the century, carried out a partition of the Indian Province of Bengal. This action was intensely resented by the Indian National Congress which started a strong agitation against the measure and demanded its cancellation. Its representations on the subject were repeatedly rejected and Lord Minto, who succeeded Lord Curzon as viceroy, announced that the partition of Bengal would not be revoked or modified. The Secretary of State for India also rejected all representations made to him on the subject.

On 11 February 1906 the Promised Messiah received a revelation (Urdu): 'Regarding the order that was issued concerning Bengal, they will now be comforted.' The announcement of this revelation was received by the Hindus of India with derision and scorn as something which was now beyond the range of possibility. Yet on 12 December 1911 King George V, on the occasion of his coronation Durbar held at Delhi, announced the cancellation of the partition and thus fulfilled the prophecy of the Promised Messiah.

On 20 December 1905 the Promised Messiah wrote and published a brochure which he called his testament. He stated therein that Divine revelation had repeatedly warned him that his end was near and went on to say:

It has been the Divine way since the beginning that He helps his Prophets and Messengers and makes them supreme as He has said: 'Allah has decreed: Most surely, it is I who will prevail, I and My Messengers' (58:22). This means that the Messengers and Prophets desire that God's will may be established on the earth and no one should be able to resist it. Therefore, God Almighty makes their truth manifest through powerful signs. He causes the seed of that truth to be sown by their hands but does not bring about its full growth through them. He causes them to die at a time which is attended with the apparent fear of failure, and thus provides an opportunity for their opponents to mock at them, and deride them. After this manifestation on their part, He exhibits His power once more and brings into operation such means through which those purposes that had been left somewhat incomplete are fully achieved.

In short He manifests His power in two ways; first through His prophets, and secondly, at a time when on the death of a prophet difficulties arise and his enemies rise up in opposition and imagine that his mission would now fail and his Community would be destroyed, and the members of the Community become a prey to anxiety and are assailed by despair, and some unfortunate ones begin to think of resiling, then God Almighty manifests His power once more and rallies the Community and saves it from disintegration. He who remains steadfast throughout witnesses this miracle as happened at the time of the death of the Holy Prophet, peace be on him, when his Companions were overwhelmed by grief and many of the desert Arabs resiled from Islam. At that time God Almighty manifested His power a second time and by establishing Hazrat Abu Bakr Siddiq as the Successor of the Holy Prophet, peace be on him, saved Islam from ruin and thus fulfilled His promise: 'Allah has promised those among you who believe and act righteously that He will surely make them Successors in the earth, as He made those Successors who were before them; that He will surely establish for them their religion which He has chosen for them; and that after their state of fear He will grant them peace and security' (24:56). The same happened in the case of Moses, peace be on him, when he died on the way from Egypt to Canaan before leading the children of Israel into the Promised Land. The children of Israel were sore distressed at his untimely death and continued to mourn him for forty days. The same happened also in the case of Jesus, peace be on him, when all his disciples were scattered at the time of his crucifixion and one of them turned against him.

Thus, my dear ones, as this has been the way of Allah from the beginning that He manifests His power in two ways so as to wipe out the false joy of the opponents, it is not possible that in this case God Almighty would depart from His established way. Therefore, do not be grieved by that which I have told you and let not your hearts suffer anxiety, for it is necessary for you to see the second manifestation of Divine power. Its coming is the better for you for it is permanent and will not be cut off till the Day of Judgment. This second manifestation will not happen till after my departure, but when I depart God will send this second manifestation to you and it will remain with you for ever, according to the Divine promise which is mentioned in *Braheen Ahmadiyya*. That promise has not reference to me but refers to you. God Almighty has said that he would make my Community supreme over the others till the Day of Judgment. Therefore, it is necessary that you should encounter the day of separation from me, so that it should be succeeded by the day of eternal promise. Though these are the last days of the world and are the days of great calamities, yet it is necessary that the world should continue till all that God has intimated is fulfilled. I have appeared as a Divine manifestation of power and I personify God's power. After me there will be other personages who will be the second manifestations of His Power. So you should occupy yourselves with supplication pending the second manifestation of Divine power. All the righteous in each country should supplicate that the second manifestation of Divine power should descend from heaven and demonstrate to you how powerful your God is. Remind yourselves that the time of death is near and no one knows when it might overtake him.

You should partake of the Holy Spirit through sympathy and through purification of yourselves, for true righteousness cannot be achieved without the Holy Spirit. Leaving aside all personal desires, you should adopt, for the sake of winning the pleasure of God, that path than which there is no narrower way. Do not run after the delights of the world, for they bring about separation from God. Adopt a hard life for the sake of God. The pain with which God is pleased is better than the pleasure which displeases God. The defeat which pleases God is better than the victory that might become the occasion of His wrath. Give up the love which brings you close to the displeasure of God. If you come to Him with a pure heart He will help you in every situation and no enemy will be able to do you harm. You cannot win the pleasure of God except by giving up your own pleasure, your joy, your honour, your property and your life, and enduring such hardship as would confront you with death. If you will endure hardship you will be taken up into the lap of God like a dear child and you will become heirs to the righteous ones who have passed on before you, and the doors of every bounty will be opened to you. But there are few such. God has told me that righteousness is a tree which should be planted in the heart. The water that nourishes righteousness irrigates the whole garden. Righteousness is a root without which nothing can be gained, but if that root flourishes everything is gained. What shall it profit a man to claim by word of mouth that he is seeking God, when he does not step forth with sincerity? I tell you truly that the person who mixes the least desire for the world with his faith will be ruined. Hell is very close to the one all whose designs are not for God, but some are for God and some are for the world. If you have the least mixture of the world in your purposes, all your worship is vain. In such case you do not follow God, but follow Satan. You should not have the least expectation that God will help you for you would be like an insect of the earth, and within a few days you would be destroyed like such an insect. God will not be in you. Indeed it will please Him to destroy you. But if you will impose a death upon yourself, then you will appear in God and God will be with you. The house wherein you dwell will be blessed and God's mercy will descend on the walls of your house, and the city wherein you reside will be hallowed. If your life and your death and your every movement and your gentleness and your wrath become solely for the sake of God, and you will not seek to try God at the time of every hardship and misfortune, and will not cut asunder from Him, but will ever go forward, then I tell you truly that you will become a chosen people of God. You are human beings as I am a human being, and my God is your God. Do not waste your pure faculties. If you will lean wholly towards God, then I tell you, according to God's will, that you will become an exalted people of God. Let the greatness of God pervade your hearts, and do affirm His Unity not only by the tongue but in practice so that God should manifest His beneficence for you in practice. Cast aside all rancour and have true sympathy with mankind. Adopt every way of goodness, for you do not know by what way you might be accepted.

I give you the good news that the field of nearness to God is empty. All people love the world and no one pays attention to that which would please God. Those who wish to enter through this door with full eagerness, have the opportunity to prove their quality and to be bestowed special favour from God [*Al-Wasiyyat*, pp. 11–13].

I saw in a vision that an angel was measuring a plot of land, and arriving at a certain spot he told me that that was the place of my burial. Then I was shown a grave which shone more brightly than silver and all of it appeared to be of silver. I was told that that was my grave. Then I was shown a plot of land which was named the Heavenly Graveyard, and it was indicated to me that these were the graves of the elect from among my Community who would be admitted to heaven. Since then I had been anxious to procure a plot of land for the purpose of a graveyard for the Community. I have now set aside for this purpose a plot of land close to our garden, of the value of not less than a thousand rupees. I pray that God may be pleased to bless it and make it truly a heavenly graveyard, and that it should be the resting place of those purehearted members of the Community who have truly upheld their faith above the world and have discarded altogether the love of the world and have become wholly God's and have carried out a holy change in themselves and have set an example of loyalty and sincerity like the companions of the Holy Prophet, peace be on him, Amen.

I supplicate again: God Almighty! Do Thou ordain that only those of my Community should be buried in this plot who have in truth become wholly Thine and have withdrawn themselves entirely from the world, Amen.

I supplicate a third time: O my Mighty and Benevolent Lord, O Forgiving and Merciful God, do Thou ordain that only those ones should find burial in this plot who believe truly in this Messenger of Thine and entertain no hypocrisy or personal motive or ill-thinking concerning me, and discharge to the full all obligations of faith and obedience, and have dedicated their lives to Thee and Thy cause, with whom Thou art pleased and concerning whom Thou knowest that they are wholly devoted to Thy love and that they have a relationship of complete loyalty, love and devotion with Thy Messenger, on the basis of sincere faith, Amen [*Al-Wasiyyat*, pp. 15–16].

As God Almighty has conveyed to me many good news about this graveyard, for instance [Arabic]: Every type of mercy has been sent down on it; therefore, I have been moved to lay down certain conditions for burial in this graveyard so that only those who comply with those conditions, out of their sincerity and perfect righteousness, should be admitted to it. These conditions are:

(1) Every one of such persons should contribute, according to his capacity, towards the preliminary expenses involved in preparing this graveyard, which are estimated at three thousand rupees.

(2) Every one of such persons should make a testamentary provision that on his death a minimum of ten per cent of his property shall be handed over to the Council that will be set up for the administration of the affairs of the graveyard, for the purpose of the propagation of Islam and other objects incidental thereto. Think not that these are merely speculative expectations; this is the design of the Mighty One Who is the Ruler of heaven and earth. I have no anxiety how these means will become available and how will those people come forward who will carry out these designs out of the eagerness and zeal of their faith. My only concern is lest after our time those who are responsible for administering these affairs should fail to observe complete integrity and should be led away by the love of the world. I, therefore, supplicate that the Movement should never lack people of integrity who should administer these affairs purely for the sake of God. It would, however, be permissible that those of them who have no means of their own to fall back upon might be helped out of these funds with moderate stipends.

(3) Every one of such persons should be pious and should be one who abstains from all that is prohibited and should indulge in no innovation or anything that savours of associating anything with God. He should be a true and pure Muslim.

(4) Any person who has no property and can offer no financial assistance, can be buried in this graveyard if it is established that he had dedicated his life to the service of the faith and was righteous.

Let no one think foolishly that this project is an innovation contrary to the teachings of Islam. It has been undertaken under divine direction and has not originated in a human mind. Nor should anyone speculate how anyone can find admission to heaven merely by being buried in this graveyard. It is not at all meant that the soil of this graveyard would make anyone a denizen of heaven. The meaning of the divine word is that only a person who is to find admission to heaven will be buried in this graveyard [*Al-Wasiyyat*, pp. 16–18].

In January 1906 the Promised Messiah established the Central Ahmadiyya Association which took over the administration of the secular affairs of the Movement which were committed to its care. It rendered notable service to the Movement, but after the death of the Promised Messiah it began to arrogate to itself a position and status which were inconsistent with the overall authority of the Head of the Movement. We shall revert to this matter in due course.

There is a very well-known *hadith* of the Holy Prophet, peace be on him, that in the latter days the sun would rise in the west. This has been interpreted as meaning that in the latter days, that is to say, in the time of the Promised Messiah, people in the West would begin to take an interest in Islam and the start of the spread of Islam in the West would be made.

The fulfilment of this prophecy began with the acceptance of Islam by Mr Alexander Russell Webb. He was born in 1846 in Hudson City, New York State. His father was the owner and editor of a daily paper, and when young Webb graduated he took up journalism and eventually became the editor of a daily paper in Missouri.

Mr Webb was deeply interested in religion, and being dissatisfied with Christianity he ceased to be a Christian in 1872 and began a research into other faiths in his keenness to discover the true religion. He studied Buddhism and did not find it satisfactory. Some time later he came across an announcement of Hazrat Mirza Ghulam Ahmad and started corresponding with him. Through this correspondence he was convinced of the truth of Islam and accepted it as his faith. He proved a sincere and devoted Muslim and was most eager to do whatever he could to spread the knowledge of Islam and its teachings in the United States of America.

Mr Webb was appointed United States Ambassador to the Philippines and at the end of his assignment he also visited India. On return to the United States he continued his correspondence with Dr Mufti Muhammad Sadiq. On learning of the death of the Promised Messiah, he wrote a letter of condolence to Mufti Muhammad Sadiq in which he observed:

Hazrat Mirza Ghulam Ahmad accomplished a great undertaking and conveyed the light of truth to hundreds of hearts, which it could not have reached otherwise. More than twenty years ago I started my correspondence with him and ever since then I have been deeply affected by the fearless earnestness with which he continued to spread the truth in the pursuance of his purpose. Without a doubt God Almighty had chosen him for this great enterprise which he fulfilled completely. I am sure that he will enjoy the companionship of the saints and prophets in heaven.

He followed this letter with another one, which was written only four days later, in which he repeated his condolences and sent his greetings to Hazrat Maulvi Nurud Din Sahib and expressed his conviction that Hazrat Maulvi Sahib's efforts towards the promotion of Islam would be crowned with success.

Thereafter several white Americans accepted Islam and joined the Ahmadiyya Movement, the particulars of some of whom were mentioned by the Promised Messiah at page 81 of *Braheen Ahmadiyya*, Part V.

Before 1891 the Promised Messiah saw in a vision that he was standing in a pulpit in London and was delivering an eloquent and well-reasoned address in English in support of the truth of Islam. Thereafter he saw that he had caught several birds that were perched among the branches of small trees and had white feathers. They resembled partridges. He interpreted this to mean that though he himself would not be able to visit London his writings would be published in England and the other countries of Europe and that many righteous people would accept the truth.

When he published this vision he observed:

So far the western countries have not shown much attachment to religious verities. It would seem that God Almighty had bestowed all the understanding of religion upon Asia and all the understanding of worldly matters on Europe and America. All the prophets from first to last have appeared in Asia and the excellences of sainthood have also been bestowed on the people of Asia. It would now appear that God Almighty desires to look upon the people of the West with mercy [*Izala Auham*, p. 516].

Though the Promised Messiah was not fully conversant with English he received many revelations in English, which was an indication that Islam was now about to be propagated in English-speaking countries. One of these revelations was: 'I will give you a large party of Islam'; which also indicated that God Almighty would establish large Muslim communities in the West.

In the late 1880s he addressed letters to H.R.H. the Prince of Wales, Mr W. E. Gladstone and Prince Bismarck, inviting them to the study of the principles and teachings of Islam and its acceptance, as mentioned at page 102 of *Izala Auham*.

In 1897 he submitted a well-reasoned brochure to Queen Victoria on the occasion of her diamond jubilee, which he named *Tohfah Qaisariyyah*, and followed it up with another communication which he designated the *Star of India*. In both these brochures he expounded the teachings of Islam and invited the Queen-Empress to accept Islam.

On 15 January 1901 he announced the publication of a monthly journal bearing the title of *Review of Religions*, which was very ably edited for several years by Maulvi Muhammad Ali Sahib, M.A. This journal was welcomed and appreciated both in Britain and in the United States of America. For instance, *The Crescent* of Liverpool wrote in 1903:

This issue of the *Review of Religions* is full of interesting articles. It contains a very learned refutation of the objections that the ignorant Christians are in the habit of raising against the Holy Prophet of Islam, peace be on him. We have not so far come across anything so well written on this subject as this article.

Mr Muhammad Alexander Russell Webb, the first American Muslim, wrote:

I am sure this journal will prove a powerful instrument for directing religious thinking into certain channels. I believe that in the long run this journal will be the means of removing the barriers which have been erected by ignorance in the way of truth.

The Church Family, an organ of the Anglican Church, wrote:

> We should make no attempt to refute the literature published under the auspices of Mirza Ghulam Ahmad, for he will create such a volumc of literature against Christianity as will destroy the authority of the Bible altogether.

On 9 December 1902 the Rev John Hugh Smyth Piggot, Pastor of a church called the Ark of Covenant, in Clapton, London E.5, announced that he was the Messiah and son of God who had descended from heaven according to His promise. He said: 'I am the same Jesus Christ who died on the cross and then after resurrection ascended to heaven.' On hearing this the congregation, with tears in their eyes, knelt in devotion to worship him. His announcement became front page news in the papers and evoked widespread interest and excitement. There was not only interest in, but a storm of opposition to, his claim.

The Rev Mr Piggot was born in 1852, and joined the ministry of the Church of England in 1882. In 1892 a church was built in Clapton by one Henry James Prince, where Piggot was invited to preach on Sundays. In his addresses he often referred to the prophecy of Henry James Prince, who claimed to be the messenger of the Holy Ghost, that the Redeemer Jesus Christ was about to appear. Prince died in 1899. Thereafter, Piggott's sermons and addresses adopted a definite line. He emphasized that the second advent of Jesus Christ was at hand. He even suggested that he might already be with them. Having thus prepared the minds of his congregation he made his announcement that Henry James Prince had come as the fore-runner of the Messiah who had promised to return to earth from heaven and that he himself was the Messiah and God who stood before them.

When the news of his claim reached India, Dr Mufti

Muhammad Sadiq Sahib, a disciple of the Promised Messiah, immediately wrote to Mr Piggot inviting him to accept the true Messiah who had appeared at Qadian. Mr Piggot ignored this letter and continued to proclaim his own Godhead.

The Promised Messiah then issued a challenge to Mr Piggot and announced that if Mr Piggot accepted the challenge God would humiliate him and demonstrate that his claim was false. *The Sunday Circle* of 14 February reproduced the challenge in the following terms:

> . . . Then follows the terrible warning of Mirza Ghulam Ahmad. The jealousy of God, he says, has been roused on account of the insult offered to His sacred name and to His messengers by the haughty assertion of a man who calls himself God and the Lord of earth and heaven, and my True Holy Perfect and Mighty God has commanded me to warn him of the punishment that awaits him. If he does not repent of this irreverent claim he shall be soon annihilated, even in my lifetime, with sore torment proceeding from God and not from the hands of man. This warning of punishment is from the God of earth and heaven. His jealousy shall consume the pretender, so that no one may defile the earth again with such false and arrogant claims.

Piggot made no response to this challenge, but became completely silent and never thereafter repeated his claim of divinity. He retreated to his country hide-out in Somerset and was forgotten by everyone. Yet, he was overtaken by divine wrath and the latter part of his life brought ruinous disgrace upon him. It was established that he was living in adultery and was defrocked by the Church.

Mr C. T. Baker-Carr, in an article on 'Bogus Messiah', printed in the *Evening News* of 1 February 1955, said:

> In July 1904, a very attractive girl called Ruth Annie Preece went to live with Smyth Piggot and his wife, whom he had married on August 14, 1886. Miss Preece was one of three sisters whose father had left them comfortably provided for. A year later there came news of the birth at Agapemonie (Abode of Love) of a child.

The record at Somerset House shows that on June 23 1905, a male child was born to Ruth Anne Preece (of independent means) and John Hugh Smyth Piggot (Priest in Holy Orders). The name given to the baby boy was Glory.

On 20 August 1908, Sister Ruth, as she was now referred to, gave birth to another boy. The Bridgwater registrar, Sidney W. Hook, was called to the Agapemonie on 18 September, when the same details of parentage were recorded. This child was named Power.

After the birth of Power, the Bishop of Bath and Wells took action and ordered that Smyth Piggot be arraigned before a Consistory Court on a charge of immorality. He was found guilty and was defrocked in Wells Cathedral in March 1909.

Public attention was then focused on Agapemonie and it was discovered that there were nearly one hundred women there and only a handful of men. Piggot lived on in ignominious circumstances in Somerset in austere loneliness and died in March 1927.

Though the promised Messiah had been warned that his life was drawing to a close and he had published his testament, had established the graveyard and had organized the Central Ahmadiyya Association, he did not sit back and take things easy. In 1905 he had completed the proverbial three score years and ten and his health, which had never been very robust, was suffering from the strains of old age and hard work. But as his entire occupation was the service of God and his fellow beings, he continued to work with more and more diligence as days and weeks and months sped past and he gave the impression as if he was working against time. The rapid growth of his Movement added to his cares and responsibilities so that the pressure upon him, instead of being relieved, became heavier with the passage of time.

In April 1908 the state both of his own health, and of his wife's health, needed attention and he decided to go to Lahore for medical advice. Before making his final decision he asked his daughter Nawab Mubaraka Begum to pray concerning a matter that he had under consideration and to let him know if she should receive any intimation in response to her prayer. She carried out his direction and saw in a dream that Maulvi Nurud Din Sahib was sitting in an upper room with a book in his hand and said to her: 'This book contains the revelations vouchsafed to Hazrat Sahib concerning me. I am Abu Bakr.' As Hazrat Abu Bakr was the first Successor of the Holy Prophet, peace be on him, this was clearly an indication that Maulvi Nurud Din Sahib would be the first Successor of the Promised Messiah, and that the latter's death was approaching. Mubaraka Begum related her dream to her father who warned her not to mention it to her mother.

He had fixed 27 April as the day of his departure for Lahore. In the early hours of 26 April he received the revelation (Persian): 'Do not feel secure against the chances of the game of life.' These and other indications created an impression on his mind that he would probably end his days in Lahore. Nevertheless, he decided to set out upon his journey as already planned, and left Qadian on the morning of 27 April. Stop ing in Batala for a day, he arrived in Lahore on 29 April and put up in Ahmadiyya Buildings on Brandreth Road, first in the portion that belonged to Khwaja Kamalud Din Sahib, and then on 9 May moved over next door into the portion belonging to Dr Syed Muhammad Husain Sahib, on receiving the revelation (Arabic): 'It is time to move; again, it is time to move.' He realized what the revelation portended, but as was his wont, he desired to carry it out literally also.

In Lahore he became even busier than he had been at Qadian as there was every day a succession of visitors, both Muslim and non-Muslim, and he gave them most generously of his time and attention.

Among his visitors was Mr Clement Rigg, an English Professor of Astronomy, to whom he granted long interviews on 12 and 18 May, during which the Professor presented many questions of philosophic and scientific character and was most impressed with the replies that he received.

Eventually, he joined the Ahmadiyya Movement and proved himself a devoted Muslim throughout the rest of his life. He continued to correspond with Dr Mufti Muhammad Sadiq Sahib right till the end of his life.

On 15 May the Promised Messiah granted an interview to Mian (later Sir) Fazle Husain, Barrister-at-law, who was accompanied by another Muslim Barrister. Mian Fazle Husain Sahib submitted several questions to which the Promised Messiah gave detailed replies.

On 17 May he received the revelation (Persian): 'Put not your trust in mortal life.' On that day a large number of leading Muslims of Lahore were invited to meet him. He addressed them from 11 a.m. till 1 p.m. after which they lunched in his company. They were all deeply impressed by his very learned discourse, in the course of which he declared:

> I claim that God has sent me for the reform of the current widespread corruption. I cannot conceal the fact that God speaks to me and honours me frequently with His converse. This amounts to prophethood, but I do not enjoy this honour in my own right. In a way this is only a verbal contention. Continuous and frequent receipt of revelation is called prophethood. The admonition of Hazrat Ayesha, may Allah be pleased with her, concerning the Holy Prophet, peace be on him, say: 'He is the Seal of the Prophets', but do not say, 'There will be no prophet after him', clearly explains this aspect of prophethood. If there is no longer any prophethood in Islam, then be sure that Islam has also died like other religions, and does not possess any distinctive sign.

On 20 May he received the revelation: 'It is time to move, again, it is time to move, and death is close.' On learning this his wife suggested that they should return to Qadian; to which he replied: 'We shall now return only when God takes us there.'

The *Akhbar-i-Aam* of 23 May 1908, in the course of a report of his address of the 17 May, observed that he had repudiated his claim of prophethood. Thereupon he immediately sent a letter to the Editor of *Akhbar-i-Aam* in which he stated:

In my address I proclaimed, and do so again, that the charge preferred against me as if I claim to be a prophet of a type who has no relationship with Islam, and that I consider myself a prophet who is not bound by the Holy Quran, and that I have instituted a new credo and have appointed a new *Qibla,* and that I claim to have abrogated the law of Islam, and that I do not follow and obey the Holy Prophet, peace be on him, is entirely false. I consider a claim of such prophethood as amounting to disbelief and I have set forth throughout, in all my books, that I do not claim any such prophethood, and that it is a calumny to attribute such a claim to me. The basis on which I call myself a prophet is that I am honoured with the converse of God Almighty, that He speaks to me frequently, and responds to me, and discloses many hidden things to me, and informs me about future events, in a manner that He adopts only towards one who enjoys special nearness to Him, and that on account of the multiplicity of these matters He has designated me a prophet. Thus, I am a prophet in accordance with divine command and it would be a sin on my part to deny it, and I shall continue to be firmly established on it till I pass away from the world. I am not a prophet in the sense that I separate myself from Islam, or abrogate any commandment of Islam. I bear the yolk of the Holy Quran and no one dare abrogate a single word or vowel point of the Holy Quran. I affirm, not out of a desire for self-praise, but on the basis of God's grace and His promise, that if the whole world were on one side and I were alone on the other side and a matter were put forward as a criterion for determining the truth of a servant of God, I would be granted supremacy by God in such a contest. God would be with me in every aspect of the contest and would grant me victory in every field. It is on this basis that God has designated me a prophet.

During his stay in Lahore he embarked upon a project which was designed to bring about an understanding between Muslims and non-Muslims, particularly Hindus, whereby both parties might be enabled to live together in peace and amity, and all bitterness and rancour might be entirely excluded from their mutual peaceful relationship. To achieve this purpose he started the compilation of a detailed brochure in which he set out his proposal and which he designated The Message of Peace. The purport of his proposal was that the members of the Ahmadiyya Movement would undertake to honour the Vedas and would always refer to the Vedas and the Rishis with respect and affection, and that if on any occasion they failed to observe this understanding they would pay a large sum of money, which would not be less than three hundred thousand rupees, to the Hindus as a penalty. On their side the Hindus were invited that if they really desired to make peace with the Ahmadis they, on their side, should subscribe to a declaration that they believe in the prophethood of Muhammad Mustapaha, the Messenger of Allah, peace be on him, and accept him as a true prophet and messenger and would always refer to him with respect and honour as behoves one who believes in him, and that if on any occasion they failed to do so they would pay to the Head of the Ahmadiyya Movement the same amount of money as a penalty. He added: 'I say truly that we can make peace with the serpents of saline deserts and with wolves of the wild, but we cannot make peace with those who make our Holy Prophet, who is dearer to us than our lives and our parents, the target of their foul attacks.'

He concluded the compilation of this brochure on the evening of 25 May. He had for a long time been subject to attacks of dysentery. During his stay in Lahore he suffered a mild attack on the night of 16 May. On the night of 25 May he had another attack of the same complaint which made him feel very weak. Despite the efforts of Hazrat Maulvi Nurud Din Sahib, who was an eminent physician, and other doctors, Syed Muhammad Husain Shah Sahib and Dr Mirza Yaqub Beg Sahib, his weakness increased progressively and he began to experience difficulty in making himself heard. All that could be distinguished of his efforts at speaking was: 'Allah, my beloved Allah.' Towards morning he inquired whether it was time for the morning service, and when he was told it was, he performed symbolic ablutions *(tayammum)* and said his prayers while lying in bed. Thereafter, he began to lose consciousness, and when at intervals he regained consciousness he was heard to repeat: 'Allah, my beloved Allah.' After

9 a.m. his breathing became laboured and about 10.30. a.m. he took one or two long breaths and his soul departed from his body. To Allah we belong and to Him shall we return. Under the impact of this grievous bereavement the members of his family set a high example of dignified steadfastness. His wife not only restrained and controlled her own grief but admonished certain women who were inclined to give expression to their grief in an unbecoming manner. She sought to console her children by pointing out to them: 'Do not imagine that your father has left you only an empty house. He has laid up for you a great treasure of prayers in heaven, which will continue to yield its beneficence to you all the time.'

His promised son, Sahibzada Mirza Bashiruddin Mahmud Ahmad, then 19 years of age, standing at the head of the bed on which his holy father's body rested, gave expression to his high resolve in these words: 'If all others should leave you and I should be left alone, yet will I stand against the whole world and shall not heed any opposition or hostility.'

His body was taken the same evening by train to Batala, and from Batala it was conveyed next morning to Qadian. It was not taken into the town but was placed in a bungalow in his garden. In the meantime a large number of the members of the Movement began to converge upon Qadian from all directions. A score of the leading members got together and agreed unanimously that Hazrat Maulvi Nurud Din Sahib should be requested to undertake the heavy responsibility of leading the Community as the First Successor of the Promised Messiah and as Head of the Ahmadiyya Movement. This request was conveyed to Hazrat Maulvi Nurud Din Sahib in a document which bore the signatures of these leading personalities of the Movement who had held a consultation over the matter and was couched in the following terms:

In the name of Allah, Most Gracious, Ever Merciful. We praise Him and call down blessings on His noble Messenger. All praise belongs to Allah, Lord of the worlds, and blessings and peace be upon the Seal of the Prophets, Muhammad, the Chosen One, and the Promised Messiah, the Seal of the aulia.

According to the command of the Promised Messiah, peace be upon him, mentioned in his testament, we Ahmadis whose signatures are appended below are sincerely convinced that the first of the migrants, Hazrat Haji Maulvi Hakeem Nurud Din Sahib, who is the most learned and most righteous of us all and is the most sincere and most long-standing friend of our departed leader, and who was declared by him as the best exmplar for us, as is indicated in his verse:

How fortunate would it be if everyone of the Community were Nurud Din.

So would it be if everyone were filled with the light of faith; should take the covenant of *Ba'iat* in the name of Ahmad from all members of the Ahmadiyya Community and from all new entrants into the Community. In future every command of Hazrat Maulvi Sahib would have the same authority for us as had the command of the Promised Messiah and Mahdi, on whom be the peace and blessings of Allah.

On receipt of this request Hazrat Maulvi Nurud Din Sahib reflected for a while and then intimated that he would give his reply after prayer. He performed his ablutions and made his supplication in *nafal* prayers. Thereafter he suggested that they should all adjourn to the garden where all those members of the Movement were gathered together who had arrived by that time in Qadian.

In that gathering Dr Mufti Muhammad Sadiq Sahib read out the request and Hazrat Maulvi Nurud Din Sahib made the following response:

I bear witness that there is no one worthy of worship save Allah, and I bear witness that Muhammad is His Servant and Messenger.

'Let there be from among you a party whose business it should be to invite to goodness, to enjoin equity, and to forbid evil' [3:105].

Reflect on my previous life. I have never desired to become the leader. I am well aware of my own condition, and my Lord is even better aware of it. I have not the slightest desire of occupying a place of honour in the world. My only desire is that my Lord and

Master may be pleased with me. I supplicate for the fulfilment of this desire; and it is out of this desire that I took up my residence in Qadian and continue and will continue to reside here. I have spent many days considering anxiously what would be our situation after the death of Hazrat Sahib. That is why I have endeavoured that Mian Mahmud's education might be completed. There are three persons out of the close relatives of Hazrat. There is Mian Mahmud Ahmad, who is my brother and my son, and has a special relationship with me. Mir Nasir Nawab Sahib is worthy of respect on account of his relationship with Hazrat Sahib. The third one is Nawab Muhammad Ali Khan Sahib. Then out of the members of the Movement there are Syed Muhammad Ashsan Sahib, who is extremely able and is a descendant of the Holy Prophet. He has served the faith in a manner that puts a person like me to shame. In his old age he has written several books in support of Hazrat Sahib. This is a service that is special to him. Then there is Maulvi Muhammad Ali Sahib who is performing such service as is beyond my imagination. All these people are resident in Qadian. From among people outside there are Syed Hamid Shah and Maulvi Ghulam Hasan, and several others.

This is a heavy responsibility and a dangerous one. It can be discharged only by one who is divinely commissioned, for such a one is supported with wonderful promises of God which serve as a support against back-breaking hardships. At this time it is necessary that all of us, men and women, should be united. For the maintenance of such unity enter into a covenant with any of those I have named, I shall be with you. I am weak and am in indifferent health and do not possess the appropriate temperament. It is not easy to discharge such a heavy responsibility. . . . You may consider it easy, but it is very difficult for the one who has to carry the burden. I call God to witness that if you elect any of those whom I have named, I shall be ready to make the covenant with him along with all of you.

If you insist upon making the covenant with me then bear in mind that *ba'iat* means to be sold. On one occasion Hazrat Sahib indicated to me that I should put the thought of my home out of my mind. Thereafter my entire honour and all thinking became attached to him and I have never thought of my home. Thus, *ba'iat* is a difficult matter. A person who makes *ba'iat* gives up all his freedom and high flights for the sake of another. That is why God

Almighty has called His creatures His servants. The burden of this servitude is difficult to carry for oneself. How can one carry it for others? Keeping in view the difference of temperaments, great courage is needed for the establishment of unity. I have always wondered at the enterprise of Hazrat Sahib. He enjoyed indifferent health and carried a heavy burden of writing in prose and verse and of several other important projects. I am of about the same age as he was, but he enjoyed the daily support of God and my condition is not worth mentioning. This is why God Almighty has said: 'You became like brethren by His grace' (3:104). All this depends upon divine grace. . . . Remember that all good proceeds from unity.

Now, in whichever direction your minds may be inclined you will have to obey my orders. If this is acceptable to you I would be willing to carry this burden willy nilly. A community that has no chief is already dead.

His address was received with great acclamation and all those who were present made the covenant of *ba'iat* at his hand. Thereafter he led the funeral prayers for the Promised Messiah, whose interment in the Heavenly Graveyard was then carried out.

Leading Muslim newspapers and journals paid glowing tributes to the Promised Messiah, drawing attention to his victorious championship of Islam and his high moral, intellectual and spiritual qualities. Even non-Muslim papers made courteous and appreciative references to him. One or two bitterly hostile critics expressed opposition to his doctrines, but on the whole in comparatively restrained language.

There were some who opined hopefully that the Movement he had founded would now disintegrate as he was no longer there to lead and guide it. The unity and speed with which the Community agreed upon the choice of his successor, whose great qualities and capacities were well known, made it clear that the expectations so fondly entertained by his hostile opponents were bound to be disappointed.

The one great reality that emerged now that his physical presence had been removed from the scene of his activities, was that he had possessed an extraordinary and astonishing personality, and that whatever view might be taken of his claim, he certainly was no impostor. His faith in God was deep, firm and unshaken, his trust in God was complete and perfect, and he was a constant recipient of Divine bounties and favours throughout his life. His death was a grievous loss not only for Islam and the Muslims, but for the entire world of religion. He had demonstrated effectively that faith could be a living reality, governing, guiding and enriching human life, and not merely an academic verbal affirmation. His devotion to the Holy Prophet, peace be on him, and his love, admiration and appreciation of the limitless ocean of verities comprehended within the Holy Quran could not be exceeded.

CHAPTER TEN

Hazrat Haji Hakeem Maulvi Nurud Din Sahib, the First Successor of the Promised Messiah, was in his own way a unique personality. He was a direct lineal descendant, in the thirty-third generation in the male line, of Hazrat Umar, may Allah be pleased with him, Second Successor of the Holy Prophet, peace be on him. Ten of his immediate ancestors in an unbroken line had, like himself, committed the Holy Quran to memory. He often said that the Quran was his nurture, his dress, his breath and his very life. This was a spiritual reality and not a hyperbole.

He was one of the most eminent physicians of India, and made a rich contribution to the development of the Unani system of medicine as practised in the country. In diagnosis he had no rival who approached anywhere near him. He did not hesitate to improvise and to experiment and was always justified by the astonishingly favourable results. He never charged a fee for his medical advice and treated poor and rich with equal attention and sympathetic care. Yet he had a large income from the voluntary gifts that some of his well-to-do patients presented to him. He was most generous towards the poor and the afflicted. His benevolence towards everyone was unbounded. So far as he himself was concerned he attached no value to money, wealth or property. He had perfect trust in God and often said that God Almighty, of His grace, mercy and bounty, had assured him that He would always provide for him in all circumstances. In his long life many occasions arose in which those who were in touch with him at the moment could not think in what manner the needs with which he was confronted would be provided for, and yet not in a single instance out of the hundreds of such occasions did this Divine guarantee remain unfulfilled.

He was not only an eminent physician and a great divine,

his intellect ranged over a very wide expanse. He was interested in a variety of subjects and the range and depth of his scholarship surprised all those who came in contact with him. He was fond of books and had accumulated a very large store of them which included copies of many rare manuscripts which he had procured at great expense. Some idea of his all-embracing interest and scholarship may be gathered from the fact that, though his knowledge of English was elementary, he had read the whole of Shakespeare in Arabic.

He belonged to Bhera in the Shahpur district of the Punjab. In 1876 he was appointed Physician-in-attendance upon His Highness the Maharaja of Jammu and Kashmir. He held this appointment till 1892.

In 1884 he came to know of Hazrat Mirza Ghulam Ahmad through one of his announcements, and felt a strong urge to visit him. He travelled to Qadian and the moment he saw him he realized that he had been appointed by God for the revival of Islam. He offered to enter into the covenant of *Ba'iat* with him, but Hazrat Ahmad told him that he had had no direction from God to bind people to himself through such a covenant. Maulvi Sahib requested that if and when he should receive such a direction, he should give him the chance of being the first one to make the covenant.

On his side Hazrat Ahmad conceived a very deep and high impression of him to which he gave expression sometime later in the following terms:

Ever since I have been commissioned by God Almighty and have been revived by the Ever-Living and Self-Subsisting One, I have been eager to meet the special helpers of the faith. This eagerness is greater than the eagerness of a thirsty one for water. I supplicated God Almighty day and night: Lord who is my helper, for I am alone and am looked down upon? As my hands were lifted time after time in supplication and the atmosphere was filled with my prayer, God Almighty took note of my humility and heard my prayer and His mercy was roused and He bestowed upon me a sincere friend, who is the eye of my helpers and the acme of my friends who help me in the matter of the faith. His name, like his shining qualities, is Nurud Din. He belongs to Bhera and is a Qureshi Hashimi by descent. He is thus one of the chieftains of Islam and belongs to a noble family. I experienced great joy at meeting him as if I had recovered a limb that had been cut off. I was in ecstacy as was the Holy Prophet, peace be on him, when Hazrat Umar, may Allah be pleased with him, made his submission.

When he came to me and met me and I beheld him I realized that he was one of the signs of my Lord, and I was convinced that he was the answer to my prayer which I had so persistently offered, and I discovered that he was one of the elect of God [*Ayena Kamalat Islam*, pp. 581–2].

Again he said: He obeys me in everything as the pulse moves in accord with one's breathing. I observe that wisdom flows from his lips and heavenly light descends upon him. When he addresses himself to the exposition of the Book of God he sets free the source of mysteries and causes the fountain of insights to flow. He discloses wonderful understanding which is hidden behind veils and digging to the roots of verities he brings out clear truth. The wise acknowledge the miraculous quality of his speech and its wonderful effects. He makes the truth manifest like a piece of gold and roots out the objections of the opponents. I praise God Almighty Who has bestowed upon me such a friend, at a time when I was in sore need of him. I pray God Almighty that He might bless his life and health and honour. I perceive a new glory in his speech and find that he is one of the foremost in explaining the mysteries of the Holy Quran and in understanding its true meaning. His knowledge and his wisdom are like two mountains facing each other. I am unable to say which of them is higher than the other. He is a garden from among the gardens of the faith. Lord, do Thou send down blessings from heaven upon him and safeguard him against harm by his enemies and be with him wherever he may be and have mercy on him here and in the hereafter, O Thou most Merciful of those who show mercy. Amen. . . . I am grateful to God Almighty that He has bestowed upon me a friend of such high rank who is righteous and most learned and far sighted and appreciative of fine points. He strives constantly in the cause of Allah and has such a high degree of love for Him with full sincerity that no one exceeds him in this respect [*Ayena Kamalat Islam*, pp. 585–9].

Maulvi Nurud Din Sahib inquired from Hazrat Mirza Ghulam Ahmad Sahib in what particular manner should he strive in the cause of Allah, and was told that he should write a book in refutation of the objections of Christians to Islam. In compliance with this suggestion he wrote his comprehensive book *Faslul Khatab*.

After his first meeting with Hazrat Ahmad he kept in constant touch with him by correspondence and meetings from time to time. On one occasion when he fell ill Hazrat Ahmad went to Jammu to inquire after his health.

In March 1889 he was the first one to make the covenant of *Ba'iat* at the hands of Ahmad as he had wished. In 1890 when Hazrat Ahmad announced that God had revealed to him that he was the Promised Messiah whose advent in the latter days had been prophecied, Maulvi Nurud Din Sahib wrote to him immediately: 'I believe and proclaim your truth. Write me down as one of the witnesses.'

In 1892 Maulvi Nurud Din Sahib left Jammu and returned to his home in Bhera where he started the construction of a large building with the design of establishing himself in Bhera as a physician. While the construction was in progress he had occasion to go to Lahore for the purpose of procuring certain materials and fittings for the building. While he was in Lahore he thought that this was a good opportunity of going to Qadian for another meeting with Hazrat Ahmad. So he proceeded to Qadian intending to return to Lahore the same day. When he met Hazrat Ahmad, the latter expressed the hope that he intended to stay for a few days, to which he made an affirmative response. After two or three days Hazrat Ahmad suggested that he should ask his wife to join him in Qadian so that he should have someone to look after him. So Maulvi Sahib wrote to his wife that she should come over to Qadian. A short while thereafter Hazrat Ahmad suggested that as Maulvi Sahib was fond of books he should arrange to have his library transferred to Qadian. Maulvi Sahib carried out this direction also without giving the slightest indication that he had come over to Qadian from Lahore only for a brief visit while the construction of the large building designed by him in Bhera was in progress. Sometime later Hazrat Ahmad indicated to him that he should settle down in Qadian and should put it out of his mind that Bhera was his home. Maulvi Sahib used often to say that after receiving this direction the idea that Bhera was his home was completely excluded from his mind. His life at Qadian was a model of perfect obedience and complete identification with his master, Hazrat Ahmad. Most of his time was taken up in teaching the Holy Quran and exposition of its verities. He also helped those who came to him for advice in his capacity as a physician; and thus he made himself a source of beneficence, physical as well as spiritual. All his activity, however, was subject to such directions as he might receive from his master.

Almost immediately after his election as First Successor of the Promised Messiah some of those very gentlemen who had insistently urged upon Maulvi Nurud Din Sahib that he should take over the heavy responsibilities of the Khilafat and become Head of the Movement founded by the Promised Messiah, and who had announced that in such an event his orders would be as binding upon the members of the Movement as had been the orders of the Promised Messiah himself, began to have second thoughts about the wisdom of the step that they had taken. The most prominent of those who felt uneasy in the situation that they had helped to create, were Khawaja Kamalud-din Sahib and Maulvi Muhammad Ali Sahib. Within a week of the election of the Khalifa Khawaja Kamalud-din Sahib, during a visit to Qadian, mentioned to Sahibzada Mirza Hahmud Ahmad Sahib, in private, that he thought that an error had been committed in the matter of the setting up of the Khilafat, in that the authority of the Khalifa had not been clearly defined and laid down. Khawaja Kamalud-din Sahib expressed the view that the functions of the Khalifa should be confined to taking the covenant of *Ba'iat* from new entrants into the Movement, leading the prayer services, making the announcements and delivering addresses on the occasions of weddings, and leading funeral prayers. To this Sahibzada Mahmud Ahmad Sahib replied that the time of defining the authority of the Khalifa was before the making of the covenant at the hand of the Khalifa elect. He had announced very clearly that after making the covenant they would have to obey him in all things, and the covenant was made after this clear declaration. They were now committed to obey him and being so committed they had no right to seek to limit the authority of the Khalifa. On hearing this Khawaja Sahib changed the subject of conversation and nothing more was said on this subject at the time.

When the Promised Messiah had instituted the Central Ahmadiyya Association in January 1906 he had appointed Maulvi Nurud Din Sahib President of the Association. He continued President even after his election as Khalifa. Those who began to think that the authority of the Khalifa should be clearly defined and strictly limited took advantage of this situation and began to refer in their speeches to the Khalifatul Masih as the Chief President; thus subtly giving currency to the notion that the Head of the Movement exercised his authority by virtue of his office of President of the Central Association and not in his capacity of Khalifatul Masih. During the Annual Conference of 1908 some of them in their speeches had recourse to this device. They urged the Community to remain united and to render full obedience to the Chief President and carry out faithfully the resolutions of the Central Association. In the record of the proceedings of the Association also, any reference to the Khalifatul Masih was carefully avoided and he was referred to only as the President of the Association.

Propaganda was carried on, especially in Lahore, stressing the importance and primacy of the Central Association and ignoring the capacity and authority of the Head of the Movement as Khalifatul Masih. In the beginning of 1909 Syed Muhammad Ishaq Sahib (brother-in-law of the Promised Messiah) drew up a set of questions on the subject of the authority of the Khalifa and the juxtaposition between the Khalifa and the Central Association, and submitted them to the Khalifatul Masih with the request for an authoritative clarification of these matters. The Khalifatul Masih directed that these questions should be sent to certain leading personalities of the Community who should be asked to send in their replies by a certain date. He also directed that those to whom these questions were sent should present themselves at Qadian by 30 January for consultation on these matters. The date of the consultation was fixed for 31 January 1909. On receipt of these questions Khawaja Kamalud-din Sahib held a meeting of the Community in Lahore in his house and explained to them that the real successor of the Promised Messiah was the Central Association and that if this aspect was ignored the Community would face a great danger and the Movement would be ruined. He asked everyone present to subscribe to a written statement that the Central Association was the real successor of the Promised Messiah. With the exception of two members all others who were present subscribed to the statement.

When the proceedings of this meeting became known in Qadian Shaikh Yaqub Ali Irfani Sahib, Editor of *Al-Hakam*, convened a meeting at his house in which a resolution was adopted upholding the supremacy of the Khalifa. Out of forty-two members who were present forty supported the resolution and only two dissented from it.

When the delegates who had been summoned to Qadian arrived they were directed to spend the night in prayer seeking Divine guidance on the matters that were to be discussed the next morning. The morning service was led by the Khalifatul Masih in person and in the course of it he recited the eighty-fifth chapter of the Holy Quran. He was deeply moved when he recited the verse: 'Those who have involved the believing men and the believing women in doubt and confusion, and do not repent, will surely suffer the chastisement of hell and the chastisement of burning' (85.11). He repeated this verse two or three times in tones that betrayed great grief and sorrow and the congregation were so deeply affected that all of them were thrown into a paroxysm of emotion and loud weeping. This spiritual experience appeared to have cleared the minds of the vast majority of any lurking doubts on the subject matter of the question that had to be discussed.

When the time came for the consultative meeting there was an attendance of about two hundred and fifty delegates representing the various branches of the Movement. They all felt that they had to pronounce on a matter that was of fundamental importance with regard to the future of the Movement.

The Khalifatul Masih arrived and delivered a short address, the purport of which was that the Khilafat was a religious institution, without which the Movement could not make any progress. He said:

> God has told me that if anyone of the members of the Movement were to discard it, He would bestow upon me a whole group in place of such a one. I am, therefore, not dependent upon any of you. I believe firmly that by His grace He will help me.

He then made reference to the replies sent in by Khawaja Kamalud-din Sahib and Maulvi Muhammad Ali Sahib, and observed:

> I am told that the only function of the Khalifa is to lead the prayer services and the funeral services and make announcements of weddings and to take the covenant of new entrants into the Movement. He who thinks in those terms is stupid and impertinent. He should repent, otherwise he will suffer loss. Those of you who have acted in this manner have caused me great pain and have affronted the office of the Khalifa.

He also expressed his displeasure with those who had convened a meeting in Qadian in support of the Khilafat. He pointed out that as he had summoned delegates to Qadian for a consultation, no one had the right to hold any meeting in support of or in opposition to any position with respect to the matter which was the subject of consultation. At the end of his speech he invited those present to express their views.

There was no one who stood up in opposition to what he had set forth. He then told Khawaja Kamalud-din Sahib and Maulvi Muhammad Ali Sahib to confer together and decide whether they would be prepared to enter into the covenant of *Ba'iat* a second time. He also directed Shaikh Yaqub Ali Irfani Sahib to enter afresh into a covenant of *Ba'iat*. All three made the covenant and the meeting came to an end. Everyone felt that God Almighty had secured the Community against a great trial. It appears, however, that Khawaja Kamalud-din Sahib and Maulvi Muhammad Ali Sahib were deeply chagrined as they felt that they had been gravely humiliated. Their subsequent conduct showed that in making the covenant again they had only submitted formally to the demand of the Khalifa and had not truly accepted him as one to whom their allegiance and obedience were due.

Maulvi Muhammad Ali Sahib in particular was deeply offended and felt that he had been deliberately insulted. He began to talk of leaving Qadian. Dr Khalifa Rashiduddin Sahib, who was an intimate friend of Maulvi Muhammad Ali Sahib, though he did not agree with him on the question of the authority of the Khalifatul Masih, came to him in great perturbation and told him that Maulvi Muhammad Ali Sahib intended to leave Qadian and that something must be done to persuade him to change his mind. The Khalifatul Masih told Dr Sahib that he should go back to Maulvi Sahib and tell him that he could leave Qadian as soon as he wished, and even sooner; at which Dr Sahib was much flustered, whereupon the Khalifatul Masih sought to comfort him by assuring him that no great harm would ensue on Maulvi Muhammad Ali's departure from Qadian. However, Khawaja Kamaluddin Sahib persuaded Maulvi Muhammad Ali Sahib that it would not be wise on his part to leave Qadian.

Differences arose occasionally between the Khalifatul Masih and the Central Association and a coterie in the Central Association became more and more critical of the Khalifatul Masih. Their attitude of opposition to him came out very clearly in some of the letters that they exchanged between themselves and which by some chance came to the notice of the Khalifatul Masih. On the occasion of the Festival of the breaking of the Fast in October 1909, the Khalifatul Masih in delivering his address stressed the importance of unity and of obedience to the Khalifatul Masih. In the course of his address he stated:

I affirm it emphatically, calling God to witness, that I shall never put aside the robe with which God has invested me. If the whole world, including all of you, were to stand up in opposition to me it would not affect me in the least. You should fulfil your covenant and you will then see how fast you will go forward and what success you will achieve. I have to say these things in view of certain circumstances that have arisen. I have God's promise that He would lend me His support. I have no need to call upon you to enter into a fresh covenant of *Ba'iat.* You should carry out your original covenant lest you should be involved in hypocrisy. If you perceive that I am in error in respect of something you should try through prayers that I might be shown the right path; but do not imagine that you can teach me the true meaning of some verse of the Holy Quran or of some *hadees* or of some statement of the Promised Messiah.

If you consider that I am foul, supplicate God that he might remove me from the world. then you will see on whom the supplication recoils.

Another mistake is that it is said that the covenant is only to obey me in that which is right *(ma'roof)* and that you are not bound to obey me in that which you do not consider right. This expression *(ma'roof)* has also been used with reference to the obedience due to the Holy Prophet in verse 13 of chapter 60 of the Holy Quran. Then have you drawn up a list of the shortcomings of the Holy Prophet? The Promised Messiah also used that expression in the conditions of *Ba'iat.* I do not think ill of any of you. I have made this exposition lest you should continue to suffer from some misunderstanding.

Then it is said that I meet people too freely. It is a sufficient answer for me to point out that you who are my disciples have no authority over me. Instead you are subject to my authority. . . . It is easy to give utterance to a sentiment but it is very difficult to eat the words afterwards. Some of you say that you have no apprehension with regard to me but that you are anxious to define the authority of the next Khalifa. How do you know that he might be greater than Abu Bakr and Mirza Sahib. . . . I had it in mind to take a certain step today but God Almighty has restrained me from taking it. I bow utterly to His wisdom. You should try to remove the defect from which you suffer. . . . I do not desire to expel such people from the Community, perchance they might realize the truth sooner or later, and lest I should become the cause of their going astray. I admonish you again to get rid of rancour and jealousy. If a matter of security or danger should arise, do not publish it. However, when something is finally decided it might be given publicity.

I warn you that you will have to carry out my directions willingly or unwillingly, and in the end you will have to affirm that you obey me willingly. Whatever I tell you is for your good. May Allah keep you and me firmly on the path of guidance and may our end be good. Amen.

Sometine in 1910 Hazrat Khalifatul Masih resigned his office of President of the Central Ahmadiyya Association and directed that Sahibzada Mirza Mahmud Ahmad Sahib be elected President of the Association. Thus the confusion between the authority of the President of the Central Association and the Khalifatul Masih was cleared up. The Sahibzada Sahib was then 21 years of age, and whenever the occasion arose that the Khalifatul Masih could not lead the prayer service himself he would direct the Sahibzada Sahib to lead the service and in case of the Friday noon service to deliver the address. This made the disgruntled section jealous of the Sahibzada Sahib and they had recourse to various devices that were aimed at reducing the activities and the growing influence of the Sahibzada Sahib in the Community.

On 18 November 1910 Hazrat Khalifatul Masih fell down while riding a pony and received serious injuries on his face and head. For some days his condition continued serious and caused anxiety. During that period, one day Khawaja Kamaluddin Sahib, Maulvi Muhammad Ali Sahib, Dr Mirza Yaqub Beg Sahib and Maulvi Sadruddin Sahib got together and sent for the Sahibzada Sahib and Mir Nasir Nawab Sahib. On their arrival Khawaja Kamaluddin Sahib, as the spokesman of the group, mentioned that the condition of the Khalifatul Masih was a source of anxiety and that they were anxious that some understanding might be reached which should obviate the risk of differences arising in case of his death. He gave the assurance that none of them had any desire to succeed the Khalifatul Masih in his holy office and that all of them were convinced that no one was better qualified for the office of Khalifa than the Sahibzada Sahib. But they were anxious that no decision on the question of succession to the Khalifatul Masih should be taken till those of them who were resident in Lahore had arrived in Qadian. It was represented that this precaution was necessary to forestall any action on the part of anyone that might give rise to differences or disturbances. Upon this the Sahibzada Sahib pointed out that the Companions of the Holy Prophet, peace be on him, had considered it unlawful and sinful to arrive at any understanding during the lifetime of a Khalifa with regard to the person who should succeed him on his death. There the matter ended.

In January 1911, after there had been considerable improvement in his health, the Khalifatul Masih felt that the effect of the injury on his right temple, which had become a permanent sore, was beginning to advance towards his heart and he apprehended that his end might arrive suddenly without warning. In this condition, on the night between 19 and 20 January, he asked for pen and paper and, making an entry on a piece of paper, folded it and put it inside an envelope. He inscribed a couple of lines on the envelope and placed it inside another envelope, which he committed to the custody of Shaikh Muhammad Taimur saying: 'In case of my death action should be taken according to the directions enclosed in this envelope.' It transpired later that the two lines inscribed on the enclosed envelope were (Arabic): 'According to the example of Abu Bakr'; and (Urdu): 'Make the covenant of *Ba'iat* with the person whose name is enclosed.'

On the piece of paper inside the envelope was written the name Mahmud Ahmad.

Thereafter his health improved and he recovered the envelope from Sheikh Muhammad Taimur and tore up its contents.

During the course of his speech in the Annual Conference of 1911, on 27 December, he stressed the need of unity through taking firm hold of Allah's rope as affirmed in the Holy Quran (3.104) and then referred to some of the differences which had occasioned him some anxiety. He said:

I am Khalifatul Masih and God has established me in this position. I had no desire at any time to hold this office. Now that God Almighty has made me wear this robe I dislike intensely all controversy on this subject. You cannot conceive how much I suffer from the apprehension that differences might arise in the Community. I desire that I should not hear of anything which might indicate the existence of differences or contentions among you, and I wish to see all of you as practical examples of the Divine direction: 'Hold fast to the rope of Allah all together and be not divided' [3:104]. But this can happen only by the grace of God. I urge you once more, and he who is listening to this should convey it to others, that there should be no contention. When I die you will have plenty of occasions for contention. Perhaps you think that I have easily become Khalifa like Hazrat Abu Bakr. You cannot conceive of the reality, nor can you have any idea of my suffering or of the burden that has been placed upon me. It is the pure grace of God that I have been able to bear this burden. There is not one of you who can feel it truly, let alone bear it. Can he who has a relationship with hundreds of thousands of people sleep in comfort?

Standing in this mosque with the Holy Quran in my hand and calling God Almighty to witness, I state that I had no desire whatsoever of becoming a spiritual preceptor. But who can have knowledge of the Divine design? He did whatever He willed. He gathered all of you together at my hand and He himself, and not any of you, invested me with the robe of Khilafat. I consider it my duty to honour it and respect it. Nevertheless, I have no desire for your wealth or anything of yours. I do not even desire that anyone should extend his greetings to me. Such money as came from you to me in token of your personal homage I used to send to Maulvi Muhammad Ali, up to last April. Then someone misled him and he said that this money was theirs and that they were its custodians. Thereupon, seeking the pleasure of Allah, I stopped sending this money to him so that I might see what they would do. He who said this was in great error, and was guilty of disrespect. He should repent; I repeat he should repent while there is still time. If such people do not repent it will be the worse for them.

Since that time I do not hand over to them such money as is presented to me as a personal gift. I put it away and spend it on purposes that should win the pleasure of Allah. For my own person and my dependents I do not depend upon your money, nor has God Almighty ever made me dependent upon you. He provides for me and provides very richly out of His hidden treasures. I can still exercise the profession that He has taught me.

Keep well in mind, and I repeat, that I am not dependent upon your money, nor do I demand it from you. If you remit any amount to me I spend it according to my understanding in seeking the pleasure of Allah. What is it, then, for which I could have wished to become your spiritual preceptor? God Almighty did whatever He willed. Neither you nor anyone else can do anything about it. Learn to be respectful for this is a blessed way for you. Take fast hold of this rope of Allah. This is also Allah's rope which has bound you all together. Keep fast hold of it.

Remember, it is not within your power to set me aside. If you find any fault in me invite my attention to it, but in a respectful manner. It is not for man to make anyone a Khalifa, it is God's own business. . . . If I have been made Khalifa this is God's doing, in accordance with His design. It is true that He has made me Khalifa for your good. No power can set aside a Khalifa appointed by God. No one of you has the power or strength to set me aside. If God Almighty wills to set me aside He will cause me to die. You must commit this matter to God. You have not the strength to set me aside. I am not grateful to any of you. The person who says that he has made me Khalifa utters a falsehood. I find it painful to hear, as someone has said, that this is the age of Parliaments and constitutions; that a constitution has been put in force in Iran and Portugal, and that a Parliament has been set up in Turkey. I say that such a one who describes this Movement as Parliamentary or constitutional should also repent. Do you not know what comfort Parliament has brought to Iran, and what benefit have others derived from it? What kind of sleep have the Turks enjoyed after setting up a Parliament? What benefit have the Iranians derived from it? How many were destroyed in the time of Muhammad Ali Shah, and now ultimatums are being served on others?

I remind you again that the Holy Quran sets forth clearly that it is Allah Who appoints Khalifas. Remember, Adam was made Khalifa by God, Who said: 'I am about to appoint a vicegerent [Khalifa] in the earth.' What good did the angels achieve by raising an objection to it? You can find it from the Quran. If that is the situation of the angels, that they had to confess: 'Holy are Thou, we have no knowledge'; then you who object to me should reflect upon your own situation. I remember well when someone said: 'A Parliament has been established in Iran and this is the age of constitutions.' He uttered a falsehood and was guilty of disrespect. The jealousy of God Almighty displayed to such people the result of the constitution in Iran. I repeat they should repent even now.

In the middle of June 1912 the Khalifatul Masih had occasion to go to Lahore and during his brief visit he delivered another important speech on the status of the Khalifa and the obedience due to the holder of that office. In the course of this speech he observed:

God Almighty of His grace saved you from disintegration after the death of the Promised Messiah by uniting you at my hands. Then appreciate this Divine bounty and do not indulge in useless discussions. I cannot understand what moral or spiritual benefit do you derive from them. God Almighty has made Khalifa whom He willed and has made you acknowledge His authority. It would be great folly on your part to take exception to this Divine determination. I have told you repeatedly and have demonstrated it from the Holy Quran that it is not the part of man to establish a Khalifa; it is the function of God Almighty.

If anyone says that the Anjuman [Central Association] has made me Khalifa, he utters a falsehood. Such thinking is destructive and should be eschewed. Listen once more that no man or Anjuman has made me Khalifa, nor do I consider any Anjuman capable of appointing a Khalifa. Thus no Anjuman has made me Khalifa, nor do I attach any value to the action of any Anjuman in that context. Should the Anjuman leave me I would not pay any attention to its action. No one has the power to deprive me of the robe of the Khilafat.

Hearken! I had never had any desire to become Khalifa. At the time when I was not yet a follower of the Promised Messiah I dressed in the same manner in which I dress now. I have met the nobility as a person of honour, in the same dress. When I became the follower of the Promised Messiah I made no change in my way of life. After his death whatever happened was brought about by God Almighty. I had not the least idea that I would become the Khalifa, but God Almighty so willed it out of His wisdom, and He made me your Imam and Khalifa. Those who in your estimation were better entitled to the office accepted me under the Divine will and are obedient to me. Then who are you that you should raise objections against me? If you have any objection, raise it against God, but beware of the consequences of such impertinence.

I do not flatter anyone. I do not need anyone's greeting, nor do I depend upon your offerings and provisions. I seek refuge with God that any such notion should pass through my mind. God Almighty has bestowed a secret treasure upon me, of which no one has any knowledge. My wife and children are not dependent upon any of you. God Almighty looks after them. You have no capacity to look after anyone. Allah is Self-Sufficient; it is you who are needy.

He who is present should listen carefully and he who is not present should be informed by those who are present, that to raise the objection that the Khilafat has not been bestowed upon someone who was better entitled to it, is the doctrine of those who rejected the Khilafat of Abu Bakr and Umar. Turn away from any such thought. Allah, the Exalted, has made that one Khalifa whom He considered best entitled to the office. He who opposes him is false and is disobedient to God. Submit and obey like the angels; do not behave like Iblis.

Despite my illness I have taken advantage of this opportunity to impress upon you that the Khilafat is no light affair. You can derive no benefit by agitating this question. No one will make any of you Khalifa, nor can anyone else become Khalifa in my lifetime. When I die it will be only that one concerning whom God so wills who will become Khalifa and God will raise him to this office Himself. You have made a covenant with me. You should not raise the question of Khalifa. God has made me Khalifa and now I cannot be set aside by any of you, nor has anyone the power to set me aside. If you persist in your attitude then remember that I have with me those who like Khalid bin Waleed will chastise you as rebels.

Be warned, my supplications are heard in heaven. My Lord fulfills my purpose even before my supplications. To fight me is to fight God. So repent and give up all these vain things. Be patient for a while; thereafter he who succeeds me will deal with you as God wills.

This address was delivered in the mosque erected within the area of the Ahmadiyya Buildings on Brandreth road, Lahore, which was the centre of all opposition to the Khalifa.

The greatest single event of the period of the Khilafat of Hazrat Khalifatul Masih I was his courageous and valiant defence of the institution of Khilafat, and the upholding of its dignity and authority. In the circumstances with which he was confronted this was without a doubt a unique achievement. Those who were opposed to him were in the majority in the Central Association and had undoubtedly rendered valuable services to the Movement. They imagined that because of those services and of their academic qualifications and their professional experience, they occupied such a position of influence and honour in the Community that even if they misconstrued and misrepresented some of the writings of the Promised Messiah, they could carry the Community with them. Though they had taken a leading part in inviting Hazrat Maulvi Nurud Din Sahib to assume the responsibilities of the office of Khalifa on the death of the Promised Messiah, almost immediately thereafter they began to be troubled by second thoughts and adopted the position that the Sadar Anjuman Ahmadiyya (Central Ahmadiyya Association) was the effective and authoritative Head of the Movement and that the Khalifa was subordinate to its authority. In their estimation the strength of their position was derived from the fact that they had a large majority in the Anjuman and as far as could be foreseen there was no prospect of this majority being reduced to a minority, inasmuch as according to the rules of the Anjuman, for the framing of which some of them alone were responsible, a vacancy in the membership of the Anjuman, which normally arose only on the death of a member, was filled by the nomination of a new member by the surviving members of the Anjuman. Thus the Anjuman was a self-renewing body in which a majority once established acquired more or less a permanency.

Where, however, the majority made a miscalculation was with regard to the character of the Khalifa. Time after time the tricks and devices to which they had recourse were frustrated by the firmness, far sightedness, courage and high resolve of the Khalifa and by his complete trust in God. They dared not come out into the open in their opposition and hostility to the Khalifa, as fairly early they had begun to perceive that the Khalifa enjoyed tremendous prestige among the Community and that if a situation was brought about in which the Community might be forced to make a choice between the Khalifa and the Anjuman, at least ninety per cent of it would support the Khalifa rather than the Anjuman.

With the passage of time they began to give currency to ideas and concepts which were designed to tone down the differences of doctrine, teaching and practice between the Ahmadiyya Community and the mass of orthodox Muslims. Their object was that they would thereby overcome the hostility of the orthodox towards the Movement and would gain popularity among them through propagating the philosophy and teachings of Islam as the Promised Messiah had set forth, but without making any reference to him. Here again they were the victims of miscalculation, the extent of which was made manifest only gradually, though for some time they prided themselves on having discovered a formula which would not only make them popular with the orthodox but would put them in the vanguard of all Islamic movements and win them credit for whatever progress was achieved by Islam and the Muslims.

Their fundamental weakness, however, was that while the

Khalifa placed his entire reliance upon the grace and mercy of God, those who were opposed to him placed their reliance upon their own qualifications and capacities, such as they were, and their plans and devices. They overlooked the elementary truth that their capacities were also a bounty of God and that any misuse and misapplication of them would draw severe divine retribution upon them as has been said: Call to mind when your Lord declared: 'If you will use My bounties beneficently, I will surely multiply them unto you, but if you misuse them, My punishment is severe indeed' (14:8).

The repeated and emphatic admonitions of the Khalifatul Masih produced no change in their attitude. They kept making hypocritical professions of loyalty and obedience to him, but did not abandon, nor even relax, their efforts towards undermining his prestige and his authority and in sowing the seeds of disloyalty and dissatisfaction towards the Khalifa in the minds of the members of the Movement.

One element that intensified their opposition to the Khalifa, and indeed to the very institution of the Khilafat, was their consuming jealousy of Sahibzada Mirza Mahmud Ahmad Sahib, the Promised son of the Founder of the Movement. They could perceive clearly the favour that the Khalifatul Masih accorded to the Sahibzada and the increasing esteem and affection in which the members of the Community at large held him. They had begun to apprehend that after the death of Khalifatul Masih I, the Community, with few exceptions, would manifest its preference for the Sahibzada as the next Khalifa. They began to have recourse to subtle devices that were calculated to restrict the activities of the Sahibzada in the cause of the Movement. He had given early proof of a very keen intelligence, a very just appreciation of spiritual values and a highly developed faculty of giving expression to his thinking in speech and in writing. His loyalty and devotion to the Khalifatul Masih were exemplary. He subordinated all his activities to the approval of the Khalifatul Masih. He was inspired by great zeal in support of the ideals and principles of the Movement.

In February 1911 the Sahibzada, in pursuance of a dream, which he mentioned to the Khalifatul Masih, decided with his permission to form a society which he called Ansarullah (Helpers of God). The main purposes of this society were to er a spirit of self improvement, to promote propagation of the ideals of the Movement, to pay greater attention to and observe regularity of Prayer services and remembrance of God, to foster the study of the Holy Quran and *ahadees*, etc. The initiation of this society furnished his opponents with another occasion for misrepresenting the Sahibzada's motives and charging him with conspiring to win support for his own succession to the Khalifatul Masih. Subsequent events established quite clearly the baselessness of any such suspicion.

In June 1913 the Sahibzada Sahib sought and obtained the permission of the Khalifatul Masih to start a weekly paper, the title of which the Khalifatul Masih himself suggested should be *Al-Fazal*. Its first issue was published on 19 June 1913. The Sahibzada was himself editor of the paper which from the very start became very popular in the Community and throughout maintained a very high standard in all respects.

The disgruntled section also started the publication of a paper called *Paigham Solh* (Message of Peace) from Lahore, the first issue of which was published on 10 July 1913. Thus they now had an organ available to them for the propagation of their point of view on different questions in which they were interested. In October 1913 two anonymous tracts were published from Lahore and were circulated within the Community in which the point of view of the disgruntled section was put forward in more offensive and aggressive language than was done in their organ *Paigham Solh*. It was soon established beyond doubt that these tracts were inspired and paid for by the leaders of dissent in Lahore. The Khalifatul Masih was grievously hurt by the publication of these tracts, and became convinced that there was little chance of those who were responsible for carrying on such propaganda against him mending their ways. On one occasion he was so annoyed at the hostile attitude of the *Paigham Solh* that he observed: 'Our people in Lahore have sent me Paigham Jang [Message of War].' Later he directed that the *Paigham Solh* should not be sent to him, and he would never bring himself to read it. About the same time someone, probably one of those who had been responsible for the anonymous tracts, wrote a most offensive and impertinent letter to Sahibzada Mirza Mahmud Ahmad in which he charged him with conspiracy and intriguing for the succession to Hazrat Khalifatul Masih, praised to the skies one of the principal personalities among the disaffected, and exhibited a most contemptuous attitude towards the Sahibzada Sahib. He also challenged him to deny the charges preferred against him on oath. As the letter was anonymous Sahibzada Sahib published a detailed reply to it in the issue of the *Al-Fazal* of 19 November 1913 in which, among other things, he also denied on oath the charges that had been made against him.

On 15 January 1914 the Khalifatul Masih recorded a note:

> Last year some stupid people attempted to create differences amongst the members of the Community in which I was also made the target of attack. The purpose of the authors of the anonymous tracts was to create confusion in the Community. But God Almighty of His grace safeguarded me and the Community against this mischief.

Despite all the admonitions of the Khalifatul Masih the nefarious activities of the dissentient group, instead of being restrained, continued to be intensified both overtly and covertly, right till the death of Khalifatul Masih I.

It is only just and fair, however, to mention that during the period of the first Khilafat the Sadar Anjuman Ahmadiyya (Central Ahmadiyya Association) carried out several useful projects for which it deserves full credit. As the majority of the Anjuman was disaffected towards the Khalifa, their activities of a beneficent character, for instance, the construction of the hostel of Talim-ul-Islam High school, of the school building itself, of the Masjid Nur, of Nur Hospital, etc., must be particularly appreciated. It is true that all these and other projects were initiated with the approval and under the auspices of the Khalifatul Masih, and were carried through with funds provided by the Community, who were motivated by their devotion to the Khalifatul Masih, yet as the projects emanated from the Anjuman, its share of the credit must be duly acknowledged.

Maulvi Muhammad Ali Sahib M.A. had settled down in Qadian during the lifetime of the Promised Messiah. When the publication of the *Reviews of Religions* was decided upon he was appointed its editor and he established a very high reputation for it within a short time. Later, during the first Khilafat he embarked upon a much more ambitious project, namely, the compilation of an English translation of the Holy Quran with explanatory notes. He continuously sought the advice of Khalifatul Masih I on difficult points of exegesis. This work was not completed till some years after the death of Khalifatul Masih I, and when it was published it was discovered that on several points Maulvi Muhammad Ali Sahib had departed from the clearly expressed views of the Promised Messiah and Khalifatul Masih I. The translation was, on the whole, a work of high scholarship and achieved great popularity.

Khawaja Kamalud-din Sahib had, during the time of Khalifatul Masih I, adopted a programme of lectures in Urdu at various places throughout the country. These lectures, in which he carefully refrained from any mention of the Promised Messiah, but which were based entirely upon his exposition of Islamic values, also proved very popular and he began to be considered an outstanding scholar of Islam. In 1912 he moved over to England and started publication of a monthly magazine which was devoted to the promotion of the interests of Islam and the Muslims, and became eventually known as the *Islamic Review*. It enjoyed great popularity during the greater part of the period during which it continued to be published. Several years after the death of

Khawaja Kamalud-din Sahib it fell into decline and its publication was stopped a few years back.

With the exceptions just mentioned, the Sadar Anjuman Ahmadiyya as a whole, quite properly, confined its attention to administrative matters and thus in practice illustrated the scope of the purposes for which it had been established. It did not concern itself with the primary purpose of the advent of the Promised Messiah, which was to establish the supremacy of Islam through the true exposition of Islamic values and their illustration in practice. That was left primarily and mainly to the spiritual Head of the Movement, that is to say, the Khalifatul Masih. That was as it should have been, if only for the reason that an Association, by the very nature of its composition, is ill-fitted and ill-equipped for the discharge of spiritual and moral responsibilities.

How well those responsibilities were discharged by the Khalifatul Masih I has become part of the history of the Movement. The greater part of his time was devoted to the exposition and illustration of the vast treasure of spiritual verities comprehended in the Holy Quran and illumined by the example of the Holy Prophet, peace be on him. In other words, he proved himself a true Successor of the Promised Messiah in every respect.

As a contrast with the preoccupations and activities of the Sadar Anjuman, the life and activities of Sahibzada Mirza Bashirud-Din Mahmud Ahmad Sahib, even during those early years, held out the promise that he would progressively continue to furnish proof of the truth of the various aspects of the prophecy of the Promised Messiah, set out in the announcement of 20 February 1886. At this stage we shall confine ourselves to mentioning only one instance from his early life. In March 1906, when he had just completed seventeen years of his life, he started the publication of a quarterly magazine, which a year later became a monthly, that was named *Tashheezul Azhan* (Stimulator of Intellects) by the Promised Messiah, and was devoted to the exposition of spiritual values.

On the publication of its first number Maulvi Muhammad Ali Sahib published the following review of it in the March 1906 number of the *Review of Religions* (Urdu):

The *Tashheezul Azhan,* a quarterly journal, has started publication from Qadian and its first number has just become available. It is an example of the high resolve of the young men of this Movement. May God bless it. Its annual subscription is 12 annas (5 English pence). The editor of this journal is Mirza Bashirud-Din Mahmud Ahmad, son of the Promised Messiah. This issue of the journal carries an Introduction from his pen extending over 14 pages. It will in any case be read and appreciated by the members of the Community, but I wish to draw the attention of the opponents of the Movement to it as a clear proof of the truth of the Movement.

The Sahibzada is only 18 or 19 [actually 17] years old. Everyone is aware of the thoughts and ambitions that inspire the minds of youngsters of that age. If they are college students, their minds are occupied with eagerness for higher education and freedom. Such zeal for the faith and such eagerness in support of Islam as are manifested in these simple words are something out of the ordinary. Not only on this occasion but, as I have observed, on every occasion this sincere eagerness of his comes to the surface. . . . It is not a casual matter that the heart of a youngster in his teens should be inspired by such eagerness and ambitions, because that is the age of sports and games, etc. Now inquire from those black-hearted people who call Hazrat Sahib an impostor whence has this true eagerness entered the heart of this young man? Falsehood is utterly foul, its effect should have been also foul and not so pure and bright as has no equal. If a person perpetrates an imposture, he might conceal it from outsiders, but cannot conceal it from his own children, who are in his company all the time and observe every movement of his, listen to every word of his and observe the manifestation of his thoughts on all occasions. Thus where there is imposture, it must become manifest sometime or other to the wife and children of the impostor. O ye unfortunate ones, do reflect whether the children of an impostor brought up during the period of his imposture can be like this. Are your hearts not human that they cannot understand such a verity and are not affected by it? What has happened to your understanding? Do reflect, can one whose instruction produces such a fruit be false in his claim? If he is false then what is the sign of a true one?

The health of Khalifatul Masih I began to be poorly in the beginning of January 1914, and suffered a serious decline in the middle of February of that year. On 26 February, under the advice of his physicians, he was removed to the house of Nawab Muhammad Ali Khan Sahib, which was situated in a garden at some distance outside the town.

On the afternoon of 4 March he wrote out his will while he was lying in bed. It was in the following terms:

In the name of Allah, Most Gracious, Ever Merciful. We praise Him and call down blessings on His noble Messenger. This humble one writes in the full possession of his senses. There is no one worthy of worship save Allah; Muhammad is the Messenger of Allah. My children are young and there is no money in our house. Allah is their Guardian. No provision should be made for them out of any fund for orphans and the needy. A loan might be provided for them which should be repaid by those of my sons who grow up into a position to do so. My books and property should be put in trust for my children. My successor should be righteous, popular, learned and of good conduct. He should exercise forbearance towards the old and new friends of the Promised Messiah. I have been the well-wisher of all of them and so should he be. The public teaching of the Quran and *hadees* should be continued. Greetings of peace. Nurud Din 4 March 1914.

After he had finished writing it he handed over the paper to Maulvi Muhammad Ali Sahib, who was sitting near him, and directed him to read it out to those who were present at the time, which was done, and it was read out a second and third time by Maulvi Muhammad Ali Sahib under the direction of the Khalifatul Masih.

After the third reading he inquired from Maulvi Muhammad Ali Sahib whether anything had been left out, on which Maulvi Muhammad Ali Sahib assured him that everything was correct.

The document was then committed to the custody of Nawab Muhammad Ali Khan Sahib.

The end came nine days later on Friday 13 March, shortly after 2 p.m. He had been born in 1841 and was thus six years younger than the Promised Messiah. He died six years after the death of the Promised Messiah and thus at the time of his death his age was the same as was the age of the Promised Messiah at the time of his death. The same was the case with Hazrat Abu Bakr, the First Successor of the Holy Prophet. He also died when he arrived at the same age at which the Holy Prophet had died.

On the evening of the same day Maulvi Muhammad Ali Sahib met the Sahibzada Sahib and suggested that nothing should be determined consequent on the death of the Khalifatul Masih in a hurry, but that everything should be settled after mutual consultation. The Sahibzada Sahib agreed and said that by the next day most people of note in the Community would have arrived in Qadian, and that a consultation could take place after their arrival. Maulvi Sahib demurred to this and proposed that as there was a difference of views on certain matters among different sections of the Community, time should be taken for full discussion so that a unanimous decision might be reached. He expressed the view that the Community should reflect upon the situation for four to five months and thereafter should come to a decision after an exchange of views. The Sahibzada Sahib pointed out the impracticability of such a course and finally said that he and those who saw eye to eye with him were prepared to make the covenant of *Ba'iat* at the hands of anyone whom Maulvi Muhammad Ali Sahib and his group might put forward for the office of Khalifa; but Maulvi Sahib would not agree.

Later the same evening the Sahibzada Sahib summoned sixty leading members of the Community who were present in Qadian for consultation. After some assessment of the situation it was unanimously agreed that before the interment of the Khalifatul Masih his successor, who should command the obedience of the Community, should be elected and should lead the funeral prayers of the deceased Khalifa and should arrange for his burial.

It was also agreed that all of them should continue to pray during the latter part of the night for Divine guidance and should observe a fast the next day.

The following day it transpired that a tract which had been drawn up by Maulvi Muhammad Ali Sahib and had been printed before the demise of Khalifatul Masih I was being widely distributed, among other places, at Batala railway station to the members of the Community who were arriving in large numbers from all directions on their journey to Qadian. The purport of the tract was that the Sadar Anjuman Ahmadiyya was the true successor of the Promised Messiah and that anyone else who might be elected as Khalifa, and there could be several such persons, would have only an honorific position, but would exercise no authority. There was a subtle hint that the Sahibzada Sahib, and those who were in agreement with him on the points of difference that had emerged, did not qualify even for an honorific position under the terms of the will of Khalifatul Masih I.

By the midday of 14 March more than a thousand members of the Movement had arrived in Qadian from outside. In the afternoon of that day Mirza Bashirud-Din Mahmud Ahmad held a consultation with all members of the family of the Promised Messiah and their close relations on the situation that confronted the Movement at the moment. After some discussion he pointed out to those present that their main concern should be to maintain, by whatever means it might be possible, the unity of the Community. With this object in view he proposed that the one fundamental requirement was that there must be a spiritual head of the Movement. If the dissident group would agree to that, then the question would be who should be elected to the office. For that purpose the view of those members of the Movement who were then present in Qadian should be ascertained and should be accepted. Should the dissident group be not prepared to agree to such a course, a person not identified with either side might be agreed upon and elected. If this should also not be acceptable, anyone of the dissident group whom they might put forward should be elected so that unity might be maintained. On his insistence all those who were present agreed to his proposal.

Immediately thereafter the Sahibzada Sahib received a note from Maulvi Muhammad Ali Sahib to the effect that the Maulvi Sahib desired to resume their conversation of the previous day. In reply the Sahibzada Sahib sent word to Maulvi Sahib that he would be welcome and he arrived accompanied by some of his friends. At the time Maulvi Syed Muhammad Ahsan Sahib, Khan Muhammad Ali Khan Sahib, and Dr Khalifa Rashidud-Din Sahib were also present with the Sahibzada Sahib. He repeated his suggestion of the previous day which he had put to Maulvi Sahib that there should be no discussion of the question whether there should or should not be a Khalifa. The only matter on which there could be an exchange of views was who should be elected Khalifa. Maulvi Sahib insisted on his side that nothing should be determined upon at the time, but after a long enough interval, which should enable the members of the Community to reflect deeply on the question that confronted them, a decision might be taken unanimously which should be given effect to. While their discussion was proceeding, the people who had gathered outside became greatly excited and in their impatience demanded that the door should be opened and they should be told what decision had been reached. At this stage the Sahibzada Sahib suggested that they should go out and try to ascertain the wishes of the people who were now gathered together in Qadian. To this the Maulvi Sahib retorted: 'You suggested this because you know who would be their choice.' The Sahibzada Sahib told him that he was ready to make the covenant of *Ba'iat* at the hands of any one of them whom they might put forward. But Maulvi Sahib persisted in affirming that the Sahibzada Sahib knew the people would insist upon electing him to the office of Khalifa. Thus the deadlock continued, and in the end the Sahibzada Sahib intimated that as he considered it essential that there must be a Khalifa and Maulvi Sahib and his group were of the view that no Khalifa was needed and there was no possibility of a compromise on this fundamental issue, which was of the nature of a religious obligation, they could do what they liked, but those who were convinced that there must be a spiritual Head of the Movement would now get together and would elect a Khalifa after consultation. That was the end of the conversation.

The Sahibzada Sahib then proceeded to Masjid Noor where he was being awaited by a couple of thousand people. After the Asr prayer Khan Muhammad Ali Khan Sahib stood up and read out the will that Hazrat Khalifatul Masih I had written on 4 March and had committed to his custody. He had scarcely finished when from every direction there arose shouts of Mian Sahib, Mian Sahib, Mian Sahib. In the midst of this uproar Hazrat Maulvi Syed Muhammad Ahsan Sahib stood up and announced in a loud voice:

> I am the person concerning whom the Promised Messiah has said that I was one of the two angels mentioned in the *Ahadees* who would accompany the Messiah on his descent from heaven. I consider that Sahibzada Bashirud Din Mahmud Ahmad Sahib is in every respect fitted that he should take the covenant of *Ba'iat* from us. I therefore request him to proceed to do so.

Thereupon Maulvi Muhammad Ali Sahib and Syed Mir Hamid Shah Sahib both stood up at the same time, each beseeching the other to let him speak first. Their altercation continued for some minutes and the audience became impatient. At this stage Shaikh Yaqub Ali Irfani Sahib stood up and announced: 'We cannot afford to waste precious time in these wranglings. I request our master the Sahibzada Sahib to accept our *Ba'iat.*' Upon this there were shouts of *labbaik, labbaik,* and it seemed that the whole body of people present was pushing forward towards the Sahibzada Sahib, who contined sitting silent and for some time gave no indication of his attitude. When he found that there was not the slightest doubt that it was the universal wish that he should assume the responsibilities of the exalted office of Khalifa, he looked for

Hazrat Maulvi Syed Sarwar Shah Sahib and on espying him in the middle of the turmoil called him and said: 'Maulvi Sahib this burden has fallen upon me suddenly and unexpectedly and I cannot even recall the formula of *Ba'iat*. Will you kindly instruct me in it.' Thus he took the *Ba'iat* of those present repeating after the Maulvi Sahib the words of the covenant. At the end of the *Ba'iat* he offered a silent prayer in which everyone joined, and after the prayer he made a brief speech. Thus the troubled, scattered and bewildered Community was, by Divine grace, again united together and Divine mercy and comfort were perceived as descending upon all hearts. Everyone appeared to be in the grip of deep emotion.

Immediately thereafter the newly elected Khalifatul Masih II led the funeral prayers of Hazrat Khalifatul Masih I in a vast open space next to the Masjid Nur. When the bier was being carried to the graveyard it was followed by a huge concourse of people of all sects and communities, Muslims and non-Muslims, as a token of their respect for and their homage to the memory of a great and gracious personality whose beneficence had recognized no boundaries and limits.

Hazrat Khalifatul Masih II was made the target of many objections, criticisms and false charges, in answer to which all that he said was:

> I would beg to be excused that I am unable to reply to all these allegations except to state that God Almighty is witness, and I make oath in His name, that I have never tried that I should become Khalifa; nor has any such idea ever crossed my mind. Those who have given expression to such an idea concerning me have been morally guilty of my murder and are accountable to God for their calumnies against me.

The entire press of the country paid tribute to the memory of Hazrat Khalifatul Masih I in superlative terms. For instance, *The Daily Zamindar* of Lahore wrote:

> In today's Indian Telegraphic News the intimation that Maulvi Hakim Nurd-Din Sahib, who was a great scholar and a dis-

tinguished divine, passed away on 13 March 1914 after an illness extending over several weeks, will be read generally by the Muslims and particularly by our Ahmadi friends with great pain and grief. To Allah we belong and to Him shall we return.

Maulvi Hakim Nur-ud-Din bore the title of Khalifatul Masih among his followers and was the Successor of Mirza Ghulam Ahmad of blessed memory. The members of the Ahmadiyya Community will continue to be agitated for a long time under the impact of the serious shock of his death. Even apart from his religious beliefs the personality and ability of Maulana Hakim Nur-ud-Din were such as to afflict the hearts of all Muslims with sorrow and grief at his passing away. It has been said that it takes a century to produce an individual possessing superb qualities. On account of his vast knowledge and his high intellect Maulana Hakim Nur-ud-Din was such a superb personality. We are sorrowful that a great scholar has today departed from our midst. We have sincere sympathy with our Ahmadi friends in their tragic bereavement, which has overtaken them like the bursting of a mountain of pain and suffering over their heads. We pray the Most Merciful One may receive the soul of Maulvi Hakim Nur-ud-Din into His mercy and may bestow steadfastness upon his followers and the members of his family.

The *Municipal Gazette* wrote:

We announce with great grief and sorrow the death at Qadian at 2 p.m. on 13 March, after an illness extending over several weeks, of Maulvi Hakim Nur-ud-Din Sahib, the Khalifa of the Ahmadiyya Community. To Allah we belong and to Him shall we return.

As is well known the deceased, on account of his matchless learning, piety and righteousness, was undoubtedly a holy and praiseworthy Khalifa for the Ahmadiyya Community, but for the Muslims of India generally also he was a great scholar and a learned divine. His love for the Holy Quran was unmatched. The way in which he expounded the verities and the insights of the Holy Quran to the Ahmadiyya Community in the latter part of his life was exemplary. He was also an expert physician. He wrote several books about Islam based on extensive research and inquiry and forcefully refuted the critics of Islam. His death is not only a great shock for the Ahmadiyya Community, it is not any the less distressing for the general body of Muslims. May Allah, the

Exalted, receive him into His mercy and bestow steadfastness upon his survivors.

The Tabeeb of Delhi wrote:

We announce with great sorrow that a famous and outstanding physician of India, Maulvi Haji Hakim Nur-ud-Din Sahib, who was also an outstanding divine and was a pious and righteous personality, and the revered leader of the Ahmadiyya Community, died last Friday, after having suffered for some time from the ills that are inseparable from old age. To Allah we belong and to Him shall be our return. The Hakim Sahib of blessed memory set a high example of compassion for all the creatures of Allah without distinction of Ahmadi or non-Ahmadi, Muslim or non-Muslim. The following are some of the special qualities that he exhibited as a physician:

(a) Friends and strangers, believers and non-believers were all equal in his estimation.

(b) Besides the systems of Yunani and Ayurvedic medicines he also had recourse to the Aloepathic system in the service of his countrymen.

(c) He based his treatment of some virulent diseases on the guidance contained in the Holy Quran.

(d) He reinforced his prescriptions with his supplications to the Divine.

(e) In his diagnosis and treatment he was not affected in the least by the worldly rank of the patient.

(f) He expected no return from his patients and exhibited a very high degree of trust in God and freedom from expecting favours from human beings.

(g) He not only treated poor and deserving patients free of charge but helped them financially also, particularly students of Quran, Hadees and medicine.

May God Almighty receive him into His mercy and bestow steadfastness on his survivors.

He was the author of several books and brochures the better known of which are *Fasalul Khatab*, which is a comprehensive refutation of Christian criticism of Islam and of the Holy Prophet, peace be on him; *Tasdeeq Brahenn Ahmadiyya*, which is a refutation of the objections raised by Pandit Lekh Ram and other Aryas against *Braheen Ahmadiyya; Nurud-Din* which is a refutation of the book *Tarke Islam* by Dharmpal, an Arya convert from Islam; and *Mirqatul Yaqeen Fi Hayate Nurud-Din* which is his autobiography.

His greatest service to the cause of Islam and humanity was the continuous courageous and valiant defence, justification and exposition of the institution of Khilafat which was vital for the spiritual survival and progress, not only of Islam and the Muslims, but of the whole of humanity. His love of the Holy Quran was proverbial, his devotion to the Holy Prophet, peace be on him, was exemplary and his obedience to the Promised Messiah was perfect and matchless. May Allah reward him richly and without measure for his devoted service. Amen.

Within a few days of the demise of Hazrat Khalifatul Masih I it came to the knowledge of Khalifatul Masih II that Maulvi Muhammad Ali Sahib was preparing to leave Qadian, as he felt that he lacked security in Qadian. The Khalifatul Masih immediately sent him a message of reassurance that he himself would be responsible for his complete security at Qadian and that he need not contemplate moving from Qadian. He followed up this message with his reassurance in person. But Maulvi Sahib was not persuaded to stay on at Qadian and soon departed for Lahore where the dissident group appointed him their Amir and where he set up his headquarters. It is worthy of note that his own subsequent exposition of the functions and authority of the Amir corresponded exactly to the functions and authority of the Khalifa as expounded by Hazrat Khalifatul Masih I.

CHAPTER ELEVEN

At the time of his election as Khalifatul Masih II, Hazrat Sahibzada Mirza Bashirud Din Mahmud Ahmad was 25 years of age. In the eyes of a worldly person he was utterly unsuitable for the discharge of great and heavy responsibilities of the exalted office to which he had been called by the almost unanimous voice of the members of the Movement, His health had always been delicate; he had during his younger days suffered from severe granulation in his upper eyelids which for long periods prevented his reading or writing anything. Consequently his attendance at school had been most irregular and he was not able to qualify even as a matriculate.

On the religious side his instruction had been confined to being taught the translation of the Holy Quran and elementary knowledge of *ahadees*. It is true that he had had the inestimable privilege of having been instructed in these matters by Hazrat Khalifatul Masih I, who, instead of forcing anything upon him, encouraged him to think for himself and thus helped him and guided him to educate himself and to develop his God-given faculties in the most beneficent manner.

At the time when he was elected Khalifatul Masih, the financial resources of the Sadar Anjuman Ahmadiyya had been reduced to almost nil. Though, with the exception of possibly half a hundred people, all those who were present at Qadian on 14 March 1919 had made the covenant of *Ba'iat* with him, yet it was not known what the reaction of the Community at large would be to the question that Maulvi Muhammad Ali Sahib had raised in his tract. It was expected that on the whole the reaction of the Community would be favourable to the Khalifa-elect, but the dissident group had announced that they had the support of 95 per cent of the Community. It had yet to be seen how far their claim was justified in fact. Such was the situation in the estimation of a secular person who had no idea of the positive and powerful assets and resources to which the newly elected Khalifa had access and which were wholly of a spiritual character.

His own state of mind at the time might be judged to some degree from the address that he delivered to the large gathering of those who were present in Qadian and had made the covenant of *Ba'iat* on 14 March 1914. This was his first address to the Community which followed immediately upon his election as the Khalifa. After a long silent prayer in which everyone present joined, he spoke as follows:

Friends, I believe with complete certainty that God Almighty is One and has no associate. Dear ones, I next believe that Hazrat Muhammad, peace be on him, is the Messenger of Allah and the Khatamal Anbiya. I believe firmly that after him no one can arise who might abrogate even a vowel point of the Law that he brought. Dear ones, that beloved master of mine, the Chief of the Prophets, possesses such high dignity that a person acknowledging him as his master can, through complete devotion and perfect obedience to him, achieve the rank of a prophet. It is true that the Holy Prophet, peace be on him, possesses such dignity and honour that a sincere servant of his can achieve the rank of prophet. This is my faith and I affirm it with complete certainty. I also believe that the Holy Quran is the beloved Book that was revealed to the Holy Prophet, peace be on him, and is the last Book and comprises the last Law. I also believe with perfect certainty that the Promised Messiah, peace be on him, was the prophet mentioned in Muslim and the Imam mentioned in Bokhari. I affirm that no part of the Islamic Law can be abrogated.

I urge you to follow the example of the Companions of the Holy Prophet, may Allah be pleased with them. They represented in their persons and conduct the result of the prayers and perfect instruction of the Holy Prophet, peace be on him. After his death the second consensus that took place was on the setting up of the system of the truly guided Khilafat. If you study the history of Islam and reflect upon it, you will find that the progress made by Islam during the time of the rightly-guided Khalifas, began to decline when the Khilafat took on the form of kingship, and Islam and the Muslims were progressively reduced to the condition which you observe today. After an interval of thirteen hundred years God Almighty raised the Promised Messiah with the rank of Prophet, according to the prophecies of the Holy Prophet, peace be on him, and after his death the system of the rightly-guided Khilafat was initiated once more. Hazrat Khalifatul Masih Maulana Nurud-Din Sahib was the First Khalifa in this dispensation. May Allah raise him to the highest rank in heaven and bestow millions of His mercies and blessings upon him. May Allah join him to the company of the Holy Prophet and the Promised Messiah, peace be on them, whose love filled his heart and coursed through his veins. We took the oath of allegiance to him on the basis of this very doctrine. Therefore, so long as this system continues in force Islam will continue to progress materially as well as spiritually.

I tell you truly that I have a fear in my heart as I find myself extremely weak. We are told in the *hadees* that we should not set a task for a slave which might be beyond his strength. At this time you have sought to make me your slave, then do not set me a task that might be beyond my strength. I know that I am weak and sinful. How can I claim that I would be able to guide mankind and would spread truth and righteousness? Our number is small and the enemies of Islam are legion, but we have high hopes in the grace and benevolence of God Almighty and in His support of the humble. Now that you have placed this responsibility on me, you must help me in its discharge; and the way of helping me is that you should supplicate God Almighty for grace and strength and should obey me, seeking the pleasure of Allah and in obedience to Him. I am a human being and a weak one. You should overlook my weaknesses and I, on my part, promise you, in the name of God Almighty, that I shall overlook your mistakes and shall forbear. Our united task is to give practical effect to the progress of the Movement and the achievement of its purpose. Now that you have established a relationship with me you should carry it on loyally. By God's grace we shall exercise forbearance towards each other; but you will have to obey me in all good things. I repeat that you must not act contrary to my directions in all good matters. If you make obedience your rule and adhere strictly to this covenant then be sure that God Almighty will lead us of His grace and our united supplications will bear fruit.

A great project that the Promised Messiah had intitiated has at its own time been committed to my care. Then supplicate and strengthen the relationship between us and try to visit Qadian often. I have heard the Promised Messiah, peace be on him, declare repeatedly that those who do not visit Qadian often run the risk that their faith might suffer a decline.

Our first duty is to propagate Islam. We must make a united effort to win the favour and grace of God. I urge you repeatedly that having established a relationship with me, after the Promised Messiah, you must fulfil the obligations of that relationship loyally and remember me in your prayers. I shall continue to remember you in my prayers. I have never made any supplication in which I have not prayed for the members of the Movement. From now on I shall do it still more. Be warned that you must do nothing contrary to your covenant with God Almighty. Our supplication should be that we should live as Muslims and die Muslims. Amen.

Among his positive assets was not only the fact that he was one of the sons of the Promised Messiah, but that he was the Promised Son concerning whom the grand prophecies, set out in the announcement of 20 February 1886, were revealed to the Promised Messiah. The fulfilment of these prophecies was gradually unfolded over more than half a century of the period of his Khilafat. His whole life as Khalifa, and all the series of his great achievements in almost every walk of life, constituted a fulfilment of those prophecies, which furnished irrefutable proof of the truth of the Promised Messiah and of the fact that the Khalifatul Masih II was the Promised Son, concerning whom those prophecies were made. There is no other single event in human history which furnishes a comparable example of Divine favour and blessing with the exception only of the events of the life of the Holy Prophet, peace be on him. These prophecies also served as a guide and pattern for Khalifatul Masih II to aim at and to conform to.

Another of his spiritual assets was that he passed the first nineteen years of his life under the supervision and guidance of his holy father when he was helped constantly by his supplications, to which were added the earnest supplications of his revered mother and her constant care for him.

That from his childhood onwards he was by Divine grace enabled to lead a pure and beneficent life is testified to by the fact that at an early age he began to have experience of true dreams, visions and revelation. While he was still at school he received the revelation: 'I shall place those who follow thee above those who reject thee, unto the Day of Judgment.' This was a clear indication that he would one day be called to a position of spiritual authority in which he would be supported by many and would be rejected by others, and that those who accept him would be always upheld above those who reject him. This has been fulfilled progressively ever since. Within a few weeks of his election as Khalifa more than 95 per cent of the Community swore allegiance to him, and the claim of his opponents that they had the support of nineteen-twentieths of the Community was thus falsified. By the date of this writing their ratio to the main Ahmadiyya Community has dwindled still more, so that they have been reduced to a position of insignificance.

Still another asset that God Almighty, by His grace, furnished to the Khalifatul Masih II was his very keen intelligence not only concerning matters spiritual but of matters relating to every aspect of individual, communal and national life. In the spiritual sphere he was bestowed deep and profound knowledge of the Holy Quran which was manifested continuously in his speeches and writings and more particularly in his two commentaries on the Holy Quran, *Tafseer Sagheer* and *Tafseer Kabeer*. In the economic and political spheres also he displayed a penetrating intelligence and a faculty of appraisal that were astonishing.

He was also greatly favoured by God Almighty through the acceptance of his prayers, which helped greatly to strengthen his relationship of affection and devotion with the members of the Community and contributed greatly to the spread of the Movement and the expansion of its influence.

Numerous prophecies of his relating to national and international events helped to impress the minds of large numbers of people in positions of authority and influence, by their striking fulfilment.

The dissident group had formed an Association of their own which they called Ahmadiyya Anjuman Ishaate Islam (Ahmadiyya Association for the Propagation of Islam), with Maulvi Muhammad Ali Sahib as its head. To start with they appointed four of their leading members, Maulvi Muhammad Ali Sahib, Khawaja Kamalud-Din Sahib, Maulvi Ghulam Hasan Khan Sahib, and Syed Hamid Shah Sahib, Khalifatul Masih; but they soon abandoned this ridiculous attempt at make-believe. Of these four gentlemen the last named made his covenant of *Ba'iat* at the hands of Khalifatul Masih II within a few weeks. Years later Maulvi Ghulam Hasan Khan Sahib also swore allegiance to Khalifatul Masih II.

Maulvi Muhammad Ali Sahib was given the title of Amir and in his sermons and addresses began to stress his own concept of his functions and authority as Amir, which was indistinguishable from the concept of the functions and authority of Khalifa as set forth by Hazrat Khalifatul Masih I. The real distinction, however, was that Maulvi Muhammad Ali Sahib, though he insisted upon it, was not accorded that sincere and wholehearted obedience and reverence by the members of the dissident group as the main Ahmadiyya Community most willingly and cheerfully accorded to the Khalifatul Masih.

Hostility towards Hazrat Khalifatul Masih II and fault finding with all that he said and did, derived from suspicion of his motives and ill-will towards him, remained for a long time a cardinal factor in the policies and activities of the group. Their principal organ for giving expression to their policies, doctrines and ambitions was the *Paigham Solh;* but from time to time they published pamphlets, brochures and booklets on matters of controversy between them and the main Ahamdiyya Community. For instance, Maulvi Muhammad Ali Sahib published his own version of the differences that had arisen over the subject of Khilafat and the election of the Khalifa and called it *The Split.* Hazrat Khalifatul Masih II rejoined with a detailed and well-reasoned account under the title *The Truth About the Split,* which established very clearly that the entire responsibility for the split lay on Maulvi Muhammad Ali Sahib and some of his close associates.

The pattern that developed and continued over a number of years without interruption was that progressively the number and strength of the Community continued to grow visibly and perceptibly, and a visible decline set in on the side of the dissident group till their activities were reduced to insignificance.

Right in the middle of the acute period of the controversy, immediately after the demise of Hazrat Khalifatul Masih I, the second Khalifa received the revelation (Arabic): 'He will shatter them.' This prophecy has been strikingly fulfilled over the years. Fairly early they presented the spectacle: 'Thou thinkest them to be united but their hearts are divided; that is because they are a people without sense' (59:15). Sharp differences manifested themselves between Maulvi Muhammad Ali Sahib and other leading figures in the group, and the tensions thereby generated became so acute that in his will Maulvi Muhammad Ali Sahib specified by name those of the group whose hostility and rancour towards him had embittered his life, and gave the direction that not a single one of them should take any part in his obsequies. Thus was fulfilled the prophecy of Hazrat Khalifatul Masih II: 'He will shatter them.' Several persons of note and a large number out of the bulk of their group had, even in the lifetime of Maulvi Muhammad Ali Sahib, left the group and sworn allegiance to Khalifatul Masih II. On the other hand large numbers of them gradually became indifferent and merged into the orthodox body of Muslims. The second generation of the group, with a few exceptions, lost all interest in religion and ceased to attach any importance to higher moral qualities and spiritual values.

Even the first few years of his Khilafat, in which differences with the dissident group continued acute and their activities claimed a sizeable portion of the time and attention of Hazrat Khalifatul Masih II, his efforts were primarily directed towards the consolidation of the Community and converting it into an effective instrument for the achievement of the purpose for which the Community had been established, that is to say, to bring about the supremacy of Islam over all other religions both through precept and through example. While his addresses and writings aimed at the stimulation of the higher moral and spiritual values in the hearts of the members of the Community and their practical manifestation in action, he did not neglect any of the multifarious factors that awaited his attention and had to be speedily attended to. One of the most important of these was the organization of the administrative machinery of the Community, that is to say the casting of the Sadar Anjuman Ahmadiyya into an effective and practical mould. This he carried out with such farsighted effectiveness as has successfully stood the test of time and trials for well over half a century. It is true that in the course of time his own dynamism and the dynamism of the Community, which was continuously stimulated under his fostering care, called for additional organs and institutions which were set up when their need arose, in such manner that the possibility and risk of conflict between the Sadar Anjuman Ahmadiyya and the new institutions was obviated altogether. The Khalifa's comprehensive supervision and a continuous flow of advice and directions contributed very largely towards keeping everyone alert and keen on doing his best.

Though this was an essential task and its successful performance was a great achievement, yet it was only ancillary and adjectival to his main responsibility, for the discharge of which he strove hard day and night. That responsibility was to maintain the Community at the highest level of activity, both in respect of self improvement and in respect of striving to carry the message of Islam to wider and wider circles by putting forth all the needed effort and making all the required sacrifices. For this purpose he called in aid all his great talents; he had recourse to continuous advice, exhortation and admonition; he set a high and shining personal example and spent a good part of his nights in supplication to the Divine, without Whose grace and mercy nothing could possibly be achieved.

Yet that was not all. His horizon was not limited to the Community. His lord and master, the Holy Prophet, peace be on him, was in the words of the Holy Quran: 'A mercy for the universe' (21:108). His father, the Promised Messiah, was a perfect reflection of the Holy Prophet; the prophecy set out in the announcement of 20 February 1886, concerning his own coming into being, described him as a sign of Divine mercy. His beneficence, therefore, comprehended the whole of mankind. He was keenly interested in promoting the true welfare of all Muslims wherever they might be, as they were the Ummat of his lord and master, the Holy Prophet, peace be on him, however much mistaken they might be in some of their beliefs and doctrines; he was also keenly interested in promoting the true welfare of all his fellow countrymen, of whatever caste or creed, and in promoting the true welfare of all his fellow human beings. Whenever any opportunity arose for service in any of these spheres he put himself in the forefront to render such service as was open to him, and he was capable of performing. He had, however, to be mindful of proper gradation in all these spheres and had to give effect to the necessary priorities. The primary field of his activities was religion, but his definition of religion was as comprehensive as was Islam itself. In his estimation, as in the estimation of all true Muslims, religion was not confined to repeating the credo, participating in the five daily Prayer services, observing the fast of Ramadhan, paying the Zakat and performing the Pilgrimage to the House of Allah. He did all this with complete devotion and sincerity and in a perfect spirit of obedience to the divine command, but he realized that all this was machinery for the generation of the true spirit of worship of the Lord and the service of His creatures.

He was firmly grounded in all his beliefs and doctrines. He believed most sincerely in the Unity of God and in all His holy attributes; he believed in God's angels and had a clear concept of their functions and beneficence; he believed in all divinely revealed Books; he believed in all Divine Messengers, without any distinction between them; he believed in the resurrection after death and he believed in the Divine determination of all good and ill. He had full faith in the acceptance of prayer to the degree of the miraculous. He had a true concept of miracles but gave no credence to legerdemain. This was his concept of Islam and all his activities must be viewed against this background.

On one occasion Maulvi Sanaullah Sahib of Amritsar, a bitter opponent of the Movement, challenged him in the following terms:

You claim to be the Khalifa of a Prophet, whom I do not accept. I am an ordinary divine and make no particular claim. I propose a very simple method of determining which of us is in the right, which I trust you will accept. We should both travel together from Amritsar to Calcutta by train, and we shall see which of us is pelted with stones and which has flowers thrown at him. The test will be that he who is pelted with stones is in the wrong and he who has flowers thrown at him is in the right. Thus let the matter be determined by the reaction of the people.

To this the Khalifatul Masih retorted:

It is not necessary for the Maulvi Sahib to incur all the expense and spend all the time needed for a journey by train from Amritsar to Calcutta. I confess readily that if we were to adopt his suggestion he would be the one at whom flowers would be thrown and I would be the one who would be pelted with stones. But that is not a true test of righteousness. Maulvi Sahib well knows who was pelted with stones during the Meccan period of the Holy Prophet, peace be on him, whether the Holy Prophet himself or his opponents.

That silenced Maulvi Sanaullah Sahib for the time being.

On another occasion Sufi Hasan Nizami Sahib of Delhi challenged him in the following terms: 'I invite you to climb to the top of the Qutub Minar, outside Delhi, along with me.

From that eminence both of us should simultaneously jump to the ground. Whichever of us survives shall be accepted as a saint and a holy man and the one who perishes will have demonstrated his falsehood.' To him the Khalifatul Masih replied that he did not believe in any such extraordinary happening, nor did he claim that he could perform such a feat. He considered such action foolish and an attempt at suicide which is forbidden by Islam as a grievous sin. He was not, therefore, prepared to accept the invitation of the Sufi Sahib. But if the Sufi Sahib felt that he could safely perform such a feat, he was welcome to climb to the top of the Qutub Minar and jump from it. If he survived, he would be prepared to acclaim him as a saint and a holy man. Let it be said to the credit of Sufi Hasan Nizami Sahib that thereafter he always treated the Khalifatul Masih with great respect and reverence. On one of his visits to Delhi, the Sufi Sahib invited him and his companions to dinner at his residence in the environs of the Dargah Nizamuddin Aulia. He asked him to lead the sunset Prayer service and himself joined in the service. In one of his books containing pen pictures of notables whom he knew personally, the Sufi Sahib set out a very appreciative and admiring sketch of the Khalifatul Masih.

On a third occasion a Muslim divine invited him to a contest of public addresses in Arabic, proposing that whichever of the two was adjudged, by a panel of umpires to be agreed upon, as having a better command of the Arabic language should be accepted as true in his stand on the matter of the truth of the claim of the Promised Messiah, and the other one as false in that respect. In answer to this the Khalifatul Masih pointed out that proficiency in any particular language was in itself not proof that a person possessing such proficiency was necessarily equipped with the spiritual faculty of distinguishing between truth and falsehood. He added that his challenger would surely agree that Abu Jahl, the bitterest enemy of the Holy Prophet, peace be on him, in Mecca, had a greater command of Arabic than the challenger and yet he failed to recognize the truth of the Holy Prophet, peace be on him.

He possessed great versatility of mind and the range of his intellect was unmatched among his contemporaries. These qualities were strikingly illustrated in his speeches and writings. His two speeches on the occasion of the Annual Conference of the Movement on 27 and 28 December were listened to with rapt attention not only by the members of the Movement but also by a large number of non-Ahmadi Muslims and scores of non-Muslims who attended the conference sessions. His speech on the 27th was a masterly and most instructive survey of the events of the year that had any bearing upon or interest for the Movement. If there was time left on the 27th he started his second speech on that day and carried it over to conclude it the next day. If the first speech took up the whole of his time on the 27th, he started his second speech on the following day. His speeches were scheduled to begin at 2.30 p.m. and generally continued till 7.30 p.m. or even later. His second speech was devoted to the exposition of some important aspect of the teachings of Islam, and was based entirely upon the Holy Quran, the practice and admonitions of the Holy Prophet, peace be on him, and the speeches and writings of the Promised Messiah. Together they constitute a most precious treasury representing the multiple facets of Islam in scintillating and attractive colours. His speeches were intellectual banquets at which those present were regaled to their great delight and enjoyment. In that guise he stimulated their intellects, enlivened their faculties, incited them to climb moral and spiritual heights and sent them home greatly enriched and determined to carry out a spiritual revolution both inside themselves and in the world around them. The experience of his listeners might perhaps be described as a moral, intellectual and spiritual Turkish bath. Everyone marvelled at the skill that enabled him to put forth the profoundest moral and spiritual verities in a language and a style which were easily comprehended and absorbed by the average listener. He did not strike poses and took no flights into the intellectual stratosphere. His purpose was to stimulate and arouse rather than to overwhelm and incite wonder and admiration. His tone was most of the time easy and conversational. The audience felt at home with him and responded to him in fullest measure. They felt that they were in the company of a deeply loving father who was instructing them in the easiest and most familiar manner in the appreciation of values that could be of the greatest benefit to them in all walks of life. No one experienced any fatigue or burden and at the conclusion of the meeting the general feeling was not of relief but of regret that the banquet had not continued longer. Everyone felt refreshed and invigorated.

By Divine grace the period of the second Khilafat extended over more than half a century and was crammed with a succession of events that covered many aspects of individual, communal, national and international life. A detailed history of the second Khilafat would take up several volumes, and would be beyond the scope and limits of this study. We are thus compelled to make a selection of certain events which might serve as illustrations of the service that Hazrat Khalifatul Masih II rendered to the cause of Islam and of humanity.

It has been noticed that Khalifatul Masih II was, under the Divine will, called to his great office at the age of 25. It was the common practice of the leaders of the dissident group to refer to him as a child or as a raw youth. They derided him and professed great concern that the destinies of a Movement of great potential had unfortunately been committed into the hands of an inexperienced young man. The record will demonstrate how mistaken was their estimation of the capacities and high resolve of that young man, and how perfect and justified was his reliance on the grace and mercy of God.

Some idea of the progress made by the Movement under the fostering care and wise leadership and guidance of Hazrat Khalifatul Masih II might be formed on the basis of the attendance in the Annual Conferences of the Movement. In the last conference under Hazrat Khalifatul Masih I in 1913, the attendance was approximately three thousand. In the conference of 1964, the last one during the second Khilafat, the attendance was over seventy-five thousand.

In the Annual Conference of the dissident group, the attendance seldom, if ever, exceeded two thousand and then began to decline progressively so that in 1976 the attendance did not reach even four hundred, of whom at least two hundred were members of the main Ahmadiyya Community.

CHAPTER TWELVE

The First World War, which had been prophesied by the Promised Messiah some years earlier, broke out within less than five months of the election of Khalifatul Masih II to his exalted office. India was then a dependency of Britain and the entry of Britain into the war automatically carried India with it. As the war proceeded Indian political leaders began to hope, and then to demand, that after the cessation of hostilities India should advance constitutionally to the status of a Dominion. In response to this demand His Majesty's Government announced in Parliament in August 1917, that the objective of British policy in India was the attainment of Dominion status by India. In pursuance of this declaration Mr Edwin Samuel Montague, Secretary of State for India, visited India for the purpose of ascertaining public opinion in India on the shape and measure of India's advance towards Dominion status after the end of the war. Representatives of political and sectional organizations were invited to Delhi to place their views before His Excellency the Governor General, Lord Chelmsford, and the Secretary of State.

Hazrat Khalifatul Masih II also received an invitation to go to Delhi to meet the Governor General and the Secretary of State and to present his views. He prepared an address in which he set out his views in some detail and went to Delhi with a delegation composed of certain leading members of the Community. The delegation waited on the Governor General and the Secretary of State and one of them read out the English translation of the address which had been prepared by the Khalifatul Masih II. He himself had separate interviews with the Secretary of State and the Governor General for the purpose of an exchange of views. The Secretary of State told him that he had been much impressed with the address that had been presented to them and sought clarification of certain points. He also said that he had taken careful note of the suggestions made in the address, two or three of which he intended to incorporate in his report so that they should not be overlooked when final proposals would be formulated. This was the Khalifatul Masih's début in the field of politics and public life. Thereafter he never let any opportunity pass without making his valuable contribution towards safeguarding the rights, interests and position of the Muslims in the political and constitutional spheres.

In pursuance of the report of the Secretary of State, the Government of India Act 1919 was passed by the British Parliament under which the system known as dyarchy was set up in the British provinces of India, and the Imperial Legislative Council at the centre was replaced by the Legislative Assembly and Council of State, both of which were composed of a majority of elected members with a certain proportion of official and non-official nominated members. At the provincial level the legislature, known as the Legislative Council, was given a large majority of elected members with a small number of nominated official members. The provincial subjects were divided into two categories, reserved and transferred. The administration of transferred subjects was committed to Ministers who were chosen from among the elected members and were made responsible to the legislature. The reserved subjects were committed to Executive Members, one of whom was generally an official and the other non-official. They were responsible to the Governor, though they were nominated members of the legislature and had to defend their policies and actions in the legislature. This system of dyarchy worked with varying degrees of success in different provinces. In the Punjab it worked with marked success due mainly to the ability, political skill and acumen of Mian Sir Fazl-i-Husain, who was senior Minister in the Punjab for five years and then became one of the two Executive Members, which position he held for another five years. In both positions he rendered great service to the cause of the advancement of India and the

Indians and the cause of all backward communities, and to safeguarding the rights and interests of Muslims.

The Government of India Act 1919 had provided that after the experience of the working of dyarchy for ten years, a Royal Commission would be appointed to make recommendations with regard to the further constitutional advance of India. By 1926 political leadership in India had begun to agitate for the appointment of the Royal Commission, in response to which a Royal Commission was appointed under the chairmanship of Sir John (later Lord) Simon, in the autumn of 1927. The Commission was composed of members of the two Houses of Parliament. The Indian National Congress took great umbrage at the exclusion of Indians from the membership of the Commission and declared that it would not co-operate with the Commission. Thus the question of co-operation with the Commission became a matter of keen controversy in Indian political circles. In an effort to placate opposition to the Commission, it was announced that the Commission would invite a committee of the Central Indian Legislature to sit with it and to participate in its proceedings while the Commission examined witnesses, and that when the Commission visited each province, a committee elected by the Provincial Legislature should also sit with it and participate in its meetings.

Hazrat Khalifatul Masih II came out very strongly in support of the presentation of the Muslim case before the Commission, both at the provincial and central levels. He made out a strong case in favour of co-operation; lest the Muslim case should go by default. He did not profess to hope for any very favourable result from the report of the Commission, but was anxious that the Muslim case should be put clearly and forcibly before the Commission.

The very strong plea that Hazrat Khalifatul Masih II made for co-operation with the Commission had considerable influence in persuading Muslims to co-operate in setting up the Central and Provincial committees which were to work with the Commission.

Parallel with the activities of the Simon Commission, the All India Congress established a committee of ten members under the chairmanship of Pandit Moti Lal Nehru for the purpose of proposing a constitution for India which should have the support of all political parties and minorities, and which could be treated as the agreed demand of the whole of India. The committee was known as the Nehru Committee. Its report was published on 12 August 1928. Hazrat Khalifatul Masih II was much perturbed on reading the report as the proposals embodied in it, if they were accepted and were given effect to in the future constitution of India, would place the Muslims of India completely at the mercy of the majority and their future in India would be put in serious jeopardy. He carried out a penetrating analysis of the report which was published in seven instalments in the *Al-Fazal,* and was subsequently issued in the form of a book entitled *Muslim Rights and the Nehru Report.* At the beginning the reaction of an important section of Muslim leaders and the Muslim press was, on the whole, in favour of the Nehru Report. But the analysis of the Report by the Khalifatul Masih alerted Muslim leadership to the dangers to which the Muslims would be exposed in case those proposals were accepted as the basis of the future constitution of India. It was then freely acknowledged that the keen intellect and the political foresight of the Khalifatul Masih had served to rescue the Muslims of India from the serious hazard to which their fortunes had been exposed by the Nehru Report.

The report of the Simon Commission proved most disappointing and was universally condemned in India as a reactionary document. His Majesty's Government was so impressed by the force of this reaction that it authorized the Governor General, Lord Irwin (later Lord Halifax) to announce on 31 October 1929 that Dominion status for India was the immediate objective of His Majesty's Government and that for the purpose of ascertaining Indian public opinion on the future constitution of India it proposed to invite the representatives of British India and of Indian states for consultation and advice to a Round Table Conference to be held in London. This announcement was followed on 12 May 1930 by the intimation that the Round Table Conference would be called together on or about 20 November 1930. On this occasion also Hazrat Khalifatul Masih II prepared and published a well-reasoned analysis of the report of the Simon Commission and put forward his suggestions with regard to the shape of the future constitution of India together with the safeguards that he considered essential in the interests of the Muslims. This booklet was published under the title *The Solution of the Political Problem of India*. It was given wide publicity both in India and in Britain and was much appreciated in thoughtful circles. It proved of great assistance to the Muslim representatives in the series of Round Table Conferences that were held in London in 1930, 1931 and 1932.

Mr Muhammad Ali Jinnah was one of the Muslim representatives in the First and Second Round Table Conferences, but he was so disgusted with what he considered the lack of reality in the discussions of the Conferences that at the end of the Second Conference he decided to withdraw from politics and settle down in London with the intention of carrying on his practice as an advocate before the Judicial Committee of the Privy Council. In his own words:

> I received the shock of my life at the meetings of the Round Table Conference. In the face of danger the Hindu sentiment, the Hindu mind, the Hindu attitude led me to the conclusion that there was no hope of unity. I felt very pessimistic about my country. The position was most unfortunate. . . . I began to feel that I could neither help India, nor change the Hindu mentality; nor could I make the Muslims realize their precarious position. I felt so disappointed and so depressed that I decided to settle down in London. Not that I did not love India but I felt so utterly helpless [*Jinnah*, by Hector Bolitho, London 1954, p. 100].

By 1933, Hazrat Khalifatul Masih was so distressed at the prospect that faced the Muslims in India that he felt very strongly that a person of the political sagacity and iron nerve of Mr Jinnah was needed to secure for the Muslims a decent political future in India. He, therefore, directed Mr A. R. Dard, Imam of the London Mosque, to get in touch with Mr Jinnah and try to persuade him to return to India and take up, and fight for, the cause of the Muslims. Mr Dard called on Mr Jinnah and had a long talk with him. He found that the task assigned to him by the Khalifatul Masih was a very uphill one. Mr Jinnah was most reluctant, but eventually changed his mind and agreed to return to India and to place himself at the head of the political struggle of the Muslims for safeguarding their position in an independent India. Mr Jinnah was approached from time to time by certain leading figures among the Muslims of India who also urged him to return to India. But there can be no doubt that what prevailed with him in the end was the persistence of Mr Dard under the directions of the Khalifatul Masih. When Mr Jinnah intimated his willingness to return to India, Mr Dard held a reception in his honour at the London Mosque which was very well attended. Mr Jinnah addressed the gathering on India of the Future. He started with the announcement that Mr Dard's persuasion had compelled him to enter the political field again from which he had withdrawn some time back. He said: 'The eloquent persuasion of the Imam left me no way of escape.' His speech was widely reported. *The Sunday Times*, London, wrote in its issue of 9 April 1933:

> There was a large gathering in the grounds of the mosque in Melrose Road, Wimbledon, where Mr Jinnah, the famous Indian Muslim, spoke on India's future. Mr Jinnah made unfavourable comments on the Indian White Paper from a national point of view. The chairman, Sir Nairn Stewart Sandeman M.P., took up the Churchill attitude on the subject, and this led to heckling by some of the Muslim students, who were, however, eventually calmed by the Imam of the mosque.

Mr Jinnah returned to India and put himself at the head of the Muslim League into which he infused a new life. He was elected a member of the Indian Legislative Assembly in which, for a time, he led the Independent Group, but soon he formed his own Muslim League Party and the Muslim members of the Legislative Assembly rallied round him.

He early put forward the claim that the Muslim League alone represented Muslim public opinion in the political field. But it took him some time and a spell of very hard work to establish that position in fact and to have it recognized by the government and his non-Muslim opponents. From the beginning, however, the trend had set in very strongly in his favour and in the very first elections to the legislatures the Muslim League representation became a factor to be reckoned with. The Khalifatul Masih and the Ahmadiyya Community throughout lent him their support and became a source of strength for him upon which he could rely confidently.

In the 1937 elections the Muslim League succeeded in consolidating its position in the Muslim majority provinces and also won almost all the Muslim seats in the provinces in which Muslims were in a minority. The Congress had won majorities in those provinces and refused to appoint any Muslim League member of the Provincial Legislatures to the post of Minister in any of those provinces. This brought about a direct confrontation between the Muslim League and the Congress. When, on the outbreak of the Second World War, the Congress Ministries resigned as a protest against the entry of India into the war without any consultation with the representatives of the people, the Muslims celebrated the occasion as the Day of Deliverance. In March 1940 the Muslim League in its Lahore session adopted the well-known resolution which has been construed as the demand for Pakistan.

The one weakness in the position of the Muslim League and of its leader, Mr Jinnah, was that in the Punjab which was to be the heart of Pakistan, the Provincial Government was headed at first by Sir Sikandar Hayat Khan, and after his death by Malik Sir Khizar Hayat Khan. The party that they headed was the Unionist Party, the membership of which comprised Muslims, Hindus and Sikhs. While Sir Sikandar had arrived at a working understanding with Mr Jinnah, the latter, not being satisfied with the arrangement insisted that Sir Sikandar's successor should fall into line with Mr Jinnah and should lead the Muslim members of his party into the Muslim League. Sir Khizar Hayat resisted this demand of Mr Jinnah and for a time the situation in the Punjab remained unsatisfactory from the point of view of the Muslim League.

In the meantime the country was marching rapidly towards independence, and the Governor General, Lord Wavell, began to work hard to set up an Interim Government at the Centre, which should be composed of representatives of the Congress and the Muslim League. Difficulties were encountered and at one time it looked as if in the formation of the cabinet the Muslim League might be bypassed. This prospect seriously disturbed the Khalifatul Masih who moved personally to Delhi and was instrumental in creating a situation, in consultation with Mr Jinnah and with the co-operation and assistance of His Highness the Nawab of Bhopal, in which the way was opened for the Muslim League to be invited to join the Interim Government on terms acceptable to Mr Jinnah.

In the spring of 1946, His Majesty's Government sent out a Commission, composed of three members of the Cabinet, to India to try to bring about a settlement between the Congress and the Muslim League. The Commission became known as the Cabinet Mission. It worked hard and unsparingly, and in the middle of the summer put forward a plan which, to the surprise of everyone, was accepted by both parties. Prime Minister Nehru, who was also President of the Congress, had, however, second thoughts on some of the features of the plan and announced an interpretation of certain paragraphs of the plan which the language was not capable of bearing. Mr Jinnah was outraged by this subterfuge and announced that unless Mr Nehru made it plain beyond doubt that the Congress would work the Cabinet Mission Plan according to its plain and true import, the Muslim league would not join in working the Plan. Thereupon, the Governor General,

Lord Wavell, sent for Mr Gandhi and Mr Nehru and tried hard to obtain from them the assurance that would satisfy Mr Jinnah that the Congress would work the Plan according to its plain meaning; but Mr Gandhi and Mr Nehru took up the position that it was for them to interpret the Plan and their interpretation must be accepted and given effect to. The situation again became deadlocked, and Prime Minister Attlee summoned Mr Nehru and Mr Jinnah to London towards the end of 1946 in the hope that he might be able to resolve the deadlock. But his hope proved vain and it became necessary to have recourse to some other device for the purpose of resolving the situation.

On 20 February 1947 Prime Minister Attlee announced that His Majesty's Government had decided to transfer power into Indian hands at the latest by the end of June 1948, and that a scheme would be worked out whereunder power might be transferred to the Central Government of India and that if this did not prove feasible all over, power might be vested in some cases in the Provincial Governments. This created a very embarrassing situation for the Muslim League in respect of the Punjab where the Unionist Party, and not the Muslim League, was in power. Fortunately, under Ahmadi advice, Malik Sir Khizar Hayat Khan was convinced of the wisdom of resigning his office of chief Minister of Punjab so as to open the way for the formation of a Muslim League Government in the Punjab and failing that for Governor's rule.

In the western districts of the United Provinces of India a large section of the rural population which had at one time accepted Islam was Muslim in name but was not distinguishable from the Hindus in the cultural pattern of their lives. Many of them even bore Hindu names. They were Rajputs by caste and were known as Malkanas. The Arya Samaj which was a militant arm of the Hindus and favoured, contrary to the thinking of the mass of orthodox Hindus, the conversion of non-Hindus to Hinduism, devised a large-scale plan in 1922 for the reconversion of the Malkanas to Hinduism. They had put this plan into effect and their campaign had acquired a certain degree of momentum before the Muslims of the Punjab and of the neighbouring districts of the United Provinces became aware of their activities. As soon as the Khalifatul Masih came to know of this development he organized and launched a counter campaign designed to safeguard the Malkanas against the proselytizing activities of the Arya Samaj. He alerted the non-Ahmadi Muslims against the gravity of the danger that threatened and appealed to them to make common cause with the Ahmadis against the challenge of the Arya Samaj. He made it quite clear that the Muslim effort should be directed towards strengthening the faith of the Malkanas in Islam and that no sectional advantage should be sought to be derived from the situation with which they were faced. On his side he made a moving and stirring appeal to the Community to provide the needed number of volunteers who should proceed immediately to the affected areas in batches and carry out whatever duties might be assigned to them over a period of three months, at the expiry of which they would be replaced by fresh batches of volunteers. Each volunteer was required to bear the expenses of his journey to and back from the area to which he was allotted and all his expenses of board and lodging, etc., throughout the period of his duty. The Community's response to the call was eager and enthusiastic, and at no time, while the campaign lasted, was there any dearth of suitable volunteers. One particular feature of the campaign was that it opened at the height of the dry summer season, and the volunteers who perforce came from urban areas and were accustomed to the amenities available in towns and cities for the purpose of mitigating the extreme discomfort resulting from the very high temperatures in the summer months, were called upon to work in rural areas at unaccustomed tasks in conditions of extreme discomfort. Their food was mostly rough and unappetizing, and cold drinking water was a luxury that was not readily available everywhere. Yet their zeal and eagerness enabled them to dispense cheerfully with all that they had been accustomed to and to be content with whatever became available from day to day. The Arya Samaj had organized a boycott of the Muslim Malkanas, many of whom were hard put to it to gather and bring in the harvest. The Ahmadiyya volunteers were thus called upon to undertake the unfamiliar tasks of cultivators and husbandmen to which they had hitherto been complete strangers. Yet they set to with eagerness, and though their performance was often awkward, the tasks were done. The whole campaign while it lasted assumed and maintained the character of the exercise of the highest moral and spiritual values. While the outward emphasis was on hard labour, the inward emphasis was on eagerness in winning the pleasure of God.

In contrast, the effort mounted by non-Ahmadi Muslims was half-hearted, sporadic, hesitant and lacking in willingness in the face of discomfort. It became apparent soon, and was freely acknowledged, that the campaign organized and set in motion by the Khalifatul Masih was alone proving effective against the activities of the Arya Samaj which were well supported with men and money.

The leaders of the Arya Samaj began to perceive within a matter of weeks that their plan had miscarried, and was not only unlikely to achieve its object but that they would soon begin to lose ground. Therefore, they proclaimed that they were anxious to avoid friction between the Muslims and the Hindus and were willing to meet Muslim leaders to discuss the cessation of all activities and the winding up of the situation. The Muslim leaders with whom they got in touch were inclined to agree to their suggestion, but it was felt that any understanding that might be reached in the absence of the representatives of the Ahmadiyya Community would be purely academic and would not affect the situation in the field where all the effort on the Muslim side was being put forth by Ahmadi volunteers. A request was, therefore, submitted to the Khalifatul Masih to send his representative to participate in the *pourparlers*. The Khalifatul Masih readily responded to the request and instructed the representatives, whom he nominated for the purpose, that as the Arya Samaj had started the whole affair and had stolen a march against the Muslims it was unrealistic on its part to suggest that the situation should be frozen. This would mean that the Arya Samaj would retain the advantage that it had already gained and could look forward to resuming and renewing its effort from that point of vantage after a few months. The Ahmadi campaign, therefore, must continue till the last Malkana who had been reconverted had been won back to the Muslim fold. The Arya Samaj thus had no choice but to beat a reluctant and rueful retreat. The non-Ahmadi leadership and press expressed great appreciation of the stand the Khalifatul Masih had taken throughout and of the campaign that he had organized and continued to direct over several months till the object had been fully achieved.

Dr Henry Leitner, an oriental scholar of note, was towards the close of the 19th Century, Principal of the Oriental College, Lahore, one of the institutions affiliated to the University of the Punjab. For a time he also acted as Registrar of the Punjab University. Before his retirement he conceived the idea of establishing an Oriental Institute in a suitable place within easy reach of London, which should have a Mosque attached to it. For this purpose he sought and obtained substantial contributions from the Muslims of India, the largest contributors being Her Highness the Begum of Bhopal and His Excellency Nawab Sir Salar Jang, Prime Minister of the State of Hyderabad in South India. Arriving in England Dr Leitner began to look for a suitable site for the Oriental Institute and Mosque, and found one outside Woking in Surrey at a distance of 24 miles from London. He acquired the site which comprised a fairly large area and proceeded with the construction of the necessary buildings for the Institute and also of the Mosque. Quite close to the Mosque he constructed a modest residential building which he called Sir Salar Jang Memorial House. He named the Mosque Shah Jehan Mosque in honour of Her Highness the Begum of Bhopal. The Mosque and the Memorial House were surrounded by a garden and formed a unit by themselves adjacent to the area on part of which the Oriental Institute had been erected. The whole project was carried through in the last years of the 19th century. Dr Leitner died some years later and the whole estate passed into the hands of his family headed by his eldest son.

The Mosque and the Memorial House were looked after by the family but were not put to any practical use. The Rt Hon. Syed Ameer Ali, a reputed Muslim scholar and Judge, a member of the Judicial Committee of the Privy council, and one or two other leading Muslims then in London approached the family of Dr Leitner with the request that as the Oriental Institute, the Mosque and the Memorial House had been constructed with funds provided by public-spirited Muslims of India, the entire estate was a Muslim foundation and its management should be committed to a Muslim body. The family of Dr Leitner resisted this demand and claimed that the estate was the property of the late Dr Leitner to which the family had succeeded on his death. Syed Ameer Ali and his colleagues continued to press their demand and eventually a compromise was agreed upon whereby the family handed over the Mosque and Memorial House to the control and management of the Muslim claimants and were permitted to retain the Institute and the area attached to it as their own property.

About that time (1912) Khawaja Kamaluddin Sahib arrived in London and started the publication of a monthly journal which ultimately became known as *The Islamic Review*. When he discovered the situation in which the Mosque and Memorial House at Woking stood he approached Syed Ameer Ali and suggested that he should be put in charge of the Mosque and Memorial House so that the Mosque could be used as a place of Muslim worship and the Memorial House could be used as the residence of the Imam.

Syed Ameer Ali and those associated with him in the project of the Mosque agreed to the suggestion of Khawaja Sahib and a formal deed of trust was drawn up and executed in the spring of 1913 whereby the management of the Mosque and Memorial House was vested in Khawaja Sahib. Khawaja Sahib thereupon transferred his residence from London to the Memorial House.

As his work and responsibilities expanded he requested Hazrat Khalifatul Masih I that someone might be sent over to assist him in his work. In response to his request the Khalifatul Masih arranged to send Chandhri Fateh Muhammad Syal M.A. to England to assist Khawaja Sahib in his work.

On the death of Hazrat Khalifatul Masih I, Chandhri Fateh Muhammed Syal swore allegiance to Hazrat Khalifatul Masih II, who directed him to move to London and start the first Ahmadiyya Mission in England.

Some years later the house and grounds at 63 Melrose Road, London S.W. 18, were acquired as the headquarters of the Mission and it was decided to build a Mosque in a part of the garden of 63 Melrose Road.

A great Imperial Exhibition was held at Wembley, a few miles out of London, in 1924. It was expected that it would attract visitors from all parts of the British Empire and a few public-spirited persons, who took an interest in comparative religion, thought that it would be a good opportunity to hold a conference of the principal religions of the Empire to which representatives of those religions might be invited to deliver addresses expounding the principles and teachings of their respective faiths. For some reason, not disclosed, no one was invited to participate in the conference on behalf of Christianity. It might well have been that the authorities of the Anglican and Catholic Churches considered it somewhat below their standing to participate in a conference of the representatives of faiths which at that time were not recognized by these two Churches as falling within their definition of religion.

Maulvi Abdur Rahim Nayyar Sahib was at that time in

charge of the Ahmadiyya Mission in London. The organizers of the proposed conference sounded him on the possibility of Hazrat Khalifatul Masih II participating in the conference and addressing it as the representative of Islam. Maulvi Nayyar Sahib conveyed the suggestion to the Khalifatul Masih and urged him to signify his willingness to address the conference, if he was invited to do so. The Khalifatul Masih took counsel with some of the leading members of the Movement and decided that he would accept the invitation. His willingness to do so was conveyed to the organizers of the conference through Maulvi Nayyar Sahib. On his part he immediately embarked upon a project to write a book setting forth in some detail the principles and teachings of Islam. He wrote it in Urdu and it was translated into English. The printing of the English translation was completed just in time before he set out on his journey to England with a dozen companions. On his way he stopped off at Port Said and visited, among other places, Jerusalem and Damascus. In London he took up his residence, along with his companions, at 6 Chesham Place, S.W.1. His arrival in London was widely publicized in the press.

The conference was held at the Imperial Institute in South Kensington, in an upper hall of commodious proportions. The Khalifatul Masih attended the conference at various times and thus had opportunities of meeting a large number of people. On the day on which his paper was to be read out he was seated on the dais with his companions and his paper was read out by one of his principal followers. The great hall was absolutely packed with people and some people not finding room inside the hall crowded the wide staircase that led down from the hall. The address was listened to in absolute silence and with concentrated attention and when the reading was finished a deep sigh was heard to go up as if the audience had been released from a spell, and everybody attempted to rush to the dais to shake hands with the Khalifatul Masih, or at least approach close to him. The address received a very good press also.

The Khalifatul Masih's book, *Ahmadiyyat or The True*

Islam, was on sale at the Imperial Institute and on one occasion, when he was visiting the Institute, a clergyman who had the book in his hand came up to greet him and said:

I obtained this book of yours yesterday and started reading it after dinner. I became so deeply interested that I went on reading it through the night and by the time I had to come down to breakfast I had finished reading it. I have been fascinated by it.

While the Khalifatul Masih and his party were still in London news arrived of the tragic death by stoning of Naimatullah Khan, a young Afghan, who had studied religion at Qadian and had returned to his own country after finishing his course of studies. He was only 19 years of age and life spread out before his imagination in attractive and alluring colours. His outstanding quality, however, was devotion to his faith. On his way back to his country he stopped at Peshawar for a short while, where his host asked him one evening: 'Naimatullah, you know that since the martyrdom of Sahibzada Syed Abdul Latif Sahib, more than a dozen of our people have been stoned to death in Afghanistan under the orders of the Amir. Should you be confronted with the same contingency, how will you behave?' His reply was:

Sir, if I said anything just now in answer to your question, my response would lack reality. I do not know and, therefore, cannot say what my reaction to the situation would be. I hope and pray that God of his grace and mercy will bestow upon me the strength and firmness that would enable me to react to the situation as the Sahibzada Sahib reacted. But I am a weak human being and all I can say at the moment is that I shall continue to supplicate for God's grace and mercy.

When he arrived in Kabul he was arrested and confined in a cell like a dangerous criminal and was charged with apostacy from Islam. He rejected every suggestion made to him that he should repudiate the Messiah of Qadian but like all his predecessors in that situation, he remained firm in his faith, in the full consciousness that he could do so only at the cost of his life. During the period of his confinement he found an opportunity of scribbling a note on a piece of paper and arranged to have it conveyed to his host in Peshawar. The note, which has been carefully preserved by his host, read: Sir, I am now face to face with the contingency that you had mentioned to me and, by God's grace, I am able to inform you that I am resolved to follow the example of the great martyr, the Sahibzada Sahib.' In due course he carried out his resolve with great firmness and presence of mind. It is worthy of note that not a single Ahmadi who was called upon to lay down his life in this cruel manner on account of his faith exhibited the slightest fear at any time or showed any inclination towards repudiating his faith. May Allah receive the souls of all of them into His mercy.

When the news of Naimatullah Khan's martyrdom was received in London, Hazrat Khalifatul Masih and his party were overwhelmed with grief and pity for the young martyr. A protest meeting was held in Essex Hall, Essex Street, which runs from the eastern end of the Strand down to Victoria Embankment. It was presided over by Dr Walter Walsh and was well attended. Several British public men spoke at the meeting and expressed their horror at the cruel murder of the young martyr and their sympathy for his parents. There was universal condemnation of the barbaric atrocity, and the authorities in Afghanistan who were responsible for it were harshly criticized.

Naimatullah Khan's execution was carried out under the orders of Amir Amanullah Khan, who advocated liberalism in every sphere of life and was anxious to modernize Afghanistan. Shortly after the execution of Naimatullah Khan, Amir Amanullah Khan set out on a tour of Western Europe with his wife, who discarded the veil and appeared to have adopted western ways in dress and deportment. In the meantime Amir Amanullah Khan had assumed the title of King and was received everywhere in Europe as His Majesty King Amanullah Khan of Afghanistan. They were accorded a royal welcome everywhere and were much gratified with all the hospitality that was extended to them and the favourable publicity that was given to their visit. But nemesis was not long delayed. King Amanullah's modernizing methods were deeply resented by the mullas who roused the populace against him. Soon after his return from Europe a scalliwag called Bacha Saqua (son of water carrier) headed a rising against him and advanced upon Kabul. He met with no opposition in Kabul, and Amanullah finding himself deserted by everyone departed in the utmost haste from Kabul, accompanied by his wife, and requested the British authorities of India to provide him with facilities for travel to Italy. Arrived in Rome he rented an apartment and settled down to an inglorious existence of degrading humiliation. His wife and daughter were disgusted with him and left him to die in lonely misery. This was the end of the line of Amir Abdur Rahman Khan, at whose instance Maulvi Abdur Rahman, a disciple of Sahibzada Abdul Latif, had been strangled to death while in custody.

Before leaving England and starting on his return journey to India, the Khalifatul Masih laid the foundation stone of the London Mosque on 19 October 1924. The construction of the Mosque was completed in the summer of 1926, and the opening ceremony was performed on 3 October 1926 by Shaikh Sir Abdul Qadir in the presence of a distinguished gathering of Muslims from all countries and British guests prominent in public life. Four English gentlemen announced their acceptance of Islam. This was the first mosque established within the area of Greater London.

In the late 1920s a graceless and shameless member of the Arya Samaj named Rajpal published a most scurrilous and disgraceful book concerning the Holy Prophet of Islam, peace be on him, which he called *Rangila Rasul* (The Rakish Messenger). The publication of the book sent a thrill of horror through the minds of the Muslims and the government prosecuted Rajpal for the offence of insulting the memory of the Founder of a religion and thus provoking feelings of hatred and contempt between the followers of Islam and Hinduism. Rajpal was convicted and sentenced to a term of imprisonment by the trial court. His appeal was dismissed, but on a revision petition to the High Court, the Judge before whom the petition came up for hearing took the view that the publication of the book, however offensive was its character, did not fall within the scope of the relevant section of the Indian Penal Code, and acquitted Rajpal. The judgment outraged Muslim sentiment and caused widespread grief and bewilderment. In effect it amounted to a sentence of death upon the wretched author of the book inasmuch as within a short time he was assassinated by a Muslim named Ilm Din who found it impossible to control his feelings of horror and outrage at the dastardly performance of Rajpal, and could find no other way of assuaging the hurt he had suffered except through the blood of the offender. Ilm Din was tried for murder, proudly confessed his guilt and was sentenced to be hanged. He went to his execution cheerfully and the Muslims acclaimed him as a martyr. The public excitement over the whole tragic affair had scarcely had time to subside when an equally offensive article against the Holy Prophet was published in a Hindu journal called *Vartman* of Amritsar. This type of performance was evidence of the diseased mind of a section of the Hindu community, the appropriate remedy for which had to be prescribed with care, wisdom and foresight. The Khalifatul Masih II considered the whole situation thoughtfully and came to the conclusion that the entire responsibility for it did not lie upon the Hindus, and that the Muslims also had been guilty of a serious default which should be set right as early as possible. The immediate need was to obtain an authoritative clarification of the state of the law regarding such offensive publications and in case of a lacuna to have it filled by legislative action. He drew up a public announcement dealing with this aspect of the matter and calling upon the government to take prompt action to secure the desired result. This announcement was prominently displayed in all the principal towns of the Punjab and evoked a wave of horror against the repetition of Rajpal's outrage by *Vartman*. The authorities felt that unless an announcement was made at once of the action the government had decided to take to deal with the situation, communal riots might erupt all over the province involving a large number of people of both religions and causing great loss of life and property. It was, therefore, decided that the editor and publisher of *Vartman* should be tried speedily by a Division Bench of the High Court, so that an authoritative construction of the relevant provision of the law might be obtained as early as possible. The Division Bench that was constituted for trial of the case overruled the judgment of the single Judge in the Rajpal case and held that the action of the accused amounted to an offence under the relevant provision of the law, and convicted the two accused and sentenced them to a term of imprisonment. The Provincial Government also moved the Government of India to put through an amendment of the particular section of the Indian Penal Code so as to put it beyond all doubt that a publication of the type of Rajpal's book and the article in *Vartman* constituted an offence under the law.

The real remedy, however, that the Khalifatul Masih devised, was to remind the Muslims that they had woefully neglected one of their principal duties, namely, to present the life and character of the Holy Prophet in their true colours to the non-Muslims. He proposed, therefore, that on a specified day in every year public meetings should be held all over the country in which speeches should be delivered by Muslims and non-Muslims on the life and character of the Holy Prophet, peace be on him. He proposed that this scheme should be inaugurated on 17 June 1928. He forthwith set up machinery at Qadian to make the scheme fully effective and appealed for speakers to address the meetings to be held on 17 June. There was a most heartening response to the appeal, not only on the part of Muslims but also of non-Muslims, and a list of speakers comprising more than fourteen hundred names was soon drawn up. In order to furnish the speakers with relevant material on the topics on which they were to speak, a set of notes was prepared of which five thousand copies were printed and were despatched to the speakers and other interested persons. In addition, the *Al-Fazal* issued a Special Number on 12 June 1927, extending over seventy-two pages, containing articles by the Khalifatul Masih, prominent Ahmadi scholars, men and women, non-Ahmadi leaders and non-Muslims on different aspects of the life of the Holy Prophet, peace be on him. The first issue of the Special Number was immediately exhausted and a second printing had to be hastily put through. The countrywide celebrations proved a tremendous success and were deeply appreciated everywhere by everyone. They helped to clear the air, to remove misunderstandings, to correct misrepresentations and to create a new, wholesome and lovable image of the Holy Prophet in the minds of non-Muslims throughout the country. These meetings have since been repeated every year and have become a permanent feature of the efforts directed towards the promotion of friendly relations between the different sects and communities of the country.

Some years later the Khalifatul Masih instituted the observance of another day in every year for speeches and addresses on the lives of the Founders of all the great religions. This was a natural and necessary sequel to the institution of the Holy Prophet's Day, and carried the purpose of interfaith understanding and appreciation still further. This Day has become known as All-Prophets' Day.

The British took over the administration of the Punjab from the Sikhs in 1845. During the last phase of their conflict with the Sikhs they were helped in various ways by Raja Gulab Singh, the Dogra Chieftain of Jammu, who deserted the Sikhs and went over to the British. Once the British control of the Punjab was established Raja Gulab Singh demanded from the British some substantial reward for his service to the British cause. He was asked what would he wish to have and he suggested that the hill country between the rivers Ravi and Indus might be made subject to his rule. The British were not at that time aware of the full extent of the territory, its resources and the character and composition of its people. They did not consider it necessary to look into any of these details and agreed readily enough to the suggestion of Raja Gulab Singh in return for a cash payment of two and a half million rupees by Gulab Singh. Thus by the Treaty of Amritsar of 1846 between His Excellency Lord Lawrence, Governor General of India, and Raja Gulab Singh, the rule of the latter over the territory just described was recognized and Raja Gulab Singh became a faithful feudatory of the British. In this manner Dogra rule was established over Kashmir which comprised the famous valley of that name and the mountainous territories of Ladakh, Poonch, Gilgit and Hunza.

This was the beginning of a century of the most savage tyranny of which history furnishes a record anywhere.

Raja Gulab Singh assumed the title of Maharaja of the State of Jammu and Kashmir. The valley had a population of roughly four million, more than 90 per cent of whom were Muslims. In the total population of the State the proportion of the Muslims was over 80 per cent. The people of Kashmir, as is well known by now, are part of the lost tribes of Israel. They are a handsome people and are given to artistic pursuits like wood-carving, silver-chasing, and woollen and silk manufactures of the finest type. Under Mughal and Pathan rule they had led happy and comparatively prosperous lives. The Mughal emperors, beginning with Akbar the Great, spent a portion of the summer in the valley as a relief from the blazing heat of the plains. The valley had been celebrated as paradise on earth.

From the very beginning of his rule, Maharaja Gulab Singh imposed a body of the harshest regulations upon the people of Kashmir and reduced them in effect to a state of humiliating bondage. He taxed severely everything needed for the support of human life, with the exception only of water and air. Even grass, growing free, on which the people were wont to pasture their cattle, was subjected to a heavy tax. Within a year of the treaty of 1846 Lord Lawrence was compelled to address a severe remonstrance to the Maharaja on the harshness and severity of his régime, warning him that if he persisted in the course that he had adopted the Paramount Power would refuse to lend him support against any uprising of his subjects against his tyranny. The remonstrance had little effect upon the Maharaja.

Matters continued more or less in that condition till the twenties of this century when the signs of a certain degree of awakening and political consciousness began to appear in the valley. By the mid-1920s demonstrations were made and processions were taken out in protest against measures of the government which bore harshly upon the people. These demonstrations and processions were suppressed by severe police action in which people were beaten up and occasionally shot down and killed. Matters came to a head by 1930 when a series of riots took place which were mercilessly suppressed entailing considerable loss of life. The Muslims of the Punjab, among whom Kashmiris who had migrated from Kashmir into the Punjab held a high position and were counted among the leaders, were deeply stirred by these happenings but were unable to think of anything that could prove effective in helping their suffering and distressed fellow Muslims in Kashmir.

Hazrat Khalifatul Masih II had started taking a keen interest in the welfare of the people of Kashmir in early 1931 and wrote several articles in the *Al-Fazal* in April, June and July of that year, drawing attention to the pitiable condition of the Kashmir Muslims and inviting the Muslims of the Punjab to take some practical step towards providing relief for the Muslims of Kashmir and designed to persuade the government of Kashmir to introduce practical and effective reforms in its policies and in the administration of the State with the view of securing substantial improvement in the condition of the Muslims of the valley.

In the meantime the situation in the valley deteriorated

rapidly and on 13 July it became so critical that it was sought to be resolved by the use of massive force, in consequence of which seventy-two people were killed and a large number were wounded. When the Khalifatul Masih learnt the details of the tragic events he invited a dozen or so leading Muslims who were deeply interested in the situation in Kashmir to meet him at Simla on 25 July 1931 for consultation over the situation in Kashmir. When they got together the Khalifatul Masih felt that there was a general air of despondence, mainly due to the fact that there was little hope of anything effective being achieved as the Viceroy of India, as the representative of the King Emperor, was bound to shield and support the Maharaja by virtue of the treaty relationship between the Maharaja and the Paramount Power. The Khalifatul Masih felt that despite all this some practical step must be taken which should convince the people of Kashmir that a body in British India was taking sympathetic interest in their affairs, and the Maharaja and his advisers should be compelled to recognize that the people of Kashmir in their struggle for securing their basic human rights had the support of a strong and active organization across the borders of the State. Finally it was decided that an All India Kashmir Committee should be formed which should take all appropriate and feasible steps to secure their basic rights for the people of Kashmir, and that the Committee's activities should not cease till the full achievement of this purpose. Agreement having been reached on the setting up of the Committee all those who were present in the consultation expressed their eagerness to become members of the Committee and thus the Committee came into being. Immediately thereupon Dr Sir Muhammad Iqbal, who was himself an eminent Kashmiri, proposed that the Head of the Ahmadiyya Movement should be elected President of the Committee. His proposal was seconded by Khawaja Hasan Nizami Sahib and everyone present acclaimed it. The Khalifatul Masih expressed strong disapproval of the proposal to elect him President, but assured the committee that he and his Community would lend their full co-operation to the Committee. In answer to this Sir Muhammad Iqbal pointed out that the Head of the Ahmadiyya Movement had at his disposal a strong organization and plenty of workers and resources of every type and that unless he assumed the responsibilities of President of the Committee its purpose would not be achieved. The Khalifatul Masih was most reluctant to assume a position which in several respects would be inconsistent with his position as Spiritual Head of the Ahmadiyya Movement, but in view of the insistence of the members of the Committee and the strong urge towards going to the rescue of a people held in bondage, he overcame his reluctance and signified his assent to the proposal of Sir Muhammad Iqbal.

With the setting up of the All India Kashmir Committee a clamour was raised in Hindu circles that the Committee was a political organization that had been set up for the purpose of securing the removal of His Highness the Maharaja and that in effect it constituted a challenge to the Hindus on the part of the Muslims. In answer to this the Committee announced that the agitation in the State was in no sense directed against His Highness the Maharaja and that its purpose was the removal of the valid grievances of the Muslims of Kashmir and to reform the tyrannical form of the administration which had prevailed in Kashmir for a very long time. It was stressed that the Committee would strive to achieve its purpose through strictly constitutional methods and would not have recourse to unlawful activities.

It is difficult at this distance of time, and having regard to the changes that have taken place in the meantime, to attempt an accurate estimate of the tremendous, complicated and multifaceted responsibilities that the Khalifatul Masih undertook to discharge by assuming the position of the President of the All India Kashmir Committee. Judged by the almost revolutionary results that were achieved by the committee and its devoted workers over the short period of two years its performance was nothing short of miraculous, the greater part of the credit for which must go to the Khalifatul Masih.

The activities set in motion by the Committee under the direction of the Khalifatul Masih were bewilderingly multifarious. In the discharge of his responsibilities the Khalifatul Masih did not spare himself at all. If it became necessary to approach the Viceroy, he did not shrink from doing so, and if it was felt that his meeting the Maharaja might prove of help he was ready to face the ordeal.

The problems that confronted the Committee and its President extended all the way from providing relief for the distressed, to urging the officials of the Kashmir Administration to perform their duties in a spirit of helpfulness, sympathy and humanity, to providing legal aid for the very large number of the people of Kashmir who were prosecuted on false charges and were made the victims of police aggression and sometimes even of judicial repression. One feature of the struggle that was carried on by the Committee and its workers was that the situation was never permitted to become stale or passive. Once the workers of the Committee had seized the initiative they never let it go and always kept things on the move towards the desired objective.

To provide finances for all the multifarious activities of the Committee the Khalifatul Masih had to supplement the modest donations made to the Committee by its well-wishers, and for this purpose he imposed a cess on all members of the Movement in addition to the contributions that they made towards financing the Movement itself. The incidence of the Kashmir cess was not at all heavy and the members of the Movement paid the cess cheerfully for several years, even after the direct activities of the Committee had been wound up. Thereafter the proceeds of the cess were utilized for providing relief to the people of Kashmir in respect of their pressing needs.

At the end of the first year of the working of the Committee, which had been carried on with great devotion and earnestness by its workers under the wise and farseeing guidance of its President, the Khalifatul Masih insisted that a new President should be elected who should take over the responsibilities of the office. The members of the Committee, led by Dr Sir Muhammad Iqbal, refused to consider the suggestion of the Khalifatul Masih and unanimously urged him to continue his direction and guidance of the Committee and its workers, particularly in view of the very gratifying success that had already been achieved by the Committee contrary to all expectations. Reluctantly the Khalifatul Masih yielded to their request and agreed to carry on as President of the Committee for another year.

In the meantime Sir Reginald Glancy, Political Secretary of the Viceroy, was appointed to make an inquiry into the causes of unrest in Kashmir and to recommend what action, if any, was needed for the restoration of peaceful conditions in the State. Sir Reginald carried out his task with diligence in a sympathetic spirit, and in the report that he submitted to the Viceroy he tried in his recommendations to meet the principal grievances of the people as far as he was able to persuade the Maharaja to agree with him. The people of Kashmir and the Kashmir Committee were not altogether happy and satisfied with Sir Reginald's report and the Committee submitted a critical review of the recommendations of Sir Reginald Glancy to the Viceroy. Eventually the recommendations that were put into effect by the Maharaja brought considerable relief to the people of Kashmir who had suffered for so long under the tyranny of an oppressive régime. The attitude of the Maharaja might be judged from his obstinate resistance to some of the recommendations of Sir Reginald. For instance, one of the grievances of the Muslims of Kashmir was that the slaughter of his own cow by a Kashmiri Muslim was prohibited in the State as a capital offence, punishable with imprisonment for life. This imposed a severe hardship upon an average Kashmiri who carried on a wretched existence in conditions of grinding poverty. For him even an old barren cow which had ceased to yield much milk was a valuable asset. Instead of letting it die of old age and decrepitude, he would wish to slaughter it in the autumn and preserve its meat as the principal source of protein for his family during the severe cold of the winter. In extreme cases a person in that situation adopted that course secretly at the risk of losing his liberty for life. Sir Reginald tried to persuade the Maharaja to agree to the abolition of this offence, or at least to the reduction of the penalty to a nominal chastisement. The Maharaja would not hear of it. The utmost that Sir Reginald was able to wrest from a reluctant Maharaja was the concession that the penalty for the offence might be reduced to rigorous imprisonment for ten years.

Another instance in which the efforts of Sir Reginald Glancy towards meeting a grievance of the Muslims of the State were completely frustrated by the stubbornness of the Maharaja, was a law under which a Hindu who became a convert to Islam forfeited his share in the family property and his right of inheritance to the property of a deceased member of the family. When Sir Reginald urged the Maharaja to agree to a repeal of this outdated instance of bigotry the Maharaja's firm reply was that he would rather abdicate than agree to the suggestion. In the face of this threat Sir Reginald felt himself unable to carry the matter further.

A short time before the All India Kashmir Committee had been set up a new political party had been formed in the Punjab called the Ahrar (the Free). Its membership was confined to Muslims and its leadership was vested in persons whose only purpose was to exploit every situation for their personal benefit. In their political outlook they supported the policies of the All India National Congress and the bulk of the Muslims of the Punjab looked upon them as the Muslim wing of the Congress. They were not, however, firmly committed to any set of principles or policies. They trimmed their sails according to the direction of the prevailing wind. The only policy to which they consistently adhered was their proclaimed virulent opposition to the Ahmadiyya Movement. This attitude of theirs was not inspired by any concern for religious doctrine or teaching but had been prompted by the consideration that opposition to and hostility towards the Movement would win them easy popularity among the bulk of orthodox Muslims.

When the All India Kashmir Committee was formed, the Khalifatul Masih requested two or three members of the Committee to try to persuade two outstanding leaders of the Ahrar to join the Committee. They declined on the ground that they would like to work on their own for the achievement of the purposes for which the Committee had been formed. The Khalifatul Masih, suspecting that their refusal to join the Committee might have been prompted by their opposition to him and the Movement, told the intermediaries that if the refusal of the Ahrar leaders to join the Committee was due to his presidentship of the Committee, he would be prepared to resign the presidentship in order to conciliate them, but even this self-denying gesture failed to overcome their reluctance to join the Committee. The Committee, however, was already fully representative of all types of political thinking and religious beliefs and doctrines among the Muslims.

During the first year of the working of the Committee the Ahrar leadership manifested little interest in the purpose, objective, or activities of the Committee, probably out of a feeling that the Committee would not be able to achieve any notable success and might only draw upon itself the opposition and hostility of the non-Muslims of the State and of the Punjab. The Ahrar were anxious to enjoy the goodwill of the non-Muslims on account of their political accord with the All India National Congress. However, when they observed that the Committee was advancing steadily towards the achievement of its objective and had established a standing both with the Viceroy and the Maharaja and the authorities of the State, the leadership of the Ahrar felt it was time for them to set up a front of their own on the Kashmir question. They tried to win the support of Muslim opinion by the utterly false representation that the President of the All India Kashmir Committee was seeking to promote the interests of the Ahmadiyya Movement in Kashmir behind the screen of the Committee. Their hostility to the Movement and their jealousy of the Khalifatul Masih were the real factors that motivated their actions in connection with the situation in

Kashmir, and not any real desire to serve and promote the interests of the Muslims of Kashmir. They had recourse to devices like picketing, etc., on the borders of the State and endeavoured to persuade the Muslims of the State to adopt measures that were more spectacular than helpful. They succeeded in persuading some members of the Committee that there should be a change in the presidency of the Committee.

The Khalifatul Masih had, throughout, been anxious that the presidentship of the Committee should not become a matter of controversy or conflict. He had taken care that nothing should be done that might be relied on to lend colour to anything of the kind to which the Ahrar leadership began to have recourse later. But when he perceived that despite all his care the Ahrar leadership was behaving in a manner that could occasion serious prejudice to the interests of the Muslims of Kashmir, he decided not to continue his presidency of the Committee beyond the end of the second year. On his resignation Dr Sir Muhammad Iqbal was elected President of the Committee. The Khalifatul Masih directed the Ahmadi workers of the Committee and the Ahmadi lawyers who provided advice and aid free of charge to the Muslims of the State to continue the work in full co-operation with the Committee. But the withdrawal of the Khalifatul Masih from the presidency of the Committee seems to have extinguished the spirit of the Committee and gradually all life departed from it.

On one occasion before his resignation from the presidency of the Kashmir Committee the Khalifatul Masih met Chaudhri Afzal Haq, President of Majlis Ahrar at the invitation of Sir Sikandar Hayat Khan, Chief Minister of the Punjab, who was seeking to bring about an understanding between the Ahrar and the Kashmir Committee. In the course of the conversation Chaudhri Afzal Haq told the Khalifatul Masih that as the Ahmadiyya Community had opposed him in the elections to the Punjab Legislative Council, the Ahrar had determined to crush the Ahmadiyya

Movement. The Khalifatul Masih pointed out that the Movement claimed to have been founded under Divine direction. If this claim was true, as surely it was, neither the Ahrar nor any other organization, or combination of organizations, nor any government would have the power to crush it. Whoever set himself up against the Movement would be crushed under Divine decree. On the other hand, if the claim of the Movement was false, Chaudhri Afzal Haq or the Ahrar need not bestir themselves to bring about the disintegration of the Movement. It would be destroyed under Divine direction. From that point onwards, for a period of about three years, the Ahrar put forth their utmost effort and had recourse to every type of device to bring about the decline and disintegration of the Movement.

Even after his resignation from the presidency of the Kashmir Committee, the Khalifatul Masih continued to take keen interest in the promotion of the welfare of the Muslims of the State of Jammu and Kashmir. Many of the workers drawn from the Movement who had rendered devoted service to the people of Kashmir under the auspices of the Kashmir Committee continued their useful activities under the direction of the Khalifatul Masih. A large number of Ahmadi lawyers continued to render legal assistance to the persecuted people of the State. This phase of voluntary selfless service continued till the Muslims of the State were enabled, by virtue of the constitutional and administrative reforms that had been put into effect under the impact of the Kashmir Committee and its first President, to stand on their own feet and push forward their struggle for further amelioration of their condition without outside help. During the initial phase of the Kashmir Committee's advocacy of the cause of the Muslims of Kashmir, the Khalifatul Masih had helped them to choose their local leaders wisely and then to give them their full support. It was at that time that Shaikh Muhammad Abdullah assumed the position of leadership in the affairs of Kashmir under the advice and encouragement of the Khalifatul Masih.

In the early thirties of this century Sir Herbert Emerson was Governor of the Punjab. He was an able officer but had an exaggerated notion of his political acumen and foresight. He had looked askance at the activities of the Kashmir Committee, and felt that as a religious leader the Khalifatul Masih should not have identified himself with the Committee. He was no doubt aware of the organization of the Ahmadiyya Community and misinterpreted it as a parallel government. He suspected that the Movement was a sort of state within a state and might one day become a danger for the government. He was, of course, not unaware of the hostility of the Ahrar towards the Ahmadiyya Movement and its Head. This was his frame of mind when the Ahrar made an application for permission to hold a propaganda conference at a place in the close vicinity of Qadian, in October 1934. It was a clumsily conceived plan as there could be no possible religious purpose that could be served by holding a conference so close to Qadian. At whom was the propaganda proceeding from the conference to be directed? The conference was proposed to be convened in an area the population around which, with the exception of Qadian, was mainly non-Muslim. If the purpose of the conference was to alienate the Ahmadis from their allegiance to the Khalifah, or to repudiate their belief in the claims of the Founder of the Movement, they knew and the government must have been aware that not a single Ahmadi would attend the conference or go anywhere near it, if for no other reason than to avoid all risk of friction or conflict. Yet the government granted permission to the Ahrar to hold the conference.

The Secretary of the Khalifatul Masih whose duty it was to make arrangements for the security of Qadian against any possible ill designs of the organizers of the conference, sent letters to branches of the Movement within a reasonable distance of Qadian requiring despatch to Qadian of a specified number of volunteers who would act as watch and ward units around Qadian for the purpose of ensuring the security of Qadian against any attempt to disrupt it. When the Superintendent of Police of the district learnt of the despatch of these letters, he proceeded to Qadian and assured the Secretary concerned that government would take adequate measures for safeguarding the security of Qadian during the period of the conference, and suggested that the letters that had been issued by the Secretary might be recalled or cancelled. The Secretary expressed his satisfaction over the assurance of the Superintendent of Police and agreed that the letters would be recalled. Thereafter prompt action was taken to recall the letters. It appears that the Governor, who had been apprised of the earlier developments and had been notified by the District Magistrate of the issue of the letters, was not immediately informed of the action taken to have the letters recalled. Acting upon his earlier information he directed the issue of a notice under the Criminal Law Amendment Act to the Khalifatul Masih calling upon him to stop the inflow of members of the Movement into Qadian during the period of the conference, to provide no accommodation or food for any members of the Movement who might arrive at Qadian during that period, and to take certain other specified measures which were designed to obviate the risk of any conflict between the Ahrar and the members of the Movement.

Apart from the fact that the need for the issue of such a notice to anyone had disappeared in consequence of the understanding reached between the Superintendent of Police and the Secretary concerned, the issue of the notice was open to serious objection on several grounds. The notice was directed to and was served upon the Khalifatul Masih, who had not been concerned with the issue of the letters to which objection was taken by the district authorities. The notice aimed at forbidding a legitimate activity, namely, members of the Movement visiting Qadian, their religious centre, freely without let or hindrance, at all times as they had been accustomed to, while no restriction was placed on the movements of those who intended to foregather in the conference. The issue of the notice created a grave situation as it affected the dignity and honour of the revered Head of the Movement.

The conference was held in this strained atmosphere, which was rendered highly explosive by the foul and fiery speeches made at the conference in which the Founder, the Head and members of the Movement were slandered and reviled and provoked beyond endurance. The situation was saved by the restraint observed by the members of the Movement and their ready and cheerful welcome that was extended to all those who desired to visit Qadian and see places of interest and offices and institutions of the Movement and observe their working. Such visitors were shown every courtesy and were taken round to see and observe whatever they wished. Some of them later joined the Movement. One of them is now the Chief Mufti (Jurist) of the Movement.

But the sequel of the issue of the notice under the Criminal Law Amendment Act brought about a situation of crisis and tension between the government and the Movement. The Khalifatul Masih explained the whole background of the situation in detail for the information of the members of the Movement all over the world in his Friday sermons and condemned the government action in strong but not provocative terms. Every Friday two police officers in plain clothes arrived in Qadian on motorcycles to note down the Khalifa's address and motored back to the headquarters of the district so that their report of the address might be translated speedily into English and despatched quickly to Government House in Lahore. Thus the Governor studied the report of the address first thing every Saturday morning. This situation dragged on for some weeks and the Governor then made an approach to the Khalifatul Masih through a prominent member of the Movement. He expressed his regret over the mistake that had been made in permitting the conference to be held in the vicinity of Qadian, and he confessed that the Ahrar had abused the opportunity that the conference afforded them by their vile abuse of the Founder and the

Head of the Movement. He expressed his appreciation of and sympathy with the point of view of the Khalifatul Masih, but he expressed the hope that the Khalifatul Masih having made his point of view and his position quite clear should now treat the matter as having been closed. When this was conveyed to the Khalifatul Masih he explained that he had aired the matter publicly not out of any desire for personal gratification or with the purpose of humiliating the government, but solely to uphold the dignity and honour of the Movement which had been grossly affronted. If he were suddenly to become silent over the matter his forbearance might be misconstrued as submission to the point of view of the government under threat of coercion. The Governor appreciated the apprehension of the Khalifatul Masih and the matter was eventually settled by means of a letter from the Home Secretary of the Provincial Government addressed to the Khalifatul Masih in which the government expressed its appreciation of the point of view of the Khalifatul Masih and its regret at the mistaken action of the government. On his side the Khalifatul Masih in his next Friday sermon announced that as the government had expressed its appreciation of his point of view and acknowledged that a mistake had been made in issuing the notice under the Criminal Law Amendment Act, the matter was now amicably settled and was finally closed. In a subsequent meeting between the Khalifatul Masih and the Governor which came about by chance, they were able to remove any lingering misunderstandings in their minds. But incidents continued to happen which demonstrated that a section of the official hierarchy still entertained feelings of strong prejudice against the Movement.

When Sir Herbert Emerson's term as Governor was approaching its end he was granted an extension for two years and a half. Before starting his extended term he took four months' leave and went home. Towards the end of his leave, when he was preparing to return to Lahore, he suffered a severe attack of internal haemorrhage while playing golf.

His medical advisers had some difficulty in determining the cause of the haemorrhage but advised him that he must not even think of returning to the tropics, and that he would have to undergo a lengthy course of treatment and observe a long period of convalescence. He was thus compelled to resign the Governorship and stayed on in England. Within a few weeks he was restored to the enjoyment of his normal robust health, but it was too late now for his resumption of the Governorship. Later he was able to serve for a term as Commissioner for Refugees under the League of Nations.

But out of evil came a great deal of good. In his three Friday addresses on 23 and 30 November and 7 December 1934, the Khalifatul Masih set forth a scheme before the Community with regard to which he had already alerted it, which made nineteen demands from the members of the Movement. Initially the operation of the scheme was limited to three years, but before the expiry of the period it was made permanent. He named the scheme Tahrik Jadeed (New Scheme). To finance the scheme he appealed to the Community to provide Rs 27,500 for the expenses of the first year. The Community made a splendid response to his appeal and in addition to all other contributions provided Rs 107,000 for Tahrik Jadeed which was nearly four times the amount for which he had appealed.

His nineteen demands, which were subsequently raised to twenty-four, were aimed mainly at rousing the spirit of sacrifice in the Community, stimulating their moral and spiritual qualities and broadening the base of the Movement by carrying its message far and wide. For instance, he urged the adoption of a simple, and in some respects even an austere, mode of life in the matter of food, dress, housing, furnishings, etc. He forbade attendance at cinemas, theatres, circuses and places of amusement generally. He urged the cultivation of the habit of manual labour. He made an appeal for a certain number of dedicated workers. He urged the unemployed to occupy themselves in some kind of work or to work honorarily, or in return for a meagre stipend, for the Movement. He invited pensioners and people who had retired from service to volunteer for work for the Movement. He urged everyone to occupy themselves most of the time with earnest supplications to God seeking His help and guidance and the bounty of steadfastness in His cause. He explained the purpose of each of these demands.

He predicted:

> Even if you should all abandon me God will provide me with resources from a hidden source. But it cannot be that what God Almighty told the Promised Messiah, the scheme for which he has disclosed to me, should not happen. It is bound to happen even if I am abandoned by everyone. In such a contingency God will descend from heaven and will complete the construction of this mansion.

On another occasion he said:

> We shall not coerce anyone, nor shall we embark on a campaign of civil disobedience, we shall respect the law, and despite all this we shall discharge all those responsibilities with which we have been charged by Ahmadiyyat. We shall carry out all the obligations which God and the Holy Prophet, peace be on him, have imposed on us, and yet the purpose of our scheme will be achieved. The Captain of the Ark of Ahmadiyyat will steer this holy Ark between fearful rocks and will bring it safe to port. This is my faith and I am firmly established in it. The reason of those to whom the leadership of divine movements is committed is placed under Divine guidance; they are bestowed light by God Almighty, and his angels guard them. They are supported by the gracious attributes of God. When they pass on from the world and present themselves before their Maker, the projects they embark upon continue to make progress and God Almighty makes them successful and prosperous.

The Community made an eager response to every one of the demands made by the Khalifatul Masih and from the very start the Tahrik Jadeed began to produce very encouraging results. In the beginning the Khalifatul Masih had made participation in Tahrik Jadeed voluntary, but before the expiry of its initial period of three years he made it compulsory upon the whole Community and made it permanent. Large numbers of volunteers were trained to work in various capacities in the different branches of the Tahrik. Literature needed for the exposition of the purposes, teachings and beliefs of the Movement was prepared and printed. In short everything in the Movement was charged with new life and a new spirit under the impact of the Tahrik.

The most striking activity of the Tahrik was the network of foreign missions that was progressively spread into many countries of the world, so that there is scarcely a region in which missions have not been established by now, or at least into which the literature of the Movement has not penetrated. Some idea of the progress made so far in the achievement of the purposes of the Tahrik may be formed from the fact that the budget of the Tahrik has risen from the original Rs 27,500 to a million and a half rupees today. This does not take into account extraordinary expenditure that is incurred in respect of special projects in different parts of the world. As time has passed the Tahrik has added to its original objectives diverse types of beneficent projects; schools, dispensaries and hospitals have been opened in widely separated regions of the earth. Mosques have been built in all the continents. For all these projects finance has had to be provided through special funds running into thousands, and on occasions into hundreds of thousands, of pounds sterling. There are flourishing branches of the Movement in more than forty countries, while individual members and small groups are scattered all round the globe.

All this activity is instrumental in the effort of achieving the ultimate purpose of the Movement, namely, the cultivation of the highest moral and spiritual qualities, seeking all the time to establish communion with God for the purpose of winning His pleasure and rendering beneficent service to His creatures without any discrimination.

In 1935 a controversy arose in which the Movement was not directly involved but in which its sympathies were with the bulk of the Muslims to whom it lent its moral support. The Ahrar ranged themselves on the opposite side. Feelings rose high and the Ahrar became the subjects of opprobrium and execration on the part of the mass of the Muslims. They rapidly lost favour and were no longer trusted or respected. Their original leadership has passed on and they drag along as a despised remnant.

CHAPTER THIRTEEN

The part played by Khalifatul Masih II in affairs that were not primarily of a religious character should not leave anyone under the impression that his main interest at any time centered on those matters. It was characteristic of him that whatever he undertook he carried through with full attention in a serious spirit, mobilizing all the resources that were needed for the purpose. Besides, the matters in which he took a lead, though not at the centre of religion, were not outside its scope. As has already been mentioned his definition of religion comprehended everything that bore immediately or ultimately on the welfare of any section of mankind. This was not a definition invented by him, but was the definition of Islam derived from the Holy Quran and the example of the Holy Prophet, peace be on him. In giving practical effect to his definition, however, he did not in the least overlook the gradations and priorities that have been established by Islam for the co-ordination of all values affecting human welfare. For him the moral and the spiritual had always top priority. He never neglected the practical upholding of this priority in the least particular. In choosing the immediate objective, in settling a policy, in adopting a procedure, he took the utmost care that the true and ultimate objective, namely winning the pleasure of God, should not be subordinated to, or laid aside even temporarily for the sake of anything else, however tempting it might appear at the moment. At no time did he neglect in the least degree the guidance needed by the Community and the constant supervision of the conduct and behaviour of every member of it, in order to secure that the Community should continue to march steadily forward on the path that led to God and should not be deflected a hair's breadth in one direction or the other. For instance, whenever he noticed a tendency on the part of anyone to exalt the

Founder of the Movement in a manner that might be misconstrued as placing him in juxtaposition to the Holy Prophet, peace be on him, he snuffed it out instantly and made it quite clear, as the Promised Messiah had himself done repeatedly, that everything that was bestowed upon him was due to his devoted obedience to the Holy Prophet, and as a spiritual reflection of the Holy Prophet, peace be on him. On the other hand, he constantly reminded the community that in the words of the Holy Prophet, peace be on him, the Promised Messiah was a just arbiter and that all his pronouncements were binding upon the community and not one of them could be contravened with impunity.

He laboured constantly to build up the organization of the Community so as to fashion it as an effective instrument for the achievement of the purposes of the Movement. For instance, in 1922 he established the Advisory Consultative Council of the Movement which is normally convened once a year to submit its advice to the Khalifa on such matters as might be committed to it for advice. It is composed of elected representatives of every branch of the Movement in the country. Practical considerations have imposed the limitation of representation in the Council to branches of the Movement in the country, but it is visualized that on the needed facilities becoming available representation would be extended to branches of the Movement outside the country also.

The Khalifatul Masih himself presides over the deliberations of the Council, except on the rare occasion when any matter involving the personal interest of the Khalifa is the subject of consideration.

The Council also discusses the Annual Budget of the Movement and submits its recommendations on it. After the session of the Council is opened with an address by the Khalifatul Masih, committees are set up for the detailed consideration of the items on the agenda of the Council, and submit their reports to the Council for discussion and the formulation of its recommendations. In the course of these discussions points constantly arise bearing upon the true appreciation of moral and spiritual values. At the conclusion of the discussion of each item the Khalifatul Masih sums up the points that arise in the course of the discussion and pronounces upon them, furnishing the needed guidance on every point. On the advice tendered by the Council and the recommendations submitted by it the Khalifatul Masih normally announces his decision at the end of his observations, but sometimes reserves the matter for further reflection. He generally accepts the advice tendered or the recommendations made by a majority of the Council, but if he is of the view that the advice or recommendation ignores or runs counter to some principle the upholding of which is an obligation that can not be contravened, he sets forth an exposition of the principle involved and rejects the advice or recommendation or announces his acceptance in a modified form which is not open to objection on principle.

Every session of the Council proves a most exhilarating experience for the participants on account of the opportunities of moral and spiritual training that it affords for every participant. The discussions in the Council are carried on at a very high level and compare very favourably with the proceedings and discussions of other bodies of a comparable character outside the Movement.

Every section of the Community is organized in an Association for the purpose of proper training in the exercise of moral and spiritual values and marching forward towards the achievement of the purposes of the Movement.

The Majlis Ansarullah (Association of the Helpers of God), is composed of all male members of the Movement over the age of 40 years. The Majlis Khuddamul Ahmadiyya (Association of the Servants of Ahmadiyyat), is composed of all male members of the Movement between the ages of 15 and 40 years. Atfalul Ahmadiyya (Children of Ahmadiyyat) is composed of male children between the ages of 7 and 15 years. Lajnah Ima Allah (Association of the Handmaidens of God) includes all female members of the Movement above the age of 15 years. Nasiratul Ahmadiyya (Female Helpers of God) comprises all female children between the ages of 7 and 15 years. Each of these associations has its own office bearers and is constantly active in promoting the moral and spiritual values inculcated by Islam. One feature of the training of all sections of the Community, which is thus bound together in affectionate ties of brotherhood and sisterhood, is that all members under the auspices of their particular association carry out without discrimination programmes of manual labour, designed to uphold the dignity of labour. The female sections also carry out programmes designed to stimulate their artistic faculties and to train them in the various branches of domestic science and household duties.

From the very beginning of his Khilafat, Khalifatul Masih II was very keen on promoting literacy and education in all sections of the Community. He paid special attention to the education of women. As the result of his directions and the methods that he adopted for the achievement of his purpose in this regard, the average standard of education among the men and women of the Movement is today considerably higher than that prevailing among the sister communities in each region. This is true not only in respect of the branches of the Community in Pakistan, Bangladesh and India but also in the case of the branches of the community in other backward regions, more particularly in Africa.

The Madrissah Ahmadiyyah which had been established for religious instruction was raised to the status of Jamiah (Higher Seminary) designed to train scholars to serve as missionaries of Islam in different parts of the world.

An Islamic solar calendar was introduced supplementing the current lunar calendar, for facilitating the comparative study of the history and progress of Islam.

The Khalifatul Masih kept reminding the Community of the obligations that lay upon it with regard to the propagation of Islam. For instance, he said:

Today the way of promoting the progress of Islam through

swords, or rifles, or cannon, or naval vessels, or aircraft has been wholly blocked. Every citadel that the companions of the Holy Prophet had constructed by shedding their blood is being demolished and there appears no possibility of safeguarding those citadels with swords, rifles, cannon and aircraft. But there is on the surface of the earth a Community whose hearts are filled with the faith and the certainty that these crumbling citadels will be restored not through cannon, swords, rifles or aircraft, but through propaganda, education, admonition and exposition. That Community is the Ahmadiyya Community. The renaissance of Islam will be undertaken by that Community. The standard of the Holy Prophet, peace be on him, will be planted again not on any height, nor on the top of any mountain, nor on a bastion of any citadel, but in the hearts of the peoples of the world. There can be no doubt that a standard planted in the hearts rises higher, is stronger and is more enduring than the one that is planted on the top of a mountain or on a bastion of a citadel.

On another occasion he stated:

I have said it several times and now repeat it emphatically that the West has been supreme in the world for a long period, but it is now the divine design to crush the Western social and cultural systems. Those who are fearful and are afraid to oppose Western values and consider that the veil can no longer be maintained and that it is necessary that men and women shall mix freely in social intercourse and that we cannot make any progress unless we follow the West in these matters, should remember that in adopting this attitude they are obstructing the progress of Islam and Ahmadiyyat. These things are bound to be wiped out and will disappear altogether. Many of you will be alive to witness the collapse of the structure of Western values and you will observe the new palaces of Islam being reared upon the ruins of Western values. These are not the words of a man; it is the decree of the God of heaven and earth and no one can change it. It is not a question of our strength. We have never said that this change will be brought about through our strength, nor shall we ever say it. What we do say is that God has promised this change and we have always witnessed the unchangeability of divine promises. After this observation there is nothing that can shake our faith or weaken our beliefs. Most certainly the world will approach us humbly on its knees and will have to accept this change. Then, have no fear that if we raise our voice in support of the veil and against mixed schools our girls will rebel against it or their parents will rise against it. Not only the girls and their parents but those who are giving currency to such ideas will apologize to us on their knees. It will never happen that our women may discard the veil and we may be put to shame and become remorseful in this context. The advocates of these new-fangled ideas will come before us with heads bent in shame and remorse and would confess that they had been following the wrong path and that the right path is the one laid down by Islam. This is a divine decree and no power, no government, no kingdom can obstruct its enforcement. . . . So prepare yourselves for these changes and keep supplicating God Almighty and cultivate certainty and confidence. The day you are filled with certainty, all your doubts and suspicions and apprehensions will disappear and you will find yourselves standing firmly on a strong and high minaret of progress.

In March 1939 Khalifatul Masih II completed 25 years of his Khalifat. During this period the Movement had gone forward in leaps and bounds and the message of Ahmadiyyat had been carried to the ends of the earth. It was felt by some members of the Movement that this was a fit occasion for a celebration by way of gratitude to God Almighty for all these numberless bounties and His guardianship and protection of the Community throughout, in the face of trials and dangers. When this idea was submitted to the Khalifatul Masih, he signified his assent to such a celebration not because of the completion of 25 years of his Khalifat but because of the completion of the first 50 years of the Movement, adding that the completion of the first century of the Movement should be celebrated with great *éclat*.

The celebration of the jubilee took place during the Annual Conference of 1939. The whole proceeding, the addresses, the march to the site of the Conference, the illumination of the white Minar, etc., were carried through with great dignity and in a spirit of prayerful gratitude to the Divine for all His bounties. The Standard of Ahmadiyyat was adopted and raised for the first time. On the occasion of the raising of the standard all those present in the Conference made the following covenant:

I promise that I shall continue to strive, to the last moment of my life, to the utmost of my strength and understanding for the strengthening of Islam and Ahmadiyyat and for their widest propagation. With the help of God Almighty, I shall make every sacrifice for the achievement of this purpose so that Ahmadiyyat, that is to say, the true Islam, should prevail over all other faiths and dispensations and its Standard should never be lowered and should fly above all other standards.

In reply to the addresses presented to the Khalifatul Masih, he made a speech in the course of which he stated:

Ever since the celebration was projected I have been troubled by the feeling that it might become a precedent for birthdays and other similar celebrations. I was afraid lest in consequence of this celebration the Community might get involved in such ceremonies as it is the purpose of Ahmadiyyat to wipe out. Our success and victory consist in reviving the faith and restoring it to the condition in which the Holy Prophet, peace be on him, had established it. We should establish it in such manner that Satan may not be able to mount an assault upon it, and no door or window or ventilator may be left open for him. I have been reflecting lest by such celebrations we might open a ventilator for the entry of Satan. I have, therefore, felt a constraint, why did I give permission for this celebration? The first feeling of reassurance was generated in my mind by the appreciation of one aspect mentioned by Maulvi Jalalud Din Shams in one of his articles that this is an occasion of celebration also because the Movement has completed 50 years of its life. Thus, I realized that this celebration can be attributed to the Movement rather than to an individual and that I can myself join in this joyous event. The second reassurance was generated in my mind when the poem of the Promised Messiah, peace be on him, named Ameen was being recited and I felt that this celebration is an occasion of proclaiming the fulfilment of a prophecy of the Promised Messiah. I, therefore, felt that my participation in it is not improper. . . . Thus, the constraint that I had felt was removed and I looked up from this meeting to God Almighty and was filled with wonder how true our God is. . . . On listening to the supplication that the Promised Messiah had made in his poem, I realized that God Almighty had heard his prayers. When these supplications were made, I was not able to decipher even elementary Readers of English, but such is the grace of God Almighty that today I can read and understand the most difficult English book on any subject whatever. Though I cannot write English, yet I can appraise intelligently the compositions of graduates and Masters. I was taken through the Holy Quran and Bokhari by Hazrat Khalifatul Masih I, who helped me to reflect myself on their meaning in consequence of which I have been bestowed an unlimited treasure. God Almighty has so instructed me in these matters that I can affirm without pride that my mind is never overcome by reading any book or any commentary, as I realize that whatever I have been bestowed by the grace of God Almighty was not granted to the authors of those books and commentaries. . . . It is the grace and bounty of God Almighty that hearing the supplications of the Promised Messiah, peace be on him, He has taught me a principle through which I am bestowed divine help on all occasions. I have always said that I am an instrument in the hands of God and that I have never felt that He has withheld from me that of which I was in need. The Promised Messiah supplicated that God may remove all darkness from me. My opponents attacked me time after time and proclaimed that they would wipe out the Khilafat. This was the darkness that God Almighty removed and the constraint that I had felt with regard to this celebration was removed by listening to this poem and I felt that the fulfilment of the prophecy of the Promised messiah was being proclaimed. My opponents had said that they would persuade the Community to turn away from me, but God Almighty said that He would bring more and more people into the Community. When He desires to manifest His light no darkness can withstand it. Thus, my heart was comforted about this celebration. Otherwise, I was somewhat ashamed that this celebration should be attributed to me. But all that we undertake is for the sake of God Almighty and as His words are being fulfilled through this celebration, I see no harm in it. All this is the doing of God Almighty. If He had not done it neither you nor I had the power to do it. Nothing has been achieved through my knowledge or through your sacrifices. Whatever has been achieved has been brought about by the grace of God. We are happy that God

Almighty has manifested another sign. The world desired to wipe us out, but God Almighty preserved us. Perceiving this the constraint that I had felt was totally removed. . . . I am grateful to all those who have expressed their joy on this occasion and pray that God may be pleased to reward them in the best manner. I also pray that the remaining days of my life may continue to be devoted through divine grace to the service and support of Islam and towards strengthening it and establishing its supremacy; so that when I am called to His presence I should not be put to shame and should be able to say: 'I have carried out the service that Thou had committed to me, through the strength bestowed by Thee.' I further pray that God Almighty may bestow His grace upon us and may enable us to act righteously and may remove any weakness that may lurk in any heart and may strengthen our sincerity and may cause our lives to be devoted to Him and may make our lives and our deaths pleasant, so that when the dwellers of Paradise hear about us they should feel happy that more pure spirits are about to join them.

At the conclusion of his speech a cheque of the amount of Rs 270,000 was presented to the Khalifatul Masih with the request that he might spend it as he pleased.

In the Annual Conference of that year the Khalifatul Masih spoke on 28 and 29 December on the Islamic System of Khilafat in a very comprehensive way and in the course of his speech said:

There is a distinction between my Khilafat and the Khilafat of those Khalifas who have passed away. Their Khilafat is today a subject of intellectual exposition; my Khilafat is related miraculously to the signs manifested in support of it. The question whether any verse is related to my Khilafat or not is irrelevant. The ever-fresh signs of God Almighty and His living miracles are sufficient proof that God has made me Khalifa and there is no one who can stand in opposition to me. If there is anyone among you who is eager to oppose me let him do so, God will humiliate and disgrace him. Not only this, even if all the powers of the earth were to join together to destroy my Khilafat, God will squeeze them out like a mosquito. Whoever rises in opposition to me will be pulled down, whoever speaks against me will be silenced, and whoever attempts to humiliate me will be humiliated and disgraced.

Therefore, O Community of believers, and O workers of righteousness, I say to you that the Khilafat is a great bounty of God Almighty. Value it as such. So long as the Majority of you continue established in faith and righteous conduct, God will continue to bestow this bounty upon you. But should a majority of you be deprived of faith and righteous conduct, then it will be for the Divine will to determine whether to continue this bounty or to withdraw it. Thus, there is no question of the Khalifa going wrong. You will be deprived of the Khilafat when you yourselves become corrupt. Do not, therefore, be ungrateful for this divine bounty and do not slight the revelations of God Almighty, but as the Promised Messiah, peace be on him, has said: 'Continue your supplications so that the second manifestation of divine power may continue to be displayed for you all the time. Do not be like those frustrated, despairing and ignorant ones who have rejected the Khilafat. Continue to be occupied with the supplication that God Almighty may continue to raise among you the bearers of the second divine manifestation of power, so that His religion may be established on strong foundations and Satan should despair forever of creating any disruption in it.'

You should know that the condition of supplication that the Promised Messiah has imposed for the display of the second manifestation of divine power is not limited to any particular period, but is perpetual. During the lifetime of the Promised Messiah it meant that in his time the object of the supplication should be that you may be blessed with the first Khilafat. In the first Khilafat its purpose was that you may be blessed with the second Khilafat. During the period of the second Khilafat this supplication means that you may be bestowed the third Khilafat. During the third Khilafat the purpose of this supplication would be that you may be bestowed the fourth Khilafat, lest the door of this bounty might be closed upon you in consequence of your own misconduct. Then continue occupied with supplications to God Almighty and keep well in mind that so long as the Khilafat continues among you no power on earth will be able to overcome you, and you will be helped and will be victorious in every field; for this is the divine promise which He has expressed in these words: 'Allah has promised those among you who believe and act righteously that He will surely make them Successors in the earth; but also remember this warning: Those who disbelieve thereafter, they will be the rebellious ones' (24:56). May God be with you and may you continue to be His chosen Community through eternity.

The Khalifatul Masih received very clear intimation through a dream of the breakout of the Second World War a couple of years ahead of the commencement of hostilities. In August of 1939 he saw another dream in which he felt that the war had broken out and that France and Britain were being hard pressed by Germany and that the British Prime Minister had invited France to unite with Britain, thus forming one country, under one government, so that the war could be prosecuted on the side of the allies with greater vigour and strength. This dream was fulfilled in an astonishing manner in June 1940 when Mr Winston Churchill made exactly that offer to the French.

In June 1940 the Khalifatul Masih saw in a dream that he was put in charge of the defence of Britain and that on taking stock of everything he said: 'There is great weakness in the air, if this could be remedied there is a good prospect of Britain pulling through.' On this, as if by way of reassurance, he saw a piece of paper which contained a news item that two thousand three hundred military aircraft were being despatched from America to Britain. A few days later the news came through that on the fall of France the orders that had been placed in the United States, by the French Military Purchasing Mission, had been switched over to the British Military Purchasing Mission and that it was expected that two thousand five hundred military aircraft would be despatched to Britain. This was followed within two or three days by the definite announcement that two thousand three hundred military aircraft had been despatched to Britain.

During the progress of the war, the Khalifatul Masih saw several dreams which indicated the course that hostilities were likely to take and which were all fulfilled according to their purport. Every one of them constituted a divine sign that he enjoyed continuous communion with God.

In the spring of 1943 he stated:

I conceive that the war will not now last much longer. In the first half of 1945 it will either come to an end or will have reached a stage when it will become clear to everyone how it is going to end. The foundation for that end will be laid in this year, 1943. But that will not be the end of all this travail. God Almighty will prolong these tribulations till the people who have to take over the governments of the world have been properly trained.

In the seventeenth chapter of the Holy Quran it is stated that Moses, peace be on him, and his companion observed a wall that was about to fall down and they repaired it and put it in good order gratuitously. Their action was prompted by the fact that under the wall there was a treasure belonging to two orphans, and God Almighty desired that the treasure should be safeguarded till they attained their maturity. The present situation is that in this case the treasure that has to be safeguarded can be preserved secure not by repairing a wall but by pulling it down. God Almighty is pulling down these worldly systems gradually and not at one stroke, because those to whom the rebuilding of this structure is to be committed are being trained in the divine academy of engineering and have not yet completed their training. If all the old structures were to be demolished suddenly there would be an hiatus. That is why God Almighty is demolishing these structures gradually. One wall is pulled down today and another is pulled down tomorrow. One roof is blown up today and another is blown up tomorrow. One room disappears today and another disappears tomorrow. In this way gradually and step by step God Almighty is pulling down, ruining and destroying all the structures, all the mansions and all the materials of the world. He does not design the complete ruin of these structures till those who are being trained in the divine academy have completed their training and are ready to take over. This is the way that God Almighty has opened for the progress of our Community. This change is bound to come about one day, but it is approaching gradually so that those who have to take over should be enabled to complete their training.

The Khalifatul Masih always worked very hard and never spared himself. At the best of times he was in indifferent health and sometimes his health broke down for weeks and months. Even during such periods he did not lay aside his work altogether. His magnum opus was a detailed commentary on the Holy Quran which he called *Tafseer Kabeer* (The Great Commentary). It is a most valuable exposition of the numberless verities comprised in the Holy Quran and is a great milestone in the history of the exegesis of the Holy Quran. It has drawn superlative encomiums from scholars of the Holy Quran. For months at a time his working hours, while he was engaged upon this compilation, stretched to seventeen or eighteen every day. The work extended over a number of years and the result was several volumes of monumental proportions setting forth the wisdom and the philosophy underlying every verse of the Holy Quran, which will not be matched for a long time to come. The truth is that the Holy Quran is an inexhaustible treasury of wisdom and truth. In every age it yields, under divine instruction, as much as is needed for the guidance of mankind in that age. While the verities that are comprehended in the Holy Quran are basic and fundamental and not subject to change, they are many-faceted, and these facets are illuminated and shine forth in galaxies from age to age. At no time, therefore, can it be said that the last word in the exposition of the wisdom and the philosophy of the Holy Quran has been pronounced.

CHAPTER FOURTEEN

The attitude of Khalifatul Masih II concerning the series of prophecies of the Promised Messiah that were published in the announcement of 20 February 1886, was that he refrained from making any positive claim that those prophecies had been fulfilled in his person, although he felt that probably that was the case. In June 1937 he wrote in a letter:

I consider that the Promised Reformer must be one of the sons of the Promised Messiah and not someone who will appear in a later age. So far as I have reflected on these prophecies 90 per cent of them are in accord with the achievements of the period of my Khilafat. As I do not consider that it is necessary for the person who is the subject of these prophecies to claim that the prophecies have been fulfilled in his person or refer to him, I do not deem it necessary to make such a claim. I do consider, however, that God Almighty has fulfilled the purpose of these prophecies to a large degree through me. Yet I would not be surprised if God Almighty should enable one of my brothers to achieve similar or even greater purposes than I have done.

Three years later he stated in the course of a Friday sermon:

People have tried that I should claim that I am the Promised Reformer, but I have never considered this necessary. It is said that my followers affirm that I am the Promised Reformer and yet I have not made any such claim. I do not see the necessity of making any claim. If I am in truth and in fact the Promised Reformer, my position is not affected by my failure to make such a claim. I believe that it is not necessary to make a claim in respect of a prophecy that relates to a person who has not been commissioned by God. How many of the Reformers whose names are entered in a list published after the approval of the Promised Messiah, made such a claim? I have heard the Promised Messiah say that he thought Emperor Aurangzeb was the Reformer of his age. Did he put forward any claim? Umar bin Abdul Aziz is revered as a Reformer. Did he make any claim? Thus it is not necessary for a non-commissioned one to make a claim. A claim is necessary only in the case of prophecies relating to a commissioned one. In the case of a non-commissioned one his achievements should be looked at, and if they show clearly that a prophecy was related to him, it is not necessary for him to make a claim. In such a case even if he disclaims being the subject of the prophecy we would say that the prophecy has been fulfilled in his person. . . . Thus I do not consider it necessary to make any claim that I am the Promised Reformer.

He did on one occasion state: 'I have no doubt that the prophecy relating to the Promised Reformer mentioned in the green announcement is related to me'; yet he did not put forward a positive claim that he was the Promised Reformer till in the beginning of 1944 it was revealed to him in a dream that he was the Promised Reformer. In view of the grandeur of the dream he decided to make a public announcement that he was the Promised Reformer. On 28 January 1944 he related his dream in detail in the Friday sermon and announced that he was the Promised Reformer. He prefaced his description of the dream with the observation: 'I wish to state something today which I find it difficult to set forth having regard to my temperament, but as some prophethoods and Divine decrees are involved in making this exposition I cannot refrain from making it despite my reluctance.' In his dream it was clearly conveyed to him that he was a reflection of the Promised Messiah and his Khalifa.

At the end of his exposition of the dream he stated:

I wish to mention that when I woke up after the dream I kept thinking over it and my thoughts were formulated in Arabic. The end of my thinking was that God had clearly determined that truth had arrived and falsehood had vanished, falsehood was bound to vanish (17:82). Today, when I was reading the announcement of the Promised Messiah of 20 February 1886, I found the same words set out in it. Thus, God Almighty has revealed the reality to me and I can affirm without the least hesitation that the prophecy of God Almighty has been fulfilled, and that He has laid a foundation through the Tahrik Jadeed in consequence of which the prophecy of Jesus that the virgins will accompany the bridegroom into the citadel will one day be fulfilled in a grand manner. The reflection of the Messiah will lead the virgins to the presence of God Almighty and the nations who will have been blessed through him will proclaim joyously: 'Hosanna, hosanna.' They will then believe in Muhammad, peace be on him, and will have true faith in the first Messiah. At present they proclaim him the Son of God, which amounts to reviling him. But it is decreed that the seed sown by me will one day grow into such a splendid tree that the Christian peoples will gather under it in order to seek blessings from the reflection of the Messiah and will thus enter into the kingdom of God, and the kingdom of God will arrive on earth as it is in heaven.

In the course of his opening speech in the session of the Advisory Council of 1944, he stated:

Every member of the Movement should realize that the revelation received by the Promised Messiah, peace be on him, concerning me that I would grow up rapidly did not mean that I would stand alone before the enemy hosts, but that, having regard to the importance of the work to be done, it would be my duty to advance rapidly against the enemy, and when I do so, God Almighty will enable those who believe in me also to advance rapidly. In the same way when God manifested to me that the earth was being compressed under my feet and that I was running rapidly ahead it meant that when I go forward rapidly God Almighty will enable my sincere companions to traverse the earth quickly and to arrive speedily at the ends of the earth. So, you must create an extraordinary change in yourselves and should prepare yourselves quickly to make great sacrifices. Do not wait too long, for the prophecies indicate that the time has come when you will not have to wait for long. Great changes are about to manifest themselves in the world which are very important in God's estimation. God alone knows what will now happen but it is clear that the foundations of certain great changes will be laid soon and the heart of him who does not keep company with me in these great events and does not advance rapidly will be rusted and he will run the risk of losing his faith.

Thereafter, he put scheme after scheme before the Community and the Community made an eager response to every one of them.

The Khalifatul Masih personally announced the purport of his dream in meetings called for the purpose in Hoshiarpur, Lahore, Ludhiana and Delhi. He addressed a message on 14 February 1944 stressing the purpose of the meeting to be held at Hoshiarpur on 20 February 1944. In this letter he stated:

> Brethren, peace be on you and the mercy of Allah and His blessings. You have read the announcement about the meeting to be held in Hoshiarpur. The only purpose of the meeting is that at the place where the Promised Messiah, in the face of very adverse circumstances, had announced a sign of divine mercy, whereby his name would be carried to the ends of the earth, an announcement should be made that the prophecy has been fulfilled in grand style. This is an occasion for the display of the fear of God and of righteousness and not for worldly celebration. I, therefore, announce that only such people should attend this meeting as are given to supplications, *istighfar,* and praise of God, and who remember God constantly. They should be determined that during their sojourn at Hoshiarpur they would not speak without purpose, nor indulge in vain talk, or laughter, or ridicule, but would maintain a serious mood and would throughout be occupied in prayers and *istighfar*.
>
> It should be kept in mind that boys and raw youths and those who are unable to exercise full control over their tempers and those who soon begin to be restless when they have to sit in silence, should not go to the meeting. Only those should go to the meeting who are determined to observe silence throughout and to devote their time to the remembrance of God or to the discharge of such duties as are assigned to them. I admonish those who intend to participate in the meeting that if they act in accordance with my advice, their participation will be acceptable to God. Otherwise, all their effort will be vain, and they will risk incurring God's wrath.

This admonition was taken so much to heart by those proceeding to Hoshiarpur for the purpose of participating in the meeting that Maulvi Sanaullah Sahib of Amritsar, a bitter opponent of the Movement, was moved to comment in his paper, the *Ahle Hadees,* of 10 March 1944: 'It appeared as if a host of the Companions of the Holy Prophet was proceeding to the conquest of Mecca.'

In the meeting at Hoshiarpur the Khalifatul Masih opened his address with the recitation of the Fatiha, repeating some of the verses in a voice steeped in emotion and followed it up with several supplications from the Holy Quran. The audience was deeply affected and repeated the supplications after him with streaming eyes and convulsed hearts. Thereafter, he described the background of the prophecy of 20 February 1886 and explained how every part of it had been fulfilled in a wonderful manner despite adverse conditions. He then set out his dream in great detail. He concluded with the declaration:

> I call to witness the One and Supreme God Who has full control over my life that the dream that I have just described was seen by me exactly as I have put it, except possibly for some slight verbal involuntary inaccuracy. I call God Almighty to witness that in a state of vision I announced: 'I am the Promised Messiah, his reflection and his Khalifa.' In the same state, under divine command, I said: 'I am the one for whose appearance the virgins had been waiting for nineteen centuries.' I therefore announce, under divine command, on oath, that God has appointed me the Promised Son of the Promised Messiah, peace be on him, according to his prophecy, who has to convey the name of the Promised Messiah to the ends of the earth.
>
> I do not say that I am the only Promised One and that no other promised one will appear till the Day of Judgment. It appears from the prophecies of the Promised Messiah that some other promised ones will also come and some of them will appear after centuries. Indeed, God has told me that at one time He will send me a second time to the world and I will come for the reform of the world at a time when association with God will have become widespread. This means that my soul will, at some time, descend upon someone who will possess faculties and capacities like mine and he will, following in my footsteps, bring about a reform of the world.

Thus, promised ones will appear in their due times according to the promise of God Almighty.

What I wish to say today is that the prophecy of the Promised Messiah, peace be on him, which was revealed to him at Hoshiarpur in the building in front of us, in which he announced in this city and concerning which he said that the Promised Son would be born within nine years, has been fulfilled in my person, and no one else can claim that he is the subject of the prophecy.

In the end he said: I draw the attention of those who have not yet joined the Movement to the fact that we are carrying the message of Islam to the ends of the earth, in the West and in the East. We earnestly wish that you should reflect on the significance of the Movement and should take advantage of the signs of God Almighty that have already been manifested. . . . It is our duty to put forth every effort for the propagation of this message and we shall continue to discharge this duty. You should not be misled into thinking that you can stop the divine decree from being fulfilled. It is bound to be fulfilled one day and this Movement will spread all over the earth. There is no one who can obstruct the spread of this Movement. I call upon heaven to bear witness and call upon the earth to bear witness and call upon every brick of Hoshiarpur to bear witness that this Movement is bound to spread. If the hearts of the people are hard, angels will massage them with their hands till they are softened and no course is left open to them except to join the Ahmadiyya Movement.

In the meeting in Lahore on 12 March 1944, which was attended not only by a large number of the members of the Ahmadiyya Movement but also by thousands of non-Ahmadi Muslims, Hindus, Sikhs and Christians, the Khalifatul Masih observed, in the course of his speech:

Who can say on his own that a son would surely be bestowed upon him, who can say that such a son would live and grow up, who can say that he would become the leader of a community, who can say that he would become known unto the ends of the earth? Most certainly no one can say these things on his own. . . . In short, the fresh evidence of the support of God Almighty has proved once more that this Movement has been established by God and enjoys His help and support. Today, the prophecy made through the

Promised Messiah 59 years ago, 'I shall bestow upon thee a son who will be a sign of My mercy and of My power, of My grace and My beneficence, and through him the message of Islam and Ahmadiyyat will be carried to the ends of the earth, has been fulfilled with great glory. Today, hundreds of countries bear witness that the name of Islam reached them during the period of my Khalifat and it was during the period of my Khalifat that they heard the name of Ahmadiyyat.

He announced: In this meeting today I call to witness God, the One and Supreme, taking Whose false oath is a characteristic of the accursed and one who is guilty of imposture against Him cannot escape His torment, that He informed me in this city in 13 Temple Road, in the house of Shaikh Bashir Ahmad, Advocate, that I am the subject of the prophecy concerning the Promised Reformer and that through me Islam will spread to the ends of the earth and the Unity of God will be established in the world.

Continuing his speech, he observed: God has bestowed upon me the swords that cut down disbelief in an instant. God has bestowed upon me hearts that are ready to offer every sacrifice in response to my voice. If I should ask them to jump into the depths of the ocean they would be ready to do so. If I should ask them to plunge down from the tops of mountains they would plunge down. If I should ask them to jump into blazing ovens, they would jump into them. If suicide had not been forbidden in Islam I would have shown you the spectacle that I would command a hundred members of the Movement to destroy themselves by plunging daggers into their bellies and they would instantly so destroy themselves. God has raised us for the support of Islam. He has raised us to glorify the name of Muhammad, the Messenger of Allah, peace be on him.

He concluded with the words: O dwellers of Lahore, I convey God's message to you. I call you to the Eternal and Ever-Living God Who has created you all. Do not think that it is I who am speaking at this moment. It is God Who is speaking through my tongue. Whoever raises his voice before me against Islam will have his voice suppressed. Whoever stands up against me will be humiliated and disgraced, he will be ruined and destroyed. God will establish a grand foundation with great honour for the progress of Islam and its support through me. I am a human being and may die today or tomorrow, but it cannot be that I should fail in the purpose for which God has raised me. . . . If the world witnesses at any time that Islam has been vanquished, if it sees at any time that those who deny me have overcome those who believe in me, then you may conclude that I was an impostor. But if that which I tell you is proved true, then reflect what would be your end, in that you heard the voice of God through my tongue and yet you did not accept it.

The meeting at Ludhiana was held on 23 March 1944. On this occasion there was very turbulent opposition to the holding of the meeting. Processions were taken out and all sorts of derisive speeches were made and slogans were shouted against the Khalifatul Masih and the Movement. In the course of his speech he stated:

We are not angry with those who have mocked at that which God Almighty has said. We supplicate God for them and pray: 'Whatever these people have done, they have done out of ignorance and lack of knowledge, forgetting the teachings of the Holy Prophet, peace be on him. Forgive them, Lord, and guide them, and open their hearts to the acceptance of the truth so that as they have ridiculed the faith today, I may be privileged to see them pressing forward to make sacrifices for the faith.' . . . People of Ludhiana, you have opposed me and I pray for you. You have desired my death, and I desire life for you. I have before me the example of my master, Muhammad, the Messenger of Allah, peace be on him. When he went to Taif to convey the divine message to the people of Taif, he was pelted with stones and was expelled from the town while his body was bleeding at several places. In this situation an angel approached him under divine direction and said: 'I could overturn this town if you would so desire.' But my master, Muhammad, the Chosen one, peace be on him, may my father and mother, and my soul, and every particle of my body be his sacrifice, said: 'No, not so. These people are foolish and ignorant and that is why they persecute me. If they were to be destroyed, then who would be left to believe?'

So people of Ludhiana, who have desired my death, I have brought the message of eternal life to you; the message of a life after which there is no death. I have brought you the message of the pleasure of God Almighty, after winning which man experiences no suffering. I am sure that today's opposition will open the hearts tomorrow and the world will see that this city, God willing, will be illumined with divine light and will become my supporter and helper in the fulfilment of my task. I supplicate God Almighty in these terms and hope that through His grace it will so come about.

In the course of his concluding speech he observed: Even if our opponents do not believe they should at least admit that whatever we say we say out of sympathy for them and as proof of our goodwill. We shall continue to say it, however great might be the suffering that they might impose upon us. They might cut us down, throw us to the lions, stone us to death, drop us down from mountains, throw us into the ocean but as we have stood up in the name of God, we cannot desist from discharging our responsibilities. So long as we have breath left in our bodies we shall continue to raise our voices. We believe that this teaching is bound to spread, and even if the strongest nations stand up against us they will be frustrated. They can, no doubt, destroy our bodies but our souls will continue to rise and this message will not be obstructed. Then it is best for you to lend your ears to our voice so that your end may be good. Listen carefully to the voice that is being raised on behalf of God Almighty and try to understand it.

Lord, I beseech Thee to open the hearts of these people and to provide the means of carrying this voice to the whole of the world. As we are Thy creatures, so are those who have not yet recognized Thy beloved Muhammad, the chosen one, peace be on him. Do Thou guide them and gather everyone under his standard. Do Thou wipe out from the world the spirit of disorder, faithlessness, injustice, disobedience, viciousness, devouring each other's property, and mutual discord, and create the spirit of peace and friendship.

The meeting at Delhi was held on 16 April 1944. In Delhi, the opposition to the holding of the meeting was much severer than it had been in Ludhiana, but the meeting was held successfully and the Khalifatul Masih repeated his announcement that he was the Reformer whose advent had been promised in the announcement of the Promised Messiah of 20 February 1886, and concluded with the declaration:

If I am true in making this announcement, and the God of heaven and earth is indeed witness to my truth, then remember that one day, through me and my disciples, the whole world will repeat the credo of the Holy Prophet, peace be on him, and a day will come when the rule of Islam will be established over the whole world in the same way, and even more gloriously, as it was established in the early centuries of Islam.

In concluding his second speech in the last session of the Conference on 29 December, he observed:

God Almighty through His revelation has intimated to me that by His grace and mercy, the prophecy whose fulfilment had been awaited for a long time has been fulfilled in my person. Now it has been made clear to the enemies of Islam that Islam is God's true religion, that Muhammad, peace be on him, is the true Messenger of God Almighty and that the Promised Messiah, peace be on him, is a true envoy of God. False are the people who call Islam false, liars are those who give the lie to Muhammad, the Messenger of Allah, peace be on him. Through the fulfilment of this grand prophecy God has furnished a living proof of the truth of Islam and of the Holy Prophet, peace be on him.

Who had the power fifty-eight years ago, in the year 1886, to announce on his own that within nine years he would be blessed with a son who would grow up rapidly and would be known unto the ends of the earth; that he would spread Islam and the name of the Holy Prophet, peace be on him, throughout the world, that he would be filled with secular and spiritual knowledge; that he would be a means of the manifestation of Divine Glory and that he would be a living sign of the power, nearness and mercy of God Almighty? No man could have made such an announcement on his own. It was God Who gave this intimation and it was He Who fulfilled it through a person concerning whom the physicians did not expect that he would grow up and live long. I enjoyed very indifferent health during my childhood and on one occasion Dr Mirza Yaqub Beg Sahib advised the Promised Messiah that I was suffering from tuberculosis and should be sent to some hill station, out of the heat of the plains. Accordingly I was sent to Simla, but felt lonely there and soon returned to Qadian. In short a person who never enjoyed good health for a day was kept alive by God so that His prophecy might be fulfilled through him, and the people might be confronted with proof of the truth of Islam and Ahmadiyyat. Then I was a person who possessed no secular knowledge, yet God, of His grace, appointed angels for my instruction and by this means made me aware of such meanings of the Quran as were beyond the imagination of a human being. The knowledge that God has bestowed upon me and the spiritual fountain that has burst in my bosom are not mere guess or imagination. Indeed they are so certain and conclusive that I challenge the whole world that I am prepared to compete at any time with anyone who might claim that he has been taught the Holy Quran by God Almighty. But I know that there is no one today in the world beside myself who has been bestowed knowledge of the Holy Quran by God. He has bestowed this knowledge on me and has appointed me the teacher of the world for teaching it the Quran in this age. He has raised me for the purpose that I should carry the name of Muhammad, the Messenger of Allah, peace be on him, and the name of the Holy Quran, to the ends of the earth and may vanquish for ever all false religions that are set up against Islam.

Let the world exert itself and gather all its strength and its hosts.

Let all Christian sovereigns and their governments combine, and let Europe and America join together, and let all wealthy and powerful nations combine and unite together to frustrate me in the achievement of this purpose, even then I state, in the name of God, that they would fail completely against me. In response to my prayers and plans God will frustrate all their projects and plans and machinations, and, through me and my disciples and followers, God will uphold the honour of Islam for the purpose of establishing the truth of this prophecy on account of the name of the Holy Prophet, peace be on him. He will not leave the world alone till Islam is established once more in the world in its full glory and till Muhammad, the Messenger of Allah, peace be on him, is accepted as the living Prophet of the world.

My friends, I do not seek any honour for myself, nor do I hope for longer life, unless God Almighty should disclose anything to me in that context. I am, however, hopeful of the grace of Almighty God and believe with certainty that in upholding the honour of Islam and the Holy Prophet, peace be on him, and in re-establishing Islam once more upon its feet, and in crushing Christianity, a great part will, God willing, be played by my past and future work, and that one of the heels that will crush the head of Satan and will put an end to Christianity, will be my heel.

I set forth this verity most clearly before the world. This is the voice of the God of heaven and earth. This is the will of that God. This verity will not be set aside, will not be set aside, will not be set aside. Islam shall prevail in the world and Christianity shall be vanquished. There is no support that can safeguard Christianity against my attacks. God will defeat it at my hands and will either so crush it in my lifetime that it will no longer be able to raise its head, or a tree will rise from the seed sown by me in contrast with which Christianity shall wither like a dry weed, and the standard of Islam and Ahmadiyyat will be seen flying on the heights.

While I convey to you the good news that God Almighty has fulfilled the prophecy of the Promised Messiah which related to the Promised Reformer, I also wish to draw your attention to the responsibilities that are now placed upon you. You have declared your support of my announcement and it is your primary duty that you should be ready to shed the last drop of your blood to bring about the victory and success of Islam and Ahmadiyyat. You are welcome to proclaim your joy at the fulfilment of the prophecy; indeed you must proclaim your joy, for the Promised Messiah has himself written: 'Be joyful and jump about in joy for now the light will come.' I do not, therefore, stop you from proclaiming your joy and jumping with joy. By all means proclaim your joy and jump about with joy. But I do admonish you that you should not forget your responsibilities in this state of joy. As God displayed to me in my dream that I am running forward swiftly and the earth is being compressed under my feet, in the same way, God Almighty had announced that I would go forward quickly. Thus I am destined to advance swiftly in the field of progress. This also imposes a duty upon you that you should abandon your slow speed and should step forward quickly. Blessed is he who matches his step with mine and advances swiftly in the field of progress; and may God have mercy upon the one who is slothful and neglectful and does not step forward quickly and instead of advancing in the field tarries behind like a hypocrite. If you wish to make progress, if you realize your responsibilities properly, then advance and march forward along with me step by step, shoulder to shoulder so that we might plant the standard of Muhammad, the Messenger of Allah, peace be on him, in the heart of disbelief and wipe out falsehood for ever from the face of the world. God willing that will surely come about. Heaven and earth can pass away but the word of God must be fulfilled.

During the lifetime of the Promised Messiah the Talimul Islam High School had been raised to an Intermediate College, but in consequence of a set of new regulations of the University of the Punjab, compliance with which was beyond the resources of the Community, the College classes had to be closed in 1905. The need of a college had, however, progressively become more insistent and eventually the Talimul Islam College was restarted on 4 June 1944, but this time the College was not limited to Intermediate classes. It was designed as a Degree College. Sahibzada Mirza Nasir Ahmad Sahib M.A. (Oxon.) was appointed the first Principal of the College, a position which he held for 21 years, till he was elected to the holy office of Khalifatul Masih.

The College continued at Qadian for 3 years and had then, on partition of the country, to be transferred to Lahore pending the construction of the necessary buildings for its accommodation at Rabwah, the new Headquarters of the Movement. Thus though the College encountered a series of vicissitudes during the first decade of its existence, yet under the wise and devoted guidance of its Principal and the constant supervision of Khalifatul Masih II, it marched forward from success to success and established a high and enviable record of academic and athletic achievement.

Admission to the College was not limited to youngsters of the Ahmadiyya Movement. Its doors were open to all students who were qualified for admission. After its permanent establishment at Rabwah the proportion of non-Ahmadi students on its rolls continued to rise progressively till almost half the students were drawn from non-Ahmadi homes, which was a tribute to the standards maintained by the College and to its universal popularity.

In course of time the College started postgraduate classes in higher physics and became the only institution in the Province, apart from the Punjab University itself, which provided instruction in higher physics at the Master's level. The college has a brilliant record in that respect. Since the start of these classes almost all the candidates it has sent up for the Master of Science Degree in Physics have passed the examination in the

First Division and some of them have established distinguished records.

On the occasion of the opening of the College in 1944, Khalifatul Masih II delivered a most learned and detailed address setting out the purpose and the objectives for which the College was being established, and the whole purpose and aim of higher education and the proper means of their achievement. In the very beginning of his address he observed:

The establishment of the Talimul Islam College has a double purpose. One purpose is to provide means of higher education without which no community can improve its cultural and economic conditions. So far as that purpose is concerned the doors of the College will be open to all students irrespective of caste and creed. All communities are in need of education and it is our duty, as human beings, that we should make education possible and easy for everyone. I have had occasion to visit one or two institutions in Lahore the founders of which had laid down the condition that no Muslim would be eligible for admission to them. When I learnt this I felt that the Muslims should also establish similar institutions but should make it clear that no non-Muslim would be refused admission to them, inasmuch as the moral point of view of a Muslim is different from the moral point of view of other people. Thus we shall make every effort that education should become easy for all people without distinction of caste or creed. The doors of this College will be open to everyone and this institution shall provide all possible help to all those who seek to derive benefit from it.

Its second purpose is related to the influence of modern education upon religion. We believe that that influence is generally harmful, as it is opposed to religion. We cannot agree that God's action can be inconsistent with His Word, or that His Word can be opposed to His action. We are positively convinced that though we may not possess the means of refuting the objections raised against Islam on the very basis from which those objections are derived, or from the subjects upon which they are based, yet it is a certainty that the objections raised against the existence of God or against God's Messengers, or against the doctrines of Islam, are false and are the result of wrong reasoning. As the centre of these types of objections are the higher institutions of learning, one of the purposes of this College is that the objections raised against religion on the basis of diverse subjects of education should be refuted through the very same subjects. The Professors of this college should charge themselves, among other things, with the duty of repelling the objections raised against Islam on the basis of their particular subjects through those very subjects. Thus while the Professors in other institutions tend to strengthen such objections the aim of our Professors would be that they should refute such objections effectively.

In the course of his address he illustrated the relationship between science and religion in great detail and pointed out that while science was still in an elementary stage of evolution and its theories and principles were under constant review and were subject to correction and modification, the fundamentals of religion and its basic verities were constant and were not subject to modification. He pointed out that though there was a certain type of evolution in the detailed teachings and commandments of religion, this did not involve any contradiction or reversal of religious verities. The whole address constituted a most illuminating discourse on the relationship between science, learning and religion, which is well worth the study and attention of all those who are interested in the cause and purpose of education.

He concluded with the supplication:

May Allah, the Exalted, cause our good expectations to be fulfilled and may the seed that we are sowing here today grow up into a splendid tree, every branch of which may be a grand University and every leaf of which may be a College. May every flower of it become a high grade foundation for the propagation of Islam and religion through which disbelief and heresy may be wiped out, and the hearts of the people may be filled with the truth of Islam and Ahmadiyyat and with the conviction of the existence of God Almighty and His Unity. Amen.

On the partition of the country in 1947 the Talimul Islam College was confronted with a series of crises in the midst of a very difficult national situation, but by the grace and mercy of Allah, under the guidance of Khalifatul Masih II and through the untiring and devoted efforts of its Principal, they were all successfully overcome and the College which was first re-established in Lahore, seven years later moved into its newly constructed buildings in Rabwah.

On 8 November 1944 the Khalifatul Masih, in a speech stressing some aspects of Tahrik Jadeed, made an important pronouncement on the system of Khilafat. He said:

Our system is based entirely on love and affection. We have no legal authority whereby we can enforce our directions. My personal view is that in Ahmadiyyat Khilafat should always be distinct from political government. The function of the Khilafat should continue to be the supervision of compliance with the commandments of the Islamic Law. We are not yet in a position of political authority in the country, but even when such a time arrives the Khalifa should remain outside active politics and should at no time seek to take over the government of the country, lest a situation of juxtaposition between the Khilafat and political parties should arise and the Khilafat should become identified with a political party. In such a situation the Khalifa would cease to be *in loco parentis* towards the community. There is no doubt that in the beginning of Islam Khalifat and government were combined in one person, but that was under the compulsion of the then circumstances. The Islamic Law had not yet been fully enforced, and as its full enforcement was necessary, Khilafat and government were combined in the same person. According to our doctrine they can be combined and they can also be separate. In my opinion when the time comes when we are in power, the Khalifa should not seek to take the government into his own hands. He should remain outside government and should supervise the government so as to secure that government should follow the directions of the Islamic Law and should settle its policies and their execution in consultation with the Khalifa. The administration of the country should be left to the statesmen and the public services. If my point of view is followed the Khalifa should not take over the government of the country at any time and should confine himself to the supervision of the exercise of the moral qualities and the enforcement of the commandments of the Holy Quran.

During the Annual Conference of 1944, in addressing the women, on 27 December, the Khalifatul Masih admonished the members of the newly established Association of Women that their first duty should be to establish literacy among all the women of the Movement. Their second step should be to take adequate measures to instruct all the women of the Movement in the principal commandments of Islam relating to the *salat,* fasting, etc. The third step should be that every woman should know the purport and meaning of the *salat,* so that her worship should not be like the cry of a parrot, not knowing what she is saying. The last step should be that every woman should know the meaning of the Holy Quran:

> . . . I would be satisfied only when every one of you knows the meaning of the Holy Quran, and I would be happy when every one of you not only knows the meaning of the Quran, but also understands the Quran, and I will be truly happy when every one of you can expound the Holy Quran to other women, and my happiness would be even greater when God Almighty becomes a witness that all of you have understood the Holy Quran and are diligent in acting upon it.

CHAPTER FIFTEEN

The last phase of the struggle for the independence of India began in London in the spring of 1945. In the Commonwealth Relations Conference in Chatham House, St James's Square, the Indian delegation was led by the President of the Indian Institute of International Relations, who was a zealous member of the Ahmadiyya Movement. In his two speeches on the opening day of the Conference, 17 February, he put forward so strong and well reasoned a plea urging Britain to move forward realistically towards the independence of India that the British press as well as British statesmen were convinced that India's demand for independence could no longer be ignored and that practical steps must be taken through constitutional procedures to satisfy Indian aspirations. The immediate reaction of His Majesty's Government was to invite the Governor General of India, Lord Wavell, to London for consultations. Lord Wavell returned to India armed with a formula for the independence of India. He announced his scheme over the All-India Radio on 14 June 1945. On 22 June 1945 Khalifatul Masih II, in his Friday sermon, urged Indian political leaders to take full advantage of the British offer. He concluded his address with a strong plea that Indian political leaders should arrive speedily at an understanding among themselves which should enable India to achieve independence without much delay. He said:

> Here four hundred million human beings are held in bondage. Their outlook has undergone a tremendous change, in consequence of which Britain has announced that it is ready to bestow independence upon India, but Indian political leaders are disputing with each other over matters of detail. . . . We are a small community and observing this state of affairs we can do little to improve it. But we can certainly supplicate the Divine: 'Lord, do Thou open the eyes of Muslim as well as Hindu leaders and bestow

upon them the vision that should make them eager to cut the bonds of four hundred million bondsmen, for this would serve not only our interest but would also serve the interest of the future peace of the world.' Had it been proper to fight on this occasion Britain would have fought, but it is a manifestation of Divine power that the Viceroy who rules India on behalf of Britain announces that he is ready to make India independent; the British industrialist who promotes his industries through the exploitation of India has announced that he is prepared to support the independence of India; the government of Britain has announced that it is prepared to concede the independence of India; the British Labour Party, which is likely to come into power soon, has announced that it is ready to grant independence to India; the greater part of the British press, whether Conservative, Labour or Liberal, is loud in its support of the independence of India; America and France and other countries, who are not directly concerned with India, are urging that India should be independent. Yet when Britain is ready to grant independence to India some Indian leaders are not ready for the independence of India. I, therefore, urge the members of my Community to be occupied in these days with special supplications to God Almighty, that He may so guide those in whose hands these matters rest that they should turn to the right path and cutting the chains of the bondage of Indians they should lead India to a high place of honour.

An English version of this address was speedily placed in the hands of Muslim and non-Muslim political leaders who had been invited by Lord Wavell to a conference in Simla.

Maulvi Sanaullah Sahib of Amritsar, despite his bitter opposition to the Khalifatul Masih and the Ahmadiyya Movement, in the course of his comments on the address said:

What the Khalifa of Qadian has said is well worth reading and listening to. He has urged the leaders to work together in amity and co-operation. His words display great and surprising courage. The speeches of the conference leaders contained no stronger expressions. The eagerness to secure the freedom of four hundred million Indians which is expressed in the Khalifa's address is not matched even in the speeches of Mr Gandhi.

No agreement could be reached in the Simla conference, mainly due to the firm refusal of the representatives of the Indian National Congress to recognize the Muslim League as the sole political representative of the Muslims. The claim of the Muslim League that it was the sole representative of the Muslims had been demonstrably established in the elections to the legislative bodies in India. Under the directions of the Khalifatul Masih the Ahmadiyya Community had throughout lent its full and enthusiastic support to the Muslim League, and continued to do so throughout the troubled period that lay ahead. By the summer of 1946, when the Cabinet Mission plan was presented to Indian leadership, even the Indian National Congress had to concede, and to reconcile itself to the position, that the Muslim League was the sole political representative of the Muslims. When the Congress leadership, after signifying its acceptance of the Cabinet Mission plan, in effect tore it up by proclaiming its own interpretation of some of its crucial clauses, which was clearly inconsistent with the language of those clauses, and the strenuous efforts of Lord Wavell to persuade Pandit Jawaharlal Nehru and Mr Gandhi to agree to give effect to the clear meaning of those clauses were frustrated, and Prime Minister Attlee made a last minute attempt to salvage the plan through his personal intervention, the only representatives summoned by him to London were Mr Nehru and Mr Jinnah. Mr Nehru was accompanied by Sardar Baldev Singh, which was only a gesture designed to secure the goodwill of the Sikh community. On his side Mr Jinnah was accompanied by Nawabzada Liaquat Ali Khan, who was his principal lieutenant in the Muslim League. Prime Minister Attlee's attempt was also frustrated by the intransigence of Mr Nehru.

On 20 February 1947, Prime Minister Attlee announced his scheme for the transfer of complete power to India, and Lord Mountbatten was sent out as Governor General in place of Lord Wavell to work out, in consultation with political leaders, the method of giving effect to the Prime Minister's announcement. Finally, on 3 June 1947, the scheme of partition was, with the agreement of the political leaders, set forth by Lord Mountbatten. Throughout this turbulent and critical period the Khalifatul Masih continued his full support of Mr Jinnah and the Muslim League.

In pursuance of the scheme of partition outlined in Lord Mountbatten's speech of 3 June 1947, Boundary Commissions were set up in the Punjab and Bengal for the demarcation of the boundaries between Pakistan and India in the North-West and North-East of the Sub-Continent. Mr Jinnah requested an eminent Ahmadi jurist to present the case of the Muslim League to the Punjab Boundary Commission. The Muslim League approached the Khalifatul Masih that he should arrange for the representation of the Ahmadiyya Community before the Punjab Boundary Commission in support of the Muslim League, with particular emphasis on the inclusion of the Gurdaspur District, within which Qadian the headquarters of the Ahmadiyya Movement was situated, in Pakistan. The Khalifatul Masih appointed Shaikh Bashir Ahmad, an able senior advocate, to represent the Movement before the Commission. When the Commission started hearing arguments, the Khalifatul Masih himself moved to Lahore and rendered valuable assistance to the Muslim League both by his advice and by procuring the services of a foreign expert on questions that the Commission would have to take into account in making its report.

As was expected the Commission, which was composed of four High Court judges, two Muslim and two non-Muslim, was not able to present a unanimous or majority report and the determination of the boundary was left to the umpire, Sir Cyril (later Lord) Redcliffe. His award came as a profound shock to the Muslims and particularly to the Ahmadiyya Community, as under it several Muslim majority areas contiguous to the rest of Pakistan were excluded from Pakistan and were included in India. The greater part of the Gurdaspur District, in which Qadian was situated, was also included within India despite a majority of Muslims in the District.

The aftermath of the partition of the Punjab proved to be a gruesome tragedy for all the three principal communities in the Punjab, Muslims (including the Ahmadiyya Community), non-Muslims and Sikhs. A terrible holocaust involving extreme human suffering and misery was let loose on both sides of the newly determined border. An irresistible wave of horror raged unchecked over the greater part of the province. The general populace, with rare exceptions, exhibited a lack of moral and spiritual values that was heartrending. It would serve no useful purpose to enter into a detailed description of the degradation of all human values that was manifested in all the areas that were overtaken by this foul maelstrom. It would be best to draw a curtain over the shameful spectacle. Neither side could be acquitted of blame. The moral guilt was shared by all.

There were noble, courageous and heart-warming individual exceptions among all the communities, in which humanity maintained its priority over bigotry, passion and beastliness. For the Ahmadiyya Community it is a matter of satisfaction that both as individuals and as a Community they came out of this terrible trial, with loss of numerous precious lives and an enormous amount of property, but with their honour bright and unsullied. The Community as a whole, and its individual members, rendered aid and assistance to their suffering fellow beings without distinction of caste or creed, in every situation in which they were capable of rendering assistance, at the risk, and sometimes even at the cost, of their own lives, security and property. This was freely acknowledged on all hands. So long as the Ahmadis were not expelled from the greater part of Qadian, under police and military action, Qadian continued to serve as an asylum for Muslim refugees who were being driven out of the areas which had been allotted to India and were fleeing to Pakistan. When the turn of Qadian itself came, and the greater part of it had to be evacuated, the Community exhibited an extraordinary spectacle of discipline, orderliness, steadfastness and courage. Despite all the adverse developments that took place hourly after the announcement of the Boundary Award, the Khalifatul Masih himself remained in Qadian, while the steady evacuation of sections of the population of Qadian and of the records and valuables belonging to the institutions of the Community proceeded in an orderly manner. It was a time of severe trial, and a testing of faith and all sterling values. By the sheer grace and mercy of the Divine not only was there no falling from grace, there were numerous instances of true heroism and heartening and almost miraculous experiences of Divine help and protection.

As soon as the Khalifatul Masih arrived in Lahore he issued directions that it was an obligation upon every member of the Community to render every assistance to such non-Muslims as were still in Pakistan. Many of them were exposed to danger at the hands of Muslims who were incensed at the brutalities and horrors to which Muslims in East Punjab had been subjected at the hands of the non-Muslims. Train after train arrived from East Punjab cram-full with Muslim refugees, some of whom had been cruelly murdered in the course of their journey by non-Muslim mobs which sacked the trains at different stops, almost all the survivors bearing marks of injuries, many of them grievous; children with their eyes gouged out, their hands and feet severed from their bodies, women with their breasts cut off. Those who managed to crawl across the border on foot, or on creaking make-shift vehicles fared even worse than those who had managed to be packed into evacuating trains. It is not surprising, though utterly illogical, that under the impact of these horrors large numbers of Muslims in Pakistan turned upon their unfortunate non-Muslim neighbours and sought to wreak vengeance upon them for the misdeeds of non-Muslims of East Punjab. Here again, under the clear directions of the Khalifatul Masih, not only did the members of the Community in Pakistan hold their emotions under complete control, but went to the assistance of non-Muslims, extended their protection to them, provided relief for them and speeded such of them as were moving towards India on their way, often at the gravest risk of their own lives and security. There has not been known a single instance in which an Ahmadi in Pakistan killed or caused any hurt or injury to a non-Muslim in those dreadful days, or was guilty of appropriating any moveable belonging of a non-Muslim. On both sides of the border immovable properties of evacuees were taken over by government and were administered by departments set up for the purpose.

It is worthy of reflection: How was it that at a time when all moral and spiritual values had suffered such large-scale stultification over large areas on both sides of the border, every member of the Ahmadiyya Movement was enabled to uphold them in situations of the gravest peril and provocation? It is true that this could only be done by the grace and mercy of God, but the question remains: How is it that such grace and mercy were bestowed in such large and perfect measure not only, as in the case of other communities also, upon outstanding individuals, but upon every member of the Ahmadiyya Movement?

Large numbers of them had suffered and passed through all the horrors that were inflicted upon the Muslims in East Punjab. They endured the suffering and the misery in a spirit of steadfastness. In their case it proved a cleansing experience and not a demoralizing affliction. Through this experience their relationship with their Maker was strengthened and their faith was invigorated. They emerged from the holocaust with renewed eagerness to march forward with greater zeal and devotion than ever before.

On 18 September 1894, the Promised Messiah had received the revelation (Urdu): 'The stigma of migration.' He himself and Khalifatul Masih II had seen dreams and visions that revealed some of the aspects of the migration with which the Community would be confronted. For instance, six years before the partition of the country the Khalifatul Masih saw in a dream that he was at some place at a distance from Qadian and was worried by a recollection that Qadian had been invaded. In his dream Sheikh Muhammad Naseeb, an Ahmadi resident of Qadian, came to him and the Khalifatul Masih inquired from him what was the situation in Qadian. The reply was that the enemy had occupied the greater part of Qadian but had been checked just outside the central quarter of the town which contained the house of the Promised Messiah, the two principal mosques, the offices of the Central Association and the heavenly graveyard. On receiving this reply the Khalifatul Masih II observed: 'If the central quarter is secure, all is secure.' It so happened that after all the upset and the taking over of the greater part of Qadian by the non-Muslims, with the active assistance of the Indian army and police, the incursion was checked right at the border of the central quarter.

These revelations, dreams and visions were fulfilled during the tribulations that followed in the wake of partition. The horrors that were let loose on that occasion arose suddenly and in circumstances in which no effective steps could be taken to avert them or to reduce their severity and impact. All that could be done was to organize the evacuation of practically the whole of the Ahmadi population with honour and a minimum loss of life. The gravest damage, however, that was suffered was that the Community ceased to have a headquarters and all the central institutions of the Movement were disrupted. The Khalifatul Masih and such of his colleagues and workers who moved about the same time to Lahore, or rallied around him from Lahore itself, or who were summoned from within Pakistan, were confronted with an enormous problem of rehabilitation, resettlement and reorganization. This was a baffling and back-breaking task in itself, but the Khalifatul Masih was still under great strain and suffered grave anxiety concerning the situation in Qadian and the branches of the Community in India who were, for the moment, bereft of spiritual leadership and guidance and had no means available of communication with the Head of the Movement.

The immediate problem was the organization of a centre for the Movement in Pakistan. The Sadar Anjuman Ahmadiyya (Central Ahmadiyya Association) was registered in Pakistan within a few months, but the educational institutions could not be rehabilitated so speedily. Everything was in a state of flux in Pakistan, and for some time it was apprehended that Pakistan might not be able to grapple successfully with the influx of millions of refugees that continued to pour into Pakistan not only from East Punjab, but also from the Indian provinces farther east. The greater part of the machinery of administration in the Punjab was occupied most of the time, directly or indirectly, with resolving the difficulties to which this great movement of the population across the borders of Pakistan and India gave rise. The Khalifatul Masih possessed a dynamic personality and his eager spirit was reflected in those who worked under his supervision and guidance. But their progress was often held up because the wheels of the administration would not move as swiftly as was desired. The consequence was that during the first year after the move to Lahore the progress of reorganization of the Movement and its institutions was comparatively slow, but not for lack of initiative on the part of the Khalifatul Masih. The two principal educational institutions, the Talimul Islam High School and the Talimul Islam College could not start functioning in Pakistan till more than six months after the move to Lahore, and even then only temporary make-shift arrangements were possible. After a few months the High School was allotted temporary accommodation at Chiniot, and sometime later the College was housed in the Dayanand Anglo-Vedic College buildings in Lahore.

In the meantime diligent search was being made for a suitable site for establishing the Centre of the Movement. The choice of a site was soon made and an application was made to government for the sale to the Community of an area of just over one thousand acres of barren, uncultivatable land across the River Chenab from Chiniot. This area was 95 miles west of Lahore and was served by the Lahore–Sargodha Road. The railway line from Lyallpur to Sargodha also passed through the area and there was every reason to expect that the Railway Administration could be persuaded to establish a railway station within the area. Such water as was available within the area was brackish but it was hoped that a supply of sweet water might be arranged.

The application for the sale of the land was diligently pursued and despite red-tape and official delays the price demanded by the government for the area to be sold to the Movement was paid into the Government Treasury on 27 June 1948, and the necessary official formalities were completed within a few days. Possession of the site, however, could not be obtained till 5 August. Nevertheless, the selection and acquisition of the site within just short of one year from the arrival of the Khalifatul Masih in Lahore was a creditable achievement. This was a necessary preliminary, but a tremendous effort was needed before the elementary facilities could be established in the absence of which even a token move to the site could not be contemplated.

The proposed town to be constructed on the barren, treeless site on which not a blade of grass had ever sprouted, was named Rabwah, which is the name ascribed in the Holy Quran to the region where Jesus eventually found shelter (23:51). A survey party soon prepared a plan of the site and in due course a plan of the town was drawn up and was submitted for approval to the Government Town Planner, who took objection to several features of the plan. For instance, he objected to the hospital being erected within the main area of the town and insisted that the hospital building should be sited at the farthest corner of the area which had been sold by government to the Movement. He also objected to a mosque being built in every quarter of the town. For the sixteen proposed quarters of the town he ruled that two mosques should be enough. He objected that no site had been provided in the plan for a cinema or a theatre. All his objections were of the same type of absurdity. The organization of every quarter of the town was based on a mosque at the centre of the quarter. Therefore, in addition to the two central mosques, sixteen mosques were needed, one for every quarter. But the Town Planner pretended that he did not see the necessity of providing a mosque in every quarter. He could not bring himself to appreciate that the Movement was a religious Movement, and that the proper and regular performance of the five daily services was incumbent upon all adult members of the Movement, and that for the proper discharge of that obligation a mosque in every quarter was indispensible. Besides, a mosque, according to Islamic tradition, is the centre of all religious, social and cultural activities of the residents of a quarter, but the Town Planner was bent upon depriving the Community of this facility.

His insistence on the provision of a site or sites for a cinema and a theatre was equally absurd. The members of the Movement were not permitted to visit cinemas and theatres, and, therefore, it was beyond comprehension what purpose would be served by providing sites for a cinema or a theatre.

Eventually the matter was taken to the Minister concerned and it did not take him more than five minutes to overrule the objections of the Town Planner. This is only an instance illustrating the crass stupidity of official red-tape which often clogs the progress of beneficent projects and undertakings.

As soon as official formalities had been complied with, temporary accommodation was erected at Rabwah to enable the Khalifatul Masih, his immediate entourage and the offices of the principal institutions of the Movement to establish themselves at Rabwah. There were few facilities and amenities available at that time at Rabwah and life there, particularly in the trying heat of the summer, was most uncomfortable and stark. But the enthusiasm and eagerness of the Khalifatul Masih and his own shining example, in the face of all the hardships to which life at Rabwah was subject, served to inspire everyone to put forth his best in every situation. In due course, better accommodation was provided for all the institutions of the Movement, a plentiful supply of sweet water became available, electricity was supplied from the grid, a telephone connection was established, trees were planted and began to grow and in due course to afford shade along the principal streets, and most of the amenities pertaining to a town of the size of Rabwah were provided. The population of Rabwah exceeds fifteen thousand, and though simplicity and even austerity are still the rule of life in Rabwah, more than a hundred thousand men and women from far and near are accommodated at Rabwah on the occasion of the Annual Conference of the Movement in the last week of December. Rabwah is still a comparatively small town but it is known all over the world as the headquarters of the Ahmadiyya Movement, whose membership already exceeds ten million. It is undoubtedly the most dynamic religious Movement in the world. All this has been consummated and has grown out of the seed sown by the Promised Messiah, and nurtured and guarded by his Successors more particularly by Khalifatul Masih II during more than half a century of his Khilafat.

The members of the Movement who were directed to stay on in Qadian, after the departure of the Khalifatul Masih for Lahore, found themselves in a situation of great peril, but they faced it with firmness and steadfastness. Their attitude was one of prayerful humility and cheerful acceptance of the role of honour that had been assigned to them of safeguarding the holy places at the centre of the Movement. The influx of non-Muslim refugees from Pakistan still continued, and though there was an apparent respite in killing and looting, there was extreme tension and currency was given to rumours which portended that violence might erupt at any moment. The police, the army and the representatives of the civil administration, instead of adopting measures that could guarantee everyone's security and could help to restore and maintain order, were only concerned with putting pressure on the Ahmadis and urging them to move out of Qadian and to proceed to Pakistan by whatever means might be available. On their part the Ahmadis were firmly resolved to hold their ground under all circumstances and at all costs, and to discharge fully and honourably the responsibility that had been placed upon them by the Khalifatul Masih. They had to be on the alert all the time, constantly seeking and relying entirely on the grace and mercy of God. Communication with the Khalifatul Masih was maintained off and on, the situation was reported to him from time to time, his guidance was sought and followed. At intervals, while the system of armed convoys was in operation, some of them were directed to move to Pakistan and replacements arrived from Pakistan. These exchanges were put an end to within a few days when the convoy system began to be resented and disturbed by the preponderating non-Muslim population along the route and had to be abandoned. By the end of the year, the situation assumed a precarious stability and the Khalifatul Masih determined that three hundred and thirteen of those Ahmadis who were still in Qadian should stay on permanently for the purpose of safeguarding the holy places, and the rest should move to Pakistan. A skeleton organization was set up at Qadian and the necessary institutions were revived and began to function on a limited scale.

Over a couple of years those members of the Movement who had chosen to stay on at Qadian were exposed to certain hazards and had to endure extremes of hardship and privation, but the situation crawled towards normality and in the end arrived at stability. The small community in Qadian was well-knit, the bonds of brotherhood held it together firmly and beneficently and all the currents of life flowed smoothly along righteous lines. The wives and dependents of the majority of those who had settled down permanently at Qadian soon joined them and the rigours of celibate life were thus softened to a large degree. The office-bearers of the revived institutions established contact with the branches of the Movement all over India and Qadian functioned once more as the headquarters of the Movement for the whole of India. All activities pertaining to the headquarters were resumed. A school was established, a weekly paper began to be published and the Annual Conference was revived. Relations with the non-Muslim sections of the people of the town, at first tenuous and hesitant, became friendly, intimate and co-operative. The factor that proved most helpful in this respect was that the daily lives of the Ahmadis presented a spectacle of the practical exercise of the highest moral and spiritual qualities. They did not, for a moment, sulk in their tents, but were cheerful, forthcoming and co-operative in matters of common concern, and were ready to give of their best in the service of their fellow citizens. The civil administration found them honest, diligent, law-abiding and, to its surprise, loyal; though they were watched suspiciously every time tension arose between Pakistan and India. The administration had been assured, time after time, that having made the choice of Indian citizenship, they were bound to be loyal citizens, not as a matter of policy, but as a matter of faith, as Islam insisted on loyalty to one's country. Nevertheless it took a long time for the administration to be convinced and fully reassured on the point.

The degree of confidence that the Ahmadis were able to establish between themselves and the non-Muslim sections of the population of the town might be judged, among other things, from the fact that after the passage of only a few years, Maulvi Abdur Rahman Sahib, Amir of the Community at Qadian, who had been elected a member of the Municipal Committee of Qadian, was later elected President of the Municipal Committee by his non-Muslim colleagues on the Committee, and discharged his duties as President to the entire satisfaction of everyone. Sahibzada Mirza Wasim Ahmad Sahib, a younger son of the Khalifatul Masih, and a permanent resident of Qadian, has, throughout, carried the responsibilities of the office of Secretary for Propagation of the Movement in India, and has now, on the demise of Maulvi Abdur Rahman Sahib, been appointed Amir of the community at Qadian. He is universally respected and held in honour by the whole population of Qadian, on account of the excellent example that he has throughout furnished of a completely devoted, God-fearing, righteous person, who has proved himself an affectionate and helpful friend and brother for everyone, irrespective of caste, creed, age or sex.

Today the Ahmadiyya Community in Qadian numbers more than two thousand and leads a totally beneficent and active vigorous existence. Qadian is a very active centre for all the Indian branches of the Movement, and as such operates at a high level. All over India the branches of the Movement continue to function efficiently in ever-widening circles of activity. The attendance at the Annual Conference of the Movement at Qadian has been growing steadily, and runs into thousands. One very satisfactory and striking feature is that a substantial proportion of those participating in the Annual Conference is non-Muslim. The Ahmadiyya High School at Qadian has several non-Muslim students on its rolls. All the central departments of the Movement at Qadian function efficiently and vigorously and the annual budget of the Central Organization now runs into hundreds of thousands of rupees and is constantly growing.

The Ahmadiyya community in Qadian is the only Muslim community in the Indian Province of the Punjab. It has throughout, in adversity and in comparative prosperity, most worthily upheld the banner of Islam and Ahmadiyyat, and has illustrated, in practice, the highest standard of moral and spiritual values inculcated by Islam.

Needless to say there is complete accord between Qadian and Rabwah, each in turn complements and supplements the other. The shifting of the world headquarters of the Movement from Qadian to Rabwah that became inevitable in the middle of the terrible holocaust of the summer and autumn of 1947, was certainly a part of the divine design and was accepted as such by the Community. The prophecies relating to that event have unfolded their purpose over the years, they also indicated, very clearly, that Qadian would, once again, become the world headquarters of the Movement. When and how that would be brought about is within the knowledge of God alone, but that it will be brought about is a certainty that cannot fail to be consummated.

On arrival in Lahore on the last day of August 1947, the Khalifatul Masih was confronted with many urgent problems. Despite his preoccupation with them, and his constant nagging anxiety with regard to the rapidly deteriorating situation in Qadian, he felt that he should give expression to his appraisal of the questions that needed the attention of not only those who were in positions of authority in Pakistan, but also of all intelligent Pakistanis. Public opinion needed to be enlightened and to be led into practical channels so that it could make its due contribution towards shaping policies and putting them into effect. With this purpose in mind, he delivered a series of addresses in Lahore, each under the presidency of a notable public personality, which were well attended and received good and appreciative press publicity. He then travelled to the principal cities of West Pakistan, Sialkot, Jhelum, Karachi, Peshawar, Rawalpindi and Quetta, in that order, and addressed large and appreciative audiences in those cities on the different facets of the problems confronting Pakistan. His analysis of each situation was masterly, but was reduced to and expressed in simple terms which made it easily comprehensible, and his suggestions, solutions and guidance were wise and most helpful. He was everywhere listened to with great attention, as his prestige at the time stood very high, on account of all the help and support that he had given to Mr Jinnah and the Muslim League in the crucial period during which the shape of the future constitution of India was being settled and the relief and shelter that was provided at Qadian for the Muslim refugees from East Punjab during the days of the terrible aftermath of the partition. It was noted with appreciative satisfaction that at no time in the course of his addresses did he make the slightest allusion to the sufferings of the Ahmadiyya Community and the loss of lives and property incurred by it during the period of terror, or to the help that it was able to render to everyone within its reach.

Hazrat Khalifatul Masih II moved from his temporary residence in Lahore to his permanent residence at Rabwah on 19 September 1949 and was now able to devote his full attention to the establishment of the new World Headquarters of the Movement, pulling together all the threads that bound the Community together and restarting the forward march of the Movement which had been so grievously interrupted by the tragic events that followed upon the partition of the country. The finances of the Community had fallen into a certain degree of inevitable disarray and were speedily reorganized on a firm basis and henceforward went on multiplying themselves in a surprising manner. In April 1949, the Annual Conference of the Movement had already been held in Rabwah, and most of the institutions of the Movement were re-established in Rabwah in the course of the year. Of the principal institutions, only the Talimul Islam College continued in the D.A.V. College building in Lahore, awaiting the construction of its own building at Rabwah. This took another five years. After the move of the Khalifatul Masih to Rabwah, everything began to hum as of yore and all the branches in Pakistan and abroad became firmly knitted together once more under the unobstructed and freely circulating guidance of the Khalifatul Masih.

The Movement had established footholds in British East Africa, as it then was, in the time of the Promised Messiah. The footholds became linked together in course of time, and during the Second Khilafat burgeoned into a network of active branches.

In the early years of the Second Khilafat, branches of the Movement had been established in the British colonies of West Africa and were doing very good work. Indeed, they were making such rapid progress that Christian missionaries in West Africa, and those interested in the spread of Christianity in the West African states, began to be apprehensive that their dream of Christianizing the whole of West Africa was likely to be frustrated in consequence of the advent of Ahmadiyyat in some of the West African countries.

Ahmadiyya missions had also been opened in some of the countries of South East Asia and were making good progress, particularly in Indonesia. Active branches had been established as far afield as Palestine, Fiji and Mauritius.

An Ahmadiyya centre had been established in Chicago, Illinois, and branches were springing up in some of the mid-western and eastern states of America. Thus, the Movement was already assuming world-wide standing. So far the only notable mission established in Europe was the one in London which had come into being simultaneously with the Second Khilafat.

A mission had, at one time, been opened in Paris but was not able to gain a firm foothold in that city, or outside it, and was closed a few years later. The persistence and steadfastness of the missionary assigned to Madrid began slowly to yield fruit and within a few years a small Spanish group of adherents of the Movement emerged in Madrid. A mission was opened in Rome, and though at one time it appeared that a branch of the Movement might be established in the capital of Christendom, that expectation has not yet been fulfilled. A beginning was made in Poland and later in Hungary and also in Albania, but political developments in those countries blocked further progress.

These instances afford further confirmation of the verity, repeatedly affirmed in the Quran, that all guidance is in the hands of God and proceeds from Him, and that there is a term appointed for every consummation. Man's part is to put forth earnest, prayerful effort in the full certainty that the divine purpose is bound to be fulfilled in all respects in due course.

Some of the other countries of Europe, however, present a more hopeful picture. Under the dynamic direction of Khalifatul Masih II missions were established also in Switzerland, Germany, the Netherlands, Denmark and Sweden. These missions made such good progress that mosques were built during the Rabwah period of the Second Khilafat in Zurich, Frankfurt, the Hague and Hamburg.

During the Third Khilafat Mosques have been opened in Copenhagen and in Gothenburg.

Recently a beginning has been made with the establishment of a branch in Poland.

All this activity has stemmed from the initiation of the Tahrik Jadeed by Khalifatul Masih II in 1934. English, German, Dutch, Danish, Esperanto, Swahili and Lugandi translations of the Holy Quran have been published, and French and Russian translations have been prepared and are being revised.

With regard to the activities of the Movement inside Pakistan the Khalifatul Masih felt the need of strengthening the machinery for propagation in the rural areas. For this purpose he instituted the scheme which was given the name of Waqf Jadeed (New Dedication). At the start the scope of this scheme was somewhat limited but after some time it became one of the regular permanent departments of the Central Organization of the Movement. The purpose of the scheme was to infuse fresh spirit and vigour into the rural sections of the Community, to urge them to greater and more eager conformity to the moral and spiritual values inculcated by Islam, and to convey the message of the Movement to wider and wider circles, both by precept and by example. The workers of the scheme were chosen with great care for their spirit of devotion and their eagerness to set an example of austerity, righteousness, helpfulness and service of humanity in their daily lives. They were not required to possess high academic qualifications, but they had to be ready to make every kind of sacrifice in the cause of duty. This institution began to yield beneficent results on a large scale within a short time. The activities of its workers achieved a remarkable measure of success among a community of non-Muslims that formed an enclave in the Province of Sindh close to the border of Rajputana. By now a large section of them have accepted Islam and within a short period most of them have carried out an appreciable cultural, moral and spiritual transformation. It is to be hoped that at no distant date all of them will be absorbed completely into the cultural and religious pattern of the Movement.

The most baffling and yet vital issue that confronted Pakistan at the very moment of its emergence as an independent state was the question of the accession of the State of Jammu and Kashmir to Pakistan. Over 80 per cent of the population of the State was Muslim, but the ruler was a non-Muslim who was anxious to bring about the accession of the State to India rather than to Pakistan. In an attempt to coerce the high-spirited Muslims of Poonch, many of whom had obtained military training during the Second World War, into opting for accession of the State to India, the Maharaja and his administration embarked on a programme of repressive measures in Poonch. These measures evoked a violent reaction on the part of the Muslim population of Poonch, who repudiated their allegiance to the Maharaja, declared their independence of him, and took up arms to defend themselves against the Maharaja's military forces. They achieved a measure of success in the early stages of their struggle in which they were helped by their kith and kin across the border in the Punjab. When the news of their heroic struggle was carried to the tribal areas of the Frontier, a large scale incursion of tribal forces into the State of Kashmir was organized, which the Maharaja's forces were not able to withstand. At this juncture the Maharaja fled in panic from Srinagar, the capital of Kashmir, to Jammu, the capital of the territory of that name, and despatched an urgent message to the Government of India offering the accession of the State to India and pleading for immediate military assistance. His offer of accession was provisionally accepted and adequate military assistance was immediately provided by the Government of India. It was announced by the Government of India that once law and order were restored in the territories of the State, the question of the accession of the State to India or Pakistan would be determined in accord with the freely expressed wishes of the people of the State.

Subsequent developments clearly established that this announcement of the Government of India was only a ruse to cover its military takeover of the State which, from the very first moment, was intended to make the State an integral part of India. The arrival of the Indian military contingents in the valley of Kashmir served to block the advance of the tribal hosts a few miles short of Srinagar, but thereafter the severe cold of the winter in the mountainous region of Kashmir brought about a stalemate and India found it difficult to drive the tribal hosts out of the territories of the State. In the meantime Gilgit, Hunza and portions of Ladakh repudiated their nominal allegiance to the Maharaja and went over to Pakistan.

In this situation the Government of India, at the beginning of 1948, placed the matter before the Security Council of the United Nations describing it as a situation that constituted a grave threat to the maintenance of international peace. Pakistan was represented before the Security council by its Foreign Minister, an Ahmadi.

The Security Council, after listening to lengthy statements of the representatives of India and Pakistan, discovered that despite their acute differences of outlook, points of view and appraisal of the actual situation, there was one matter on which there was enough agreement between the parties which could form the basis of a settlement of the dispute between them. The Indian representative had made a clear submission to the Security Council that the policy of the government of India on the question of the accession of a State to India or Pakistan was that in cases in which the ruler of a State adhered to one religious persuasion and the majority of the people of the State professed allegiance to the other religious persuasion, the question of the accession of the State should be determined in accordance with the freely expressed wishes of the people of the State. This was acceptable to Pakistan. When, however, the Security Council framed a resolution which would ensure a free expression of their wishes by the people of Kashmir on the question of the accession of the State to India or to Pakistan, India embarked upon a course of subterfuge, chicanery and quibbling, against which the Security Council, and the Commission appointed by it, felt helpless. The Commission did succeed in persuading the two governments to accept two resolutions proposed by it with the object of ascertaining the wishes of the people of the State on the question of accession, and in consequence to agree to a ceasefire on 1 January 1949. A ceasefire line was settled and demarcated on the ground, and there the matter has stuck for nearly thirty years, so that now the Government of India pretends that there is no longer any dispute over the question of the accession of the State as India has unilaterally carried out its original design of making the State of Jammu and Kashmir an integral part of its dominions. The question is still formally on the agenda of the Security Council, but no one knows how to move it towards a solution that would be acceptable, not only to Pakistan and India, but also the people of Kashmir, whose interests are vitally involved. Despite all that has happened and all the efforts that India has made towards winning the goodwill of the people of Kashmir, there is no doubt in anyone's mind that if the wishes of the people of the valley were ascertained under conditions and in a manner that would guarantee their free expression, there would still be near unanimity in favour of the accession of the State to Pakistan, rather than to India.

From the moment of his arrival in Lahore at the end of August 1947, the Khalifatul Masih had been at pains to point out that the accession of the State of Jammu and Kashmir to Pakistan was vital, not only from the point of view of the defence and security of Pakistan, but also for the commercial and industrial development both of Pakistan and of Kashmir itself. He also urged that the question of the accession of Kashmir to Pakistan or to India must be approached keeping in mind the future of the State of Hyderabad in South India. He maintained that a clear and unequivocal understanding must be reached with India that these two problems should be resolved by the application of the same principle to both, that is to say, it should be agreed that the question of accession of the two states should be determined either according to the wishes of the respective rulers in each case, or according to the freely expressed wishes of the people of each State. His own inclination was in favour of securing the accession of Kashmir to Pakistan and not in any way obstructing the accession of Hyderabad to India. Unfortunately, his strong pleas in that behalf were ignored by the authorities in Pakistan with dire consequences in the long run.

Towards the end of April 1948 it was realized that India had decided to seek a solution of the problem of Kashmir through the use of military force, and military intelligence indicated that India was making preparations for a military advance in strength all along the line in Kashmir. The Prime Minister of Pakistan received a report from the Commander-in-Chief of the Pakistan forces which stressed the perilous situation in which Pakistan would be placed in case of a military advance in force by India along the Kashmir border. The report concluded with a strong recommendation that Pakistan should post its regular forces along the border of Kashmir in sufficient strength to block the advance of the Indian forces. Acting upon the advice of the Commander-in-Chief, the Prime Minister, who also held the portfolio of defence, authorized military dispositions to be made along the Kashmir border in conformity with the recommendation of the Commander-in-Chief, so that from the first week of May 1948 the regular forces of both Dominions were engaged in combat against each other along the Kashmir border.

The Khalifatul Masih was not content with offering well-reasoned advice to the Administration of Pakistan. He made a substantial contribution in terms of men and money towards the struggle that Pakistan was now waging with India over the accession of Kashmir. The number of Ahmadis serving in the Pakistan forces at the time, both as officers and other ranks, was much higher than their proportion in the population. Those of them who were serving in the units that were engaged in combat on the Kashmir border established an enviable record of good service and outstanding achievement in battle. The Community had suffered terribly in respect of personnel and resources in the tragic aftermath of the partition. Nevertheless, under the directions of the Khalifatul Masih, an entire battalion of Ahmadi volunteers was organized and was placed at the disposal of the Commander-in-Chief, for deployment on the Kashmir border in the late spring of 1948. It was called the Furqan Battalion and continued in active service on the Kashmir front till the cessation of hostilities on 1 January 1949. The entire cost of maintaining the Battalion at the front was borne by the Ahmadiyya Community. The Battalion established a high reputation for discipline, courage, bravery and an eager spirit of service and sacrifice, an appreciation of which was conveyed by the Commander-in-Chief in his letter to the Khalifatul Masih, when the Battalion was disbanded.

The first grave crisis encountered by the Movement was the death of its Holy Founder on 26 May 1908. By the grace and mercy of Allah, the Movement was enabled to negotiate it successfully through the unanimous election of Hazrat Maulvi Nurud Din Sahib as Khalifatul Masih I.

An even graver crisis arose in March 1914 on the death of Hazrat Khalifatul Masih I. For a while it threatened to rip the Community apart right down its middle. Again, by the grace and mercy of Allah, it was surmounted by the wisdom, sagacity, tact, farsight and prayers of Hazrat Khalifatul Masih II.

Sir Herbert Emerson and the Ahrar combined to confront the Movement with a third crisis twenty years later, in the autumn of 1934. The grace and mercy of Allah again came to the rescue of the Movement, and the blessed initiation of

Tahrik Jadeed opened the way of farther and faster progress of the Movement.

In 1953, the orthodox Muslim divines made a tremendous effort to incite the masses to wipe out the Movement by violence. While no great harm was done in Karachi, which was still the seat of government, murder, grievous hurt, arson and large-scale destruction of property were let loose against the members of the Movement. Yet again, the grace and mercy of Allah enabled the Community to weather the storm. The aftermath lingered yet awhile, and bitterness and rancour rankled in some bosoms.

In March 1954 the Khalifatul Masih completed forty years of his Khalifat. It will be appreciated that from the moment of his election to his sacred and exalted office, the Khalifatul Masih had been continuously preoccupied with problems of a baffling variety and volume calling for the exercise of the highest qualities of astonishing diversity, and that on no occasion was he found wanting. If he had confined himself entirely to urging the Community towards the maintenance of a high standard of moral and spiritual qualities, that in itself would have been a full-time occupation, calling for the very best that any human being could put forth. Under his wise and fostering care, reinforced by his continuous humble and earnest supplications to the Divine, in all seasons and at all hours, but more particularly during the latter part of the night, the Community had grown vastly in numbers and was now spread all around the globe. Its constant care and supervision, the provision of comfort and consolation for different sections in diverse situations of trial and tribulation, the constant urging towards higher achievement in all walks of life, the demand for the upholding of the highest moral and spiritual values, imposed upon the Khalifatul Masih a heavy strain which, but for the grace and mercy of God, would have destroyed a lesser person within the space of a few years. His high and sterling qualities and characteristics had, however, been presaged in glowing and superlative terms by God Himself in the galaxy of prophecies set out in the announcement of his revered father of 20 February 1886. Every one of them was illustrated and fulfilled in an astonishing manner, in the face of the most adverse combination of circumstances during the course of more than half a century of his Khilafat. To the members of the Movement he was, at all times, a deeply loving father to whom they could look at all times and in all circumstances for guidance, advice, help, encouragement, appreciation and admonition; to all intelligent, reasonable people of goodwill he proved himself a wise friend and counsellor; towards his opponents he was forbearing and truly sympathetic over their lack of understanding; to the afflicted he was, without discrimination, a ready source of comfort, consolation and relief. Yet, there were those who, through error, bigotry, misunderstanding or sheer perversity entertained bitter hostility towards him and were capable of subjecting him to the most heinous outrages.

One day in March 1954 a young man belonging to this last category managed to take his stand in the first line of worshippers immediately behind him, while he was leading the afternoon service in the principal mosque at Rabwah. In the middle of the service he suddenly advanced upon him from his rear and drove the blade of a long sharp knife into his neck with murderous force. There was profuse bleeding from the injury which the efforts of those who were nearest to him failed to staunch completely. With a wad of cotton cloth pressed closely against his neck he was able to walk across the few yards that separated him from his residence. In his state of agony, characteristically, his first thought was for the safety of his assailant. He directed: 'Secure the young man but do him no harm. This is an order.' His direction was loudly announced to the bewildered congregation in the mosque and served to secure his assailant against the least harm. He was, in due course, handed over to the police and was eventually sentenced to a substantial term of imprisonment.

The injury inflicted upon the Khalifatul Masih was deep and grievous and had a serious effect on his nervous system. The surgeons who attended upon him made a diagnosis which they put in reassuring terms. The speed with which the injury was apparently healed also served to reassure everyone; but its after effects persisted and it soon became apparent that he was not able to maintain his activities at the level at which he was accustomed to work. He was 65 years of age, had never been in robust health, had always driven himself hard and had given himself little respite. He was now called upon to pay part of the price. On the other hand, but for the sheer grace and mercy of God, the injury might have proved instantaneously fatal. Indeed, the surgeons were surprised that his life had been spared. The blade of the knife had penetrated into his neck a distance of four inches and its point had stopped right at the jugular vein. The examination of the surgeons and the X-ray impressions failed to reveal any injury to the vein itself. But as the patient, even after the apparently complete healing of the wound, continued to suffer discomfort and unease, he was not satisfied that all was well with him; though the repeated examinations carried out by the surgeons disclosed no cause for the discomfort. They hoped that the passage of time would complete the process of inner healing and the slight strain on the nervous system would gradually be eased and would ultimately be removed altogether, but this prognostication was not completely fulfilled, and the Khalifatul Masih decided in 1955 to proceed to Europe and seek expert medical and surgical advice.

He was examined very thoroughly by top experts in Zurich, Hamburg and London with such assistance as could be drawn from X-ray impressions, etc., and the unanimous conclusion was that the point of the knife had broken at the jugular vein and was embedded in it. The expert advice was that no attempt should be made to extricate it as the risk to his life involved in any such operation was too serious to be worth taking. It was hoped that the pressure on the vein and the consequent effect on the nervous system might be slowly eased and the patient be able to resume his activities at a reduced tempo. He was advised to adopt a restful pattern of life and to avoid hard work and long periods of sustained labour. For a person of his temperament and high capacities this was a disappointing prospect. But there was no help for it. He was still able to carry on a comparatively active life, but the pressure on his nervous system, instead of being eased with the passage of time, tended to be intensified progressively.

One of his prophetic titles was Fazle Umar, indicating his spiritual affinity to Hazrat Umar, the Second Successor of the Holy Prophet, peace be on him. The Khalifatul Masih not only became the Second Successor of the Promised Messiah, the spiritual reflection of the Holy Prophet, but several of the projects undertaken by him, and his achievements in diverse spheres, bore a close resemblance to the achievements of Hazrat Umar; even the almost fatal tragedy to which he was subjected by his assailant was identical with the tragedy that brought the Second Khilafat of the Holy Prophet, peace be on him, to a sudden and premature end. Hazrat Umar was also attacked in the middle of the Prayer service that he was leading by a non-Muslim who had worked up some grudge against him and who inflicted with a dagger severe injuries upon him which proved fatal.

During his visit to Europe in 1955, the Khalifatul Masih inspected the various missions in Europe and held a conference in London of all the missionaries working in the different European countries, in which he checked up on their activities and progress and gave them directions and furnished them with guidance with regard to their future work.

Having in mind the crisis with which the Movement had been confronted on the demise of Khalifatul Masih I, he had already established an Electoral College for the election of a Khalifa, when the sacred office should become vacant by the Khalifa's death. The college was composed of the following, subject to the essential qualification that every elector must be a member of the Movement and should be a supporter of the Khilafat:

(1) The surviving sons of the Promised Messiah.
(2) The President of the Sadar Anjuman Ahmadiyya.

(3) All Secretaries of the Sadar Anjuman.
(4) The Director General and the Directors of Tahrik Jadeed.
(5) The President of Waqf Jadeed.
(6) The Principal of the Talimul Islam College.
(7) The Headmaster of the Talimul Islam High School.
(8) The President of the Theological Seminary.
(9) The President of Ansarullah.
(10) The President of Khuddamul Ahmadiyya.
(11) Representative of Lajna Imaullah.
(12) Missionaries who had worked abroad for a minimum period of three years.
(13) Missionaries who had worked within Pakistan or India for a minimum period of five years.
(14) Amirs of circles in Pakistan.
(15) Members of the Movement who had joined the Movement in the lifetime of the Founder of the Movement.

The total membership of the college is approximately one hundred and fifty.

The health of Khalifatul Masih II entered upon a prolonged process of slow but progressive decline and the end came on 8 November 1965. His demise shook the Movement to its foundations. Every member of the Movement was overwhelmed with grief, the depth and intensity of which were beyond measure. The shock was bewildering and baffling. It seemed that the vacuum thus created would be hard, if not impossible, to fill. Everyone, however, realized that the divine will was supreme and no human being was immortal.

The members of the Community converged in large numbers upon Rabwah for the purpose of seeking comfort and consolation from each other's company and to pay their tribute of love and devotion to the sacred memory of the holy one who had guided the destinies of the Movement for more than half a century and had given freely of his love, sympathy and support to everyone without discrimination.

The President of the Sadar Anjuman Ahmadiyya, in conformity with the constitution of the Electoral College, convened a meeting of the College on 9 November for the purpose of electing the new Khalifa. The interval between the demise of Khalifatul Masih II and the meeting of the Electoral College was spent by everyone in humble and earnest supplication to the Divine, that the members of the Electoral College may be rightly guided in their choice of the Successor to Khalifatul Masih II. The College met in a deeply prayerful mood and Sahibzada Mirza Nasir Ahmad Sahib, eldest son of the departed Khalifatul Masih, who had been Principal of the Talimul Islam College for 21 years, was elected Khalifatul Masih III by an overwhelming majority of the Electoral College. As soon as the choice of the Electoral College became known it was universally felt as if comfort and consolation were descending upon every heart from heaven.

The funeral prayers over the beloved departed, led by the newly elected Khalifa, and his interment later on the same day were a deeply moving experience for everyone, which was born of conflicting emotions of grief and bereavement on the one hand and steadfast submission to the divine will, and a firm resolve to march forward in earnestness, giving of one's very best, on the other. The bonds of brotherhood were felt to be gaining in strength, and the urge towards greater uprightness and righteousness in every sphere appeared to be the prevailing mood.

Tributes in superlative terms were paid to the memory of Khalifatul Masih II by the entire press of Pakistan. It would be enough to set out as an example the one that was published in *The Light,* a weekly publication of the dissentient group published from Lahore. In its issue of 16 November 1965, under the caption 'A GREAT NATION-BUILDER', the editor wrote:

The death of Mirza Bashirud Din Mahmud Ahmad, Head of the Ahmadiyya Movement (Rabwah) rang the curtain down on a most eventful career, packed with a multitude of far-reaching enterprises. A man of versatile genius and dynamic personality, there was hardly any sphere of contemporary thought and life during the past half century, from religious scholarship to missionary organization, even political leadership, on which the deceased did not leave a deep imprint. A whole network of Islamic missions and mosques scattered over the world, the deep penetration of Islamic preaching in Africa, transplanting the long-entrenched Christian Missions, are a standing monument to the imaginative planning, organizational capacity and unflagging drive of the deceased. There has hardly been a leader of men in recent times who commanded such deep devotion from his followers, not only when alive, but also after death, when sixty thousand people rushed from all parts of the country to pay their last homage to their departed leader. In the story of the Ahmadiyya Movement the Mirza Sahib's name will go down as a Great Nation Builder, who built up a well-knit community in the face of heavy odds, making it a force to be counted with. We offer the bereaved family our deep condolences in their great loss.

The fulfilment of every aspect of the grand prophecy of the Promised Messiah set out in the announcement of 20 February 1886, in the person of Hazrat Khalifatul Masih II, furnishes irrefutable proof of the truth of the Promised Messiah. From whatever point of view it is approached, the impossibility of the prophecy having been the product of the workings of a human mind becomes patent. The prophecy is studded with innumerable contingencies the non-fulfilment of a single one of which would have demonstrated its falsehood, had it been an imposture. The fulfilment of the whole cluster of the grand predictions comprised in the prophecy leaves no room for a shadow of doubt that the prophecy was made under Divine direction and its fulfilment firmly establishes the existence of God, the truth of the Holy Prophet of Islam, the divine origin of the Holy Quran, the truth of the Promised Messiah and the righteousness of Hazrat Khalifatul Masih II, and the fact that he was the Divinely appointed Successor of the Promised Messiah. His outstanding qualities and his astonishing record of high achievement in so many fields of human endeavour, all related to the revival of the faith and the supremacy of Islam over all other religions, marked him out as a great and shining figure in the annals of the Renaissance of Islam in the latter days.

CHAPTER SIXTEEN

Hazrat Mirza Nasir Ahmad Sahib, Khalifatul Masih III, was 56 years of age when he was elected to his exalted office. Under the directions of his revered father he had at an early age committed the whole of the Holy Quran to memory. His education and training had comprised the religious as well as the secular in both of which he attained high proficiency. All through priority had been given to the religious over the secular and to the spiritual over the intellectual, yet neither was neglected. After having completed his course of theological and oriental studies at the level of High Proficiency, he graduated from Government College Lahore and obtained the Bachelor of Arts Degree of the Punjab University. He then proceeded to England for postgraduate studies at Balliol College, Oxford, and in due course obtained the Honours Degree of the University of Oxford, and later became Master of Arts of the University.

On return from England he was appointed a professor in the Theological Seminary at Qadian and later became its Principal. On the establishment, in 1944 of the Talimul Islam College, which was affiliated to the Punjab University, he was appointed its first Principal, which office he filled with distinction for 21 years, and which he relinquished on his election as Khalifatul Masih III. Under his devoted care and guardianship the Talimul Islam College went steadily forward and established a record of both academic achievement and athletic performance, as one of the foremost educational institutions in the province. For a number of years Sahibzada Mirza Nasir Ahmad Sahib also served as a member of the governing body of the Punjab University in which capacity he rendered valuable service to the cause of higher education in the province.

While for more than twenty years the college had a prior claim on his time and attention, he was ready to serve in whatever capacity he was called upon. For a period he served as the President of the Sadar Anjuman Ahmadiyya, which office, though honorary, involved the discharge of heavy responsibilities at the Centre of the organizational pattern of the Movement.

He possesses a firm but gentle disposition which is characterized chiefly by shyness and modesty. It has been observed, however, that when the occasion so demands he does not fail to provide dashing leadership.

He was called to his exalted office at a mature age in the face of the most poignant tragedy of his revered father's death, and by the grace and mercy of God, has proved himself an inexhaustible source of comfort and consolation to all members of the Movement, not only at that critical juncture in the fortunes of the Community but through the series of crises with which the Movement has been faced from time to time during his Khilafat.

From the beginning of his Khilafat he has given proof of great zeal and drive in the pursuit of the objectives of the Movement. One of the very first projects that he initiated was the setting up of the Fazl-i-Umar Foundation in memory of Hazrat Khalifatul Masih II, the purpose of which was to push forward all the designs in which the late Khalifatul Masih had taken particular interest. It was made clear that the Foundation would not take over or intervene in the exercise of any function that had been allotted to any of the existing institutions or departments of the Movement, though it could be called upon to render aid or assistance in carrying out any project which the department concerned was unable to put through for lack of adequate personnel or resources. An appeal was made to the Community to provide two and a half million rupees as the capital of the proposed Foundation, the income of which would be utilized by the Foundation for the achievement of its purposes. The Community responded readily to the appeal and provided over two million rupees in cash contributions to serve as the capital of the Foundation. This was a gratifying indication that the spirit of devotion and sacrifice that had inspired the Community under Hazrat Khalifatul Masih II had not only survived the shattering shock of his death, but had in effect been stimulated by the consciousness that a heavier burden of responsibility now rested on the shoulders of every member of the Movement.

As soon as the Foundation was set up it began to occupy itself with the study and formulation of such projects as were designed to forward the purposes for which the Foundation had been set up. For instance, it initiated a project for the purpose of stimulating the intellectual capacities of those members of the Movement who were interested in scholastic pursuits. It announced that it would make five awards every year of the value of one thousand rupees to each scholar who would prepare and submit to the Foundation a thesis on any of the diverse intellectual topics specified by the Foundation, which in the estimation of the Foundation gave proof of high intellectual endeavour. The response to this initiative of the Foundation has been encouraging but has not been as enthusiastic as it had been hoped. The Foundation is continuing the project and expects that in the course of time the standard and number of theses submitted to it every year will continue to rise.

With the development of Rabwah as the Headquarters of the Movement, the need of an adequate library to which the intellectual sections of the Community could have free access had been felt. But the Sadar Anjuman Ahmadiyya had not been able to make financial provision for the housing of such a library and providing the necessary cognate facilities. The Foundation came forward with the offer that it would undertake the construction of the building and other facilities pertaining to the library on some suitable site to be provided by the Anjuman. The offer of the foundation was accepted, the building was erected and on completion was handed over to the Sadar Anjuman.

As a result of the opening of new Missions of the Movement and the proliferation of its branches across the globe, the number of members of the Movement in foreign countries visiting Rabwah in all seasons of the year, but more particularly on the occasion of the Annual Conference in the last week of December, has grown every year. The Tahrik Jadeed had built a modest guest house simultaneously with the construction of its offices which was maintained in good condition, but the accommodation provided therein was limited and soon became inadequate for the demands made upon it. Thus the need was felt of a much larger hostel for foreign visitors which should be fitted with all the facilities to which they were accustomed at home. Again the Foundation came forward with the offer to construct such a hostel on the scale and to the specifications that would meet the need that had arisen. Its offer was accepted by the Tahrik Jadeed and the project went forward. As everywhere else, the country was about that time caught in the grip of severe inflation and the cost of the project, despite every effort at keeping it down, went up progressively and the Directorate of the Foundation began to be apprehensive whether the resources of the Foundation would prove equal to the liability that it had undertaken. Through the grace and mercy of God, the first stage of the project, which alone had been undertaken to start with, was successfully and satisfactorily completed at more than twice the cost originally estimated. The hostel was then taken over by Tahrik Jadeed. The demand for hostel accommodation of various types has continued to grow and a number of smaller hostels have been constructed or are in course of construction at the instance of institutions of the Movement other than the Fazli Umar Foundation.

The Foundation has published the first volume of the addresses delivered by Khalifatul Masih II. Other volumes will follow in due course. An authoritative biography of him has been taken in hand, of which the first of three volumes have been published.

The Founder of the Ahmadiyya Movement had

announced very early: 'Truth will be victorious and Islam will again experience the day of light and freshness which it had experienced early in its history, and the sun will rise again in its perfection as it had risen before.'

In those early days a beginning had been made of the advance of Islam in East Africa. Hazrat Khalifatul Masih I had announced during his last illness: 'God Almighty has promised me that half a million Christians would accept Islam in Africa'; and had added: 'Education will spread in West Africa.'

On 18 February 1945 Hazrat Khalifatul Masih II said, in the course of an address:

God has reserved these African countries for Ahmadiyyat and they have a close relationship with the progress of Islam. Our future is bound up with Africa. . . . God Almighty diverted my attention to these countries in good time and then of His grace He opened the door of extraordinary progress in those countries. . . . If our younger men do not proceed quickly to these countries and do not make an attempt to win the whole of that region for Islam in the shortest possible time, no chance will be left for us to make further progress. . . . If we make even a small effort we will be supreme in those countries, not only because we are established on the truth, but also because the African temperament will support us. We shall be at an advantage against our rivals for they seek to succeed through power and force, and we shall have the support of the truth. Thus those people will, in any case, turn to us and will not turn to them. . . . This is a time of great tact and alertness for us. This is a time for great speed and swiftness for us. We must spread all over Africa in a matter of days and months and we must establish the Kingdom of the One God in those countries in place of the Trinity.

In April and May 1970 Khalifatul Masih III visited Nigeria, Ghana, Ivory Coast, Liberia, Gambia and Sierra Leone, in that order, to check up on the activities of the Missions of the Movement in those countries and to make an appraisal of the opportunities of further progress. At the end of his visit to those countries of West Africa he arrived in

London and, in an address to the Community in a meeting in which all the branches of the Movement in Britain were represented, gave a brief account of the impressions he had gathered in the West African countries that he had visited, and stressed the great need of pressing forward in West Africa. He announced a scheme that he had conceived under Divine direction, of expanding the activities of the Movement in West Africa through the establishment of a substantial number of schools and hospitals which were the great need of the people of West Africa. He mentioned that the programme that he had in mind for the next three years would require an outlay of one hundred thousand pounds sterling and called upon the Community to furnish a substantial portion of that amount as early as possible so that there should be no delay in launching the programme. The Community in Britain responded with promises of fifty-one thousand pounds, of which eleven thousand pounds were contributed within ten days. The total amount pledged by the Community for the Nusrat Jehan Scheme as the programme was named, far exceeded the hundred thousand pounds which was the original target. But this was only the financial requirement. Teachers, physicians and surgeons were needed for the schools and hospitals that were to be set up in West Africa. The response of the Community in that respect also proved quite adequate.

On his return to Rabwah the Khalifatul Masih described some of his impressions of West Africa in the course of his Friday sermons. For instance, he said in his very first sermon:

> I stand before you today to announce to you the bounties of my Beneficent Lord. It is not possible to express in words the manifestations of the Greatness and the Majesty of God Almighty and of the dignity of the Holy Prophet, peace be on him, that my companions and myself experienced in West Africa. When we arrived in that part of the world we had no idea how lovable are the people of that region and how their hearts and bosoms throb with the love of Allah and of Muhammad, the Messenger of Allah, peace be on him, and of his great spiritual son, the Mahdi. My first

impression was that the intensity of their love bordered on lunacy. They stared at me and went on staring and though they did not give verbal expression to their emotions, their love shone forth from their eyes.

On another occasion he said in the same context: 'The great day of the supremacy of Islam has dawned. No power on earth can frustrate it. Islam and Ahmadiyyat are bound to triumph. I assure you that your future is most glorious.'

On 26 June 1970 he called upon Ahmadi doctors and teachers to volunteer their services for work in West Africa, and indicated that in case he found that the number of volunteers did not correspond to the need, he would select the teachers and doctors who would be required to proceed to West Africa under his directions. He announced that he had promised the African countries that he had visited, to establish a minimum of twenty-five health centres and seventy to eighty schools in those countries.

A cluster of problems had to be resolved and pushed out of the way, before the scheme could begin to operate. But these were overcome fairly rapidly under the dynamic directions of the Khalifatul Masih and in consequence of his continuous humble supplications to the Divine. The details in each case furnished an astonishing record of beneficent achievement in the face of formidable difficulties. The success achieved by all the institutions that were set up in pursuance of the scheme was most gratifying. The efforts of the devoted physicians and surgeons to bring relief and healing to the suffering people within the range of their activities were often blessed with a degree of fulfilment that was almost miraculous. By the end of 1972 sixteen new hospitals and thirteen new secondary schools had been opened and were in full operation. The success of the medical centres was so remarkable that in many instances they became self-multiplying. In deserving cases relief was administered free, and yet the income from several of the centres not only enabled the need of suitable buildings and necessary equipment to be met but the surplus helped to establish new health centres in areas where their need was most urgent. In this manner the scheme has so multiplied itself since its initiation in 1970 that by now the financial outlay alone has exceeded a quarter of a million pounds at a modest estimate. The schools also are doing very good work and are being steadily multiplied. Fortunately the governments of the countries concerned have been most co-operative, helpful and appreciative of the service that the Movement has so eagerly and enthusiastically rendered and is rendering to their people as a practical expression of the bonds of brotherhood that operate to hold the whole of humanity together. In one or two instances red-tape held up the initiation or the progress of units of the scheme, but the persistent efforts of the workers of the Movement, helped by the prayers of the Khalifatul Masih, succeeded within a short time in overcoming the obstructions put up by the officialdom concerned.

Altogether the success achieved by the Nusrat Jehan Scheme has been most encouraging and gratifying and the Movement is now accepted in the countries concerned as an extremely beneficent dispensation. At several places the institutions established by the Movement have had to operate in beneficent competition with Christian missionary institutions. In every one of those cases the institutions of the Movement, starting years later than their rivals and working initially under a complexity of handicaps, soon overtook their rivals and have by now left them far behind in several instances. It is beginning to be realized in Christian Missionary circles that Islam and not Christianity would ultimately prevail in West Africa. The Nusrat Jehan Scheme limited originally to three years has by now become permanent, and it is expected that its activities will soon begin to be expanded into the neighbouring countries of West Africa. While the success of the scheme in every one of the countries in which it has been in operation has been most gratifying, perhaps its impact has been most striking, from a certain point of view, in the smallest of those countries, namely Gambia. That country is not only the smallest but was also the most backward of all the countries of West Africa so far as medical and educational facilities were concerned. For instance, anyone who was in need of dental care or attention had either to reconcile himself to the continuous endurance of the deficiency from which he suffered, or had to undertake a journey to Dakar, the capital of Senegal, which was the nearest place where dental attention was procurable. Under the Nusrat Jehan Scheme half a dozen health centres have been established in Gambia, including a dental clinic and a centre for the treatment of tuberculosis. There is an excellent secondary school just outside the capital which is running so well that there is already keen competition for admission to its classes.

While the success of the Nusrat Jehan Scheme in its initial stages is most encouraging, it is recognized that this is only the pioneer stage of a grand project and that the work so far initiated and in progress touches only the fringe of an enormous human problem. It is hoped, however, that by the grace and mercy of God, the start that has been made will go on expanding and multiplying till not only West Africa but the whole of the continent, hitherto designated as the Dark Continent, is illuminated with the heavenly light of Islam, and the standard of Muhammad, the Messenger of Allah, peace be on him, is planted on all the heights and in all the valleys of that vast continent.

The Movement was formally initiated in March 1889 and will complete its first century in March 1989. Hazrat Khalifatul Masih II had directed that the centenary of the Movement should be celebrated with great *éclat*. In view of this direction Khalifatul Masih III decided to make an announcement concerning the celebration of the centenary of the Movement in the Annual Conference of 1973, in which he enumerated a number of projects which he had in mind in connection with the centenary. These projects include, among others, the building of mosques in different parts of the world; the publication of the translations of the Holy Quran in French,

Russian, Italian, Spanish and other languages; publication of the philosophy of the teachings of the Quran in suitable brochures in one hundred languages; opening new Missions of the Movement in countries where no Mission is at present established; the setting up of a large printing press at the Headquarters of the Movement; the establishment of a broadcasting station in some country of West Africa where permission for such a station might be forthcoming. It is contemplated that some form of celebration would be launched as a token in March 1989 to be continued during the rest of the year to its culmination in the Annual Conference of that year. The Khalifatul Masih called upon the Community to pledge the amount of twenty-five million rupees to finance the projects and the celebration of the centenary. He suggested that as sixteen years intervened between his announcement and the culmination of the celebrations at the end of 1989, every contributor to the Centenary Fund should pay up one-sixteenth of the amount of his contribution every year. As by the grace of God the Community is expanding daily, and a certain proportion of its youth joins the ranks of workers in gainful employment every year, it is expected that the target of financial contributions aimed at when the announcement was first made would be more than doubled by the end of 1989.

In the meantime some of the projects included in the centenary programme have already been put in hand and are being proceeded with. One of them was completed in August 1976. This is a beautiful mosque built on an eminence in the city of Gothenburg which serves as a beacon of spiritual light for miles around. The opening ceremony was performed by Khalifatul Masih III and attracted a large concourse of people from all over Europe. There is a large Community of Ahmadi Muslims in Gothenburg, the membership of which was enlarged by several people joining the Movement on the occasion of the opening of the mosque.

The bigoted section of orthodox Muslim divines in Pakistan was much perturbed by the announcement of the Khalifatul Masih concerning the centenary celebrations which he made in December 1973. Time after time the plans that they had devised for the purpose of arresting the progress of the Movement had been frustrated, by the grace and mercy of God, and from each trial the Movement had emerged in greater strength and reinvigorated in spirit. Rather than learn a lesson from their repeated experiences their bitterness and hostility towards the Movement had continued to mount and the announcement of the centenary celebrations put them in a mood of desperation. In the middle of 1974 they devised a plan which was aimed at provoking anger and rancour against the Ahmadiyya Community which unfortunately succeeded only too well in its immediate purpose. An incident was staged at the Rabwah railway station, which was so managed that a party of students who belonged to an organization bitterly hostile to the Movement succeeded in provoking a number of Ahmadis, who happened to be present at the railway station when the train carrying the students arrived, into a conflict in which slight injuries were inflicted on some of the students in the party. At the next stop of the train preparations had already been made to receive the students as heroes who had suffered grievous injuries in the cause of Islam at the hands of the members of the Movement. Fiery speeches were made and the incident was painted in lurid colours. The utterly false and misleading accounts of the incident were further embroidered in the press next morning, with the addition of such false, fictitious and horrifying details as that the students had been cruelly maimed, that some of them had their tongues cut out and that others had their genitals cut off. This sent a wave of horror throughout the province and all sorts of premeditated atrocities were let loose against the members of the Movement. In the inquiry subsequently conducted by a Judge of the Lahore High Court into the incident, it was established by the medical evidence produced that all the injuries alleged to have been received by some of the students were simple bruises and scars and not a single one of them was grievous.

For reasons undisclosed the report of the inquiry has not

been published so far. This lends colour to the speculation that the administration does not come out too well in the report. Be that as it may, it is a fact that in the widespread disorders that followed upon the Rabwah incident, as it came to be known, a number of Ahmadis were killed, maimed and injured, and there was large-scale looting and destruction of properties of Ahmadis. In not a single instance did the police or the civil authorities intervene to extend their protection to the victims of violence, no investigation was made into any of the numerous outrages committed against the persons and properties of the Ahmadis, no one was arrested or tried in respect of any of them, and no compensation was awarded to any Ahmadi for the loss inflicted upon him. There were several instances in which the police openly and actively encouraged the unruly and disorderly elements to do their worst.

At Sargodha, during the perpetration of large-scale outrages against the Ahmadis, the then Chief Minister of the Province was present in the town and, though apprised of what was going on, and made aware of it by observing the columns of smoke rising above the gutted buildings, did not stir his little finger to check the course of the outrages. The same was the attitude of the Deputy Inspector General of police who was also present in the town in attendance upon the Chief Minister.

Some of the guardians of law and order explained their inaction and their dereliction of duty as having been imposed upon them by orders from on high.

The community again set an example of perfect steadfastness under extreme suffering and complete confidence in God. The bereaved and the afflicted managed to make their way to the Headquarters of the Movement, where the Khalifatul Masih applied the healing balm of compassion and love to their lacerated souls and sent them back comforted and consoled. They came with grief stricken, gloomy faces and went back smiling and cheerful.

Certain measures of relief and rehabilitation had to be

undertaken by the Community, and by the grace of God these proved most fruitful. Within a short time were witnessed numerous striking instances in which those who had suffered heavy, and in some cases crippling, losses were not only able to re-establish themselves but achieved a degree of prosperity higher than that which they had enjoyed before the disturbances. Boycotts of the Community were organized in several places which imposed great hardship upon the members of the Movement who were affected by them, especially women, children and old people. On the whole, however, the Community at large emerged from the trial stronger, more united and in greater vigour than had been the case before the trouble started. This was something that puzzled the opponents of the Movement and which they were not able to comprehend. They felt that a greater effort on their part was called for in order to coerce the members of the Movement into submission. They began to agitate that the Movement should, by legislative action, be declared outside the pale of Islam. They prevailed upon the Prime Minister to make a declaration that appropriate action would be taken in the National Assembly to achieve that end. At the start of the session of the Assembly a resolution sponsored by the government was moved, the purport of which was to declare that the members of the Ahmadiyya Movement were not Muslims for the purpose of the law and the constitution. During the debates on the resolution the Khalifatul Masih was invited to make an exposition of the beliefs and teachings of the Movement before a committee composed of the total membership of the National Assembly. He was examined at great length by the Attorney General on the minutest details of the beliefs, doctrines and teachings of the Movement. The whole proceeding boomeranged upon the sponsors and promoters of the resolution and served to make them appear inconsistent and ridiculous even in their own eyes. Nevertheless, the Assembly was dragooned into adopting the resolution with the requisite majority and it was sent up to the Senate for its approval, which was accorded within a few hours. Despite repeated requests the proceedings of the Committee of the National Assembly have not yet been made public, which is sure proof that the opponents of the Movement did not emerge with any credit from the proceedings, though through their large numbers and by outrageous abuse of the process of legislation they achieved their immediate objective. Nobody appears, however, to be certain what exactly is the import of the resolution. Attempts have been made to manipulate the resolution for the purpose of depriving the members of the Movement of the benefit of the fundamental right embedded in the constitution guaranteeing to every citizen freedom to profess and practise his religion and to establish and maintain his religious institutions. Such attempts as have been made the subject of judicial determination have only backfired against their proponents. There is no doubt, however, that the Constitutional Amendment, brought about by the resolution of the National Assembly of 7 September 1974, has placed the Movement and its members in a position of some embarrassment, if not of difficulty.

But as has always been the case in the history of the Movement, this is only one side of the picture. The whole chain of events, beginning with the Rabwah incident, stimulated a surprising degree of interest in the Movement in the minds of the serious section of the people of Pakistan, so much so that within a few weeks of the adoption of the resolution of 7 September by the National Assembly, all the material for propaganda at the Headquarters of the Movement was exhausted by a very brisk demand for it. Seekers after truth began to arrive at the Headquarters daily in large numbers to look at everything themselves, and to ascertain by direct personal inquiries the differences that separated the Movement from the bulk of the Muslims and to determine where did the truth reside. This type of curiosity was most welcome to the workers of the Movement and they strove to satisfy it completely objectively with most beneficent results. But the factor that proved most effective in this context was the personality of the Khalifatul Masih, his urbane temperament, his winning smile, the love that shone forth from his eyes and his uniform courtesy extended to everyone without discrimination. In a large majority of cases the visitors decided to join the Movement while they were still at Rabwah, and the rest followed suit within a few days of their return home. A final decision to keep out of the Movement was extremely rare. The enthusiasm and eagerness of the new entrants into the Movement has been most remarkable; their conformity to the teachings of Islam as interpreted by the Movement has been exemplary. Under this impulse membership of the Movement has risen steadily at a rate much in excess of that which had come to be regarded as normal, and a large number of new branches have been established. The hostility of the bigoted Muslim divines towards the Movement has by no means been assuaged, though the eruption of violence against the members of the Movement has subsided in a large measure. Thus the Movement has every reason to be beholden to its extreme opponents for serving as a stimulant arousing healthy curiosity about the Movement.

Such was the crisis of 1974. These crises have so far recurred with surprising regularity in the history of the Movement at intervals of approximately twenty years: 1914, 1934, 1953–54 and 1974.

As has been noticed the Holy Founder of the Ahmadiyya Movement announced almost eight decades ago to an incredulous world that according to the Holy Quran Jesus had not died on the cross but had been delivered from an accursed death by the grace and mercy of God. Thereafter he had travelled through the countries in which the lost tribes of Israel had been settled after their dispersal, and had finally arrived among a portion of them in Kashmir where he died and is buried. He had also announced that now that the knowledge of these events had been revealed to him, God in

His wisdom would progressively manifest historical evidence in support of the truth, so that the world might gain sure knowledge of the reality. So it has come about. By now a mass of evidence has been accumulated which goes to establish the accuracy of the thesis set forth by the Promised Messiah. In recent years interest has been stimulated in the central issue in this thesis, namely, whether Jesus did or did not die on the cross. A striking piece of evidence upon which attention has progressively centred more and more, is whether the piece of linen cloth in which the body of Jesus was wrapped up when it was taken down from the cross, which is now known as the Holy Shroud, furnishes evidence of a type which can help in the final and conclusive determination of the issue, one way or the other. The research so far carried out tends to lend strong support to the thesis that the body that had been wrapped in the linen cloth was that of a person who was alive and was not dead. The Holy Shroud has for some centuries been preserved in the chapel of the Dukes of Savoy in Turin Cathedral, and is exposed to public view at intervals of thirty-three years. The next public exhibition of the Holy Shroud is due in April 1978, and it is expected that permission might at last be granted by the relevant authorities to permit a small piece of the Holy Shroud, no more than a few square centimeters, to be detached for the purpose of further scientific research which might enable the age of the shroud to be determined within a matter of fifty years, one way or the other. Hitherto, scientific research into the mystery of the Holy Shroud has been carried out only on the basis of enlarged photographs of the Shroud. The possibility of submitting a piece of the Shroud itself to radio exposition has aroused great interest in the result of such research. As it seems likely that, if such research becomes possible, its results would become available by the middle of May 1978, the Ahmadiyya Movement has announced its project of holding a conference in London, in the first week of June 1978, when the subject of the deliverance of Jesus from the cross will be brought under discussion.

It is understood that the Head of the Ahmadiyya Movement will address the conference in its final session. It is expected that a mass of information relating to the reputed tomb of Jesus in Srinagar, the capital of Kashmir, will be exhibited in the conference.

The central question of the delivery of Jesus from death on the cross is of fundamental importance to the three great religions of semitic origin, Judaism, Christianity and Islam. It is therefore expected that the discourses delivered at the conference and the evidence exhibited at it will engage the attention of the religious leadership of these three faiths. Incidentally, the conference will serve to place the Ahmadiyya Movement in the van of research into the mystery that has hitherto surrounded the question of the death of Jesus upon the cross.

EPILOGUE

In the early eighties of the 19th century, a pious, middle-aged, revered personage, identifying himself completely with Islam, a faithful servant of Allah, a devoted follower of the Holy Prophet, Muhammad, peace be on him, announced that he had been a constant recipient of revelation for some years and that God had informed him that the day of the renaissance of Islam was about to dawn and that this revival would be brought about through him. This voice was raised in a small town boasting a population of no more than a few hundreds, situated in a corner of the most backward province of India, lacking all facilities for communication with the rest of the world, and bereft of all amenities which could help to soften the rigours of existence in such a milieu. This person was Hazrat Mirza Ghulam Ahmad, scion of a noble house of ancient lineage whose fortunes were now at an ebb. He had not received much formal education, but had made a deep study of the Holy Quran and was richly endowed with knowledge of the profound eternal verities.

The revelation vouchsafed to him held out, among other things, the promise that the message with which God had charged him would be carried to the ends of the earth, that he would be greatly blessed, so much so that kings would seek blessings from his garments, that the seed of spiritual revival if Islam sown by him would have a splendid sprouting, that it would flourish and grow into a strong tree that would afford shelter to multitudes, that no one would be able to arrest its growth and that the greater part of mankind would eventually seek shelter under it.

On 20 February 1886, he announced that God, of His grace and mercy, had informed him that He would bless him with a son who would be possessed of superlative qualities, which were set out in the announcement, and that he would resemble him in beauty and beneficence. This was a multi-faceted prophecy. The promised son was born on 12 January 1889.

In 1889 Hazrat Mirza Ghulam Ahmad claimed that he was the Reformer of the century whose advent had been predicted by the Holy Prophet of Islam, peace be on him. In March of that year he laid the foundation of the Ahmadiyya Movement. By then revelation descended upon him in a constant flow. He was informed that he was the Mahdi and the Promised Messiah whose advent in the latter days had been predicted. He was also told by the Divine that in his person were fulfilled the prophecies handed down in all the great faiths of the Second Advent of a great teacher in every one of those faiths.

These claims of his aroused bitter opposition towards him on the part of the religious leaders of all the principal faiths. The greater was the opposition to him, the stronger and more frequent were the Divine assurances of support, success, victory and triumph. Here and there he found acceptance among the serious minded and the truly pious, who yearned after righteousness. Their number swelled progressively from scores to hundreds, to thousands and even to hundreds of thousands in his lifetime. He was bestowed great treasures of moral and spiritual wealth which carried with it firm assurances of success and triumph, but of material resources he possessed little. This was in accord with Divine practice. His success had to come through the moral and the spiritual and not through the material or the physical, though a modicum of these was, of course, needed and was constantly provided. He predicted that material resources would also be provided in great abundance, once the moral and spiritual foundations had been firmly laid and there was left no danger of their being engulfed by the material and the physical. He warned against any tendency towards assigning priority to them over the moral and the spiritual.

A single instance might be mentioned as illustration of the paucity of his financial resources. His own near collaterals were bitterly hostile towards him and he suffered every type of hardship at their hands. At one time one of them erected a wall outside his residence, a part of which was used as a mosque, so as to block egress and ingress except by a round-about way which imposed great hardship both upon the members of his family and his visitors. This obstruction was fortunately removed through judicial action, but the apprehension of recourse to some similar action in future lingered. In this situation he decided to sink a well in the courtyard of his residence so that a supply of water for drinking and domestic purposes might be assured. The cost of the sinking of the well was estimated at Rs 200 (£13.33). He wrote to some of his followers inviting them to participate in providing the amount that was needed. He assessed the contribution of one of them, who was a physician in easy circumstances at the equivalent of two pence of the then sterling currency!

It will be appreciated that his entire dependence was upon God, in full confidence that He would provide the means whereby the purpose of his advent would continue to be fulfilled. How this happened is nothing short of the miraculous. His claim of being a recipient of revelation in an age steeped in materialism made him an object of ridicule in the eyes of the worldly. His announcement that he was the great teacher whose advent in the latter days had been foretold in all the great faiths, aroused against him the bitter hostility of all religious circles. Orthodox Muslim divines condemned him as a disbeliever and an apostate whose assassination would be an act of the highest spiritual merit. None of this caused him any perturbation. He had been divinely assured: 'God will safeguard thee against harm by people.' Throughout his life he was exposed to the evil designs of his enemies, and throughout he was miraculously safeguarded. He had appointed no bodyguard and no one was assigned the task of watching over him.

He led a wholly blameless, pure and beneficent life, which followed in the minutest detail the pattern that had been established by the Holy Prophet, peace be upon him. LIke the Holy Prophet he challenged his opponents to point to a single default in his conduct which might raise a doubt concerning his claim that he was favoured with constant communion with God. The revelation vouchsafed to him was replete with prophecies having the widest range, pertaining to all spheres of life, and every one of them has been fulfilled according to its purport and at its due time.

He founded a Community, the members of which were required to illustrate in their lives all the social, moral and spiritual values inculcated by Islam, and of which the highest example was furnished in the life of the Holy Prophet of Islam, peace be on him. The members of the Movement have been drawn from every walk of life; they are practical men pursuing the whole range of beneficent activities permissible in Islam. They are not cranks, recluses or ascetics who reject the normal values of life; they have set enviable examples of full, successful and highly beneficent lives. The distinguishing feature of their lives is the upholding of the moral and the spiritual above the material and the physical in a pattern of beneficent co-ordination. As taught by Islam, they believe that the faculties and capacities bestowed upon them by God Almighty are a precious bounty and should be beneficently developed and exercised at their proper time and occasion, and not to be suppressed or stultified. They believe that everything bestowed upon man has a beneficent purpose which should be sought to be achieved and fulfilled at the highest level. The moral and spiritual code to which they seek to conform imposes no handicap upon them. Indeed it enables them to live their lives at a high level of beneficent activity, much above the average standard of life of those around them, judged by a true standard of beneficence. There have, by the grace and mercy of God, appeared among them men possessing high eminence in almost every sphere of human life.

The most outstanding instances of the moral and spiritual revolution that is worked in the lives of the members of the Movement as a result of the teachings, exhortations and example of the Holy Founder of the Movement and his

Successors, are to be found in Africa, among the indigenous communities of that continent. It is their example which has become the effective instrument for the wider spread of the Movement in those countries. When their fellow countrymen observe the beneficence wrought in the lives of the members of the Movement through their adherence to the standards of the Movement, they are in turn drawn strongly towards the Movement and need little persuasion to identify themselves with it. The Movement has thus a bright future before it in several parts of Africa, more particularly in West Africa.

The world today presents an ironic spectacle of the highest progress in science and technology, beyond the wildest dreams of even half a century ago, on the one side, and the rapid deterioration of moral and spiritual values on the other. This rift is widening daily, more especially in the West, and if it is not drastically narrowed and then eliminated at an early date, it would bring about universal disaster of the highest magnitude. It might mean the end of civilization as it is conceived today. At the root of the trouble is the woeful lack of moral and spiritual leadership among the so-called advanced sections of humanity. Large sections have become completely alienated from God. In the West scarcely anyone believes truly in the possibility of communion with God, which is of the very essence of spiritual life. Such halting and sporadic effort as is put forth towards the stimulation of moral and spiritual values, is based on human speculation and is not derived from Divine direction. This tendency is patently observed even among the orthodox Muslim divines. They render lip-service and verbal homage to the doctrines and teachings of Islam, but their conduct does not furnish an illustration of those values. By denying the possibility of revelation in this age they have closed firmly upon themselves, and upon those who seek guidance from them, the only door through which access might be gained to the Almighty. They talk of things divine and sublime, but in the conduct of their lives they merely ape and copy the West, though they go on proclaiming loudly that the West is heading towards disaster. They fail to recognize that the only way of deliverance is through the re-establishment of man's relationship with God. In today's world the only claimant of such a possibility is the Ahmadiyya Movement. It not only puts forward such a claim, it furnishes practical illustration of the truth of the claim. To mention only one aspect of such proof, there is frequent and continuous experience of the acceptance of prayer among the members of the Movement which acceptance is often indicated through some form of revelation, and is confirmed by the achievement of the purpose of the prayer in the face of all types of adverse circumstances and considerations. It is only through such experience that a person can arrive at the absolute certainty of faith in the Divine which alone can work the needed moral and spiritual revolution in the lives of people. This is the challenge that the Ahmadiyya Movement presents to an incredulous world. It is the challenge of a revived, strong and invigorated Islam.

Islam is the distilled essence of all truth. There is not a single fundamental verity that is not comprised in the Holy Quran. It requires faith in all the prophets and in the revelations that were vouchsafed to them. By the acceptance of Islam a Jew is not called upon to repudiate Moses and the Prophets, he is invited to fuller acceptance of Moses and the Prophets and the fulfilment of their prophecies; a Christian is not called upon to repudiate Jesus and the Gospel, he is invited to believe in the true capacity of Jesus as set out in the Gospel, and his interpretation of the Law and the fulfilment of his prophecies relating to the Comforter and the whole truth. A Zoroastrian is not called upon to repudiate Zoroaster and the Zendavesta, he is invited to accept the fulfilment of the teaching and message of Zoroaster; a Hindu is not called upon to repudiate the Rishis and the Vedas and Rama and Krishna, he is invited to accept the fulfilment of their message and teachings; a Buddhist is not called upon to repudiate Sakia Muni Gautam as the Buddha, he is invited to accept the fulfilment and culmination of the teachings of the Buddha through the highest manifestation of enlightenment; a follower of Confucius is not called upon to repudiate the way of Confucius, he is invited to accept the fullness and culmination of that way; a Sikh is not called upon to repudiate the saintliness of Guru Nanak, he is invited to accept the truth as Guru Nanak saw it, as is testified to by his relics: the holy mantle preserved at Dera Baba Nanak and his vade-mecum preserved at Guru Har Sahai.

The Holy Quran is thus a universal possession and a perfect guide. Anyone who makes it the law of his life and conforms to it down to the least particular, will see God in this very life, than which there can be no greater proof that he is treading along the straight and true path. That is the only true salvation and there is no other salvation beside it. That is the perfect fulfilment of life here and hereafter.